She Took to the Woods

A Biography and Selected Writings of
LOUISE DICKINSON RICH

Alice Arlen

Down East Books • Rockport Maine

To family, friends, and fans of
Louise Dickinson Rich

Copyright © 2000 by Alice Arlen

ISBN 0-89272-483-8

Book design by Lurelle Cheverie
Printed and bound at Versa Press, East Peoria, Ill.

1   3   5   4   2

Down East Books
P.O. Box 679
Camden, ME 04843

BOOK ORDERS: 1-800-766-1670

Library of Congress Cataloging-in-Publication Data

Arlen, Alice.
    She took to the woods : A biography and selected writings of Louise Dickinson Rich
        p.   cm.
    Pt. 2 contains selections from Rich's essay's, stories, journals, and letters.
    ISBN 0-89272-483-8
    1. Rich, Louise Dickinson, 1903–91. 2. Authors, American—20th century—Biography. 3. Women and
literature—Maine—History—20th century. 4. Wilderness areas in literature. 5. Maine—in literature. I.
Rich, Louise Dickinson, 1903–91 Selections. 2000. II. Title.

    PS3535.I244 Z56 2000
    818'.5209—dc21
    [B]00-43112

She Took to the Woods

A Biography and Selected Writings of
LOUISE DICKINSON RICH

Enjoy!

Also by Alice Arlen

Contents

Unpublished Writings

Photographs follow page 54

Introduction

My acquaintance with wilderness writer Louise Dickinson Rich began years ago in the midst of research I was doing for a book on traditional Maine sporting camps. I heard her name and glanced down the "Carry Road" (originally a canoe portage trail) leading to her place by the Rapid River in the Rangeley Lakes region of western Maine. I also took note of a log home occupied, I was informed, by Louise's longtime friend and neighbor, Alys Parsons. At that point, though, there were places to go, people and a deadline to meet, so I moved on.

My sporting-camp book came out and I started receiving mail from readers. Several petitioned, "Please write a book about Louise Dickinson Rich." A librarian from the Midwest was very specific: "*We Took to the Woods* [the 1942 best-seller that launched Rich's career] is still checked out on a regular basis. There has never been a biography written about her and I feel you are the person to do it."

I started to pay attention.

Soon it seemed I was stumbling into Louise wherever I went. Events accelerated until it became clear that I was almost destined for the job. Even the name was right. All her life, Louise was closely connected to one Alice or another. When a neighbor told me Louise's son lived just two towns away, I realized the time had come to step up to the plate.

"Ayah," drawled his answering machine, "This is Rufus. If you want to leave a message, fine. If not, that's the way it goes." Hmm. Two more encounters with this message and I was rewarded with a real voice. He seemed wary, but perhaps willing to set up an interview.

"Would next Thursday be convenient?" I ventured.

"Hell," he blasted back, "I don't know what I'll be doing that far away!"

"Well ... um, how about tomorrow at three?"

"That's more like it!"

Next day I found his trailer (surrounded by mechanical objects and conscientiously protected by a loudly barking black dog). No one came to the door. The dog, on an aerial leash, could reach the front steps. I took a deep breath and, with what I hoped were soothing yet firm tones regarding the validity of my visit, reached the door. I knocked (the dog frantic). Sounds of rustling inside. Waited. More knocking, more dog. Finally the door opened. A man with a shock of gray hair filled the entire door frame. He looked at me slowly. "I see you got past my dog...."

"Oh ...yeah."

"Well, I guess you'd better come in."

That was my introduction to Rufus Rich. We feinted and parried until he mentioned the town of Andover, Maine, where he'd lived for a time. "Don't suppose you know where it is," he assumed.

"Sure do. I lived there myself for a little while."

He sat up in his chair. "Really?"

"Mm. Lived with Mary and Phil Learned."

"No kidding!" He leaned forward. "Phil taught me how to fish!"

From then on, it was clear sailing. My host proved to be kind, informative, and generous. As I was leaving, Rufus wrote something. "You might want to call this person. Here's her number."

"Who is it?" I reached out my hand.

"My sister."

Several months later, Dinah, a very private person, invited me for lunch. A rare pleasure. At the end of the meal, she came out with a shopping bag. "This may be of interest," she said, with what apparently is the family gift for understatement. In it were her mother's scrapbook, her writer's journal, and a five-year diary. And as I was poring over this gold mine, she made a call to her mother's friend of seventy years, Hester Rich Hopkins, who was willing to see me that day on Dinah's assurances that I was "OK."

The responsibility of being entrusted with another person's life is not something to be taken lightly—especially a person whose work you admire. My early catapult devolved into a series of frustrations with intractable data, wildly conflicting oral reports, and unresolved questions. But Louise Dickinson Rich is a very engaging person. She speaks across time. At least she spoke to me, offering insight and reassurance. One day I was at her home, Forest Lodge, above the thunderous Rapid River. I'd been totally immersed in musty *Woman's Day* magazines all afternoon, and felt in a 1940s time warp. The sun was dipping low when I came upon a July 4, 1946, short story Louise had written about the Maine Indian woman Mollyockett. I laughed out loud and shook my head in wonder. In the piece, Louise was expressing perfectly the turmoil, inconclusive musings and meanderings, the joyous, brief moments of epiphany one receives as a biographer—in other words, the evolution of her own biography. Gladly and humbly, I defer to Louise's inimitable way with words. Let her give you a sense of what went before and what lies ahead:

Did you ever try to determine the character of an individual from the reports and opinions of a variety of persons, from the known facts about him [her] and the conjectures concerning him [her]? It's a fascinating occupation, a sort of psychological hare-and-hounds. This fact is at wide variance with that; this opinion contradicts utterly the other. Somewhere through the maze of fact and personal bias and legend and distortion flees the hare, the true identity of the individual; but where? Every[one] has as many personalities as he [she] has acquaintances.

My intent in what follows is to stay in the background as much as possible; to provide context and data; to share insights and impressions from friends, foes, and family; but mostly to let Louise speak to you herself through her work. I've even included some out-of-print and some unpublished pieces that, as they say in the Rich family, "you might want to see. . . ."

PINE POINT
Lake Umbagog

FOREST LODGE
Rapid River

RUMFORD POINT

THE SANDS
Prospect Harbor

CROWLEY ISLAND
Gouldsboro

CRANBERRY POINT
Gouldsboro

Islesboro

LOCATIONS WHERE
LOUISE DICKINSON RICH
LIVED IN MAINE

-- PART I --

Biography

Childhood

The year is 1905. Teddy Roosevelt is the U.S. president and the Russo–Japanese War is on. More fundamentally, there is a major shift underway, affecting time and motion. Twenty-six-year-old Albert Einstein has just published the theory of relativity, and Orville and Wilbur Wright have introduced machines that fly. Trains are faster and cleaner, and—along with trolleys and subways—lines and service areas are being extended farther. More than 25,000 personal automobiles are tootling around at "breakneck" speed. The *New York Tribune* buys its first typewriter and wireless telegraphy links the United States and Europe. The world is opening up and getting smaller. The pace of life is ratcheting up a notch, inventions are in the air, risk-takers are on the move, and over all is a sense that "anything is possible."

James H. Dickinson, former newspaperman with the Westfield Massachusetts, *Valley Echo,* and his wife, Florence Stewart Dickinson, have this year traveled two hundred miles from their home and relatives in Huntington, Massachusetts, to make good on a dream. James, a wiry five feet eight inches, with blue eyes and blond, wavy hair, wears glasses and dresses fastidiously in tie and jacket. Florence, tidy and handsome, has brown hair and eyes. They arrive in Bridgewater, Massachusetts, a typical midsize New England town between Boston and Cape Cod, where they have recently bought the weekly *Bridgewater Independent.* James, owner and editor, and Florence—typesetter, advertising salesperson, copy editor, and reporter—have two daughters: infant Alice Eldora (named after her maternal Aunt Alice) and two-year-old Sarah Louise (after her paternal grandmother, Sarah Bullock).

As Louise described in *Innocence under the Elms,* the wonderfully reminiscent and readable account of her childhood, the Dickinsons did not fit neatly into the tight social structure of their new hometown. In a time when people in small New England communities "stayed put," they were "from away." Instead of immediately buying a home and improving its yard, as expected, the Dickinsons opted to proceed from one rented house to another, moving along as owners died off or sold.

In addition, due to the financial constraints of buying and running a small business, and their insistence on living within their means, most of the Dickinsons' rentals were in poor to terrible condition. Thus, even though they came from solidly middle-class ancestry (founders of the towns of South Hadley and Northfield, Massachusetts), in Bridgewater they were members of the "genteel poor." In her memoir, Louise created the impression that her family was unique in this regard, but they probably were in very good company. The reason they lived in big, old homes (which, though unmodernized, sometimes had such classic, elegant features as dumbwaiters and fine cabinetry details) was that the owners probably also were in need of downsizing. For the first five years the Dickinsons lived in Bridgewater, the entire U.S. economy was in crisis. Foreign turmoil and domestic disasters, such as the San Francisco earthquake of 1906, drained the U.S. treasury. In 1908, many banks closed, and by 1920 the average worker earned less than $15 for a fifty-five-to-sixty-hour work week. Most people had vegetable gardens (Louise and Alice were adept child gardeners), and even though thousands had flocked to major cities, America remained primarily a rural society. So living in rented homes, growing one's own vegetables, and counting pennies would not have been particularly suspect. The Bridgewater of Louise and Alice's childhood did not have the stigma of a "poor section." In fact, they loved the adventure of acquiring new rooms, neighbors, and backyards. These changes served as touchstones for developing keen curiosity, creativity, and vivid imaginations. The girls learned to live without electricity or bathrooms; they learned to haul wood and coal, clean the woodshed and henhouse, read by kerosene lamps, and wash in tin tubs. Louise wrote: "We lived almost primitively in a time and place that was not primitive and not geared to primitive living."

On the other hand, as intellectual blue bloods (relatives included Cyrus Field, transatlantic cable genius, as well as the eccentric poet Emily Dickinson), the family went against the grain. "In a time and place where the line separating the sheep from the goats was identical with the impassable chasm between good, reputable Republicans and riffraffish, disreputable Democrats," James Dickinson was a Democrat "and ran a Democratic newspaper, a fact that curtailed appreciably his circulation." It was the family's intellectual rigor and blunt honesty, its self-sufficiency and shyness, that removed it from the general fray.

James and Florence's political incorrectness and peripatetic lifestyle could have marginalized them within the community had it not been for the fact that these oddities were very much offset by strong Christian virtues and affiliations. Both parents abstained from drink and idleness, living their lives (and expecting that their daughters would do likewise) with decorum, discipline, and integrity—a quiet, self-contained family. On the matter of religion, the family came by its upstanding genes honestly. Louise's paternal grandfather, a Yale graduate, "bee-keeper, observer of the stars, student of Greek and many other . . . unworldly things," was a much-respected Congregational minister. "In his home it was as natural as breathing to start each day in communion with God." Her maternal grandfather Stewart, "a wheelwright and politician," was a Congregational deacon, "when being a deacon was an important seven-day-a-week job." Louise claimed that he was such a "martinet," or strict disciplinarian, that the church probably appointed him to the position because "they knew if he couldn't be a deacon, he wouldn't play at all. He brought the full weight of his not inconsiderable personality and powers to bear upon the problem, ran the church with an iron hand, and decreed family prayers in his own bailiwick. . . banned all Sunday papers and would allow only absolutely imperative work to be done on the Sabbath." One of the first things James and Florence did upon settling in Bridgewater was to become fully ensconced in the Central Square Congregational Church and its activities.

Louise and Alice lived out their pious, frugal, disciplined heritage in a number of ways. Every breakfast, James read the Bible (Louise related that he got through all of it and started over again while she was still living at home), and the family then repeated the Lord's Prayer. Both habits were "not common practice then, no matter what it may have been at an earlier period." They also went to church and then to Sunday School every week. In addition to living in rented homes, the family ate a chicken every Sunday dinner (and Christmas and Thanksgiving) culled from the hens they raised. Practical gifts were the norm (although Aunt Julia Dickinson broke the mold with lavish, bountiful Christmas presents). Louise always received handmade outfits of the most understated material possible so they would not look particularly obvious when Alice wore them a year or two later.

As for discipline, Louise wrote that because of the newspaper's demands on their parents' time and minds, it was tacitly expected that she and Alice would not be sick Monday through Thursday—especially Thursday when the paper went to press. By then, she pointed out, it was the end of the school week, their mother had time off, and they all had the weekend before them. Consequently, the girls learned to live with all sorts of minor ailments that eventually went away of their own accord. They were required to be sturdy and to stay within certain boundaries (not stray too far from their house or prescribed behavior). When they crossed the line, Florence first gave them a "good talking to," then resorted to the dreaded "Black Stick," a thin bamboo cane strung between the wires holding up the kitchen mirror. This stick traveled with them from house to house and was a powerful disciplinarian. It may have been something Florence, the oldest of eight children, remembered from her childhood. Louise recalled: "It wasn't because applications of The Black Stick hurt so much. All our mother ever did with it was switch our legs a few times. And yet just the threat of [it] reduced us to abject whimpers. I guess it was a case of good old applied psychology, in a day when even the term was unknown. Recourse to The Black Stick was The End. When we'd been that bad, we'd put ourselves outside the pale, and what was more, we knew it. I guess that knowledge was the real burden of our penalty. Our own black hearts were punishing us."

Despite their stern discipline, James and Florence also served as role models for departing sharply from some traditions. For one, they had left the family fold. On top of that, they had some "downright lax" attitudes—in comparison to their own upbringings—such as allowing Louise and Alice to play with dolls and read books on Sunday. And they always had a Sunday paper. James "claimed he needed it in his business; and anyhow, most of the work involved in its publication had been done on Saturday. If you had to skip a paper on the grounds of Sabbath breaking, he said, the one to skip was the Monday morning edition. So Alice and I were very familiar with the doings of Billy the Boy Artist, the Katzenjammer Kids, and Hairbreadth Harry and the Beautiful Belinda."

The inexorability of getting out the paper not only gave the family a focus and sense of purpose, but it also served as a counterpoint to the transitory aspects of their lives. The *Bridgewater Independent* was almost a presence—rather like a fascinating but highly demanding relative who requires chunks of intensely focused ministrations followed by moments of reprieve. This relative, however, nurtured in Louise the characteristics necessary to become a successful writer. The job of working with words, of transforming events and ideas into print, was something she knew intimately. In addition, house-hopping developed her imagination, as well as tolerance for and keen observation of new places and people. And her immediate and extended family provided the template for diligence, self-sufficiency, and discipline.

Louise's immediate family also provided the source of her very best childhood friend—her sister, Alice. The duo was inseparable. They were born exactly two years apart, on June 14, and for years assumed all siblings had identical birthdays. They also had the delusion that their particular birthday was celebrated with flags waving all over town. Eventually they learned, to their chagrin, that the display was actually in honor of Flag Day.

Louise described Alice as her "second self. Everybody always spoke of us, and probably thought of us, as linked—the Dickinson sisters, or Louisenalice Dickinson." They looked, thought, sounded, and dressed alike (Louise's color was pink and Alice's blue: "We hated pink and blue!") and were a year apart in school because Alice skipped second grade. (Alice's report cards were always "monotonously" all As, whereas Louise sometimes received a C in arithmetic.) But Alice made up for this brilliance by staunchly supporting Louise when her big sister was held responsible for their generally harmless and childish escapades.

The girls were both shy and sensitive, and their strategic defense was to make a pact that they would not cry, if at all possible, in public. "Perhaps one of the reasons she and I made such a Thing of never crying was that normally we cried very easily. We had tender hearts where others were concerned and were self-conscious enough to be easily hurt on our own accounts." Louise was so shy that she nearly fainted one day when introduced to a stranger. Thereafter, in Emily Dickinsonesque fashion, she tried to hide when someone new arrived.

On top of that Louise recounted, "We were the worst cases of retarded development as far as maturing emotionally went that I have ever heard of. Sex wasn't a closed book to us. It just wasn't, period. We'd never even glimpsed the cover of the book. Boys to us were simply more fortunate children who were allowed for some reason we couldn't fathom to wear sensible clothes which gave them an unfair advantage in climbing trees or leaping brooks." This became a point of contention, because both girls developed such a love affair with nature and collected so many treasures for future identification that Florence capitulated and sewed secret pockets (a female fashion taboo) into her daughters' frocks. Their scientific curiosity extended to wild berries and plants that they munched with abandon (luckily avoiding a poisonous demise)!

They even managed to survive one episode when they *tried* to succumb. Louise and Alice were in the sixth and fifth grades, respectively, when rather than attend a party in which the new kissing game Post Office would be played, they decided to get sick. It had to be a real sickness, since pretense wouldn't wash with their mother. Consequently, they overcompensated by gorging on green apples and grapes, rubbing poison ivy all over themselves, and drinking pints of salt water. After spending a week in bed with fevers, vomiting, itching, and diarrhea, they both agreed: "The reward was worth the sacrifice. That's how unsociable we were."

Louise and Alice gathered their solace, strength, and pleasure from books, nature, and the company of each other and the family. Each year, Florence took the girls to the Stewart cottage on Lake Whitehall in Woodville, Massachusetts. Here the girls saw their mother in a new light: a relaxed, giggling Stewart girl. Surrounded by aunts and uncles, grandparents and cousins, they swam, fished, reveled in nature, and contemplated the immensity of the universe. Before Louise and Alice reached their teens, James bought the *Advertiser,* the *Independent*'s competitor, which kept Florence from leaving for a vacation. Shortly thereafter, the Stewarts sold the cottage. But its lessons and pleasures had already become embedded.

While Louise and Alice struggled with the social complexities of party-going and loss of the family lakeside retreat, the world went to war. Louise, in keeping with the upbeat tenor of her books, did not mention World War I, the economic crises before and after, or much of anything outside the Bridgewater area. Her book was aptly named *Innocence under the Elms* because it looked at childhood through the eyes of youth. That was her genius: the ability to put herself squarely and empathetically in the shoes of specific people at a particular time and place. What was important to thirteen-year-old Louise in 1916, and what she described, was her first job (substitute librarian), where she discovered there could be more than the classroom's prescribed view on various subjects; her mother's first absence from home (due to a mastoid operation), when she learned the responsibility of running a household; and her heightened awareness (upon looking at the summer stars) of the insignificance of humanity against the grandeur of the universe. As the book ended, she was, in other words, growing up.

Adolescence

The year is now 1920. A white clapboard house, surrounded by lilacs, sits on the right corner lot of a quiet, dead-end street. Nine other two-storied homes face each other from behind tidy front lawns. A little dirt path leads into a grove of trees and a tangle of shrubs. Similar streets bracket this one: a small, residential maze. Tucked in the midst of this modestly gracious, tree-lined neighborhood, the house, at 83 Dean Street in Bridgewater is an easy five-minute walk from the town common and its encircling shops, churches, town hall, brick library, and tall, white-clapboard high school. The streets, shops, and factories in town suddenly begin filling with men returning from war. Families are trying to return to "normal," but the world, and consequently the meaning of the word itself, has changed. And continues to change rapidly. It seems there is no turning back. The war has turned out to be a sort of fault line. The resulting friction creates upheavals that dramatically change the accustomed cultural landscape. Like social tectonic plates, the waning Victorian era rubs and buckles against the encroaching "roaring twenties."

The unremitting tectonic action of opposing, almost ironic, forces is everywhere apparent. Survivors of war return home only to be killed off, along with 5.5 percent of the 100 million U.S. population, by the Spanish influenza pandemic. Prohibition has just been signed into law, but speakeasies and hard liquor abound. D. H. Lawrence's *Lady Chatterley's Lover* is available on the bookstands, along with A. A. Milne's *Winnie the Pooh*. The music of Irving Berlin and Debussy vies with atonal pieces and jazz, impressionism meets abstract expressionism. The Nineteenth Amendment gives women the right to vote as scores are fired from "male" wartime jobs and sent home. Both Hitler and Gandhi are current headliners. Overlaid on all this, short-wave radio and sound films are about to alter the way people communicate and perceive their world, themselves, and each other.

It is all very confusing, liberating, and overwhelming to a stoic populace that has held its collective breath for four years. It is a time for exploring inner and outer worlds: Astronomers see the form of the Milky Way for the first time; other scientists expound on psychology and the inner workings of the mind. Some decide it's time to play: The American Football Association is formed, waterskiing is invented, table tennis enjoys a revival, and families head off in droves to newly constructed "motor inns" in cars that now have an adequate supply of gasoline.

• • •

Closer to home, Louise at seventeen was also living on a fault line—the one commonly known as adolescence. She was becoming more aware of the larger world and described in *Innocence Under the Elms,* her father's reaction to a series of events that occurred during the months before her high-school graduation. It says much about her inheritance of intellectual rigor, integrity, and individuality.

Our father felt justified in tearing his whole front page to pieces on the December day when there was an attempted holdup of the L. Q. White Shoe Factory payroll, down on Hale Street, just below where we lived. . . . Violence really is a serious and shocking thing to the peaceful and peace-loving, and our father wrote an editorial to that effect. About four months later the forces of evil struck again in a town not far north of us, and this time the paymaster was killed. Two or three weeks later arrests were made, and again our father happily . . . dug out his seldom-used banner type, and blazoned the tidings to the world. There was at this point no doubt in his or anybody else's mind as to the guilt of the prisoners.

But as time went on and hearing after hearing was held, the *Independent*—which was our father—began to be less certain. There were discrepancies in testimony which he thought needed to be explained a little more convincingly, and he wrote editorials saying as much. This attitude was considered a little peculiar in face of the overwhelming popular certainty of guilt, but nobody was very much surprised that our father took it. He was known to have peculiar ideas. He was probably the only respectable person in town to vote against both local and national Prohibition, although he'd rather have died The Death, than allow a drop of alcohol to pass his lips. He was convinced that what a man ate and drank was his own business, and that any attempt at regulation was an infringement on his rights.

In this case of the holdup men, he honestly thought they were being given a raw deal. "They're not on trial for their politics," our father stated mildly. "They're on trial for a murder that I for one don't believe they committed. The time has passed in this world when a man can be executed for his political beliefs." Oh, my poor, innocent father! But then, he was living in an innocent era.

The years dragged on, and everybody became bored with the

case of the anarchists who had killed the paymaster, except my father. Alice and I went into the Office one morning to find our father seated at his desk, doing nothing. This in itself was unusual enough so that we asked what was the matter. He turned a stricken face to us. "We've finally murdered them. I never thought, after keeping them penned up like cattle all these years. . . ."

"Who?" we asked timidly.

"Nicola Sacco and Bartolomeo Vanzetti." He gave them their full names in a kind of solemn requiem. "We shouldn't have done that. We didn't have the right—" his voice died sadly.

I don't remember ever hearing him mention them again, but he never forgot. It hurt him more deeply than it's easy to realize, that the men whom he believed—whether rightly or not I can't say—to be innocent should have been done to death by a system he endorsed. I wish I was as capable of single-minded devotion to an ideal as my father was. But at least I have an example that I can try to follow.

Five months after the paymaster murder, on September 15, 1920, James and Florence Dickinson's firstborn embarked on a new stage in her life. Sarah Louise entered Bridgewater State Teachers' College—what townspeople called the Normal School. She joined a class of forty-eight students, almost exclusively female, along with neighborhood friends Enid Buzzell and Ruth Hunt. Ruth—tall, gorgeous, and brilliant—had unorthodox views on female sexuality. Enid ("Buzz") had the spirit of an explorer. She would, as the school yearbook, the *Normal Offering,* boasted, "make possible the reflected glory of the whole class by biking from coast to coast in the summer of 1922." But it was Louise ("Dicky") who would lead the pack and become a real force on campus.

The 1921/22 *Normal Offering* shows Louise, a clone of her sophomore classmates, in a flowing white dress with ruffled collar and three-quarter-length sleeves, both edged in lace. Her hair hangs just to the ears, curled at the sides and pulled back, exposing a high forehead and straightforward expression behind glasses. Her byline reveals active involvement in school life: Library and French Clubs in 1920/21, and membership in Alpha Gamma Phi sorority. The next year she was assistant editor of the yearbook and active in the Dramatic Club, the Tennis Club, and O.I.C. (Out and In Club, a social and athletic organization).

By 1922/23, Louise was president of the Dramatic Club and editor in chief of the yearbook (with Alice serving as assistant editor). The two sisters posed dead center in the editorial-board photo. Nearly everyone was wearing a sweater, plaid skirt, and white blouse with a rounded Peter Pan collar from which fell a thin, dark, bowed ribbon. But that year, amid the sea of sameness, of upswept hairdos and clear foreheads, Louise and Alice Dickinson sat, demure mavericks. Only they sported the new "Dutch boy" bob: straight hair cut to the ears, plus bangs (a daring statement in those days). In addition to all these activities, and perhaps most significant, Louise served as president of her class for three years straight.

Louise's teacher training consisted of spending thirteen weeks during the fall of 1922 at the teacher-training school within the college, where she practiced "writing lesson plans, learning rote songs, making reading and arithmetic charts, and working out projects." Then, during the winter semester, the students dispersed to nearby schools to try their wings as student teachers. In addition to this heavy workload, her responsibilities as class president and editor of the yearbook, Louise was also doing some writing. The 1922 *Normal Offering* featured the first published pieces by S. Louise Dickinson:

The Lure of the South Seas

Through all my life I've never been
Beyond these bleak New England skies.
I've never heard the boom of surf
On coral reefs; nor watched the rise
Of mellow tropic moon; nor seen
Slender and black against the rose
Of South Sea sunrise, graceful palms;
Nor, when the raging typhoon blows,
Trembled with high, ecstatic joy.
Yet oft when in the silent night
I see the march of distant stars
Before the moon, serene and white,
And see the Dipper's stately wheel
Above the black waves heave and toss
Around the steady, blue Pole Star,
I'm homesick for the Southern Cross.

Appreciation

These are the things I like about the night,—
That bring a throbbing ache into my throat:

The high white splendor of the autumn moon,
The thrill of whip-poor-will's recurring note,
The road, agleam between the shadowy trees,
Or mottled with the restless black and white,
And over all, a brooding mystery.
These are the things I like about the night.

And then one that seems almost prescient:

Swamp Maple

Upon my wooded hillside all is still
Save when some bird, sending his plaintive call,
Flits through the branches, or last autumn's leaves,
Weathered and browned and seared, stir; that is all.
But ah! I know that life starts now anew,
For in the swamp, amidst the green-black pines
I see the maples' scarlet haze, just touched
With golden rays and dulled by shadow lines,
As April's setting sun sends through the trees
That top my rocky crest, its slanting ray
And kindles all the glory of the red
Against the dark pines and the forest grey.

Apparently, most of the students in Louise's class left at the end of their third year (1923). "When we united in the spring," notes the 1923/24 *Normal Offering*, "there were but a few weeks of jolly companionship before graduation, when the majority of our class left to take up work in schoolrooms of their own. On September 12, 1923, but thirteen of the original forty-eight started on the last quarter of the journey, hence we were eager to welcome two new members."

Louise, Enid Buzzell, and Ruth Hunt (now class president) were still together, and one of the new students, Hester Rich, soon joined their threesome. Hester's recollections from this time period forward are invaluable. She and Louise are from the same era, and they were kindred spirits and dearest friends for the rest of Louise's life.

Hester greeted me for our first interview dressed in a white oxford-cloth shirt and denim skirt. Her short gray hair reveals a high forehead. She looks, acts, and thinks decades younger than her ninety-plus years. Her narrative is punctuated with a wonderfully expressive laugh. She looks right at you, instantly assessing if you're "with her"; then, eyes twinkling, the laugh starts in her chest, bubbles up to a grin, and one chuckle/hoot emerges. She clearly enjoys the memories of her "antics" with Louise and has great respect for the character and talents of her best friend. We are getting very close to Louise when we listen to Hester:

> I first met Louise in 1923. I had been, a year and a fraction after the death of my father, at Framingham State College. Because a friend of mine was going to Bridgewater State, I made a deal with the school to give me a bachelor's degree if I did two years' work in one.
>
> Louise was a year older than I and a year ahead of me, but because of the conditions I mentioned I entered as a senior, skipping my junior year. She at that time had two fast friends. One was Enid Buzzell and one was Ruth Hunt. They were inseparable; they had been since kindergarten. Each was exceedingly brilliant, and by some luck I was included into this, and it became a very unusual and satisfying relationship. It sounds egotistical, but it's absolutely accurate, that our records in school were among the highest.
>
> We paid no attention to anyone else. And because the work seemed easy, and we traveled in a pack, we did things that were sheer rebellious because we were bored. And we earned quite a reputation for that! Ruth Hunt was the daughter of the psychology professor at the school, a perfectly gorgeous girl. She had tendencies toward being a lesbian. But the other three of us weren't interested in that. Neither were we interested in men, for some reason. We just had an awfully good time together. Alice was a year behind us and didn't move with us. She was very sober, more a loner, a quiet person really who loved to study. Anyway, we apparently were attractive to other members of the school population. We got along with them and we got along with the teachers. But we broke rules.
>
> We did things like taking a history teacher, whom we liked enormously (she was a very good teacher, and we learned a lot from her)—taking her out canoeing before breakfast, quite a long distance on the Taunton River. This, of course, was forbidden. We'd brew coffee in tin cans, this sort of thing, and always managed to be just a little late for classes. This teacher always took the brunt; she never squealed. In these expeditions and the other things we

managed to get ourselves into, it was Dicky and I who more or less paired together. She took me into her home and life, and I met her mother and father. Her mother particularly was very much like Dicky herself: a very able and very stout (and I mean this in the sense of strong, stouthearted) person. And her father was quiet, a substantial man in town.

Dicky was very attractive. She always dressed well and looked very nice. And she had wonderful eyes: big, brown, and upsettingly penetrating. They looked right at you. Dicky, as a person, was one of the staunchest, most honest friends a person could have. She simply related in terms of her own confidence and ability and just made friends. People were attracted to her. And she could empathize with people. She had the quality of being able to put herself in the position of sensing someone else's feelings very clearly and still go on with her own life. But at the same time, she'd convey to them her understanding and her complete support, which is really rare in a person. At least that's what I felt to be true.

Well, back at Bridgewater, toward the end of the 1924 school year I was told by the administration that they'd changed their mind about giving me a degree and letting me graduate. They didn't want to set a precedent, that sort of thing. I was furious about it, just felt terribly let down. I was partially earning my way and this was very serious to me. Plus they'd broken a promise and didn't tell me until the end of the year. They told me if I came back the following year I needn't do anything. I could just take some gardening, play some cards, golf, sit around, or whatever. I was so cocky and so mad I said I'd have no part of it and told them I was leaving.

Now just about this same time, Dicky was put on probation, or actually expelled from Bridgewater for smoking—which seemed absolutely asinine! So that meant two more of us, Dicky and myself, who weren't going to graduate with our class that year. And to show just how cocky we were—there was a tradition that each year the graduating class would plant ivy at a certain spot on campus. And then they'd have an Ivy Day parade and speeches. Well, Dicky and I went in and planted poison ivy where they had planted the regular ivy. Then we just went into hysterics at the Ivy Day parade knowing it was poison ivy. So we fixed that one! This was the typical cockiness of us. I think people may have become contaminated, but they never knew who did it.

And on the day of graduation, we went down on the baseball field which was right in front of the graduation exercises. Everyone showed up for the ceremony and as soon as it started, Dicky and I played tennis—back and forth, back and forth—and made as much noise as we possibly could. This was not behind everything, or to the side, mind you, but in full view. So we weren't very popular!

On the contrary. Bridgewater State Teachers' College 1924 class superlatives found in the *Normal Offering*: Tallest: Ruth Hunt; Most Exclusive: Enid Buzzell; Most Popular: Louise Dickinson.

> And here's to our Dicky, the friend of our youth,
> With a head full of genius, a heart full of truth,
> Who travell'd with us in the sunshine of life,
> And stood by our side in its peace and its strife.

Records show Louise received a three-year diploma (not unusual at the time) dated June 16, 1924. It was now off to the real world. . . .

The Real World

In the fall of 1925, Louise, according to a 1942 interview in the *Maine Sunday Telegram,* took a teaching job in Lebanon, New Hampshire and during the following summer she and a fellow teacher took a trip to Europe. Then, as Hester puts it, "It was in New Hampshire, or somewhere along the line, that she met 'this man.'" Prior to my interview with Hester (and Dinah), I visited Bridgewater and stopped at the town office in search of Louise's marriage certificate. I was surprised to find one, dated November 24, 1926, between Sarah Louise Dickinson and a John Davis Bacon—not the name I had expected! Louise was twenty-three years old and Bacon thirty-one. Both bride and groom were listed as living at their childhood homes. Louise's occupation was recorded as "teacher" and Bacon's as "bond salesman."

Louise's husband, son of John C. Bacon, a banker, and Elizabeth Davis, grew up in White River Junction, Vermont, a hop across the Connecticut River from Lebanon, in a house that had been in the family since 1891. John's father had died at age forty-six, when John was only fourteen years old. A generally above-average student, John lived at home with his mother after completing his education. This should not necessarily be seen as lack of independence on his part, but rather what was expected at the time. Family members cared for widows and orphans and men provided for women. And the Bacons followed conventions. However, as Louise explained in *Innocence under the Elms*: "In a day when it was neither fashionable nor common for wives and mothers in good standing to work outside the home, our mother worked. Nobody else's mother did, and we tried hard to convince ourselves that what she did was not really working, but just helping our father. For some reason, that made it seem a little less peculiar, and us a little less unlike other children. Our mother worked, all right, no matter how we chose to regard it."

Now, although Louise worked as well, she held a socially acceptable job for a woman "in good standing." By marrying John Bacon, she was, consciously or not, attempting to be even "less unlike"—moving toward mainstream, even conservative, conventions. After their marriage, John's mother went to live with them in Brattleboro, Vermont. The 1927 poll tax records show Louise at 10 Linden Street. From 1928 to 1930, Louise and John are both listed as living at 1 Williston Street.

Hester recalls meeting John Bacon:

My impression of Dicky's husband is that he was rather much of a playboy. By that I mean, I don't think he worked very hard at anything. A few months after she'd been married, Dicky invited us all [Enid, Ruth, Hester] to come visit. And I think we just overwhelmed the poor guy, and his mother, too! I mean, to have three of us land, as tremendous a power as we seemed to be, and take over, and Dicky too, in this little quiet town of Brattleboro, Vermont. But I don't seem to remember anything more about him. I think I probably decided I wouldn't like him, and I have a great capacity for forgetting people I don't like.

That same year, I was teaching high-school history—at age nineteen. The following [school] year, 1927, I took a position in Waltham [Massachusetts]. So summers I would be on Cape Cod and Dicky would come down. In the fall of 1928 or 1929, because I was going to Boston University on weekends, I do remember once meeting her at a Harvard football game with this guy, I think his name was Bacon. And then, after the game, they went to the Copley [Plaza Hotel] and to parties. It was that kind of life she was leading, and I don't think she liked it. It wasn't her style.

It is interesting, in hindsight, to observe Louise trying to find her own "style." There was an obvious tug between the legacy of her family's "otherness" (rented homes/transient neighborhoods, working mother, intellectual rigor, teetotaling parents, contrary opinions) and her need/ desire to fit in—a universal exercise, and one made more strenuous by the extent to which one believes one's family diverges from some perceived golden mean. Louise started her college days looking identical to all the other young women and ended up going beyond approved limits. In reaction, the pendulum swung way back: small-town teacher/wife/daughter-in-law attending Ivy League football games, teas, and dinner dances. She was finding her way by trying things—by default, by discovery and reflection. And indeed, life with John Bacon, his mother, and high society went against the grain.

On March 18, 1931, Louise filed for divorce, returned home to Bridgewater, and visited often with Hester in nearby Waltham:

I don't think it was a bitter divorce, they just weren't on the same wavelength, intellectually or emotionally. I think it took Dik [Hester's diminutive of Dicky] a while to rationalize this whole thing and calm herself down. It wasn't that easy. But I don't remember her ever complaining or talking about it. She was just happy to be with me. This was typical. If anything troubled her very deeply, she wasn't known to verbalize about it. I could always tell by her quietness if something was wrong. She would work it out until she was confident in the line of action she was going to take. And then she took it. This was a thing I respected in her very much. I guess I tend to be the same way so I understood her and it was part of the good relationship that we had.

The supportive space her dearest friend and her family provided allowed Louise to take stock of her life and make some formative decisions. Marriage to Bacon—and, by extension, to conventional society—proved a disappointment and loss of innocence. What to do next? By this time, she was twenty-eight years old. She had experienced the realities of work, marriage, and small-town life. She wanted more: culture, adventure, a challenge. She wanted to move ahead and try again. The pendulum swung back....

Louise and Hester dreamed and schemed and decided they would both apply for teaching positions in or around New York City. Louise reasoned that she should finish her degree in order to strengthen her job prospects. This was, after all, in the midst of the Depression. On April 7, she reentered Bridgewater State Teachers' College under the name of Mrs. Louise Dickinson Bacon. According to the registrar, she "carried a heavy program," and received her full four-year degree on June 15, 1931. On July 1, her divorce was granted and she resumed her maiden name.

Hester and Louise were successful in their job searches: "Dik found a good one in Bound Brook, New Jersey, and I got one in Mount Vernon, New York." The Bound Brook Board of Education personnel files show that "Ms. Dickinson was approved for employment on June 9, 1931, as an 8th grade English teacher in the Washington Grammar School and was employed until June of 1933." The Bound Brook Chronicle, a decade later, reported that Louise lived with a "Mrs. B. A. Copeland on Mountain Avenue. Her friends knew her as Dicky. To them she was outstanding for her unconventionality, her rather blunt manner, an interest in outdoor sports, a less than the average woman's concern about clothes, though she was an inveterate knitter, and a not too enthusiastic attitude toward teaching."

Hester picks up the story:

From 1930 to 1933 we were together practically every weekend. This was great fun because we thought going to New York City was just the living end. We would save $10 apiece each week. Then around behind the Astor Hotel, one of us would book a hotel room for all of $1.50. And it usually ended up that Enid and Ruth appeared from someplace. I don't know whether they were teaching, or if Enid was married at this point, but they'd show up occasionally, and we'd all pile into this single room, scared to death we'd be found out! And on our $10, from Friday night until Sunday night, we did practically every theater show that came out. We did everything that anyone would ever want to do. Dik and I would take a map of New York City, and we'd block out the area we were interested in. And then we'd walk it. We literally walked everything from Brooklyn to the Connecticut boundary. And even though this was during the Depression, strangely, it was the healthiest time to be in New York. It was very open, people were generally kind, we learned a great deal, and nothing unfortunate happened to us.

One Saturday morning we were walking along Amsterdam Avenue and we came to the photographer Alfred Stieglitz's studio. I guess our noses were pressed against his window, and he asked us in and talked to us quite a lot. Then he said, "Would you like to come to tea next Saturday? Artists visit and my wife, Georgia O'Keeffe, will be here and perhaps you'd like to meet her?"

Well, of course we were familiar with her work and said, "Oh yes! We'd like to do that!" So, we arrived the next Saturday and, lo and behold, Georgia O'Keeffe was there, along with a number of prominent artists, and he introduced us to them all! I don't know, but these things happened to us all the time. We were curious and just absorbed everything, and so we always had great fun together.

Then, it was in 1933, I believe, when Alice went up to the area around Rangeley, Maine, liked it very much, and suggested that Louise come up. So she left here, on the Cape, sometime before the summer was out—say, August—and she went up to some camp to be with Alice. And, on a canoe trip, Ralph [Rich] was there and it was love at first sight. Dik just really never came out. She stayed from that point on. And through letters and telephone—I would hear from her frequently, maybe as much as every week—I pretty much knew what made her happy, the hardships, what was going on, and so forth.

Actually, records show that in September 1933, Louise was in Bridge-water, at the Malden High School, teaching sophomore English (salary: $1,500). Why did she decide to leave New York? Perhaps the pendulum was swinging gently back, away from society and the city? At any rate, she was home, with a signed teaching contract. Her heart really wasn't in it, though. That belonged elsewhere.

Ralph

Ralph Eugene Rich, born April 11, 1890, was the son of Isaac Baker Rich, Boston theater impresario (originally from Bucksport, Maine, and a long line of shipbuilders), and Pauline Van Babo Rich, born in Boston and daughter of Leopold Van Babo, a German chemist. From all accounts, he had a childhood reminiscent of the Plaza Hotel's famous book character Eloise—living in hotels, eating room-service meals, and befriending hotel staff, guests, and theater people. Once, as the family story goes, young Ralph found a hotel storage room full of old mattresses and quickly set to bobbing from one to another to his heart's content. He also hung around backstage in his father's various theaters. A production of *Ben Hur* was playing to a packed audience when Ralph, lolling on the sidelines, inadvertently hit the button for the moving-sidewalk apparatus to simulate the chariot race. The actors suddenly were conveyed offstage—much to their chagrin and the audience's amusement. Years later, he used to sneak school buddies backstage to see the shows.

Ralph attended the Noble and Greenough School in Dedham, Massachusetts, where he fortuitously linked up with one of the teaching masters, a Mr. Wiswell, who led small coveys of boys on expeditions to the wilds of Maine. Here they tented and hiked, fished and boated—for hotel- and school-bound Ralph, it proved a heady experience. Their destination was the Richardson Lakes area of western Maine: beautiful expanses of clear water surrounded by virgin forest. They boated on Lower Richardson Lake and stopped at Lakewood Camps, owned by Charles ("Captain") Coburn. There they saw the "middle dam," used by the timber industry to sluice logs down the aptly named Rapid River. And they lugged their gear down the Carry Road (for portaging) to a cabin with several outbuildings tucked next to the river. The complex, noted on old maps as the Oxford Club Camp, was owned by Edwin Abbot of Cambridge. On November 29, 1905, Abbot sold the place to Robert Davis from Chelsea, Massachusetts. One of these gentlemen may have been an acquaintance of Wiswell's—hence the connection to the area.

This letter, dated June 30, 1904, when Ralph was fourteen, clearly shows that he had made connections to places and people in the area. It was addressed to Royden ("Dick") Allen, son of local guide George Allen:

Dear Dick

I hope you are well. Is our camp all right? I am going to send up a package by express addressed to you. Please do not open it before I arrive. I will come on the 18th of July. Hope your father is getting better and will be all right when I get there. Come down to the boat [landing] and meet me. Give my kind regards to everyone.

Yours truly,
Ralph Eugene Rich

P.S. Be sure not to open the package.

In another note to Dick, sixteen-year-old Ralph was definitely smitten by a new boat, and particularly its engine—the first in a lifetime of such romances.

Dear Dick,

I have had the slickest luck you can think of. Ma has promised me the motor boat and today Mr. Wiswell and another gentleman and I went down town and looked the boat all over. Mr. Wiswell thinks she is a little beauty and she is too. She is eighteen feet long, about four feet wide, and has a 3 horsepower gasoline engine. It will go about 7 or eight miles an hour. She has a seat in the stern, back of the engine and seats running on each side in front of the engine. The engine is a little aloft of midships. She has a small deck in the bow and one about the same size in the stern. The one in the bow covers the gasoline tank which holds about fifteen gallons, enough to run about 150 miles. The stern deck covers the muffler. She has a coaming running all around the cockpit, and has a small wheel. She will cost about $270, and to get her up and all ready it will cost about $325 to $350. Tell me do you think you can raise any money toward it and how much. If you can't why you can repay it in meals and board etc. Tell me about the fish caught last fall, the sizes, who caught them and the flies. Did you catch any big ones. Were any of my big ones at the Pond [Pond in the River] caught. I did not send you my Christmas presents because I thought that I could bring you up something next spring that you would like better. Write me as soon as you get this.
Give my regards to everybody.

Yours truly,
Ralph E. Rich

P.S. Please ask George York or Ed or any engineer about getting a
license to run a gasoline engine, when you can be examined,
how, where you go and how much it costs and who will do it
and all about it and let me know everything. Find out fully. Write
very soon. R.E.R.

Ralph continued to spend winters in Boston and summers in Maine,
and by 1909 he went off to Harvard. Family and class photos show a handsome young man with dark hair, high forehead, and deep, dark-blue eyes.
He was six feet seven inches. Ralph was at Harvard until 1912, in an interesting coincidence, also not finishing his senior year (although neither
did 154 other students out of his class of 661). Louise and Ralph's "three-
year degree" clearly was not unique at the time and did not prevent them
from getting good jobs. In addition, world events and societal expectations, especially for young men, were pulling would-be graduates away.
As President Lowell told Ralph's classmates in 1913: "I cannot myself con-
ceive how any man with a heart in him can see the battle of the world
going on before his face and not take a part in it."
However, by the time of this speech, Ralph was already otherwise
occupied, and his work would, in fact, make a contribution to the war effort. Here is his description (an amalgam of various class reports) of what
happened after college:

I left College in May, 1912, and continued in the work of ex-
perimenting in various mechanical ideas regarding automobiles.
Moved to Pasadena, California, in May, 1913, and entered the employ of Thomas D. Campbell Company, Los Angeles, real estate,
that same month. This lasted about a year, when I luckily became
connected with Bob Burman's automobile racing crew. A year of
this gave plenty of excitement and a lifetime of thrills. During this
time I worked out a new type of bearing metal that became widely
used in racing circles and I began to manufacture the same com-
mercially in July, 1914, in Los Angeles. Was joined in this during
August, 1914, by J. W. Brooks Ladd, '11, and we moved the business to Chicago, Illinois, in June, 1915, under the name of Amalgamated Metals Company. Throughout the entire war this company
was manufacturing government materials exclusively, in fact its entire production was eventually taken over by the United States
Shipping Board. I, being the President/production man, was taken
with it. I remained on my old job with the Amalgamated, getting

plenty of grief during the slump after the war, plenty of orders—all for automobile manufacturers—during the boom times following, and still more grief during the subsequent slump. So as the capital was getting thin and neither of us wanted to get clubby with the Sheriff, we liquidated.

In January, 1922, I left the old vale of tears and entered a new one known as Silver Reduction Company, hiring on as Vice-President and Chief Engineer. My duties are variable, consisting of going out and "bulling" our customers when things go wrong, all the way down to training the Company's Airedale watchdog to do tricks. However, I like it, get paid for it, and am getting on in the world, so what more could anyone ask?

Ralph was still unmarried as of that report, but by the spring of 1924, which coincided with Louise's ignominious departure from college, Ralph also entered a new stage in life. With Euterpe Fitz Gerrell, from Chicago, Ralph created a Massachusetts-based fund, the Rich Trust, and, on March 25, 1924, he and Euterpe ("Terpe") bought the Carry Road cabin along the Rapid River, naming it Forest Lodge. (The Registry of Deeds in South Paris, Maine, shows a later quitclaim deed stating that Ralph and Euterpe, "both of the town of Upton," where Forest Lodge is located, for $1.00 convey to the Rich Trust land "up river from the abutment of the old Richardson Bridge on the river which runs from Lake Richardson to Lake Umbagog about one-fourth of a mile below Pond-in-the-River, so called, with all buildings and appurtenances, containing about two acres con-veyed by deed of Robert Davis dated February 26, 1929.") At any rate, Ralph finally owned property in that corner of the world in which he felt a sense of continuity and belonging. In August 1924, he and Terpe were married, and on March 19, the following year, their child Sara ("Sally")— named after her maternal Aunt "Sadie" Sara Fitz Gerrell—was born.

According to Sally, her mother was a very glamorous woman. Terpe had not gone to college; she had married and divorced a wealthy man from Nashville, Tennessee, before she met Ralph in Chicago. "My mother's family was from Marion, Illinois, and she had been brought up to under-stand that a lady never does any housework." Terpe made fancy clothes for her young daughter, and the couple had a big, green touring car and unusual taste in food—for that time—serving artichokes, for example. Ralph enjoyed eating raw eggs. Each summer, the family traveled to Maine. Sally fondly remembers the annual train trip from Chicago and later from Ohio: the bunk and little blue light of the sleeper bed, the meals in the elegant dining car.

In 1933, the twentieth-anniversary records of the Harvard class of 1913 carried some of the details of Ralph's life:

> I then went with an outfit that refined silver from wastes and got up a new process for extracting the silver from photographers' waste hypo solution. This went finely for a couple of years, until the movie laboratories decided to move out of Chicago, so I started to write articles and books on Costs and allied subjects for *System Magazine* and the Shaw Co., which I did off and on for a couple of years.
>
> Rather inadvertently I got wished into a job running an ailing manufacturing business for one of the Chicago banks, and when I got the bank's money out, this led to another, and so on until I finally got put into one that made nuts (not the kind that grow on trees but, nevertheless, an apt business).
>
> After a couple of years of no capital, etc., I finally sold it for the benefit of its many creditors of many years' standing, to a competitor. But while I was there, I designed and built some very ultra, ultra high speed and precision nut machines. Among other things I got up a new form of tap (for the uninitiated, a tap is the cutting tool used for cutting the threads in a nut) and, after moving the plant down to the purchaser's place in Ohio and getting it running, I sold the tap, together with a design of a machine for using it, to the company I am now with [the National Machinery Company, Tiffin, Ohio]. During the following two years I commuted between Tiffin and Chicago, holding down a manufacturing job in Chicago with one hand and a job as consulting engineer on the tapper with the other.
>
> The slight dip in the Stock Market finally put the kibosh on the Chicago job, so I moved permanently into the simple life of the wilds of the Ohio country. And what a life—not even a decent speakeasy within 93 miles.
>
> To digress for a moment, I sometimes wonder why I became a manufacturer instead of a banker. Our salary cuts over the last year have been only 66%, then 50% of that, and again 20% of that, while the bankers have swell bank holidays, moratoriums and what not. And now some of them are even taking vacations in jail

(as if they hadn't had enough time off just sitting around saying No!).

Well, anyway, we finally have the tapper developed, tested by a couple of years of actual use, and in production, so when we get around the next "corner" we will have a machine and tap that will, so our customers tell us, revolutionize the nut threading industry. So until then—here endeth the 20th lesson.

Ralph was still married to Terpe as of the writing of this "lesson," and still working on his nut-threading invention. With the invention, he had success; with the marriage, he did not. The pressures of working during the Depression are clearly evident in Ralph's report. Life in Ohio was not as cosmopolitan as in Chicago, and Ralph's dwindling salary and many debts undoubtedly made it hard for him to provide the high-flying lifestyle to which his family had become accustomed. For Ralph Rich, bounced around hotels as a child, shuttling to various cities as an adult, Forest Lodge and its environs constituted home—not only in the physical sense, but in the mental/emotional sense as well. It was a template for simpler, happier times. But for Terpe, the remote cabin on the Rapid River, containing the barest of necessities and requiring heavy maintenance, held no childhood memories and was far too simple to suit her tastes and desires. Forest Lodge may have been the final straw, the dividing line.

Before the summer of 1933, Terpe and Ralph separated. Terpe headed south and Ralph—after his mother, Pauline, arrived in Ohio to take up residence—headed north. Fed up with manufacturing, socializing, "keeping up with the Joneses," the economic crisis, his life in general, Ralph sold his nut-threading patent, liquidated some of his assets, and set off in August of that year for Forest Lodge, where he had always been happiest. In other words, he went home.

Meeting of the Minds

As Ralph unpacked his gear at Forest Lodge, Louise and Alice dipped their paddles in unison. Their party of four canoes slipped past stands of fir, spruce and pine, toe-to-toe at the water's edge. Louise sighed in deep satisfaction. Marriage, high society, divorce, the hustle of New York, teaching, her return to Bridgewater—all had left her feeling unsettled, restless. The beauty of the Maine landscape, Alice's presence, and the daily physical challenges provided a soothing catharsis. It was as though they were adult versions of their childhood selves, out exploring a new vast backyard, and Louise was finally beginning to relax and feel at peace.

It was August 1933. Alice had signed up for a camping trip (via auto, canoe, and trail) in the Rangeley Lakes region offered by the Richardson family's venerable Pinewood Camps. She called Louise at Hester's on Cape Cod to ask her sister to join her, because she knew Louise was trying to make some decisions. The change of pace and place might do her good. Besides, the trip would be infinitely better with Louise along. No one could get Alice laughing so much and take off on so many interesting conversational tangents. In *Happy the Land,* Louise described how friends would ask them, "What in the world do you two talk about that you can go on for hours?" Louise's answer was typical: "Oh, we can yak about almost anything. We just love the sound of our own voices."*

As they pushed off for the start of their camping adventure, Louise piped up: "You know, Alice, the thing about paddling a canoe is this. When you first start out after not having pushed one around for awhile, you make a conscious effort with every stroke. Your arms start aching, you get a crick in your shoulders, and you think, 'Why was I ever fool enough to let myself in for this? We've got fifteen more miles to go today. And fifteen tomorrow. And my arms are dropping off right this minute. I'll never be able to take it.' " Alice laughed and nodded and Louise added: "Then after an interval in hell you discover that your aches and cricks have vanished and you are paddling automatically, the operation completely apart from your personal life. It's like breathing or the beat of the heart, which goes on no matter what you are thinking or doing."

Their little party of eight men and women started at a campsite at Little Boy Falls (just above Parmachenee Lake, tucked in the western corner of Maine near the New Hampshire/Canada border), a wild, remote area

---

* [I've based the following reconstructed dialogue and trip events on Louise's description in *Happy the Land.* —A.A.]

that their guide, John Lavorgna, knew intimately. Louise decided John looked the part, with his plaid shirt, deerskin moccasins, and Indian features. The first night, around the campfire, he gave his "pedigree: one-quarter Indian, one-quarter Italian, and one-half Yankee." Whatever it was, she and Alice agreed that Joe was the "best guide imaginable. He worked like a horse, had the economy of motion and grace of a dancer, told a story like an experienced after-dinner speaker and could take anything his 'sports' dished out without getting flustered or run over."

Next day, they paddled south to sixteen-mile-long Aziscoos Lake, with islands and inlets and a gravel bottom. Joe found a lovely site on a peninsula and set up camp. After everyone was settled, the gear in order and the fire started, he walked to a little promontory and began fishing in the early evening calm. Louise went over and sat down on a rock to watch. "Here, let me try that, will you?" She soon discovered that fishing definitely was not as easy as it looked. But she also was "hooked, as they say."

As they approached Umbagog Lake, Louise was dreading the end of the trip. She had felt more her real self out under the stars, surrounded by trees and wild water, than she had back in her other self, surrounded by people and cities and teaching duties. Her chest constricted as she thought grimly of the daily restraints, restrictions, and regulations—the real "three Rs."

John planned that the party would head across the northern portion of Umbagog to a protected cove where they would then portage the canoes along a carry road to Lower Richardson Lake and thence to civilization. At this, the intrepid paddlers balked. The thought of lugging canoes along a five-mile trail was not exactly what they had in mind at that point. But Joe stuck to his itinerary, and when they reached Sunday Cove, they hoisted the canoes and started trudging.

It soon became clear why they had to portage their canoes—the river they were skirting was totally unnavigable. Joe told them that the aptly named Rapid River drops 185 feet in three miles—one of the swiftest rivers in the entire country. After about three miles of portaging, they reached the welcome sight of a house, cabin, and small outbuildings. Louise could see a man chopping wood and hear the roar of the tumultuous river in the background. The man put down his axe; the party lowered their canoes. All were glad for a break.

The initial pleasantries were so amiable that Ralph Rich invited them into his home. He explained that he had just arrived that morning and was chopping wood to build a fire and cook his first meal. Would they like to help him celebrate by staying for lunch? Over the meal, Ralph extolled the quality of the fishing more or less out his back door, and it didn't take much more to induce the group to spend the afternoon. He gave them a guided tour of his wilderness kingdom, pointing out the intended garden plot, opening up all the buildings and explaining his plans for improvements.

Later, as the happy company gathered on the porch of Forest Lodge, they readily accepted their host's generous offer to stay for dinner and the evening. As the talk and time proceeded, Louise Dickinson and Ralph Rich slowly became aware of how much they had in common. They appreciatively appraised each other's keen and curious minds, their comparable senses of humor, their similar wariness and weariness with the trappings of civilization, their hearty sense of adventure, and their knowledge and love of the outdoors. They were at the same spot emotionally: that fragile, vulnerable, early post-relationship freefall where one opens a door, steps out into thin air, and hopes a floor will rise up. Ralph shared his dream with his inaugural guests: He was fixing up the place because he planned to spend the rest of his life along the Rapid River. Louise was touched, intrigued, and secretly thrilled by his enthusiasm and bravery, his freedom. It sounded absolutely wonderful. The next morning, as the travelers prepared to leave, Ralph went over to Louise, reluctantly packing, and obtained her address.

Finally, the group headed off. Ralph picked up his axe, split a piece of wood, and then, standing in the front yard in the early morning sun, he watched quietly as the group rounded the driveway and dipped down out of sight. Slowly, pensively, he bent down to pick up another log and resume his preparations for the coming winter.

Meanwhile, on the Carry Road, Louise was finding it hard to put one foot in front of the other. With every step, she became increasingly convinced that she had just met her destiny and was walking away from it. She felt bereft, almost frantic. Her intuition said, "Drop the canoe and run back." Her intellect said, "Don't be impulsive; you know it gets you in trouble." What to do? What to do! Just ahead, Alice's enthusiastic impressions about the encounter, the locale, and the host began to peter out. She cocked her head at Louise: "Gosh, you're awfully quiet all of a sudden."

Forest Lodge

It took all of Louise's willpower to return to Bridgewater. Her life, the place, everything seemed flat and mundane after Forest Lodge. She lay in her bedroom on Dean Street and became obsessed with the conviction that she absolutely had to see a lot more of Ralph Rich. Fortunately, Ralph had come to the same conclusion. He started writing—prolifically. He also was writing to Pauline and Sally. He told them he'd had six inches of snow at Forest Lodge by October 24, that he had acquired a "Plymouth Rock hen named Fanny to keep me company," and that he had been visiting with a local guide and friend, Will Morton. Ralph began wiring and telephoning Louise day and night, asking her to come to Forest Lodge. Ralph was forty-three and Louise thirty, but the closeness of their aspirations and inclinations narrowed the thirteen-year gap.

Barbara Libby, one of Louise's sophomore English students in Bridgewater that fall of 1933, described the surprise that awaited her and her classmates when they returned from Christmas vacation. Their "quiet, athletic looking, good teacher" had left school quietly and "she never returned." Decades later, she still says wistfully, "We thought it was so romantic!"

The reality, of course, was much less romantic—a drafty, decrepit cabin with absolutely no amenities in the wilds of Maine in the middle of winter. But this, while arduous, was merely a superficial challenge. The underlying reality, resolve, and romance was their intense mutual need to be away from it all, yet with each other. They figured that with hard work and a lot of laughter, they could repair the buildings and themselves. And this they set out to do.

Then Pauline Rich became ill. (Ralph's father had died before Sally was born.) The doctors said that only rest and absolute quiet could save her. Fortunately, Louise, Ralph, and Pauline were in agreement that Forest Lodge was the lifesaving prescription for all of them. On March 19, 1934, Sally received an encouraging ninth-birthday note from Ralph: "I've been working all winter fixing up Grandmother's house inside and I've got a lot of it done."

Sally also received a card from her mother, who at that point was in Trinidad. Although both Ralph and Terpe expressed hopes of seeing her, neither of them was in a position to offer their young daughter educational stability. When her grandmother left for Maine, Sally went to live with Aunt Sadie Fitz Gerrell. Although Louise only mentioned once—

obliquely, and two decades later—that Pauline lived with them, she did, in fact, spend the last years of her life in the small "Winter House" that Ralph had been fixing up. She was in residence before Ralph and Terpe's divorce became final on July 23, 1935.

The years from 1934 to 1938 were full of activities critical to winter survival. During this time, Louise and Ralph acquired a right-hand man, Ralph Gerrish. Gerrish, as they called him (to distinguish between the Ralphs) had four children and a capable, strong-willed wife that "he liked to keep at arm's length," as the Riches' neighbor, Alys Parsons, puts it. He apparently was indispensable, particularly early on, in helping to forge something livable out of the dilapidated complex. Gerrish stayed in the small "Guide's House," near the Winter House, and took his meals with Ralph, Louise, and Pauline.

Alys Parsons during this period was waitressing at "Captain" Coburn's Lakewood Camps, Ralph's childhood haunt. (Still in operation, it's tied for the distinction of being the oldest continuously running sporting camp in Maine.) Alys says she was so busy getting used to the new job and surroundings, and falling in love with her soon-to-be-husband Larry (they were married in 1937), that she didn't pay much attention to what was going on two miles down the road. She doesn't remember Pauline (who was an ailing recluse at this point). The Riches' only other neighbors were Renny and Alice Miller, the damkeeper and his wife, who lived at Middle Dam ("Middle") year-round with their family. The Millers had taken over from Merna and Albert Allen, Ralph's friends, another set of Allens, from his childhood visits. Merna and Albert had moved to Upton—the nearest town through the woods, and Louise and Ralph's legal residence.

Ralph, Louise, and Gerrish (with intermittent help from friends, family, and periodic boarders such as loggers and road crews) battened down the hatches, cleared land, and planted and policed a garden. The soil there is poor—rocky and acidic from the pine trees—so they began the arduous process of hauling in loads of manure from Middle. ("Captain" Coburn had a cow, and there were several horses.) Then, after finally getting something to grow, they watched as the wildlife decimated their harvest. They lugged in fencing; it all slipped down the slope in the melting snow and rain. They began anew, constructing a soil-enriched, fenced-in, terraced garden. It all took patience, and a hellacious amount of effort. Everything from "Outside" had to be hauled in from the point of purchase, then fifteen miles down a dirt road to the South Arm boat landing, then boated across Lower Richardson Lake to Middle Dam, and down two miles of the Carry Road.

Louise and Ralph recalled those early years in a 1942 interview with the *Maine Sunday Telegram.* Louise: "For a few years we were prosperous enough, then hard times came along." Ralph: "When I went into the woods I thought I had sufficient investments. I did not figure on a wife and children. Naturally I would not have married unless I saw my way clear to get along, but the loss of investments left us stranded nearly high and dry." Louise: "Sometimes I borrowed from one family or the other of the two who live in this section [Millers and Parsonses]. And often, I just scraped the bottom of the flour barrel. We had no baby then, and it didn't seem so hard. Ralph asked me if I wanted to go back to Boston. But I said, 'No, we'll hang on for another month.' Which became months."

Life on the Outside might not have seemed all that much better at the time. The U.S. economy in the mid-1930s was scraping the barrel, too. President Roosevelt closed the banks throughout America for three days straight. He revalued the dollar, set up civil projects, and established social security programs. Hitler, meanwhile, was building concentration camps, destabilizing governments, and occupying land. There was a revolution in Austria, a general strike in France, disaster legislation in Great Britain. The reach of the worldwide economic panic was far indeed, stretching to the cupboards of remote Forest Lodge.

Louise and Ralph had something else to think about. By April 1936, Louise was pregnant with her first child. She wrote that she and Ralph were alone at 3 A.M. on December 18 when Rufus (named after Ralph's childhood pet parrot) was born. Gerrish was out visiting his family for the holidays, Pauline presumably was in the Winter House. Ralph and Louise had been sliding on the ice the day before at a pond upriver, and Louise took a number of spills. This may account for Rufus's slightly premature birth and their lack of preparedness for his arrival. They were still in the big house, Forest Lodge (although they usually moved to the Winter House in November) and apparently were planning to have Christmas there together and go out to the hospital in Rumford. Ralph would then return to Forest Lodge, make the winter move, and return to Rumford to pick up mother and baby. As it was, Louise wrote that she delivered Rufus while Ralph was downstairs boiling water. He came in, sized up the situation, and took his newborn son down to the warm kitchen, where he oiled him all over with olive oil he had been saving for making insect repellent. He wrapped him in a blanket he'd heated near the stove, and the new Rich family threesome was in business.

Being a family was one thing, but what next? With deep winter and a newborn child staring them in the face, Louise and Ralph must have seriously discussed the business of bringing in further income. Ralph had taxied a few "sports" and loggers along the Carry Road and guided a few fishing trips, but recently they had had to barter and borrow. Fortunately, they were now cornered into acting on one particular part of what undoubtedly had been the original dream: lead a simple life, away from the mob, tinkering with engines, hosting interesting guests, reading good books, and—writing. Both Louise and Ralph hoped to become published writers. Ralph had written some technical pieces. According to Hester, Louise had submitted work for publication while she was in New York, but to no avail. Now the wilderness parents had motivation, spare time while tending the baby and the fires, and nothing to lose by acting on their dreams. Plus, living where and how they did, they had stories to tell.

"Why did I write my first story?" Louise answered in an interview. "Desperation, I guess." She said her sister pointed out a contest advertisement in a *Scribner's* magazine left by a guest at Lakewood Camps. The ad solicited stories and offered a first prize of $1,000, with five others ranging down to $300; six regional prizes of $200; twenty-five prizes of $100. In fact, Louise's first published story was a collaboration with Ralph called "Why Guides Turn Gray." Given the time it took to write a story, walk it out to be mailed, wait for a magazine editor to receive it and respond, they must have worked on the story either prior to Rufus's birth or very shortly thereafter, because only eight weeks after Rufus showed up, a $50 check arrived from *Outdoor Life*. Desperation turned to determination, and they now *really* were in business.

During the spring of 1937, a man named Rush Rogers came in to work the annual log drive on the river and to "dry out" after the death of his wife—a Russian countess—and son. He met Louise and Ralph, who invited him to stay on with them for the weekend, after the log drive was over, to help with a wall-building project. The two-day visit ended up being a two-year stay. Rush occupied the second bedroom in the Guide's House with Gerrish, worked on what needed doing, and encouraged Ralph and Louise in their literary pursuits. He had had an Ivy League education, had once started a small, innovative private boys school, and was a born teacher. Louise worked up another version of the Maine Guide story, called "Wish You Were Here," for the *Scribner's* contest. She finished it in May and since the contest deadline wasn't until August 1, they decided to send it to the *Saturday Evening Post*.

But full-time writing was not an option. The arrival of twelve-year-old Sally for the summer meant that there were, at the very least, seven mouths to feed: Louise and Ralph, Rush and Gerrish, Sally, ailing Pauline, and baby Rufus. Gerrish sometimes guided and worked outside Forest Lodge, guests and friends often brought in food and supplies, but it fell primarily to Louise and Ralph to keep it all going. Sally remembers that her grandmother was installed year-round in a tiny room in the Winter House. She recalls picking raspberries on a summer's day as a frail Pauline watched her from the back porch; the family would deliver meals to the Winter House and occasionally look in on Pauline.

Alys Parsons describes the place as being like a hippie commune, thirty years before the term was coined: people living together in back-to-the-land fashion, long-term visitors coming and going, everything fairly loose, and all very bare-bones. But the tide was turning. In July 1937, not only was "Why Guides Turn Gray" published, under Ralph's name, but a letter arrived from the *Saturday Evening Post* regarding "Wish You Were Here." Inside was a check for $350—a hefty sum in those days, definitely enough to fill the cupboards and boost morale. And the *Scribner's* contest was still out there. The topic: Life in the United States, Brief Articles of Personal Experience. Amid the summer gardening, cooking, and cleaning, and the usual flurry of visitors, Louise somehow managed to submit "First Monday in March," a down-home story of a typical New England town meeting. It is intriguing that her byline appeared as S. L. Dickinson. This was the first and only time, outside of the college yearbook, that she was anything other than Louise Dickinson Rich. Was it a desire to use her own name? Or, considering the time constraints, was the story something she actually wrote much earlier and decided to resurrect? Whatever the case, it does not diminish the outcome. (Louise's later insouciant, "Gosh, it just happened," belied her own previous efforts at being published.)

On September 4, 1937, Louise had the satisfaction of seeing her name (as Louise D. Rich, for the "Wish You Were Here" story) in the national print media for the first time. In October, she received notice that she was one of the winners in the *Scribner's* contest. The $100 prize enclosed was a godsend toward the coming winter. The risk of acting on their dreams had paid off, literally. (Out of the three dozen other contest winners that year, Louise was the only writer who would go on to national prominence, or be a name one could recognize today.)

The winter of 1937/38 was a turning point. Ralph and Louise had established a foothold in the wilderness; now they turned their attention and efforts toward trying to live there on an extended basis. On the strength of their published stories, and/or their literary connections they acquired a New York literary agent, Willis Wing. After Rufus's first birthday and the holidays had passed, Louise, at Willis's suggestion, wrote a short story, geared to particular publications and a general audience, which she called "Husband on Ice."

February 1938 was marked by two pivotal events. Pauline, age seventy-nine, died of a blood clot on February 14. Although no mention was made in the records of the disposition of the body, apparently she was cremated and buried at Forest Lodge. One door closed and another opened. . . . Shortly thereafter, Louise received a whopping $450 check from *Woman's Home Companion* (a magazine no longer in circulation) for "Husband on Ice," which had been retitled "Don't Worry." Willis clearly was working on her behalf. "First Monday in March" came out in *Scribner's* March 1938 issue, once again giving Louise national exposure. She worked on two other pieces: "Skunk in the Home," which appeared in an April edition of the *Herald Tribune,* and "Party for Phyllis," which *The American Magazine* bought in August for another heady $450. Then came

Section of a 1920s map showing Louise's neck of the woods. The Carry Road runs alongside the Rapid River from Anglers Retreat (Lakewood Camps) past Oxford Club Camp (Forest Lodge) to Sunday Cove on Umbagog Lake. Total distance: five miles. Pine Point, purchased by Louise in 1942, is at the western edge, right on the New Hampshire border (not labeled on the original map). COURTESY OF ALDRO FRENCH, FOREST LODGE.

a brief hiatus in Louise's writing, because Mother Nature had other plans.

On September 21, Fred and Edith Tibbott, close friends and frequent visitors, were "in," and apparently Rush and Gerrish were "out" (as in back to the outside/civilization). Fred and Ralph had gone up to Middle. Three days of pouring rain had turned into a howling wind, and a hurricane struck. As Louise and Edith sat horrified at Forest Lodge, one tree fell across the front porch and another sent the kitchen porch into the cellar, twelve feet below. Yet another tree crashed onto the roof right over Rufus's crib and started a leak that dripped onto his pillow. Ralph and Fred rushed back, dodging falling trees all the way. By morning, twenty-eight of their largest trees were strewn over the yard, the roads and paths were all blocked, telephone lines were down. In the aftermath, Ralph made a deal to acquire the board-size lengths of trees that were cleared from the roads. Just as their financial situation had started to stabilize somewhat, the Riches now would have to make extensive repairs to Forest Lodge. They spent a backbreaking fall patching roof leaks, constructing makeshift porches and a cellar, sawing trees, and hauling brush. The garden was a shambles. But whenever there was the slightest lull, Louise continued to write. They were desperate again.

This is not to imply that Louise only wrote to make money. She wrote because it was in her blood, it was a skill she had and enjoyed using. Nonetheless, Louise's writing talent was absolutely instrumental in helping the Rich family live at Forest Lodge. In December 1938, she carefully recorded story sales in the back of the diary she had been given for Christmas. The list attested to Louise's growing success as writer and breadwinner:

"Important Events" Subject: Story Sales

1937	"Why Guides Turn Gray"	Outdoor Life—Feb.	$50.00
	"Wish You Were Here'	S.E.P.—July	350.00
	"First Monday in March"	Scribners'—Oct.	100.00
		TOTAL:	$500.00

1938	"Don't Worry"	Woman's Home Comp.—Feb.	$450.00
	"Party for Phyllis"	American—Aug.	450.00
	"Skunk in the Home"	Herald Trib.—Apr.	50.00
	"Little Matter of Politics"	W.H.C.—Dec.	450.00
	"Another Breed of Cats"	Liberty—Dec.	270.00
		TOTAL:	$1,670.00

This diary (perhaps given to her by Rush?) covers the years from 1939 to 1943 and provides invaluable insight, in her own words, into the life, personality, and work of Louise Dickinson Rich. The excerpts in the next chapter I hope will give a very intimate sense of the Rich household, and the time and place in which they lived.

The Diary:
1939–43

The most striking thing about Louise's five-year diary is that every single day is filled in. Anyone who has kept a daily journal knows it is remarkably easy to skip a day, a week, or even a month. The immediate impact of Louise's diary—page after page covered in her relatively neat teacher's script—is that, all humorous self-effacements to the contrary, here is a person with tremendous discipline. And it isn't as though she had long, languorous days in which to record her impressions. The truth is just the opposite. In light of all that was going on, this completely filled diary is almost startling in its impact.

Furthermore, Louise was able to get an amazing amount of information into a small space, to create a sense of the day in very few words. Major events are given equal weight as the daily weather—a sometimes startling juxtaposition. There is remarkably little analysis, either of self or others, even in this very private medium. Emotions do permeate the pages—anxiety, frustration, exaltation, and so on—but often with only one or two words ("feel bum") or an exclamation point. Louise's evident honesty and restraint provide an interesting contrast to today's milieu of almost competitive public angst and self-justification. The diary also provides insight into the ambiguity between Louise's sense of privacy and her reported "bluntness." Perhaps she was able to cope with many of her feelings by living her life "out loud"?

Although the following entries comprise a shortened and edited version of the original, especially toward the last years, there is still a great deal of material. Hopefully, the accumulation of minutiae will draw the reader into Louise's daily world.

In the diary Louise frequently mentions the landmarks they would pass along the five-mile Carry Road. Here they are listed in order: Middle Dam/"Coburn's"; Club Pool Trail; Black Valley; up Birch Hill; Pond in the River, the logging camp/wangan; Forest Lodge—two miles. Next, Smooth Ledge; then the "Spike" logging camp/wangan—four miles. Finally, at the northern end, Sunday Cove, where there was a shack, telephone, and the boathouse in which Louise and Ralph stored their Chris-Craft on Umbagog Lake.

--1939--

The diary starts off with a wallop, the very first entry dealing with the personal consequences of a hotel fire that occurred in Rumford. Here are excerpts from the winter of 1939:

January 1: Rush [Rogers] killed last night in Rumford Falls View Hotel. Miller [Renny, the damkeeper] went down & identified body. 2: Larry [Parsons] & Will Morton dropped in for drink. First trip down with new snowboat "Black Maria." 3: Ralph broke out road to Middle in Essex. Took two hours. Joe called up—just got Magallaway bills for road—mailed two weeks ago. [Ralph plowed the backwoods roads with his 1929 Essex truck to bring in extra cash.]

January 4: Henry Bemis & Arch Hutchins hauling our wood from Birch Hill [Louise and Ralph's woodlot]. 6: Rain, for God's sake, and temp. up to 45 all day and night. 7: Started story, and wood splitting on big pile left by Hen. & Arch. 8: R. walked to Middle ["M"] with mail. Couldn't make it with car. Finished red and grey mittens. 10: *Woman's Home Comp* came with first published story "Don't Worry"—nee "Husband on Ice." [This is puzzling, since there had been three published stories prior to this date. Perhaps she was talking about the first piece for *W.H.C.*? Perhaps this was her first non-collaborative story?] 11: Rufus [age two] had first convulsion, nearly scaring us to death. 12: R. attempted M. in Essex [truck]. Went into swamp at head of Pond & Arch Hutchins had to pull him out with horses. Probably last trip. Al lent me "All This and Heaven Too." 17: Cold. Split some wood in p.m. R. finished "White Elephant." [Unpublished. Clearly, both Ralph and Louise were writing, and doing their own pieces.] 18: Larry's ice cutter fell in lake. Starting to house break Rufus. Walk to Smooth Ledge looking for shovel. No luck. Lost Kyak [the dog]. 19: Cold as the devil. Wrote Sally. Split a little wood. Finished maid of all work story. *Bum!* Name of story—"Edna Takes an Interest." 21: R. walked to M. Letters from Stumpy [one of group of yearly visitors from Fitchburg, Massachusetts]. Airplane brought in mail (1st time ever). 23: Coldest day yet—14 degrees when we got up & 3 at 2 p.m. R. finished rewrite of "In Memory." Calls it "The Great Fish Spouts Music" [unpublished]. 24:

Larry [Parsons] & Renny [Miller] went out, bringing in Gerrish, library books, and mystery package, probably stove parts. 26: Started new Jed & Caro [Caroline] story. Thermometer never got above zero all day. 27: Twenty below zero when we got up. G & R spent day sharpening tools in kitchen. 29: Above freezing all day. Mail. Very nice letter from [Willis] Wing about "Edna Takes an Interest."

During the rest of the winter, the "two Rs" [Ralph and Gerrish] dealt with trees felled by the fall hurricane. Louise's diary continued to reflect her interest in nature: daily weather conditions, wildlife sightings; in literature, opinions, and events on the Outside; and in her family/writing life.

February 5: Finished story about Jed, Caroline & a siren ["A Wife's a Working Woman"]. 9: Learned how to whip canned milk: Put on stove in cold water; bring to a boil, boil 5 min.; chill thoroughly & whip. 10: Pope Pius died. 11: Started story about Latana Ripley. Helped G. saw up birch near house. He thinks I'm a good sawyer (I am!). 14: Finished Latana story and like it pretty well. 15: Poured. Typed "A Good Day for Spring Cleaning" all day. 16: Below zero all day. Got mildly approving letter from Wing about "A Wife's a W.W." Not too keen.

February 22: Big snow storm. Rufus loves his Bingo Bed that came yesterday. Started revision of "The Great Fish Spouts Music" [Ralph's story]. 24: Got letter from Sally saying they [Terpe and Sally] are going to Haiti (Why? for godsake?) where she'll enter convent school. Ralph working on story, I on fish story. Bum futile day.

Sally had been living with Terpe in Liechtenstein before needing to move on: "Germany had just taken over Austria and there was barbed wire all across Switzerland. My mother and I got one of the last tramp steamers out and sailed to Haiti where we stayed at the Hotel Splendide for one month, and where I had a very fancy fourteenth birthday party. We then sailed to Baltimore and up to Boston."

March 1: Warm and very windy. Kitchen chimney caught fire. Very enthusiastic note from Wing about "Latana." Ward's catalog came. 3: Finished "The Great Fish" (rewrite) [first indication that

Louise did Ralph's rewrites]. Sawed up birch with G. behind
Guide's House. 5: R. & G. went over to Upton to attend town
meeting. [Entries for all five years show that only the men attended town meeting. On March 6, she was alone with Rufus,
unusual enough to note in the diary.] 7: Electric lights authorized
in town meeting. 10: Got word we sold "Latana" to *W.H.C.* Joe
called up & said "Another Breed of Cats" is in March 18 *Liberty.*
12: Logging crew came back in. 13: Biggest snow storm since
1888. We got 18"—about an inch an hour. 16: More snow and
down to zero again. Got winch frame and motor out of bedroom.
Made pop-corn balls—my first. 23: [Leon] Wilson [game warden]
in to dinner, bringing G.'s application for guide's license. 26:
Around 40, sleet. Terribly depressed all day. [This was the first
time in three months that Louise expressed specific feelings.]
Cooked bread & doughnuts. 28: Worked on "A Little Matter of
Business." R. & G. went to B. Pond after loot. [When logging
crews went "out," their cooks left food in the wangan, or store-
room. These leftovers were often godsends to the financially
strapped Rich household.]

April 3: Snow, raw. Larry came in—4 hours to Arm from Andover
[a fifteen-mile trip!]. Terpe called Miller from Baltimore. [As
Louise wrote in *We Took to the Woods,* Terpe had decided, if all
went well, to place Sally in their care at Forest Lodge. Louise
then went on an early spring-cleaning jag—lugging water from
the frigid river, washing down walls and floors of the Summer,
Winter, and Guide's Houses—on account of Terpe's visit.] 7:
Telegram from Terpe in Baltimore. "Wine of Good Hope" from
[sister] AED. Millers saw geese in lake. 10: Terpe and Sally came
in. Walked down from M. 11: Ralph's birthday. Sally took care of
Rufus so I could write. 12: Finished "Little Matter of Business" &
G took it up to M. 14: Snow. We now have still about 40 inches.
Cooked all a.m. Takes too many desserts for this crew. 21:
Warmest day yet—over 50 degrees. snow going fast, altho' still
have plenty. Washed curtains & started third Madonna [idealized
woman] story. 23: Letter from Wing—mildly pleased with "Little
Matter of Business." 24: Ice out of Sebago [Lake in southern
Maine; Louise recorded this event each year, in anticipation of
the much-awaited local ice-out]. Terpe cleaned Guide's House.
R. & G. laid stringers for bridge to Spirit Island. [They continued

working on this cable pulley bridge for several weeks.] 25–27: Rufus sick—finally had convulsion at 11 p.m. Terpe up all night with him. 28: Warm & sunny. Ice out a year ago to-day. Gerrish went smelting—first trip this year. No luck.

May 1: Went fishing at Dam with G. First time. Saw nothing. Snow mostly off gardens. Narcissus up. Snow boat went into lake off Coburn's dock. Coburn came in. 3: Finished "Little Matter of Child Welfare." G. went smelting. 11: Hole in Dam collapsed & Ted [dam foreman] came in. G. gone up to cook for [maintenance] crew. First mail in week. 19: Finished planting flower seeds. Letter from Wing, not liking last story much. [Louise worked on the rewrite daily through May.] 22: First trip to Middle in Essex. Crew finished cat walks on Dam & went out. 25: Terpe left [after a month and a half!]; moved to big house; AED came. 26: Fire started at C Meadows, but under control late at night. 27: Lovely day, but windy. Fire started up again going to B. Brook. Very alarming. Showers at night damped it. 31: John Lavorgna, Charlie Barney in with Perry Greene, PG=champion chopper of world. Goes thru' 8" log in 15 sec.

June 3: Alice went home. 4: Finished "A Hard Row to Hoe." 6: Heard Barnett [Jim, logging contractor from Upton] coming in here to cut. "Globe" subscription started. 9: Went swimming for first time. Cold. Started "A Present for the Baby." 10: Swimming. Finished story. Went down road with R. and saw game warden behind tree. [He reported the next day that a prison gang had run the upper river.] 12: Hot and windy. Washed kitchen floor. Letter from Wing mildly approving "Hard Row." 14: Thirty-six today. Rainy. Walked up to Middle to see Alice, Gertie. Took Gert's baby some rompers of Rufus'. Got dollar from James [Dickinson] for birthday. Broke & practically no food in house. 16: Open & shut [clear and cloudy]. Food situation continuing critical. Feel very bum. Gave G. horse hair belt, denim pants, and shirt. Rufus fell down cellar hole. 19: Richardsons came in & we had no coffee. [The Richardson family had two out-cabins for Pinewoods—also called Pinewood Camps. One was at B Pond, the other beyond Forest Lodge toward Sunday Cove.] 20: Hot, lovely. Letter from Wing turning down "Present for the Baby" flat. Started new story. Ralph started hauling for Barnett [until the end of June]. 21:

Worked on story. John [Lavorgna] & party left. Gave us steaks which came in handy. 26: Bugs awful. Finished "Wednesday Night Off." First radishes. Got food from Barnett. Letter from Wing saying he's coming in July. 28: Hot, buggy. Rufus & Sally swimming. Road crew came in to eat at Wangan. Lewis beat Galents—[boxing match] fourth round.

July 4: Hot & clear. All hands went to Deep Pocket swimming. R. & G. first swim of season. Lost Kyak. Flies bad. 8: Still very hot—86 degrees in shade. Tried to start revision of "Astral Lure." Book on writing arrived from Fred Tibbott. 11: Horse came and hauled out logs in yard. Jim B's truck stuck at Cove. 13: Cleaned winter house partially [three days of heavy cleaning for the upcoming Wing/Tibbott visit]. Started "Ordeal." Swimming nice. Rufus loves it. 17: Overcast. Wings & Tibbotts came, not getting here until late p.m. *Awfully* nice people. 18: Rather grey. Talked quite a lot about writing. [Later entries indicate that the topic of Louise's writing a book about life at Forest Lodge came up, or solidified, on this day.] [Next day, everyone went fishing.] July 20: Hot with big storm. Hail 6" deep down below. Wings and Riches went down to haul out Barnett's truck. Snow shoveling in July. [Wings left the next day.] 22: Hot & clear. Went swimming twice. Had Round Table about R & Fred's stories. Heated arguments.

There is no published record of any Ralph/Fred stories. A local-color piece, by Tibbott, appeared in the May 1938 *Saturday Evening Post*—perhaps with input from Ralph? The Tibbotts left on July 24 as John Lavorgna came in with a party of people.

July 28: Four Fitchburgers [Massachusetts] came in. [Stumpy et al.]. 30: Hot, muggy. Fitchburgers big help in Black Valley. Drove tractor. Big thrill. 31: Stumpy & Fixit to Pine Island. Bill fishing. B. & I got tight. F's went home.

August 1: Lovely, brisk. R & G to Black Valley taking Rufus who had swell time with tractor drivers. 2: Worked on story. "Shattered Schedule" of Ralph's back from Wing. 3: Hot. Worked on "Wed. Night Off" all day. 4: Muggy, enervating. Worked on story most of day. 5: Lovely day. Edgar Worcester burned arm on tractor in a.m. Dr. Kreida from M. attended. Says Rufus has rickets &

needs leg exercises. 6: "Middle Dam Day." Sally sucked G into rowing her to M. in eve. Finished "Wed. Nite Off." 7: Hot. Sally being *very* helpful. Gov't man came to see about P.O. route here. R & G hauling gravel for Barnett to fill in ruts made by twitching [dragging logs] across Carry.

For the next two weeks, they moved gravel, and Ralph hauled canoes occasionally for sports. Meanwhile, Louise, Sally, and Gerrish picked fourteen quarts of raspberries and twenty-eight quarts of blueberries, getting lost in a blowdown (a section of fallen trees) once in the process.

August 8: Wrote Terpe to come here. Sent off "Wed. Nite Off." 9: Got Rufus' shoes fixed to make his toes turn in. Sent flowers to Dr. Kreida's wife. 10: Rufus cut thumb—first big cut. Proud of bandage. "Wilderness Wife" from Wing. [About the wilderness experiences of Daniel Boone's wife, Rebecca. Wing probably sent it in regard to the discussed book project.] 24: Kyak in fight with Edgar W's dog. Also fell in river & flushed bevy of half-grown partridges. Baby rabbit [kept three days]. 27: Nice day. Rufus up at 5:00 and spilled potatoes all over floor. Gerrish brought me pond lily. 28: "Fold" boats here. Fun. [Precursors to kayaks, they were used to run the Rapid River during a yearly three-day festival.] 30: R & Mr. Little ran from M. Dam to here in foldboats. R took 3 dumps. Rufus swam alone for first time.

September 1: Littles left. "Each to the Other" for me from Willie Little. Germany invaded Poland. 3: Thunder storm. Went to call on Allens [Upton]. Fr. & Eng. declare war, take "Bremen." 5: Gerrish back from visiting wife. Edgar hauled downed trees in yard with tractor. Ned brought bacon fat from Mrs. Lamont [Upton]. Story in *American* ["Party for Phyllis"]. 6: Started fold-boat story ["The Dry Trip"]. R & G hauled enormous pine around front drive. 7: Windy, raw. Sold 40 cukes to Barnett for $2.00 Tried to write, but no go. 9: Rain and bleak. Started story about free trip to Bermuda, shelving fold boat. Letter from Alice in Guatemala. 10: Cold and rainy. Wrote. Eva [Gerrish's daughter] gave me $3.00 for sweater. [Louise took on knitting projects for supplemental income.]

September 19: Lovely crisp day: Finished story—not too good.

Practically out of food. 21: Anniversary (1) of Hurricane. Gerrish
to M. to listen to Pastor–Lewis fight [boxing match]. 26: Snow
squall. Barnetts started clearing river for drive. [This was the last
long-log drive in the east—needed to clear the woods from the
previous year's hurricane.] 27: Barnett drove some out of Pond.
Finished Arch's sweater. Food almost gone—no funds in sight. 28:
Cold, pleasant. Drive goes on. R & G fishing in eve. Walked
Rufus to Richardsons. Still no food. 29: Cold. Drive. Miller gave
1 case milk ½ pay for checked coat. [Were they bartering
clothes?] 30: Word came that winter mail route had been allowed. Books (review copies from Personal B.S. came).

October 1: Overcast, raw. Reporters & news reel men in for [log]
drive. Dinner at Barnett's camp. Three visitors stayed here. 2:
Started story about propaganda which may be good. 4: Raw.
Drive way past F.L. [Forest Lodge]. Worked on story. R fished
radio table out of lake where Coburn dumped it. Pkg. of clothes
from Huntie [Ruth Hunt] & Louise. 6: Indian summer day. Fan
letter about "Party for Phyllis." R & Sally have colds—first of the
season. 8: Warm. Ralph sick on couch with cold. Worked on
"Stillwater Front." Barnetts truck off road. 11: Worked on "Clear-
water [sic] Front" finally finishing it. R & G better. I have sore
throat. 12: Cold & raw. Got story ready to go out. Throat still bad.
Drive over.

October 14: Rufus discovered possibilities of nail & hammer &
pine block. Saw rainbow in p.m. 15: Feel bum—cold. G gone to
Larry's to work. Fred Cyr & Eddie Hibbard in, one about boarding
wife, another for hair cut. 20: R, Sally & Rufus to Spike for gravel.
Letter from Wing thumbing down story on propaganda. 21:
Warm, hazy. Tried to start drive story. Finished Eva's sweater. Fred
Cyr called & brought me two apples. 24: Snow squalls. Ground
white. Food situation acute. Started Gerrish sweater. 25: Warm
and lovely. Worked on Gov't Pine story. We are practically starving. Don't know what the outcome will be. 26: Rain—warm.
Opened last big can of hot dogs. Worked on story. Gov't scaler
[measures tree stumpage/footage] came in to borrow deck of
cards. 27: Rain. Mail Day. Worked on story. Fred Cyr in to visit. R
painted around lot line for benefit of wood cutters.

November 2: Open and shut. Sports in to hunt. Did good stint on drive story. 4: Lovely fall day. Worked on story. Fred Cyr in with proposal for me. Don't know whether to be insulted or flattered. 10: Moved to winter house, using car. Settled fairly comfortably. 14: Nice letter from Fred Tibbott offering us use of his house if necessary. 15: Cold. Worked on G's sweater. Dumb, uneventful day—feel very low in mind and spirits. 17: Raw. Barnett's truck folded, so R. hauling. Essex gear shift busted. Wing liked "Hurricane Timber." Gang [logging] from camp in eve. 25: Sunny day. F. Cyr fired. G missed 8 point buck on Carry Road. Worked on story. Harvard 7–Yale 20, R. at Parsons to hear game. Started Edward Miller's sweater. 27: Grey, brooding. Finished "Bless This House." Rufus has a little cold. Fight with Ralph about general messy situation. 30: About 50 degrees. Thanksgiving Day—no celebration. Skating in p.m. with kids. McGinley in [clerk from logging camp].

December 1: Like spring. Skating with kids & Edw. Miller & friend. Fun. WHC wants rewrite of "The Dry Trip." 2: Bunch of supplies from Barnett. Cooked all day. Army 0–Navy 10—listened to game in p.m. 5: A little snow—½". Walked to Pond with kids. Hills in sun lovely. Mail—Wing liked "Bless This House." 8: Lake all broke up again, blasting hopes. Snowed. Mail—letter from Supt. of Sch. about Sally. McGinley in to sharpen pencils. Feel rotten. 9: Made first ice cream of winter. Knit on Miller's sweater. Walked with R & kids to Lamont's Isle. Man came to see me about doing washing. 12: Lovely, clear day. Letter from Mass. Psych. Hosp. saying Terpe is there under observation. 13: Snow. Gerrish back for few days. Finished Edw. sweater. Brit.–Ger. naval battle off Montevideo. 15: R & G to Spike for sandwiches. Sent Mark Peabody (cook) a chair. Doug. Fairbanks dead. 20: Letter from Alice about seeing Terpe in hosp. Decided T should come here. Found beaver house under boat float. Took on another woodman's wash. 21: Found trap (illegal) for our beaver. A Judkins up with cigarettes in pay for A. Hulbert's wash. 22: Got good revis. of "Dry Trip" worked out. G back drunk. Pkgs. from Wings, Huntie & Louise. Xmas "card" from Ezra Baker, bless him. December 23: Cold (18°) windy. G with very bad hang-over. McGinley in in eve. to hear "Gangbusters." Worked on story—

should be good, I think. Rufus learned to soap bubble. 24: Cold
(8°) G better. McGinley in again. Finished new "Dry Trip."
Sounds good to us. Opened a couple of Rufus' presents. 25:
Went to Millers for Xmas dinner. *Very* pleasant day. Edw. & Angel
put Ford in ditch. Rufus had fun. R & G tried skating. 29:
Warmer—over 20. Game warden and two Barnett cars drove in
from [South] Arm. More damn traffic! G started work for Barnett.
31: Lovely a.m., cloudy snowy p.m. Family all went for walk on
Pond in a.m. Syd. Abbott here for eve. and supper. Hope next
year is better than this!!

--1939--
Stories Written and Sold

Louise and Ralph, between them, wrote sixteen stories in 1939:

Louise	*Ralph*
"Edna Takes an Interest"	"White Elephant"
"A Wife's a Working Woman"	"The Great Fish Spouts Music"
"A Little Matter of Business"	"Shattered Schedule"
"A Little Matter of Child Welfare"	
"A Hard Row to Hoe"	
"A Present for the Baby"	
"Wednesday Night Off"	
"Astral Lure"	
"Ordeal"	
"Clearwater Front"	
"Hurricane Timber"	
"Bless This House"	
"The Dry Trip"	

Only two stories actually sold during that year—"A Good Day for
Spring Cleaning" ["Edna Takes an Interest"] and "Latana."
Louise recorded year-end sales of $450, though probably it was more
like $900, counting "Latana"—still frighteningly low. As Louise put it,
"Total lousy."

--1940--

The year 1940 dawned to much the same economic roller coaster.

January 1: Down to bare poles again on food. 2: Check ($35)
from *Field and Stream*. The Lord is looking after us! Letter from
Alice D. saying Mass. has taken Terpe's welfare over.

The family all had bad sore throats the beginning of January, but that
didn't seem to stop them from sawing, shoveling out the wood pile,
walking up to Middle to get the mail, working on the house/cars/tools,
and writing:

January 6: Ralph working on rewrite of "Schedule" ["Shattered
Schedule"]. 19: *WHC* bought "Most Important Thing." 21: Ralph
working on fishing story. 23: Check came in from Wing—regular
rate [$450]. Wrote on new story some. R. paid Jim Barnett and
got groceries. 25: Worked on story, but finally tore it up to start
again. Seems swell to have house full of food for once.

In February, Sally took Rufus, age three, on walks to the wangan. He
was learning to dress himself, and he had a rabbit, "now definitely named
'Rober.'" Gerrish was working on the woods crew for Jim Barnett, Ralph
was fixing broken down cars and hauling wood. The adults sat up for
Lewis's boxing matches, kept tabs on Harvard football scores and current
events (such as the big storm in Boston, the most snow in forty years). And
Louise sewed, quilted, knitted—for cash or barter—and wrote steadily.

February 11: Third anniversary of our first sale (*Outdoor Life*—
"Why Guides . . ."). 19: Walk with R & G to Long Pool, exploring
pulp landing. Went off & left Rufus. 24: Whole family taking
baths. G. worried about self. Walks to wangan, Middle & Pondy
Dam. 27: Ten below in a.m. Split wood. Rufus threaded needle
all alone. Saw five planets at once. Wrote Terpe about outrageous
dresses of Sally's. 29: Ralph finished long nut manufacturing story.

March 2: General exodus to Town Meeting: Sally, Ralph, F. Judkins, E. St. Peter, A. Judkins. Spent eve. chewing with G. [The Jud-
kinses, from Upton, were staying or visiting at Forest Lodge while
working in the woods; they were two of many such boarders and

long-term visitors over the years.] 6: Worked on R's long nut
story, snapping it up some. 8: Stumpy, Bill & R. Smart arrived in
full flower. Glad to see them. [During this time, Gerrish quit
Barnett's crew and "went out for eye exam."] 11: Gang went out.
Returned mattresses. Felt bum. 17: Palm Sunday & St. Pat's Day.
Finished damn nut story of R's, thank God. Shoveled out tree by
dump in p.m. Read "Beer for the Kitchen." 19: Sally's [fifteenth]
birthday. Gifts from Albert Judkins and Buster Williamson [an-
other young Upton man] & relatives.

Toward the end of the month, the area was busy with logging: a "kid
from #1 [logging camp] and horse down twitching pulp all a.m. All out
working on pulp operation. Rufus' first horse ride." Crews from the logging
camps, Spike and #1, moved out, leaving "edible loot." They corded and
split wood in back of the hen house, shoveled out the old wood pile, and
lugged firewood. Meanwhile, Sally was being wooed, Alice Miller had an
appendicitis operation, and Louise write steadily on a "Box Supper Story."

March 30: Thawed all day. Worked on story. Rufus cut hand with
ax giving me awful sinking feeling.

In April, Ralph tapped maple trees for syrup. Gerrish was "out." The
river crew came in to fix the log booms [log corrals used to contain and
transport logs]. Louise finished the box supper story and "Rufus learns to
look like an angel." Spring cleaning for Louise began in earnest. On
Ralph's birthday, April 11, Louise made a cake, Albert Allen came in to
dinner on a tractor, and Larry Parsons came down.

April 12: Letter from Wing on "Sapphire." WHC like but had another. Sewed on Sally's clothes. Knitting for R & S. Read "Flames
Come Out at the Top." 16–20: Gerrish back. Non-committal letter
from Terpe. Mild approval of "Box Supper." Worked aimlessly on
"Hurricane Time" rewrite. R fishing for first time (none). Sally un-
strung by Buster–Albert affair [rivals for attentions], R & G making
smelt net and saw mill parts. 24: Finished "No Fit Place." Buster
brought Kyak home. Sap ran swell. Wrote Alice D. Marvelous
northern lights. Made homespun sweater for Rufus.

The rest of April, the roads were washed out and they had to fix the
Guide's House roof. They all continued to smelt, and Louise recorded
seeing her first swallow.

By May 2, the "ice is out of Sebago," the first thunderstorms arrived, and plants were just coming up.

> May 6: Started new story about adopted child. Fly tying and smelting with G. Letter from Wing approving "No Fit Place." Census taker went out. 9: Miller down with Jr., Rufus delighted. Four drowned hunters surfaced in Umbagog. Holland invaded. Saw three deer feeding at Long Pool. 11: Sunny & nice. Ice out on Umbagog. Raw p.m. G & I on ill-starred fishing trip to B. Pond. Ice out there. No fish. Saw sea gulls arrive. [See chapter 10 in *We Took to the Woods.*]

Crews came in to repair log booms and the roads damaged from winter twitching, and Ralph was busy taxiing them up and down. Soon the first of the guests (other than loggers and hunters) began arriving.

Between May 19 and 23, they moved to the Summer House, the cook for the log drive came in to Pond in the River wangan, a cabin at Coburn's Lakewood Camps burned down, and Rufus went barefoot for the first time. Louise planted flowers, Ralph and Gerrish spent days hauling manure to the vegetable garden, a check for $15 arrived from *American Home* for a seedbed piece Ralph wrote, and Albert and Buster were still in attendance. On May 24, Alice Dickinson arrived for a ten-day visit, followed by Edith and Fred Tibbott "with much food."

> May 27: Fish flown in to B. Pond. G spaded veg. garden. Sunbathing in p.m. John Lavorgna in. Edith had heart attack in middle of night. 28: Heavy thunderstorm: 2½" rain. Lightening struck pine in yard. Tibbotts went home, taking Sally. Telephones all shot. Alice, R & I fox hunting at 3 a.m. [full story in *We Took to the Woods*].

In June, the "war news is very bad." There were Coburn/Lakewood guests "all over the place," mosquitoes were bad, a semi-hurricane downed telephone lines, and the Alligator (the boat used to haul the log booms from dam to dam), broke down. More bodies surfaced from winter drowning and on June 10 Sally returned from visiting the Tibbotts. Louise had been writing "My Daughter" (an adopted-child story), and on June 14, she turned thirty-seven (with no mention of any celebration). Ralph and Gerrish were getting booms "strung" (connected) in the cove for their salvaged hurricane timber.

June 18: Kyak's birthday—3 years. R to Middle to help Miller on
Ford. Rufus too. Sally fishing. G replanted corn. Rolled first log
into cove. Marmon fixed, then busted. [The family was busy with
the log-drive operation, as were the commercial log drivers, who
left at the end of June.]

In July, the Schaffer family came for the river-running festival over the
Fourth of July weekend. "Rufus is so happy with other kids" around. With
the arrival of Stumpy et als, and visitors stopping in from Lakewood, Forest Lodge was brim-full of guests. Alice continued to send books. Louise
noted: "'They Shoot Horses, Don't They?' seems strangely haunting & impressive." After the guests left, Louise took a canoe "below dam in eve.
and fished. Started thinking about story."

July 18: Writing. Rufus laid up with lame leg. Buster in swimming. Went swimming alone. Swell. Out to Island with R. (R in
for first swim) S picking strawberries. 22: Weigh 169 lbs. [This is
the first recording of her weight.] Started writing refugee story.
Radishes. Peas in blossom. G caught small salmon. Logs all
hauled to Pond. Larkspur out.

July 24: Sally & I sick & up much of night. G on road for Coburn.
John L. in with party. 27: Hot, overcast. R & G fixing rock at back
door. Swimming with kids. Scene at dinner between R & S about
reading. I can't stand it much longer. Row on Pond with Ralph in
eve. 30: Hot, humid. G on road. Showdown with R about Sally.
Almost no food & no money. Larry down to fix Ford left last
night. First beet greens.

August 1: R & G pulling stumps in yard. Worked on Refugee
story, but no go. Decided to start over. Raspberry picking. Erect-
ing gravel tower by lily of the valley bed. 3: No meat, so veg.
dinner. Swimming with kids. Finances desperate. R & S got blueberries. Moving firewood. Swam with Rufus. Nice to be alone. 7:
Tried to write, but Rufus pesty. Practically no food or money in
house. First new peas. R & I got 4 qts. blueberries at Long Pool.
8: Howey Reed in with VT girls' camp. Gave us leftovers, thank
God! Mrs. Lamont brought ginger marmalade. Letter with $10
from AED. My faith is renewed.

Louise wrote steadily in mid-August and finished her refugee story, "No Safer Refuge." Alice came for another visit—three weeks this time. Gerrish and Louise picked raspberries and blueberries and Louise gave Gerrish her old boat. Louise wrote "Sadie [Sally's Aunt] about Sally going to school in Upton" and Louise and Ralph rented a house in Upton for this purpose. On August 27, Terpe arrived, "looking awful." Sally developed strep throat, Gerrish began to guide for Coburn, and visitors continued to pop in.

> September 3: Muggy. Call from Wings. R asked Terpe to stay on—I am mad. Alice, Rufus & I walked to *Alligator* & talked about Barbados. Geographic survey in. 4: G gone out. Alice not well—very worried. [She was OK the next day.] 7: Bob Kingsley family with Wings arrive. Sally and Alice out to Upton/[then] Newton. 9: Rufus feeling sick. Terpe being *very* helpful—couldn't do without her. 10: Terpe went home. Barnett started coming in. [There was a new #3 logging camp as well as his #1 camp.] R hauled for B. all day. A. Miller saw Sally in Andover. 13: Wings went home. Signed agreement with Will for income for year.

This Wing visit was the turning point in Louise's career. It is clear that the grating poverty and instability of their writing/wilderness efforts were becoming almost intolerable. The agreement Louise signed provided hope for the future. It recognized Louise's worth as a writer and allowed for a small but steady income with which she could work. By the time of this visit, the Riches' savings had dried up, they had had three years with very little money coming in, and they were trying to squeak by on a frightening $550 in story sales over a full eight months.

The agreement was crucial, and motivational: Willis Wing would send Louise a monthly check, Louise would send Wing a monthly story. Not only did it become possible, but artistically important, to stay together at Forest Lodge. Although a copy of the agreement has not surfaced, further diary entries reveal that an additional element was the plan for Louise to prepare sample chapters and an outline for a book on her wilderness experiences. Louise began to write in earnest.

> September 16: Office hours start. Wrote. Walked to Oxford [camp] to see new bridge. Quite an affair. Blueberrying in p.m. Feel run-down, tired, nervous, and cross. S. to go in grade 8.

18: Wrote. Went to *Alligator* in p.m. to try to close boom. First check from Will Wing on new deal came.

While Louise wrote, Ralph and Gerrish worked on the hurricane timber boom. Ralph started fixing vehicles and got batteries for his saw mill for the hurricane timber extraction. Lakewood closed and there was a killing frost on September 27.

October 1: Ralph begins working for the geodetic survey over by B Pond. Gerrish gone for winter. Rufus & I alone. Cut wood, made bread, etc. 2: R with survey. Took Mann [surveyor] home & forgot Rufus. Had to go back for him. 3: R still with survey. Came home exhausted and scratched. 4: Will [Wing] OKing "Two Weeks Grace." Gov't paid R $10.50 on survey. Miller brought in our potatoes. Cleaned up woodshed and sawed wood. 8: Ideas for Town Report story. Cincinnati won World Series. Books from Miss Hall and Alice—swell lot! Yarn and candy from Florence. R & Rufus hauling firewood. 12: Read "King's Row." Michigan beat Harvard 26–0. Tried to write—stuck. Went down road in p.m. with R to haul wood. 15: Wrote, conceiving "No Story." Letter (first) from Travis Hoke [a whitewater guide]. Check (monthly) from Will. [Every day that week, Louise was "writing like mad" in the morning and sawing or splitting wood in the afternoon.] 22: R has lumbago [a painful rheumatism of back muscles and tendons; Ralph was fifty at this point]. Letter from Willis saying WHC will take "No Safer Refuge" if we'll make a few changes. Hope we can. 23: Wrote all day, finishing "No Story." S in for a few days—teacher's convention. R & Rufus to Island for ice."

Then at the end of October and during November, an interpersonal drama developed. Sally went back to Upton with Ban Barnett. "Jim Barnett told clerk not to sell us any more stuff. Why?" Then the sawmill battery died. Despite this, Louise managed to send off "No Story" and start the rewrite of "No Safer Refuge." "October 30: Young James Barnett in to camp & Jim is apparently really mad at us. Why?"

November 4: Went to see Millers, Effie, Alice & baby. Feel depressed over this apparent conspiracy against us. Nov. 5 is election day and Roosevelt is elected to his third term. Sat up til midnight listening to returns. Started wood pile on Winter House porch. Will approved "No Story." 6: Sawed up big pile of wood. Heard *very* odd tel. con. betw. Alice M. & clerk Shirley implying that we are thieves. War is on! and I am mad. 7: Jim B in—refused to talk to Ralph. R up to Parsons twice with books & mail. I am still very mad & think to hell with Millers. They shall suffer. 10: Split wood a.m. entertained Rufus p.m. Feel very tired & depressed. 13: R finished his damn "For Tech." story. Cooked, split all wood. Wheelbarrow finally broke for good. Road in terrible shape. 15: *WHC* accepts "No Safer Refuge" raising rate to $600, Thank God! Sawed wood, put up new stove pipe in kitchen. Started thinking about column for *WHC*. 18: Wrote. Sawed wood. Took Rufus up to M. to see Jr., Alice & Effie. R tried to square up with Renny who was very odd. 19: Washed. Worked on Will's idea for column. Mail late, but check [$600] came—whoops! Spent eve planning how to spend the money. 20: Food down to zero altho' plenty on order when Larry goes out. Albert Allen in today. Spent day writing checks and orders. 21: Got A&P groceries, but not Armour's [meats]. Got *WHC* column done & ready to send to Will. R making cabinet for typewriter supplies. 25: R paid Larry and Miller (who seems smarty as hell). Rufus played with Jr. Alice very friendly. Sally walked in from Upton with Albert & three hunters. 28: Thanksgiving. Sally, R & Rufus to M. for chairs & mattresses on loan. Turkey for dinner. [The neighborhood crisis then seemed to have calmed down, a testament to the necessity of interdependence when there are so few neighbors). Life reverted to the normal roller coaster.] 29/30: Moved to Winter House. Stuff from Wards arriving. Sally out. Larry pulling boat out. Rufus threw up. Barnett's truck off road at Spauling Hill.

The first week in December, Louise read *For Whom the Bell Tolls* and *Native Son*, received *Woman's Home Companion* with her story "Latana" in it, and "got idea about Jewish Dr. story." Meanwhile, the weather was very cold, with sixteen inches of snow on the ground. Larry got the snowboat running and Ralph hauled the axle out of the back bedroom. By the second week in December, Louise moved the "author department to kitchen for peace." The Winter House was small, and by doing her writing in the kitchen of the Summer House, Louise could get right to work in the morning after breakfast. (Most meals were prepared in the equipped Summer House kitchen and brought over to the warmer Winter House.)

PHOTOGRAPHS

The 1922–23 editorial board
of the *Normal Offering*,
the Bridgewater Teachers' College yearbook.
In the center, with bangs and glasses,
is editor-in-chief Louise Dickinson.
Seated beside her, also with bangs, is the
assistant editor, Alice Dickinson.

RIGHT: One of the Dickinson homes in Bridgewater, Massachusetts. Louise lived here, at 83 Dean Street, while she attended college and then prior to her first marriage, while she dreamed of moving to Forest Lodge. Here, too, she finished out her second pregnancy and completed *We Took to the Woods*.

PHOTO BY ALICE ARLEN.

LEFT: The old Bridgewater High School.
To the right is the library, site of thirteen-
year-old Louise's first job as substitute
librarian. (It was a short-lived tenure since,
as Louise described in *Innocence Under the Elms*,
she and Alice deemed it part of the job to
inform patrons which books they should read.)
PHOTO BY ALICE ARLEN.

Ralph Eugene Rich
as a schoolboy at
Noble and Greenough.
COURTESY OF SARA R. DUN.

Ralph Rich,
mechanical engineer,
in the mid-1920s.
COURTESY OF SARA R. DUN.

Ralph at Forest
Lodge (1933)
with Fanny,
his Plymouth
Rock hen.
COURTESY OF SARA R. DUN.

Louise Dickinson
Rich at Forest
Lodge in the
mid-1930s.
COURTESY OF SARA R. DUN.

RIGHT:
Forest Lodge in 1996.
PHOTO BY ALICE ARLEN.

BELOW:
Louise's and
Ralph's bedroom,
overlooking the
Rapid River. Rufus
was born here.
PHOTO BY ALICE ARLEN.

BELOW, RIGHT:
Louise's typewriter.
PHOTO BY ALICE ARLEN.

OPPOSITE PAGE, TOP:
Rufus and Ralph at the
sawmill Ralph constructed.
COURTESY OF SARA R. DUN.

OPPOSITE PAGE, BOTTOM:
The Forest Lodge
living room in 1996.
PHOTO BY ALICE ARLEN.

ABOVE: Sally and Rufus
with their father, Ralph,
on the porch at Forest
Lodge in the late 1930s.
COURTESY OF SARA R. DUN.

LEFT: Louise.
COURTESY OF DINAH RICH CLARK.

BELOW:

Right to left, front: Dinah and Vaughn.
Right to left, back: Larry Parsons with his
1937 Ford Woody station wagon, Bon, Rufus,
Katie (Catherine) Gerrish Jacobs, and Louise.
Photo taken in 1944. COURTESY OF VAUGHN JACOBS.

OPPOSITE PAGE, TOP:
Book-of-the-Month Club
author Louise about 1946.
COURTESY OF SARA R. DUN.

OPPOSITE PAGE, BOTTOM:
Louise at Rumford
Point in 1945.
PHOTO BY BUD DUNTON.
COURTESY OF VAUGHN JACOBS.

RIGHT:
The Sands, a 1790 cape
on Prospect Harbor, in
Gouldsboro, where
Louise moved in 1961
and continued to write.
PHOTO BY ALICE ARLEN.

LEFT:
The log cabin on Cranberry Point,
in Corea, where Louise spent
the summer of 1954. This marked
the beginning of her life on
the Gouldsboro Peninsula.
PHOTO BY ALICE ARLEN.

ABOVE, LEFT: Rufus in his army days.
COURTESY OF SARA R. DUN.

ABOVE, RIGHT: Dinah with Hero
in Gouldsboro, with Louise's
1930 Model A in the background.
COURTESY OF DINAH RICH CLARK.

OPPOSITE PAGE, TOP LEFT:
Rufus at his home in
Maine, with Damion, 1996.
PHOTO BY ALICE ARLEN.

OPPOSITE PAGE, TOP RIGHT: Dinah,
at her home in Cape Cod in 1996.
PHOTO BY ALICE ARLEN.

RIGHT: Louise and Hero at
The Sands in the 1960s.
COURTESY OF CONDON RODGERS.

Right to left: Alice Dickinson Hoke,
Hortense Condon, Rufus Rich,
Louise Dickinson Rich.
Gouldsboro Peninsula, 1960s.
COURTESY OF DINAH RICH CLARK.

December 18: Rufus' [fourth] birthday. Washed curtains in
Rufus' room. Pkgs from Ward's for Rufus: top, slippers. 19: Finished Jewish Dr. story ["They Came to the Place"]. 20: Earthquake at 3 a.m. Typed on story. *Oliver Wiswell* came from Alice
D. R built shelves for Rufus, painted motor red. Terpe reports goi-
ter improving. 23: To Middle to send out story, see Alice & Effie
and take them Xmas presents. 24: Earthquake 9 a.m. Mail today:
card from Ezra, many others. Radio batteries, airplane for Rufus
from Tibbotts. 25: Rufus had nice Xmas—liked gun, tools, etc.
Walk on Pond in p.m. 31: Cloudy, warm (34 degrees). Wrote. R
to M. in car for mail & groceries. Tough going. We went sliding
with Rufus. This year better than last, thank God. Still room for
improvement.

The year 1940 had most definitely been better. There had been un-
pleasantries—brutal weather, backbreaking chores, a houseguest's heart
attack (Edith Tibbott recovered), teenage romance, Terpe's mental health
issues, and other interpersonal tensions such as the "neighborhood" spat.
But on balance, the Riches were beginning to see themselves clear of the
hurricane damage and enjoyed a steady stream of visitors and guests. At
year's end, the family was relatively healthy, Rufus was beginning to be a
little helper, Gerrish was out with his family, Sally was going to school and
boarding in Upton. Ralph and Louise were both writing, but Louise was
more persistent, and thus prolific. She continued to write in the face of
the usual daily difficulties and distractions. This year her efforts had
begun to pay off. By the end of 1940, sales from "Most Important Thing,"
Ralph's "Seedbed in Maine," a reprint of "Don't Worry," and "No Safer
Refuge" in *Woman's Home Companion* (which had raised its rate to $600,
of which Willis, under their agreement was taking 10 percent) totaled
$1,038.50. In addition, there was Louise's monthy check (unrecorded). Fi-
nally, in their seventh winter together, life was beginning to stabilize for
Louise and Ralph. Thanks to their daily preparations and Willis Wing's
monthly checks, there was wood in the woodbox and food in the cup-
board. Although life was simple, sometimes austere, that year it was not
desperate.

- - 1941 - -

On January 3, 1941, Louise sent out two significant sample pieces she
called "Dept." They served as precursors to a full-fledged book, showing

that the summer discussions with Willis Wing clearly included plans for Louise to write about her wilderness experiences. Louise more than kept to her one-story-a-month schedule with Wing. On January 23, she submitted a piece called "Tenth Reunion," plus a rewrite of "They Came to the Place." She entered an Ivory soap writing contest and came up with a story idea for a romance about a camp hostess. In February, she wrote "One of These Ideal Things," the camp hostess story (called "Spruce-haven"), and "Imagine Mary" (a rewrite/renaming of "Tenth Reunion"). In March, she sent off an outline for a 25,000-word serial in *Woman's Home Companion* and wrote "The Silver Platter."

Although Louise was carrying a heavy writing load that required her attention most mornings, of course other events were occurring throughout the day and around her which she recorded. In January, Stumpy and the gang arrived as usual, and there was a session of ice cutting. Louise and Rufus (and often Kyak) enjoyed many nice walks together, seeing a big buck and visiting with the Millers. James Joyce died. Louise sewed and knitted; one night she cooked artichokes and hollandaise for dinner. They made the winter ice cream. Rufus got his first bloody nose, played with clay for the first time, and had his longest walk—three and a half miles. A man named Russell came in with Camp Spike and became a constant drop-in.

In February, the two teachers from their rented house in Upton arrived with Sally for the weekend. Louise received mail from classmate Ruth Hunt, and she started on a diet. Her mother, Florence, contracted shingles. Ralph became stuck in the snow in their own driveway. Camp Spike moved out. Louise received a check for the Swedish rights to "Don't Worry."

In March, Ralph headed off for town meeting. Louise received a letter from Willis Wing about "Fred Tibbott's failure" (as a writer?). Logging crews were busy around Forest Lodge. Louise received a letter from Catherine ("Katie") Jacobs, Ralph Gerrish's daughter. Camp #1 moved out.

> March 14: Started another love story. 15: Finished Delilah—liked it enormously. 16: Got a vague idea for story, "Silver Platter" [which went out two weeks later].

Outside it was snowy and cold. Ralph fixed Larry's broken gear for the snowboat. The roads were "plugged up—definitely on foot now." In the mail came a "new, snappy *Independent*" from Bridgewater. With the advent of spring, Louise was busy with cleaning chores and started "planning a detective story. Decided on old maid school teacher and librarian for main character." (The character may have been patterned after sister Alice, then single and a librarian and children's book writer/editor living in Newton, Massachusetts.)

The following five entries relate to a full-blown six-page story that appears in *We Took to the Woods*.

> April 2: Two tractors came in to tear down Spike. Edgar W[orster] suggests I go out to-morrow. Spent p.m. getting clothes ready if I go. 3: Lovely day. Rode to Upton with Rufus, P[aul] Fuller & Edgar W. on tractor. Road terrible. Night at Allen's—stopped at store & Jim Barnett's. Nice time. 4: Gorgeous warm sunny day. Rode back from Upton with E & P & Sally & Phyllis Barnett. Got sunburn. Cooked hot dogs at B. Brook. 5: Lovely, warm, thawing. Sally & Phyllis went out on tractor. We rode to bridge. Rd maple trees. I cleaned guide's house & dining room. Spike all burned.

The end of the Spike logging camp meant the loss of a spring/winter neighbor and the end of an era of sorts for Louise and Ralph. The Pondy logging camp/wangan was still nearby, and other camps dotted the area, but the absence of Spike meant a loss of companionship, fallback help, and leftover supplies. The winter of 1940/41 had been relatively solitary for the little family, but the season of visitors started right up.

> April 8: Travis Hoke in. Stayed up until 1 a.m. listening to him. Letter from Gerrish announcing arrival soon. 9: All went fishing at dam for first time. No luck, of course. Spent eve. being highly entertained by Hoke's uncle Will. 10: First robin. Travis fishing—got strikes. Ice out of Sebago. Fished myself in p.m. 11: Ralph's birthday—he caught two salmon at dam—2 & 3 lbs. First of year. Coburn came in. Letter from Will OK-ing book idea.

This entry marks the beginning of *We Took to the Woods*. The following day, spring arrived in the symbolic forms of Gerrish returning and the family moving to the Summer House. Gerrish went to work at Lakewood Camps until "ice out," Larry lost their order of meat on the lake, the dam had a leak. Louise took a "wild canoe trip with Travis Hoke and Gerrish" while getting two quarts of smelts, and she was "down to 147 pounds."

> April 26: War is going badly. Walk with Rufus across the dam— see deer swimming. 27: Rufus falls in the river. 28: Sold "The Sil-

ver Platter" to *Good Housekeeping.* 29: Fire started on C Meadows. Gerrish caught first trout of year. Rufus put water in the
Marmon gas tank.

May 2: Snow. Wrote. Rufus back in good graces. R and G
wrecked Reo. G caught two small trout at Dam. Upton fire out.
3: Sally comes in alone. First sports at Coburn's.

And the winter was officially over: The dam was fixed, boats were put
in, flowers and visitors began to emerge. Louise was working on "Day Off
from Love" [which went out the end of August as "Day Off for the Heart"].

The *Alligator* was launched, booms started moving, and the log drive
was underway for another year. Once again, Ralph and Gerrish hauled
crews working the river and fixing the roads, manure for the garden, and
canoes for Coburn. Louise visited Ruth and Fred Adams, friends/visitors
at Lakewood, who the previous year had taken pictures of the log drive.
On May 14, "Adams came down and took pictures for book [*WTTTW*]."
Alice and visitors arrived. Travis Hoke and Gerrish were in the Guide's
House, so the place was chockablock full. Fortunately, a $540 check for
"The Silver Platter" also arrived. The rest of May, Louise worked on her
book outline and another monthly story, "A Sweater for the British." When
Louise and Alice weren't visiting, Alice and Travis spent time together.
May was very dry and because of the high danger of forest fire, "the
woods have a ban on." Ralph went with Alice to Boston for his lumbago
(the visit apparently a "success"). Also, in terms of the Outside, Louise
reported that the "war news is bad in Crete." On the last day of May, she
noted: "Finished planting flower seeds. Lamont's men in to put in our
water pump [in kitchen]. Started final copy 'Sweater For Brt.' Wilson in.
Fun OK'd Travis' guide license."

On June 3, Louise noted a "funny green fog at dawn. Cooked, & Rufus
spilled aspic & jelly on front porch. Went swimming." Next day, she
"started outline of book in question form." She called her book *Some of
the Answers,* and the question format turned out to be an organizational
device that served Louise well. The season continued dry. June 6: "Sky
hazy from Canadian fires." Sally came home for the summer and, in
spite of a busy schedule, Louise wrote and sent off her book outline.

June 14: thirty-eight today. Rainy, thank God on act. of garden. R
fixed Coburn's spring on Studebaker. Went to Coburn's in eve.

Travis and G caught fish. 15: Sample chapter for *Some of the Answers*. Finished a story called "Semantics." A stupifyingly big bill came from Coburn for month, depressing me terribly. 19: Lovely day. Drive done. Sally to Upton. John Lav. Went out, leaving loot. G back from B Pond—caught fish, had a good time. Finished Chap. 1 of book. Rufus & I went swimming. [A couple of days later, Travis left and Louise received a copy of *Woman's Home Companion* with the story "Malvena" in it.] 25: Windy, hot day. Started to plan driving Chap. Second sample of book. To Middle for drinks with Lowe's & got tight. Fun, but disgraceful. 26: Terribly hot. Had bad hangover. R & G setting kitchen chimney with cement. Letter from Will approving first Chap. Enthusiastically. Went swimming. Walked to dam in eve.

July 1: Hot again. Wrote all a.m., ironed all p.m. Ralph's first swim—liked it! Letter from Fred Tibbott inviting us to Chesterville [Maine, southeast of Farmington]. Rumford people (34) drowned on cruise. 2: Got winter house ready for guests [for foldboat races]. I am sick with summer complaint.

This was actually no "summer complaint" but rather the early stages of their next child—Louise was pregnant. On July 9, the Wings arrived, and Louise had another sample chapter and ten pages of a proposed final chapter ready for Willis. Next day, he read and approved them. During the Wings' twelve-day visit, there were many "talks," Louise's "Imagine Mary" was sold to the *Family Circle* after a quick touch-up, and the *Good Housekeeping* issue with her story "The Silver Platter" arrived. She revised "An Ideal Thing," entertained the Wings, and picked quarts of berries. On July 22, the day after the Wings left, she noted with surprise, "Weigh 139 lb!"

July 23: Started re-write for *Chatelaine*. Food very low, but check in offing. 24: Finished re-write for *Chatelaine*. Sally to lunch at M. John out with party, left loot. Swimming with R, R & G. Check came for *Family Circle*, but gave all to Coburn. July 25: Typed all day on "Ideal Thing" for *Chatelaine*. Got it done. Hope they take it. Walk to dam in eve. Very nice. 30: Read "Justice Be Damned" in a.m. Sally, G & I got 8 qts blueberries in p.m. 31: R, G, Al[ys], Al's sister & I raspberrying all a.m. Picnic at Smooth Ledge. Getting ready to go to Tibbotts.

The family had a good time being summer visitors for a change at the Tibbotts' in Chesterville. The first day, August 1, was a working vacation for poor Louise: "Read Fred's story all a.m. & think gave some good criticisms." Next day they helped Fred build a pontoon and then all went swimming; "Rufus good as gold." Then Ralph was roped into hauling Fred's "Model T down from hill & took to pieces," while Louise read *Lost Horizon;* "Fair."

> August 4: Went to Boothbay Harbor with Tibbotts. Lovely drive. Rufus saw a *million* new things. Nice to see ocean again. Rufus stung by bee—first time. 5: Came home from Tibbotts. Nice letter from Will about Angus Cameron's reaction to book samples. New bathing suit from Wards—yellow & nice.

The next week, Louise moved her typewriter downstairs and started back on her detective story. Ralph and Gerrish worked on finishing the kitchen chimney. Rufus fell down the cellar hole, and Sally was back and forth from Upton. The river was high and all hands were swimming. Raspberries were thick, as were thunderstorms. Louise found herself needing to take naps.

> August 14: Feel bum. Little Brown wants nine chap. samples, so Wing offering manusc. to Lippincott. 16: Alice came. Went raspberrying in p.m. around Smooth Ledge. Annie & Bessie [Sally's friends] went home. G. sick. R's Salem pals in to Richardsons. 21: Gerrish sick with something obscure. Alice, Sally & Rufus walked to M. Got story started & it will be good, I think ["Day Off for the Heart"]. 23: Wrote on story. Got word from Lippincott they will take book. Packed toys to send to BrH_2O [Bridgewater]. Rufus played with Gordon Wright. Wonderful time. 25: Kyak sick, so took to Bethel at night. Terrible rain. Back at 1:30 a.m. Very tired. 26: Big wash. Finished story. R & G tore hole in kitchen for chimney. 30: Typed up story to go out. Letter from Will saying deCassitt against whodonit.

By September, Louise knew she was pregnant (although there is no mention of it in the diary!). At some point, the decision had been made for her to go to Bridgewater to have the child and enroll Sally and Rufus in school there (thus the August 23 packing of toys). Visitors, including Travis Hoke, came in and had to spend the night because of high winds.

September 2: Up at 4:30 a.m. to get Woodmans off. Walked in
p.m. to *Alligator* with Alice & Ruf. Alice is engaged [to Travis]. 3:
Ironed, cooked, rode to Spike in p.m. Went swimming with
Rufus. Cold. G caught 2 3/4 lb salmon above dam. Chewed with
Travis all eve. 4: Went swimming with Rufus, got ready to leave.
Fishing with R above dam in eve. Gerrish got 4 lb. Salmon. 5:
Came to Bridgewater in eve. Travis as far as Rumford. Huntie
[Ruth Hunt] & Louise met us at North Station. Letter here from
Will liking last story.

On September 6, Louise's first full day back in Bridgewater, a book
contract and $225 advance from Lippincott & Co. arrived in the mail—
making *Some of the Answers*, a.k.a. *We Took to the Woods*, an official
project.

On September 6, Louise also looked into the children's schooling
and, not surprisingly, obtained library cards for both of them. The next
day, Sally went to church with the family and Alice headed back to Newton in the evening. Sally and Rufus went off to school. Louise had Rufus
vaccinated and took them all to the Brockton Fair, Duxbury Beach, and
Plymouth Rock. She caught up with family and friends, had a permanent,
and attended dinner parties. But by the second week, in Bridgewater,
she was back to her writing schedule and had started work on chapter
two of the book. She had also heard from Ralph, who reported that the
new chimney was up and running at Forest Lodge. Rufus, a young four
and a half, was understandably having a rough time adjusting to school.

September 16: Scene in school with Rufus, but finally OK.
Mother's meeting in p.m. 17: Tub in yard for Rufus. Man with
bagpipes came by. Wonderful northern lights. 18/19: Rufus
played all day with a pal. 20: Rufus cried about school again.

Meanwhile Ralph reported that a fire, which started at one of Jim
Barnett's logging operations, had spread, Upton was in danger, and a
burning ban had been put on the woods in Maine. As September ended,
Louise "mailed chapter 2 to Will, thank God," and received a letter from
him saying she "*must* come to NYC, Ralph or no Ralph."

On October 1, Louise began writing chapter 11 of *We Took to the
Woods*. Things evidently were going better for Rufus, because in spite of
a stomachache, he "insisted on going to school." Louise attended *Arsenic
and Old Lace,* went to the Boston arboretum with Ruth Hunt, and did all

the housework while Sally and Florence were down with intestinal flu. On October 6, Ralph arrived. The next day, they visited Rufus's kindergarten in the morning and traveled to Wilton, Connecticut, in the afternoon to meet the Wings. Then they spent five days "doing" the New York literary scene: luncheons with publishers/editors of *Good Housekeeping*, *Woman's Home Companion*, Lippincott, *The American Magazine*,

Pages from the five-year diary. February 4, 1942 was a red-letter day for Louise: she finished the manuscript for *She Took to the Woods*.

FEBRUARY 3

1939- Alice M. went to Rumford to the Carnival, and the Parsons went to Boston to the Sportsman's Show.

1940- Raw, overcast (12°) windy. Nothing much. Wrote A. P. & Mrs. Hall notes of thanks. Made ice cream. Kids on walk to camp.

1941- Warm, grey. Washed. R + R to Middle in car with mail. Bau up from Spike to get sock drills fixed. Worked some on story.

1942- Very cold day. Wrote all a.m. on final chap. In p.m. R— & I to library & for groceries.

1943- Nice day. Warm. Larry down hauling wood. Brought 17# fresh pork which we had for dinner. Hauled 5 loads, Fred + Ralph sawing. I wrote some. R Packard to aem & photo Larry.

Collier's. Louise wistfully commented on the hoopla: "Hope it is profitable." By the end, she was getting tired: "Had an exhausting trip home. Shopped for Rufus' school smock in Boston. Alice still home. Sally to Parkers. Rufus glad to see us." Ralph went back to Maine on October 15 and Louise resumed work on her book.

October 18: Raw and grey. Rufus outdoors playing all day long. Wrote, cleaned house, asked Ralph to come down for winter. 20: Letter from Will saying *Family Circle* would take two stories long since abandoned ["Sapphire in Her Shoe," and "No Fit Place" for

FEBRUARY 4

1939 - Finished Gerrish's mittens. Otherwise, usual schedule.

1940 - Warmer (35°) sunny, lovely. Moved out of bed-room onto front porch. Cut of blue cotton flowered blouse.

1941 - Lovely day. Worked on story. Mail, Russell, P. & Rufus in ear. New Yorkers from Alice & pkg. from Filmena - pretzels, animal crackers, book plates, etc. au diet still.

1942 - good day. FINISHED BOOK. Gladys Bryant Taylor down in p.m. with some interesting old letters. Fine. Rufus pl. ev. Sonny Gattuckal

1943 - Warm & mild. Fred & I wrote some. Worked up wood in p.m. to clear woodshed. Irene still here. Al & Alice still out. sent out query list.

$100 each—$90 for her after Will]. 22: Wrote all a.m., copied all p.m. Word from R saying Kyak must be killed on act. of mange. Letter from Terpe about her own sadness & futility!! 23: Wrote all day. Got cutting on "No Fit Place" done. Walked in field with Rufus in rain in dusk. [Louise and Alice took a lot of walks with Rufus that fall.] 25: Went in town [Boston] with Sally. Lunch with Terpe. *Let's Face It* (Danny Kaye) with Alice D. [her sister]. Swell. All three came to BrH$_2$O. Huntie & Louise in eve. 27: Couldn't write—too much disturbance around. Letter from Ralph. Guess he's coming down for the winter. Sally stamping papers for Mr. Isreal. 29: Sent out chap. 11 to Will. Rufus not very good. I seriously begin to wonder if he is normal. He is awfully spoiled. 30: Tried to think up new story. No luck. Made jack-o-lant. For Rufus. Sally walked to school dance. 31: Halloween. No school. Started on new story. Sally working at *Independent* office. Took Rufus out with jack-o-lantern in eve. He was thrilled.

In November, Louise started "You Haven't Changed a Bit" and received a letter from Will "approving Ch. 11 highly & sending $50." A letter from Ralph came nearly every day, and Rufus played outdoors for hours. Louise read Pinkerton's *Two Ends to Our Shoestring* ("Not much good") and *Wolf in the Fold* for Alice ("No good").

November 10: Finished "You Haven't Changed...." Felt rotten. Letter from Will saying *Good House.* would like article on "When a Man Fails." Sally, Rufus, James [Dickinson] to parade in West Br. 12: Finished typing story. To HS for parent's night. Sally seems to be doing OK. 13: Thought about article on "Failure." Wrote Terpe to come to-morrow. Special from Ralph saying he comes tomorrow. [The next day, she met Ralph in Boston and they went out to dinner and the movies.] 15: Home from Boston with Ralph. Got Rufus at school; he was funny. Terpe here. R & I uptown in eve. Nice to have him here.

Terpe left the following day, and Ralph and Louise worked together on rewriting "When a Man Fails." They walked uptown to the post office: She received a $22.50 check for the Canadian rights to "Imagine Mary," and *Family Circle* was buying "One of those Ideal Things" for $100. Ralph got his library card, and they all had a typical and happy Thanksgiving, complete with a football game and lots of friends and family. Louise finished "Day Off for the Heart" and turned her attention to chapter 8, "Aren't

You Ever Frightened?" By the end of November, it was out the door, and she also received a check from the *Toronto Star*. After a checkup from her doctor, she was happy to report: "I am in good condition."

Rufus and Sally seemed to be settling in nicely, and as December rolled around, Louise tackled chapter three, "But You Don't Live Here All Year Round?"—which by her analysis: "Should be OK, I think." And they received word from Willis that he "wants 'When a Man Fails' done *again*, damn." Ralph got a typewriter for his own use as well as a pair of glasses, "which should help." Terpe was "mending dolls for Jordan Marsh" [department store]."

> December 6: Japanese situation bad. 7: Cold & windy. Wrote all a.m. Took Rufus and Colby kids to walk in woods & gravel pit in p.m. Japan bombed Honolulu. Made Xmas door décor. 8: Cold & windy. Listened to declaration of war by US on Japan. Radio broadcasts all day. Also wrote quite a stint on book. Sally in bad [graces] for being out late. December 9: Nice day, altho' cold. Wrote on chap. 3. First air raid alarm—proved unfounded. Uptown in p.m. Saw Army go thru. Pres. Speech at night. Excellent. 10: War news bad. *Pr. of Wales* sunk off Malaya. Went uptown with Ralph. Wrote on Ch. 3. 11: US declared war on Italy & Germany. Did a lot on chap. 3. Note from Stump saying will call Sat. 12: Cold, grey. Finished chap. 3 of book. Dec. check from Will. Went uptown in p.m. with Ralph. Correcting mms. all eve. 13 Stumpy came in eve. Took us to dinner at Howard Johnson's. Good time. Rufus to parade with Grandpa & Colbys. 19: The war goes on. Japs doing too well.

Rufus made Louise and Ralph "an invitation to the kindergarten Xmas party." One day, the three went uptown for groceries and took a taxi back home: "Rufus delighted." Rufus also walked home alone from school for the first time and was "very proud of self." Sally was still working at the newspaper after school and attending school and church functions. Louise finished the third stab at "When a Man Fails" (which fortunately was approved), worked hard on chapter 4, and noted that Will was pleased with chapter 3.

> December 25: [Rufus saw "his first Xmas tree."] He was thrilled. Finished Chap. 4. Alice, Ralph & I called on the Hunts. Alice back to Newton in the eve. with Huntie & Louise. Sally with

Terpe in Boston. 27: Alice came in p.m. *Family Circle* with pine
drive story came [hurricane logs]. Helped James with Review of
Year for *Independent* in eve. 29: Snow & sleet. Started chap 5 on
children. Ironed. Rufus played out in snow all day. Helped James
with yrs. review in eve. War not going so very well. 31: Rufus
first hair cut at barber shop. Uptown to library with Ralph. Alice
came out with Huntie & Louise. [Alice had] attack in night, scaring all, and depressing me.

Although 1941 ended with a nationwide shock in terms of Japan, and
a personal shock in terms of Alice, by all other measures the Rich family
was doing better than they had in years. Simply figuring story sales, their
income was up slightly (from $1,000 to $1,100 for the year); Will's monthly
checks were on top of that. They were warm and safe together near a hospital and a support system of family and friends. Sally (sixteen) and Rufus
(five) were managing well with the move. Ralph's lumbago/back had
a break from heavy labor. Louise did not critique 1941 in her diary, but
it was definitely better than the previous year.

--1942--

Although Louise and Rufus in particular were clearly chafing under
the confinements of a town, they managed to be outdoors as much as
possible, and Rufus developed a sixth sense for urban excitements.
Louise's diary for January 1, 1942, reads: "Nice day. Rufus went to prison
riot & fire with Colbys. R & I walked down to The Pike in p.m. & then to
Carvers with kids. Alice back to Newton."
In Louise's sixth book, *Only Parent,* she elaborated on that nine-word
entry about Rufus. It was her second "Thanksgiving-when-Rufus-was-four"
story. In *Happy the Land,* her second book, Louise wrote of the time she
and Ralph and Rufus had tea, canned beans, canned milk, and crackers
at the summer camp of their friends the Richardsons over on B Pond.
When they got home, in a snow squall, and turned on the radio for the
evening, they were surprised to discover it was Thanksgiving. Years later,
when they were sitting down to a sumptuous Thanksgiving feast, Rufus
fondly recalled that meager meal. In *Only Parent,* she situated the prison
riot and fire on the same day and used the story to relate Rufus's early
descriptive abilities, his curiosity, and his love of action. "That day started
his career of always managing to be on the scene of the crime." Actually,
the "no celebration" Thanksgiving happened, according to the diary,
in 1939, just before Rufus's third birthday, and the riot/fire was on New

Year's Day 1942, when Rufus was five. The real four-year-old Rufus sat down to a classic Thanksgiving meal at his grandparents' house, followed by a football game for the grownups—in other words, nothing particularly exciting to write about. The events related in the stories actually did happen, but at different times. As Alys Parsons says about Louise's books, "They are based on fact, but she embellishes a bit here and there."

On January 2, Louise and Ralph paid a visit to her doctor, and "all is OK. US lost Manila. Started Chap. 6. Alice came in eve. Seems much better, been to Dr." During early January, Rufus experienced a number of firsts: Sunday school, a spanking the next day for being late for supper, a "shiner" from sliding at the Colbys'. Ralph and Sally went to lectures at the high school "on bombs" and Sally started babysitting. Louise worked hard on chapter 6, "What Do You Do with All Your Spare Time?" She "did 3,000 words" one day and mailed it all off in one week's time. Next day, she started on chapter 10, "Do You Get Out Very Often?" which is a lovely tribute to her wilderness land and shows a bit of her homesickness. She also met Alice Folsom for the first time, her sidekick in later years when she returned to Bridgewater.

> January 15: Thawing. Worked on book. Jacket for book arrived. Nice. Also news of selling "Swing. from Birch" ["Swinging from Birches"] to *Chatelaine*. 16: Finished and mailed Chap. 10 [also completed in a week]. [The next few days:] Rufus not well at all. Temp. 103 degrees—fluid on lungs. Worried. Got word story about Bermuda trip in *WHC*. 21: Rufus a little better & getting cross. Letter from Will not much liking, & saying *Good H.* took "When a Man Fails." 22: Dr. says Rufus has pneumonia. Very much upset by it. He is quite sick. Stayed with him all day. [Rufus slowly got better, but then Ralph became sick.] 28: Florence is impatient. 29: I feel awful: cold. Went uptown in p.m. and did some shopping. Florence not feeling well. Home from work early. Ralph also not well. I am discouraged.

No wonder! But by the end of January, Rufus was out of bed and playing outdoors all day again, Ralph had visited "the doctor who pronounced him ok," and Louise had finished chapter 9, "Don't You Get Awfully Out of Touch?"

> February 1: Ralph feeling miserable. Got a typhoid shot from the doctor. 3: Wrote all a.m. on final chap. In p.m. R & I to library &

for groceries. To PO at midnight to mail R's Civil Service blank. 4:
Good day. FINISHED BOOK. Gladys Bryant Taylor down in p.m.
with some interesting old letters. Fun. Rufus played with Donny
G. [Louise then took five days off from writing.] 9: War Time Daylight Savings Time started. Went to Brockton to hosp. Everything
ok. Started white baby sweater. 11: Finished dog team addition to
book. *Independent*–Larkin deal seems sure [the sale of her parents' newspaper]. 12: Tried to work, but got talking with R. Willis
writes it is ok with Lynn Carrick (Lippincott) if I have a baby. 13:
Started work with Travis' "Story Builder" on draft story.

The contacts Louise made in New York finally began to pay off. Bob
Endicott at *Family Circle* bought "No Story" and "This Is My Daughter."
Louise and Ralph had lunch at Boston's Copley Plaza with Lynn Carrick:
"nice guy, and with personal book gang." The family continued to have
bouts of sickness: "Everyone ailing. To bed early to hear Ralph coughing
all night." They still continued the job of moving the *Independent* operation, Ralph worked at "Wylie's," Sally worked for the Soldiers' Committee,
Rufus went to school, Louise and Ralph saw *The Man Who Came to Dinner* at the movies and went on walks uptown.

By the beginning of March, Louise wrote: "Lovely spring day. War
going badly. Very homesick for Middle." Everything was getting on her
nerves: her pregnancy, weekends with the kids/family, God-fearing Sundays. By March 8, she entered an atypically scorching pronouncement:
"I *hate* Sundays in civilization."

March 10: Windy wash day. Helped Florence. Tried to write
"Hero's Daughter" ["This Is My Father"]. In a state of nervous jitters. 13: Letter from Gerrish wanting to go to Middle. Letter from
Fred Tibbott. He's sold his book! Rufus remarkably good all day.
15: Received news of Stumpy's death. Shock. Whole place a
wreck because Sally was out last night. Letter from Terpe who has
been sick again. MacArthur in Australia. 18: Went to hospital
with Ralph. Am ok. Correcting book proofs in p.m. 20: Lovely
day. Finished "Hero's Daughter," typed 4 pp. Got pains in p.m.
and finally went to hospital in police car. Dinah born at 8:13
p.m.—breach [*sic*] presentation—7 lbs. 6 oz. [While in the hospital, Louise finished the second batch of book proofs. Dinah lost
ground, and Louise began to breast-feed her (after three days).
After six days, everyone had had enough of the hospital.] 26: Ok

day. Rather depressed, altho' Dinah better. Ralph up—talked over story ideas. Feel he is having tuff time, poor guy. Lot of mail.

The next day, Louise got up for the first time and sat in a chair. Dinah was doing better but weighed only six pounds seven ounces. Louise finished "Mr. Moto" (a story that doesn't show up in any records). By day nine, Louise went home from the hospital to find "things here not as bad as feared, but bad enuf. Sally's fiasco party at Crane's too bad." Soon, "nerves are raw" again. A letter came from Terpe, who "is in a bad way." Louise began work on "a hospital story" and recorded that she was down to 135 pounds.

In April, *Atlantic Monthly* picked up the serial rights for *We Took to the Woods,* Ralph returned to Forest Lodge, and Louise finished "The People in the Street." She was so homesick for Maine that in the backyard she planted a pine tree and chopped down an old apple tree, "spending time working on wood." One weekend, Sally visited Terpe in Boston, Alice came over and went to bed with a cold, Rufus had an earache and "howled like hell," and Louise wrote: "Another lousy day with Florence being noble. Tried to write. R & G. caught first fish—5—at dam." The following weekend, she started a "story about a wonderful woman," and took off for the movies: *How Green Was My Valley.*

In May, she sold "A Hard Row to Hoe" to *Household Magazine* and finalized plans with Alice to head back to Maine. She paid Sally's fare to go with Terpe to live in Marion, Illinois, and made preparations for Forest Lodge: "Fixed glasses, deposited money in Maine bank, got sugar ration cans, mailed clothes/supplies, tried to find toothpaste without the tube."

> May 13: School gets out early—due to gas rationing. Rufus contracts dogwood poisoning. 15: Went to see *The Chocolate Soldier* with Florence. 16: Brought Rufus to his first movie—a Gene Autry cowboy film. 17: Collecting last articles for going home. [Last-minute anxieties before the grand departure provoked the following:] Florence driving me wild with half-witted attitude toward Dinah—baby talk, etc. 18: *Went home to Middle!* Both kids behaved marvelously! Alice with me. Middle looks wonderful. Got drunk. R sick.

The log drive was under way, Gerrish was planting the garden, a new oil stove was installed, and on May 21 a telegram arrived from Lynn Carrick saying Book of the Month Club had selected *We Took to the Woods..*

May 23: Letter from Will about B of M.C. terms. We can hardly
believe it! Swell! Saw Alice Miller for first time. [The rest of the
month was rounded out by walks to favorite spots, Fred and Edith
Tibbott's visit, and an almost-daily fish offering from a suitor for
Alice.]

On June 1, Alice left and Kyak came back in (apparently having recovered from his mange), "looking swell." Louise then finished "The
Sewing Circle's Mrs. Rogers" and started a "new Town Report series."

June 13: Check for $4,050 from Will, advance from Lipp.
Whoops! 14: Rained 4½ inches during night. Thirty-nine today.
Went to Middle in p.m. spent a.m. paying bills, etc.—a swell
birthday occupation.

If the Rich household was suddenly overflowing, so was Mother Nature. It had been a very rainy spring, and the day after Louise's birthday,
she wrote that the area was in "flood conditions: All the dams are open
and water gaining." The roads were washed out, Jim Barnett's bridge
went down, and there was no mail in or out. A fawn was found and they
offered it Dinah's bottle for its feeding. By June 19, the waters had receded enough so Ralph could go out for a big load of supplies. Apparently he also stopped at the doctor's office, because Louise reported that
his blood pressure was 218. Ralph clearly was having health problems.

June 21: Wrote 10 letters for Ralph who is not using glasses to
see if that makes him feel any better. 27: Big mail order arrived
including checked overalls—a birthday present from Ralph.
Started a town meeting story. 27/28: Washed both houses. [Not
surprisingly, by June 29 she notes:] Lovely day, but I am so tired.
Washed & ironed. Drive done. Washing machine came & yarn
from Chelsea. Ralph getting a new outboard motor.

July began with the usual onslaught of guests and canoeists for the
races. Alice and Travis renewed their romance: "Affair between Alice &
Trav. app. serious. What a mess!! Trav. drunk."

July 5: Wilson in to dinner & supper. Took Va. Beal to B. Pond &
swimming. Alice all blah about that damn Hoke. Left after supper. 6: Used washing machine for first time. It is Wonderful. Read

det. story to Ralph all eve. Tired from week-end. 7: Ordered
refrig. Heard that Catherine Gerrish Jacobs [Gerrish's daughter]
will come work. Sally wrote wanting [to come] back. Blue. and
rasp. beg. to ripen.

July 11's entry is interesting—not only by what was said, but also by
what wasn't. There had been no previous mention of a dog(?) named
Tom: "Rainy & cold. Tom bit me. Went to Dr. in Andover. G. shot Tom."
The only other mention of this incident is oblique. In the next day's entry,
Louise mentioned that she was "down with bum hand all day." And on
July 22, she headed to Rumford with Coburn, Freeman, & Mrs. Grants to
get a permanent, shop, and "get G's gun." End of story. However startling
the incident, it caused barely a ripple in the diary. Louise seemed more
interested in her new washing machine, in the arrival of Catherine and
her son, Vaughn, and in the installation of new piping for gravity-fed water
in the kitchen. On July 16, she announced: "Water pumped into the
kitchen at 9 a.m.!" For many years, Louise had shouldered the backbreaking job of keeping clothes, houses, and people clean by lugging
water up from the river for washing and cooking. With new amenities, and
Catherine ("Katie") Jacobs's help as housekeeper and child sitter, some
of the strain was finally relieved. Naturally, all was not perfection. "Will
thumbed down 'Too Bad She Never Married.' " So she started an "Abbott
Notch/snow plow story." They had running water, but it runneth over,
and the kitchen flooded. Rufus had someone to play with, a sort of
kid brother, but then, on July 29: "R. discovered water in Reo tank (kids).
Feeling vaguely mad & discouraged." No wonder. . . double trouble! The
Rich menagerie was still operating under the motto "Never a dull
moment," as the entries for August attest.

August 3: Big wash. *Love* w. machine. R & G to Middle—brought
back refrig. It's huge! Works swell. 6: Scene about water in Ford.
Got dope on Jim Barnett failing & #C maybe not opening. Made
first mousse (cranberry). 8: Went to lunch at Pine Point [on Lake
Umbagog] with Mr. Leman and some people called Condon. Awfully nice time. 9: Ralph hit Rufus with pliers cutting face. Bull-
dozer came in to work on road. 10: Ralph feeling bum—finally
went to bed with temp. of 102.

August 11: Alice came. Spent most of day chasing a dr. for Ralph
who has temp. of 104. Finally got Dr. Greene from Rumford in

eve. 12: R about the same—getting nasty tempered. John Lav. in. A mess of fan mail. 13: Ralph no better. Rufus developing temp. It's getting me down—running upstairs, etc. Called Dr. in eve. New medicine. 14: Edsons [?] left at 5:30 a.m. Got ambulance & took Ralph & Rufus to hosp. in Rumford. Dinner with Dr. & Mrs. Greene. 15: Came home from Rumford. Got kitten [named Carter Glass] from Freeman Wisener's mother. House seems empty. 16: Very quiet without Ralph and Rufus. Got house straightened around. Wrote letters. Kitten very much at home. John Lav. in. 17: Cath. & I did big wash. Got house cleaned. Alice stayed in bed, sick. Margaret & Rufus (from hosp.) came. 18: Wings came. Ralph out of hosp. Cath & I found hawk in road. It died. 19: Loafed around. Alice still in bed. Wrote answers to fan mail. Got ready to go canoeing. 20: Windy. Started on canoe trip. [See chapter 4 in *Happy the Land,* and the original, unedited account that follows on pages 274–88]. Night at Pine Island. A little shower. Swam in p.m. on beach. Fun. John, Gerrish, Wings, and Riches. 21: Funny, windy, smoky day. Paddled to Upper Dam, up big lake [Mooselookmeguntic] to Cupsuptic. Swell night on island. Had fun. Headwinds all the way. Tough going on bay. 22: Hot. Carried across to Brown Farm. Paddled down Magalloway. Spent night at Pine Point with Mr. Leman. Slept on dock. Swell liquor. Good time. 23: Heavy showers. Mr. Leman & Willard took us to Sunday cove with boats. Stopped at Cliff's [Wiggins]. John here to dinner. All tired & silly. Talked with Wings about buying Pine Point.

Louise fell in love with Pine Point the first time she saw it: a house with a cluster of buildings and a view, a peninsula of "five hundred acres of woodland bounded by seven miles of shoreline" on Lake Umbagog, the next lake down the chain from Forest Lodge. There was no road near it, so the only approach was by boat—a seven-mile trip. The place had a guide's house and a powerhouse with a generator for lights and a water pump. The rafters in the house were all "eight-by-eight hewn pine. The living room is two stories high, with a fieldstone fireplace that will take four-foot logs. The shingles on the outer walls are two feet long. Every room has a stove, set on a stone hearth that springs from the earth." There were screened-in porches where one could sit or sleep and listen to the sounds of lapping water and breeze in the trees—quiet and peaceful after the omnipresent roar of the Rapid River.

August 24: Carricks [Lynn and Virginia] came. Book gossip all eve. 25: Killing frost everywhere but here. Gang went to B. Pond in p.m. I wrote Mr. Leman about Pine Point. To Middle for mail with Will. Saw deer and fawn. 26: Swimming with A.E.D. Ralph reconciled to Pine Point. 30: Perfect day. Wings, Carricks, Alice, Gerrish on picnic to Pine Point. Men to Errol Dam; sheered prop. blades. Had a lovely time.

[The Wings went home September 1] September 2: Walked to C Pond with Alice, Va. & Lynn. Very successful trip. Ralph sore about something when we got home. [See chapter 7 in *Happy the Land* for the whole story.]

The Carricks and Alice left after a day of recouping and gloating over their bushwhack to C Pond. Louise received a check from *Liberty* and a letter from *Country Gentleman* about rewriting her blizzard story, "Road Commissioner's Report." On September 6, Louise and Ralph and the kids went over to Pine Point for dinner and "arrived at a partial agreement with Leman." Catherine, Gerrish, and Vaughn left for a week's vacation, Dinah's first tooth came in, and Willis was negotiating with Mr. Leman on Louise and Ralph's behalf, probably as a guarantor.

September 13: Rufus to school [in Upton]—Ralph goes with him. Did wash alone. Slept all p.m. & read all eve. Nice day. 14: Gerrish died. Talked with Ralph in Upton on phone & with Katie—had to walk to Middle. R. came in in middle of night from Sunday Cove. 15: Packing & getting ready to go to funeral & Boston. Very sad about Gerrish & feel rotten. Check from Will on act. *Reader's Digest* [about Rufus's birth. Louise also wrote a tribute to Gerrish for *Reader's Digest*'s "My Most Unforgettable Character." See also chapter 2, "Gerrish," in *Happy the Land*]. 16: Hot, muggy. Gerrish's funeral. Met Catherine in Andover. Very sad occasion. Fred Tibbott & Ralph among bearers. Over to Fred's a few minutes & then on to Boston, arr. 10:30. 20: In Boston. Met with Leman. 21: *Bought Pine Point.*

The purchase price of $15,000 included all the contents (aside from Leman's personal effects). On the way home, they stopped in Rumford, where Ralph had four dentist appointments. Katie had "held down the fort fine." A *Life* photographer came in for a few days, Katie left for

California to see her husband off to war, and "Ralph's new teeth came."

At the beginning of October, Louise and Ralph moved to Pine Point for nearly a month. In the process, Louise "busted the typewriter," but that didn't stop her from writing and answering fan mail. Mr. Leman came to take what he wanted: "Evening in attic. He left most of it. Dinah being an angel." Ralph and Louise then began clearing some of the brush outside and rearranging things inside. Louise worked on a *Harper's Bazaar* piece. Alys and Larry Parsons were their first Pine Point guests. They took the boat *Puss* to Upton, and it was Louise's first trip down the length of Umbagog. They went "up the hill" to Upton in the afternoon to "see a few natives" and Rufus, who was homesick and sad when they left the next day: "poor kid."

> October 21: Heme Woodman, Vee Akers [an artist], Doc Hayden
> arr. loaded with food & drink. Like the place. *Co. Gent.* Raised
> my rate to $700 voluntarily. Adv. copy of *WTTTW* came!

At the end of October, they picked up Rufus, who blessedly had a few days off due to a teachers' convention. Ralph and Rufus boated over the seven miles to Middle to get the mail. Umbagog is a wild lake that Louise feared. It takes its toll of bodies each year. While they were out, Louise reoriented a lost hunter and worried. That October 28 was very windy. The boat came back and stalled right off Pine Point, "but they got ashore."

> October 29: Shut the place up for the winter. Started for F. Lodge
> about 3:30. Home & fires going before dark. Rufus a real help.
> Brought Carter [cat] in bread box.

The *Life* article with a photo spread of the author was waiting for them, as were their Middle Dam friends. To top it all off: "Harvard beat Princeton 19–14. Ralph frenzied."

On November 1, Rufus reluctantly headed back to school and Ralph went with Larry Parsons to Rumford, where "food is very scarce." But they enjoyed a "triumphal tour on act. of *Life* pics." The mail of November 5 included a letter to Louise from Lynn Carrick saying that Book of the Month Club had ordered 200,000 copies of *We Took to the Woods.* From that high, she headed out the door with Ralph to rescue the "busted" Essex down at the Cove. "Some ride!! Drained cars."

November 6: Started planning story. In p.m. cleaned up yard. Big mail. Clothes for me came from Ward's [which she packed in a trunk "for emergency"]. BOM order changed to 250,000. 8: US invaded North Africa. This is IT, I think. Started mittens for self and knit socks for Dinah. R to M. with mail. Meant to write, but didn't get to it. 13: Friends in for hunting came across a man looking for his daughter and new husband who are lost in Umbagog. Father, brother, Fred Judkins searching, spent night here.

Early the next frigid morning, the search party left, followed by the hunting party, and Louise and Ralph moved over to the Winter House. Louise "got idea for novel on the death of a town like Grafton," and on November 18 "received a telegram from Lynn and Stevens about publication day," which read: "Congratulations on publication of *We Took to the Woods* putting you in higher income bracket." Ralph went out to Upton to bring Rufus in for his fifth Thanksgiving. Rufus "can read a little now. Very proud." The family walked up to Middle for dinner at the Parsonses'. Next day, a photographer from a Maine paper came in for the day. When he left, Louise wrote: "We are alone for the winter now."

December 1: Gray, raw, with snow squalls. R out with Larry to take Rufus back to Upton & dentist. Got involved & didn't come in. Alone all night. 2: Rain, snow, wind. Barom.=27.9 the lowest ever, even hurricane. R & Larry unable to get in. Alone all day. Shoveled paths, lugged wood, etc. 3: Very high winds, snow squalls. R & Larry got as far as Arm, but not in. Read, wrote letters, got in wood & water. Talked with Alice Miller on phone several times. 4: Snow, not too cold. R started to walk from Arm at 9 a.m. Got to Middle [a half-hour boat ride] at 6:00. Terrible trip. Stayed at Parsons overnight. 5: Snow spits. Ralph, Larry & Blair Lamont arr. in 2 cars about noon. In p.m. R & I to Middle in Reo. R to bed early—sick. 8: Lake skimmed over part way. Did 3 weeks wash. Loads of fan mail. Cookbook from Hester Rich [Hopkins]. 10: Started work on "Killing's No Cure." Road to Middle in p.m. with Dinah & R & called on Millers. Edith Tibbott died. 18: [Rufus's sixth birthday] R & Larry to Rumford & Upton for Rufus. Home about 6:30 p.m. Wrote a lot on "K's no C." Weigh 148. 19: Minus 24 in a.m. apparently cold everywhere. R & R & I to M. in p.m. & got groceries OK, thank God! Bitterly cold; frost never off kitchen. 20: Horribly cold & windy (–22). Stayed in most of day, never opened back room. Breakfast in

Winter House. This is long cold spell & terrible. 21: Bitterly cold, never up to zero. Wild cat came in finally—starved. Rufus & I went out back snow shoeing. 22: Slightly warmer. Grey. Mail day. Rufus' skis came. Fred Tibbott wrote accepting invitation to stay here. Foot of ice on lake. Sink frozen up!! 23: Thawing—thank God! Rufus on Xmas skiis most of day. 24: Rufus & I cut and trimmed Xmas tree. Stuffed turkey. Arranged presents under tree. Nice day. 25: Warm & nice. Rufus liked tree. R & R took presents to Millers. Edward in. 29: Fred Tibbott came in with his dog. Rufus enchanted with Butch—runs him ragged. R & Fred to Middle for Fred's things. Tough going. Probably last trip by car. 31: Snow, cold, raw. Sat up til midnight eating crackers & cheese & drinking Singapore Slings. This has been a *swell* year for us. At last.

--1942--
Stories/Work Written and Sold

With the close of 1942, Louise's sales of her writing jumped dramatically. In addition to chapters 6, 9, 10, and 12 of *We Took to the Woods*, she completed several stories:

"This Is My Father"
"The People in the Street"
"The Sewing Circle's Mrs. Rogers"
"Too Bad She Never Married"
"Road Commissioner's Report"
"Let's Get Away from It All"

For sales, she signed a contract with Lippincott for *Some of the Answers* (*We Took to the Woods*) and sold thirteen shorter pieces:

"Swinging from Birches": *Chatelaine*
"When a Man Fails": *Good Housekeeping*
"No Story": *Family Circle*
"This Is My Daughter": *Family Circle*
"A Hard Row to Hoe": *Household Magazine*
Serial rights to book in *Atlantic Monthly*
"Astral Lure": *Farm Journal*
"You Haven't Changed a Bit": *Chatelaine*

"The People in the Street": *Liberty*
"Rufus' Birth": *Reader's Digest*
"My Most Unforgettable Character": *Reader's Digest*
"Road Commissioner's Report": *Country Gentleman*
Excerpt of *We Took to the Woods*: *Liberty*

After the lean months of 1941, with only $1,154 in sales, 1942 was "a swell year" indeed, bringing in a total of $13,170.

It was also an eventful year. *We Took to the Woods* shared the December 1942 Book of the Month Club top billing with Cornelia Otis Skinner's and Emily Kimbrough's travel frolic, *Our Hearts Were Young and Gay. We Took to the Woods* gained instant popularity and was translated into several languages. Rufus says it was also issued in a small pocket edition for soldiers overseas. Generally considered to be Louise's signature book, it received very enthusiastic reviews, although a few critics, in a condescending (even dismissive tone), described it as escapist reading. Of course it was, and is. Books are that. You stop the real-life/real-time thing you are doing, sit down, take pages in hand, and let the mind go elsewhere. You inhabit the disembodied world of the imagination for a time, are moved in some subtle or profound way, and rise from your chair a slightly altered person. The depth of the change is matched by the author's skill in luring you into his or her world.

An even though it did not make "Best Books of the Decade 1936–45" (a thirty-seven author list), *We Took to the Woods* has stood the test of time better than many on the list (which included *Our Hearts* ..., truly escapist reading that has scarcely been heard of since). Although the story of *We Took to the Woods* superficially, and wonderfully, is dated, its underlying themes are universal. It (and much of Louise's other work) has the status of a classic because its author was able to bend time; to reach beyond the present to the timeless.

- - 1943 - -

The winter of 1943. The world was in the midst of war, but at the Rich household, the wolf of starvation no longer bayed at the door. They owned Forest Lodge, a woodlot nearby, and a gracious summer home on Pine Point. As the new year began, everyone but Louise was down with a cold. She took on the task of housebreaking Fred Tibbott's dog Butch and talked with Merna Allen (six-year-old Rufus was boarding with the Allens in Upton) about Rufus's "stuttering."

January 19: Heavy snow. Radio says ice storms bad nearer coast. Dinah very cute—10 mos. weighs 20 lb. Ralph forged trailer hitch in p.m. 21: Bitterly cold. Never hit zero all day. Larry not able to get in. Andover cut off from Rumford. Terrible winter, so far.

Fred Tibbott was in residence, settling in with his typewriter. Louise worked on "Killing's No Cure" and a piece for the *New Yorker* about fan mail.

In February, a man named Swene came in to work their woodlot and they hauled logs to the sawmill Ralph had devised.

February 7: Clothes rationing starts tomorrow. *WTTTW* on Radio Readers Digest in eve. 10: Larry down, brought mail & hauled 5 loads of wood which Fred & Ralph sawed. Woodshed full of wood now waiting to be split and piled. Duhme to publish my letters [to publisher]. 12: Got BOM club payment of over $16,000 and paid Sadie [for taking care of Sally] through March. Tried to write. Split & piled wood in p.m. Garage starting to buckle under snow load. 16: Coldest a.m. of winter 28 below. Feel rotten—neuritis and cramps. Stayed in and wrote letters most of day. Xmas checks to James and Flor. All bills paid up!! Hurray. 17: Dinah stood up for first time. R's soap came and my wax paper. Larry down to haul wood. Swene staying until wood is done. [They were sawing wood to sell.] 24: Heavy rain. Swene finished 30 cords wood in a.m. In p.m. he, Fred & I sawed, split & stacked wood in shed. Ray Thurston killed. Dinah in kitchen at noon. 26: Talked with Joe Mooney—story out in *Co. Gent* ["Road Commissioner's Report"]. Fred about finished [his] story: "Mr. Sheffington." Delightful. 27: Larry & Swene down. Brought groceries, grapefruit, mail. Hauled & sawed last of wood. Had round of drinks. 28: Wrote check for Sally's birthday present. Ordered green mocs. from Ward with #17 stamp—first time to use book on rationed clothes. Klatched [talked] about Fred's story in eve.

March 1: Started *Liberty* article ["When Our Ship Comes In"]. Fred walked mail to Middle barefoot [no snowshoes]. Talked with A. Miller on phone about NY trip. Worked on income tax. 2: BOM ordered 25,000 more copies. We are 8th on the *Herald Trib.* book list. 9: Up at 5:30. 22 below zero. Down lake, hectic

drive to Andover with Fred, Butch, Ralph, Al & Larry, Dinah and
me to Rumford. Got permanent, went shopping. Dinah to Miss
Colpitts [babysitter, where she stayed for nearly a month].

Ralph and Louise continued on to Boston, where they paid their income tax; met up with Alice, Mr. Leman, and others; had a "Personal Bk.
Shp. Cocktail party"; and bought "old" furniture [antique Windsor chairs].
Then followed a flashy literary week in New York City: "Orchid from Will.
BOM luncheon, dinner at Lafayette, lunch at Plaza, cocktails at Hoboff's,
dinner at Penthouse club, drinks in Algonquin Bar, Reviewer's luncheon
at Park Lane & interview with Driscall in Ritz Bar. . . ." Louise did two broadcasts [Martha Dean and Dorothy Wheelock shows], managed to see *Life
with Father* with Ralph, and "had lunch with Hester Rich H. Fun." They
spent four days at the Wings' new house, where Louise and Will "chew
[ed] the fat" and had "conferences." On March 23: "To NY with Will. Lunch
with Bernie [*WHC*]. Made column deal. Shopped in p.m. Home to hilarious eve. for no good reason." Then it was off to Philadelphia with Ralph
and Will and meetings with "*Co Gent.* people, *Sat. Eve. Post* and *Liberty,*
and the Lipp. [Lippincott] gang." Back to New York to see *Lady in the Dark*
with publishing contacts and the midnight train to Boston. They went to
Bridgewater for a week and saw Ralph's Boston friends (Ezra, George
Myer). Louise had an interview with the New Bedford newspaper and
they went to dinner in Newton with the Dave Tibbotts, brother Fred, Alice
and Travis (who "has pneumonia").

April 1: Return to Maine with Fred. Talked with Joe Mooney
about Dinah, whose picture is in paper. 2: Much fuss over us in
Rumford. Went to the ration board. Finally hit Arm at 2:00, lunch
at Parsons and home to tons of mail. 3: Washed and tidied and
thought about speech. Read fan mail. Worried about poor homesick Rufus. 4: Called Merna about Rufus who seems better. Wrote
Knights of P speech. 5: To Rumford. Speeches at Rotary and K of
P. Very festive reception. 6: Did much shopping. Got Dinah. Larry
came for me. Lunch at Poore's [Andover]. Home—terrible on
lake. Fred & R glad to see me.

Louise played with Dinah, read William Saroyan's "*Human Comedy*—
which I loved," *Butterfield 8,* and *Cause for Alarm,* by Eric Ambler. She
wrote three *WHC* stories. Ralph, Swene, and Fred rebuilt the Guide's
House roof and buried the water pipe into the kitchen—"sink drain free

at last!" The log-drive wangan/cook crew came in, as did their delivery of furniture from Boston. Dinah was "loose on floor for first time—loved it." Louise sent Sally a hundred dollars for her boarding-out money (she was in Bridgewater) and got word on April 29 that Captain Coburn had died. "Great suspense over hotel."

> May 1: Snow for May Day. Sponged R's clothes for Coburn's funeral tomorrow. Read most of p.m. Coal strike. 3: Swene back. Ralph sick & up most of night with cramps. 5: Wrote. Cleaned our summer house room. Smelting in eve. with Alice M., Parsons & Ralph. Supper at Parsons. They are taking over Lakewood. Larry out tomorrow to see about help, rationing etc. for hotel. [Louise and Ralph bought insurance, the log-drive crew came in, and the annual batch of drowned bodies started surfacing.] 20: Ice out 21: The first [log] boom is on its way down from Narrows. 24: R, Fred & Ed Coombs to Pine Point. Catherine is coming back!! Norwegians [houseguests along with Ed] fished L. Richardson all day. No luck. 26: Norwegians, Ed left. River almost at flood pitch. Alice M. waiting on table at Hotel. R. to Rumford to see gas board. Came out ok on F.L., PPt. under consideration.

The *New York Herald Tribune Weekly Book Review* (June 6, 1943) announced: "Refusing to Forsake Hide-Away to Comply with Point Rationing, Author of *We Took to the Woods* Receives Special Office of Price Administration Dispensation." People on the Outside were allowed six to eight items of canned food a month. Louise and Ralph, who often went through that much in a day, were allowed extra so they would not have to leave Forest Lodge. At the end of May, Louise went to Upton: "Rufus glad to see me." She bought him an ice cream, had his hair cut, and visited school, where she noted he "did fine."

> June 1: Dinah fell out of bed. Rufus very tired and sensitive. 2: Rufus' Graduation Day. His first public speech. Did very well, but obviously scared. 3: School picnic. Merna, Dinah & I picnicing [sic] on blanket in pasture. Fun. Got a little sunburned. Rufus took off shorts. [Louise and the children headed back to Forest Lodge, where Rufus was promptly "mislaid and found at Wangan." Sally wrote, asking permission to stay with them for a couple of weeks.] 14: Gorgeous day. Forty to-day. Telephone from Wings. Made tentative deal with Woodward about wood lot. OPA will let us have some gas for Pine Point.

Over the next few days, the area was in a flood alert: "Brown Farm flooded, Pondy Dam went out. Boat skid [launching platform] busted up and the first pier washed out. Drive halted." The water receded and Louise helped get the "logs for boat skid re-arranged. Ralph, Rufus & I went & looked for salvage. Found a lot."

> June 21: Drive starts up again. Sally arrived. Parsons are doing well at Lakewood with lots of guests. 24: Lovely day. Wrote. Finished story ["Health Commissioner's Report"]. Check from *WHC* ["Ten Paces to the Left"]. Catherine and Vaughn are back. Vaughn and Rufus in groove at once. 27: Down to Cliff [Wiggins] for lunch with Woodward. Bought the old Mason lot back of Pine Point from Woodward.

> July 1: The bantam [hen] from Goleta, Calif. arrived. Rufus all agog. Wrote. Outlined possible movie plot for *WTTTW*. Cath. & I helped Fred & R move sawmill parts off Winter House porch.

The annual foldboat throng came and went, Ralph hauled for the log drive, Louise worked on a "freeze-up story," Whit Roberts and his wife arrived to take care of Forest Lodge, and by the middle of July the family repaired to Pine Point, where teenage suitors, camp followers, and literary types descended. In her endearing canine/human descriptions (she "housebroke Rufus," for example), Louise reported that after encounters with unnamed summer visitors one day, "Fred is in heat." After a few days of "doping around sick," he left for his place in Chesterville with Catherine and Sally's friend, Doris, to work in Fred's garden. In their absence, Ralph, Louise, and Whit did a score of odd jobs. Although Louise commented how "quiet and peaceful" it was at Pine Point, she was referring to the tranquillity of the lake. Socially, they were as busy as ever, and logistically there was still a huge amount of shuffling. Louise went back and forth to Forest Lodge in order to use the washing machine, they had to go seven miles by boat to pick up their mail at Middle Dam, and the nearest town was still a day trip away.

During the August berrying time, Katie, Doris, and Fred made another vegetable-garden foray, returning with thirty-five quarts of canned beans. Next, Fred, Ralph, and Rufus disgorged the motor out of an old Packard and lugged it down the Carry Road to Ralph's sawmill. Dave and Dorothy Tibbott [Fred's brother and sister-in-law] arrived for the month and immediately helped move over "Twitchell's [neighbor's] boat house. Very gay supper and evening." On August 10, Louise celebrated the Tibbotts' twenty-fifth anniversary with her "annual pancake night." Dave fell down the hatch of *Puss*, and *Iggliffe* nearly swamped on one run. They lost the shaft of the Chris-Craft at Sunday Cove (after "much hurrah," Louise had to dive for it). A couple of dynamiters came in (dynamiting—what is not said—for several days). Sally's friends came; Rufus visited a friend for a week; Dinah—about a year and a half—was busy toddling around; Alice came for her annual stay. There was a constant flow in and visiting out.

In spite of all that, Louise continued to produce stories: a rewrite of "Health Commissioner's Report," "The Grapevine," and "Mine Enemies [*sic*] Heart" (in September retitled "The Talisman"). Rufus says that for as long as he can remember, mornings were inviolate: "From eight or nine in the morning until lunch you did not bother Ma on pain of death." On August 27, Louise headed over to Forest Lodge to do the washing and prepare her speech (presumably in relative quiet) for an OPA broadcast at the state capital the following day. On August 28: "Nice day. Traveled to Augusta, met the press and prep broadcast which went ok."

> September 1: Heavy rain. To Errol with Alice, Stevens, kids in a.m. Soaked! To Upton in p.m. to see Jim's [Barnett] house. Hired it. Alice & Stevens went home. [As of this entry, Rufus would no longer board out during the school year but will be with Catherine and Vaughn in this rented house. Louise's justification for sending Rufus out was that it was important for him to be socialized, but it is also clear that a highly attuned sense of motherhood was not part of Louise's nature.] 3: Nice day. Cleaned, washed sheets. Wrote "Self-Sufficiency." Put cots back in attic for winter. Getting Pine Point ready to close is sad. [The next entries make wonderful reading in *Happy the Land* (chapter 9).] 5: Packed for Upton. Rode down with Ralph in *Puss*. Cedric took us uphill. Bought groceries. Got settled some. Kids excited. Then, at 11 p.m., bed bugs in Rufus' bed!! 6: Nice day. Saw Jim about B.Bs. He upset. Fumigated room. Cleaned house partially. Took kids down to see Merna. *Two* teachers arr.!!! [They had agreed to board "one" schoolteacher in order to rent the house.] 7: Kids [Vaughn and Rufus] first day at school. Washed back room with gasoline.

The next day, Ralph picked her up and they headed off to Forest Lodge. The following day, they went to Pine Point, where they were greeted by Carter (the cat) and discovered that a coon had stolen their bantam rooster. Louise spent a few days rewriting "The Talisman" and reading *Prodigal Women,* while Ralph and his two helpers, Whit Roberts and Phil Learned, cleared some of the wood around the property. On September 11, she wrote, went swimming, painted their dinghy, and slept out "on the porch, as I was alone." By the middle of September, they moved back to Forest Lodge, having delivered the hen to a friend to be boarded out for the winter.

September 18: We visit Katie [Catherine] and the kids in Upton. All doing well. Had fun. Heavenly on Umbagog. Phil and Whit cranberrying. 20: Another perfect day. Took Adamses [photographer friends staying at Lakewood] and Stewarts to Pine Point on picnic. Place looks swell. Phil left for marines. 21: Nice day. Spent most of it writing loads of letters and tidying house. Leaves turning fast now. 25: Got Reo home. I drove Ford up from Long Pool alone. [Ralph had taught her to drive, and this was her first recorded solo.]

Ralph and Whit (with help from visitor Dudley Dorr and a "new man Jack Robertson," who "showed up looking for work") spent the month of October renovating the kitchen in the Summer House. They tore out the old icebox and cleaned out the cellar. The day after they laid a cement floor, Whit, Jack, Ralph, and Louise headed for Pine Point, picking up Katie and the kids, for a few days of respite. Once the kids were back in Upton, Louise resumed her writing.

October 13: Gorgeous day. Got article ["Drama in Everyday Life," for the *Reader's Digest*] ready to mail. Closed spare bedrooms. Partridge stew for supper. R & I to Forest Lodge [where they picked up the last-minute things they needed for a trip to Boston with Katie and the kids]. 16: Hot & nice. Lunch and shopping with Alice who is marrying Travis. Out to Bridgewater in p.m. Called on Sally and Cranes. [Next, Louise had three Boston appearances.] Speech at book fair, on Yankee Network in a.m., at Symphony Hall in p.m. Did ok. [Ralph and the kids stayed in Bridgewater while Louise headed on to the Wings' house in Georgetown and heard that] *Reader's Digest* bought "Grandma and the Seagull." [After several days,] Ralph called up so took night train home. Dinner at Commodore. [Next day, they all went back to Maine, stopping at the Ration Board in Rumford. Once ensconced at Forest Lodge, the inexorable events of the place once again took hold.] 29: Cold. Walked down to Richardsons. Three hunters drowned in Umbagog near Red Spot.

Ralph spent the first two weeks in November trying to get the water pump working again. Louise compiled and sent out their winter supply list, did massive amounts of cleaning, knitted, and wrote consistently.

November 15: Ralph worked all day on pump & finally abandoned for winter. 16: Typed "Cousin Althea" [later called "The Pretty One"]. Ralph decided to abandon finishing kitchen for winter. Dismantled gravel chipper. 18: Nice day. Whit & Ralph got cellar decked over. Big improv. Anniversary of *WTTTW*. Letter from Fred [Tibbott] saying Will [agent] has chucked him. 21: Started "Game Warden & Refugees" for *WHC*. Whit & Ralph cleaning yard and in p.m. to Middle to haul Whit's boat. Snow in eve. 22: Heavy snow all day. Worked on "Game Warden." In p.m. R. took Whit & duffel to Middle in Reo. Whit stayed. 18" snow at 7 p.m. Talked to Catherine. 23: Still snowing. Biggest storm on record—40"! All roads blocked and tel. lines down. Started to move to Winter House. 25: Thanksgiving. Walked to Middle for dinner at Millers. Hard going. Arm still blocked. Lines still out. 26: Lovely day. Carried wood, etc. Nice to be out. Larry started for Andover at 7:30 p.m. Arm froze last night. 27: Larry got to Andover ok. Arm no longer frozen. Larry hauling for Pete Baker like mad. 30: Tried to call Katie again, but Upton line still out.

December 1: Gray and raw. Walked to Middle for mail. Letter from George S. saying book sales spurting. Ralph & I had party in eve. 2: Read, knit. Upton line still out [nine days now]. Lugged wood. Finished *USA*. Started *Lady Chatterly's* [sic] *Lover.* Dopey day. 3: Mail day, but Larry to be late on acct. has to go in kicker [motorboat]. Upton telephone still down. 4: Rain. Ralph up for mail. Word from Katie [telephone finally working] that kids smashed up Ladies' Aid china. [See chapter 9 in *Happy the Land.*] 5: Grey. Wrote a mess of letters. Thinking of story about Demeter in Upton. 8: Larry down with mail. Check from *R. Digest* for $1,350. Whoops! Cooked, started Demeter story. Income tax bill—about $10,000!! 12: Lake froze over for first time. Wrote on story. R & I did Xmas cards—over 100. Artichoke hearts and hollandaise for supper. Weigh 157. Must lose.

On December 16, Ralph and Louise left the cat with the Parsonses, took Kyak to Bethel, and headed for Portland for a doctor's visit for Ralph. He was diagnosed as having either "multiple or disseminated sclerosis." He was fifty-three but looked at least ten years older. While in Portland, Ralph and Louise shopped for Christmas presents, had dinner at Boone's restaurant, and went back to the Eastland Hotel for oysters. Next day: "Ralph and I both feel bum. Too many oysters." They returned for Christmas in Upton to be with Katie and the kids, who were "all agog about Xmas." Ralph visited with Albert Allen.

December 23: Cold. Ralph cut Xmas tree & Katie & I trimmed it. Looks nice. Worked on "Miss Pollard." Kids cute and good. 24: Sally arrived. Kids glad to see her. Xmas tree [at church]. Rufus spoke piece. Chewed fat with Ken Hinckley about Arthur's place [to buy?]. 25: Christmas. Tree great success. Finished "Miss Pollard." Shoveled out Ladies' Aid broken crockery. Jim Barnett in. 27: Katie left for Hinckley to see Bon & I took over. Ralph down to lake burning Durkees boat for him. Sent out Demeter story ["Miss Pollard"]. 31: Cold. Word from Will "Miss Pollard" sold. good way to end a year. Tel calls from Katie who arr. tomorrow. Been a good year.

--1943--
Short Stories Written and Sold

"Letter to the *New Yorker*"
"Killing's No Cure"
"The Ship": *Liberty*
"Ten Paces to the Left": *Woman's Home Companion*
"Carter Glass, Pinky & Democracy": *Good Housekeeping*
"Mind Out of Time"
"Health Commissioner's Report": *Country Gentleman*
"The Grapevine"
"The Talisman": *Country Gentleman*
"When Our Ship Comes In"
"Supposing Something Happens": *Glamour*
"Drama in Everyday Life": *Reader's Digest*

"Althea": *Woman's Home Companion*
"Grandma and the Seagull": *Reader's Digest*
"Game Warden and Refugees"
"Miss Pollard"
"Yours Truly"

All of Louise's stories from 1943 sold during that year, except "Killing's No Cure," "Mind Out of Time," "When Our Ship Comes In," "The Grapevine," and "Game Warden and Refugees." Several of those stories sold in 1944 and one ("The Grapevine") in 1945.

The sales list included British rights to "Rainbow Chase" and "Mother Takes a Holiday," radio rights to the chapter on Rufus's birth from *We Took to the Woods*, and royalty payments for *WTTTW*, for a grand total of $41,343.95 ($36,500+ after taxes)—all that in 1943 dollars.

The tone of Louise's diary, even the look, changed subtly over the years. Initially, her handwriting was the large, careful script of a schoolteacher. By the end, it was smaller and much more angular. Up until the whirlwind success of *We Took to the Woods*, Louise recorded her short-story titles with the humble delight of ownership. By the end, she often just wrote, "finished story." The early entries showed an intensity of perceptions and emotions—of newness and wonder. Simplicity, a certain naivete, and vulnerability honed the senses—at that time she was literally a starving artist.

It is understandable that Louise would want to celebrate after at least half a dozen years of financial deprivation, but, as is universally acknowledged, getting all you desire can have its drawbacks. Her energy became more diffuse (more houses, people, money, outside commitments and influences). She was faced with life lessons about maintaining creative and personal integrity. She even tried on a forty-year-old-famous-author persona (shades of her high-school drama days?) when deluged with fame and celebrity seekers.

Steve Kovar, a longtime visitor to the area, remembers seeing Louise in 1937, "barefoot with a baby under her arm," and Ralph hammering away at one of the many engines littering the yard, and thinking to himself, "How do they live?" By the summer of 1943, while at Lakewood Camps on leave from the navy, he and three companions decided to pay a call on the famous author. "Alys informed us visiting hours were from two to four p.m. So we all got dressed up in uniform and went down. A woman met us at the door and offered us drinks. Then Louise showed up wearing high heels, black slacks, a green sweater, hair all done up, and a long cigarette holder. Ralph was down by the dam in the same old clothes I remembered from six years before. He had white hair and we talked a bit about fishing. He didn't seem to want any part of what was going on. She was a snob, turned her back, and wouldn't talk to me twice. I mean, she was at the top of the heap—people coming from Europe! Some of us think that Ralph wrote the book anyway, and she was getting all the credit and attention."

The Dark Years

Louise and Ralph headed into 1944 on a roll. The bills were paid, Rufus and Dinah were with Catherine in Upton (the Ladies' Aid crockery had been replaced...!), and Sally was in Bridgewater. The usual pattern continued: a cold, snowy winter with logging crews nearby. The tiny winter community cut wood, traded visits, tried to keep vehicles and fires going. Louise wrote the short stories "Tolerance" in January, "Paid Notice" and "The Red Slipper" in February. Spring thawed the frozen lake, making it hazardous for travel. In April, *We Took to the Woods* was printed in Swedish (it was also translated into French and German). Finally the ice melted, the booms came downriver, and the logs tumbled out the dam. Gardens and visitors popped up. Alice married Travis Hoke, and Ralph constructed the new kitchen ell. In summer, they moved over to Pine Point and conducted the usual summer-camp scene for adults, pets, and children and their classmates.

With the beginning of the school year, Catherine, Rufus, Dinah, and Vaughn moved to the Swett house at "Windy Corner" in Andover and Louise and Ralph moved back to Forest Lodge. At that point, Louise had written "What to do When They Write" for the *Saturday Review of Literature,* and "Luck for the Bride," "Share My Secret," and "The Gift" (all featured in various 1944 issues of *Woman's Home Companion*). Thanksgiving came and went, a modest affair due to the war and rationing. December 17 marked the one-year anniversary of Ralph's diagnosis of multiple sclerosis. On December 18, Rufus celebrated his eighth birthday in Andover. The next morning, Louise wrote, most likely, and then chopped/hauled wood with Ralph. The hired help, visitors, and woods crews had all gone home, and they were "alone for the winter." The evening came early and brought a few flurries. By the time supper was over and they were settled comfortably by the fire, the snow fluttered down steadily in the still night. Louise took out her knitting and Ralph made comments that soon had them laughing.

Then, in midsentence, Ralph uttered a strange little sigh and stopped talking. Suddenly the room was quiet, time stopped, and Louise knew something was very wrong. Looking up, startled, she saw a man, in a room, in an orb of lamplight. Outside the snow was falling ... falling. All was still—the silence almost solid. Fighting the evidence, someone who looked like Louise carefully, slowly, put down her knitting and floated over to find the man, Ralph, dead.

Louise described the event in *Only Parent:*

> Between one minute and the next, Ralph suffered a cerebral
> hemorrhage. One minute he was laughing with me, then he gave
> a sigh, then he was dead. I now realize what a wonderful thing it
> was to have happened. He might have made a partial recovery,
> and been crippled and paralyzed in a wheel chair. He couldn't
> have borne that. Life without action would have been hell for him.
> I'm glad now that he was so lucky. But after the shock and the grief
> of the moment passed, I realized only one thing: that I was alone
> now and that for all the rest of my life I was going to be lonely.

Ralph was fifty-four. Alys Parsons says that as soon as Louise called,
they went to Forest Lodge to help transport Ralph's body and offer support. Louise frantically packed and did the bare essentials to close up the
place for the winter. Her mind wasn't on it; she just wanted to flee the
deathly quiet. Ralph's body was taken out to Rumford, and the medical
examiner, Dr. Stewart, diagnosed "sudden death, probably due to cerebral
hemorrhage." Albert Allen, Ralph's old friend and the Upton town clerk
at the time, signed (undoubtedly with great sadness) the death certificate. The day after Christmas, Ralph was cremated. Sally says she remembers taking the train to Rumford for her father's funeral, but Rufus
and Dinah did not attend.

Louise was forty-one years old. She and Ralph had been together
ten years. I say "been together" because various people I interviewed confided that they thought Louise and Ralph never married. Simply because
many suspect a thing does not make it true, so I checked marriage
records from the town offices in Upton and Andover. No record in Upton,
and the Andover records from 1933 to 1939 apparently were destroyed
by fire. Nothing in Bridgewater. Ralph's twenty-fifth-anniversary report
from Harvard said they were married in Portland, Maine, in August 1935,
but Portland City Hall had no such entry, and neither did the records
from the period 1933 to 1943 for the entire state of Maine.

Records from the states of New Hampshire, Massachusetts, and even
Vermont failed to supply confirmation of a marriage. Rufus's 1936 birth
certificate states they were married, Ralph's death certificate says they
were married. Legal transactions occurred (real estate purchases, for example) as a married couple. However, it slowly became clear: Louise
Dickinson and Ralph Rich were never legally married.

Nonetheless, the integrity of their life together makes the issue almost
irrelevant. By every other indicator except a piece of paper, they were in-

deed married. They had forged an interdependent partnership, acquired property that each bequeathed to the other, conceived two children and raised three, and lived with and cared for both sets of in-laws. They were by each other's side "in sickness and in health, for richer or for poorer," through joy and sorrow, crisis and calm, and—at least from the diary indications—remained faithfully committed to each other. Most important—they simply loved one another.

Alys says: "I have rarely seen a more compatible couple, and I've seen a lot. They just seemed to enjoy each other's company and be on the same wavelength. It was a real love match." Hester agrees: "Louise was extremely happy with Ralph, she truly loved him, and you could see it was mutual." They certainly were married in their own minds. My intuition (or perhaps romantic heart!) tells me that August 27, 1934—which most often appears as "the date"—may well have been the anniversary of that summer day Ralph and Louise first laid eyes upon each other along the Carry Road. When they were later required to come up with a specific date, that may have been their private joke in a relationship where laughter was the main ingredient. Perhaps they had even made a private pact with each other that day in celebration.

Without Ralph, bereft and beside herself, Louise spent the winter of 1945 in Andover with Catherine and the kids, and Vaughn says that, according to his mother, Louise started to fall apart. Whereas she had previously been a social drinker, now she applied herself vigorously to the bottle. It must have been a volatile time for all concerned.

By March, Louise wanted to get back to Forest Lodge—before the woods "started crawling with logging crews and fishermen." Leaving Eva, Catherine's sister, in charge of two-year-old Dinah, Vaughn, and eight-year-old Rufus, Louise and Catherine hitched a ride on Larry Parsons's snowboat. Louise was immobilized, awash in indecision, feeling very alone and responsible. She had not been able or inclined to write for months. Fortunately, she had written "Secret of the Island" and "The Martyr Wife" (*Woman's Home Companion*) and "Grapevine for OPA" (*Liberty*) before Ralph's death, and these Willis had been able to sell.

The first days back home, Louise wrote (in *Happy the Land*), "were perhaps the queerest two weeks I have ever spent in my life—two weeks lifted entirely out of time. It was only March, but every day shone as hot as August." Surrounded by all the old familiar things, her mind ranged back to the early days, the desperate/wonderful times together with Ralph, Rush, and Gerrish. She reflected on those men she loved—one as a husband, one as a brother, the other as a father figure—with much tenderness and gratitude. And quietly, slowly, lying in the sun, the weight of her grief began to melt and the outline for another story started to emerge. She wrote a tribute to Gerrish, sent it off to Willis, and turned her attention to the neighborhood crisis.

The abnormally hot spring was forcing an unusually early opening of Lakewood Camps. Louise and Catherine flew around helping to ready the cabins. The ice was out on April 14, the earliest on record, and the sporting camp opened April 19. For about the next two months, until school was out, Catherine waited on tables while Louise cleaned cabins, served as assistant cook, did laundry duty, and put in a stint behind the front desk. Unfortunately, surrounded by couples and slews of single men, Louise became lonelier than ever, and, liquored up, became something of a loose cannon. "Red" Johnson, the cook, says she returned to her cottage one day to find Louise "in bed, my own bed, with my husband." And this was not an isolated incident. She was emotionally volatile, running wild and hard, trying to flee the dark emptiness within.

Soon the children returned from school and the onslaught of guests began. Willis urged Louise to use her Gerrish story—which came out as "My Most Unforgettable Character" in the August issue of *Reader's Digest*—as the basis for a chapter in another book. Louise left the happy chaos of Pine Point to visit Hester and think. As Hester tells it: "She didn't cultivate any new friends. Huntie had a place in Plymouth and we visited her. We talked nonstop from the time we got together, not about ourselves but about things that seemed important. None of us ever agreed, and it seemed like we were all talking and listening at the same time. It was one of the joys of my relationship with Dicky. I remember once the two of us went to the beach and were so completely absorbed we sat down on the path and talked till we were lying down. People were walking over us to get to the beach!"

Louise used her respite with Hester to take stock of her circumstances. Hester says she was very much unto herself: "So much of her life was internalizing her experiences, which of course proved useful in her writing." Louise's pattern was to deal with a crises head-on and then step back and evaluate what to do next. She removed herself from the trees in order to see the forest—in this case, not only emotionally but also literally.

Here's what she knew: She had debts, practically no money to pay them off, and everything suddenly seemed to be more expensive (the cost of living had, in fact, risen almost 30 percent during the year). She owed $3,000 to the Woodwards for the three Pine Point lots; and $5,000 was past due (as of January 1945, and accruing 69 cents interest every overdue day) to J. Howard Leman for Pine Point. She needed to raise some money, to get to work writing again.

No sooner had she settled down to write than Louise, as executrix of Ralph's estate, received a formal claim against her for payment of an old debt Ralph owed to his former classmate and business partner J.W.B. Ladd. On June 1, 1943, while Louise was in Upton attending Rufus's graduation, Ladd (unbeknownst to her? and on the strength of her literary success?) had come to collect some of the debt Ralph owed from their business liquidation twenty years earlier. On June 1, they signed a written agreement that Ralph would pay Ladd $5,000 ($2,000 of which he paid at the time of the signing). The claim Louise received demanded payment of the remaining $3,000 in yearly installments of $1,000 (starting in June 1945). Although that may not sound like much by today's standards, it, along with Ralph's other debts (totaling approximately $9,000) was money Louise simply did not have. She was once again broke—worse than broke—and it must have been a huge additional strain. Ironically, the greatest high point in her career was also the lowest point in her personal life.

As for assets, she and Ralph had $80 in bank savings and about $700 in salable items (cement mixer, lumber, tools, etc.). And she had property that she could either sell or maintain. Ralph's will (recorded April 25, 1945) gave her "the Forest Lodge Lot, the Pine Point property and the [3] Woodward Lots, in Magalloway Plantation, together with equity in any other real estate." She would be surrounded by memories, but that could be a solace. Besides, they were home—particularly Forest Lodge, which fortunately had been paid off years earlier (March 1943). Given the choice between Bridgewater and Forest Lodge, there was no question. Nothing was wrong with Bridgewater itself, she was simply spoiled for the woods and the wild. But her property was remote, and the sheer bulk of buildings, and the systems/machinery involved, required huge and constant maintenance—something Ralph had been good at doing or overseeing. Would she have to hire an additional person?

As for the family, what if someone became seriously ill? Rufus had been diagnosed as "an infector" with a blood abnormality. Dinah was only three. What about schooling? What about the logistics of getting supplies and services? Andover was still a long drive off the main road. She made up her mind. She would try to keep Forest Lodge and Pine Point going, and they would all move somewhere closer to a larger town. But how would she raise the money to make all that happen? She could go back to teaching, find some other steady income, or she could continue to write. Writing was risky. It functioned, as Louise would say, on conscientiously "applying the seat of your pants to the task at hand." It was fraught with rejections, false hopes, delayed gratification, and fickle and undermining stardom. However, according to Hester: "Louise always knew writing was what she wanted to do. It was in her gene pool. She was passionate about wanting to be the best possible writer she could be." Writing was her work, her skill; but even more it was her lifesaver. Writing about Gerrish had been a catharsis. Yes. She would write her heart out....

Louise went back to Maine and rented a house for Catherine, the kids, and herself in Rumford Point. Vaughn remembers that they lived "by Johnny Martin's store, across the street from the Congregational church."

In spite of (or perhaps because of) this financial burden, Louise's literary output was noteworthy, the tangible evidence of her determination, practicality, and self-discipline. Before 1945 was over, "Secret of the Island," "Grapevine for OPA," and "The Martyr Wife" were published, and she was working on what would become *Happy the Land*, her second book. Louise's personal life may have been dark and chaotic, but she doggedly wrote her way back into her own courage, one word at a time, and those words ultimately offered light and meaning to others in a world winding down from a war.

Happy the Land: Those who have drunk lonesome water are not in their right minds. It's more than loving the land. It seems for me the thing for which you spend your whole life to build, if you would be whole, is not a bank account, or an unimpeachable social position, or success in any one of a thousand lines of endeavor; it seems to me that the only thing worth having is a certainty of yourself. People who have this knowledge are people who have kept their edges intact, people with what I can only call core; by which I mean the indestructible skeleton of character, showing through manner and mannerism, as good bones show through flesh. It's one thing you know you can count on in yourself and in others, and it's not easily acquired.

Here in this country I have found the circumstance that will make a woman of me if anything will. Here I have my feet on the solid earth, literally, and that is good; for it seems to me that the earth is the only permanence we can know. In spite of war and pestilence and destruction, in spite of the unthinkable cruelties man inflicts upon man, in spite of political upheavals and personal disloyalties and treacheries, the earth remains unchanged.

Every individual must find the proper ground on which to work out his [her] own salvation. For some it is city; for some it is farm; for some it is laboratory or monastery or tropical jungle. The important thing is to find the place in which you can be the best person you are capable of being, in which you can develop your potentialities most nearly to the utmost; and the implication is that that is the place in which you can be most useful and happiest, the place in which you feel at home. I have found my place.

In Rumford Point, Rufus and Vaughn went to a two-room schoolhouse Vaughn explains:

Rufus was like a big brother. Actually, Catherine adopted me (I was her sister Maggie's baby), and her other son, "Bon" [Bonhomme], was ten years older and away at school. Catherine really was mother to Rufus, Dinah, and me. It seemed like Rufus was always coming up with ideas to make mischief and I just went right along. There were two tracks in the snow—Rufus's were first and mine were right behind. Once, at Forest Lodge, he dumped kerosene in an old woodstove and flames shot out all over the place. In Upton, he and Bon (home for Christmas) teased me out on the roof at 6 a.m., in my pajamas. They closed the window and it was freezing out there! I finally had to jump off the roof and run around and knock on the door. Not long after that, we drank the ginger ale Louise had put out in the snow to cool for a ladies' get-together. When I was around five, Rufus fell through the ice in Andover and I had to haul him out. Then there was the day we put our hands in the cement steps for the new kitchen at Forest Lodge. Ralph was so mad he spanked us with his trowel. Ralph Rich was a good dad to us, though. He didn't play any favorites. He was always out doing something or other. He had a whole bunch of plans: he was going to make a waterwheel and put it out in the river and generate electricity, and he had a blueprint for a square peg. I don't remember Louise getting mad, but Mother used a yardstick to spank us. I remember the time of the Ladies' Aid broken dishes we squirmed so much the yardstick broke. Leon Wilson was watching and said, 'Here, I'll give you a hand.' Well, he took off his belt and, I gotta tell you, after a few whacks that belt seemed *very* wide. . . .

Dinah picks up her story:

> Rufus put me in the rain barrel at Forest Lodge, and that's how I learned to swim—by treading water. Then we'd go down the sluice gates at Middle Dam in inner tubes together. We'd bicker, of course, like any kids, but Rufus always looked out for me. I remember Ma always said she didn't care if any of us got all As, but if conduct was graded from 1 to 4, she wanted us to get 1s and 2s. I'm afraid we didn't measure up (more times than I want to remember), but our mistakes were usually stupid rather than mean-spirited.

Louise meanwhile made a few friends in Rumford Point, most notably Virginia Hutchins, according to Virginia's sister-in-law, Dotty Dunton:

> The Hutchins house was like a French salon, full of interesting people. When we all got together, we would read poetry—sometimes until two or three o'clock in the morning. Louise had her own code. She was not opinionated in a harsh sense—she'd make a strong statement, but always add something like, "that's the way it is for me." She was completely herself, almost self-deprecating, with a wonderful natural sense of humor. A very generous person—and had a lot of people she gave money to. And, believe it or not, she spoke even better than she wrote. She had perfect diction, with a deep, rich voice. She could see the ridiculous in what others took seriously. Both Louise and Virginia were ahead of their time in many ways, and behind in some. They thought alike, and would have fit in with Gertrude Stein or any literary circle.

Over the next few years, Louise would spend a month at a time with the Hutchinses.

Jim Barnett was once again in the picture. He still owned their old rental house in Upton, but he had retired from logging and was running a taxi service in the Rumford area. Jim had been a friend in the early, desperate days and now began showing signs of wanting to be more than a friend. Perhaps it was a combination of Jim's attentions, Louise's financial crisis, and the imminent arrival of her estranged husband home from the war, but by the end of 1945, Catherine had decided to leave. Vaughn: "She felt she wasn't doing Louise any favors at this point by taking responsibility for everything." On December 13, another claim—from the Rumford National Bank on behalf of Leman—arrived, demanding a Pine Point payment of $5,051.39.

By February 1946, Catherine and Vaughn left and Jim and Louise recorded their marriage intentions at the Upton Town Office. Alone with two young children, and confronted with property and personal expenses, creditors howling, and virtually no savings, Louise perhaps saw Jim as a man of means who could help provide security for the future. Dinah (four) and Rufus (nine) would have a friendly father figure and she would have a congenial companion. Jim, for his part, perhaps saw a lonely friend, a rich and famous woman who could help provide security for the future. Whatever the motivations, on March 28, 1946, at 9 a.m., James Barnett, born on Prince Edward Island, and Louise Dickinson Rich, were married in a double-ring ceremony at her Rumford Point home by Reverend Linwood Potter of Andover. The marriage certificate says it was Louise's second marriage—which of course was technically true. The local paper stated: "After a short honeymoon trip to Boston, they will reside in Mrs. Barnett's home at Rumford Point until school vacation. Their plans beyond then are not definite although Mrs. Barnett expressed a desire to go to Alaska."

On April 13, 1946, just two weeks after her marriage, Louise received a claim demanding payment for the "Woodward lots." Louise now owed $11,500, and on April 25 her lawyer filed a Representation of Insolvency, telling the court that Ralph's estate was "insufficient to pay all the just debts which deceased owed." During the spring, Louise wrote the short stories "Backstairs" and "Molly Ockett." The latter story was the tale of a strong and valiant woman Louise said was her role model at that point. (See page 241.) When the school year ended, the family shuffled from Upton to Forest Lodge and Pine Point, where Jim must have had an uncomfortable time at "Camp Rich" with the intellectual, literary talk. Hester: "This was the period when I lost track of Louise—she just stopped things cold. I couldn't understand this because it was so out of character. I realized later it was because she had married this man, Barnett, who had helped them buy land early on, I believe, and Ralph had trusted." But, once again, she had married someone with whom she had very little in common.

Her marriage quickly turned sour. Needless to say, under such a veil of illusions, the relationship was doomed from the start. By summer, it was clear that neither was a pot of gold, or even a vaguely suitable companion. They were drowning their disappointments and had turned bitter and angry. People interviewed in Upton reported overhearing heated arguments and screams and seeing both parties with black eyes and bruises. This particular household certainly was not going to be a gentle and supportive place for anyone, especially a feisty boy and a vulnerable little girl. In October, Jim and Louise separated.

For the 1946/47 school year, Rufus and Dinah were out of harm's way in Chesterville at "Uncle" Fred Tibbott's farm. Fred was raising pheasants for the state of Maine and keeping Rufus on a short leash by invoking the wrath of Ralph when he misbehaved:

> I remember him telling me, "Your father would have expected better." Uncle Fred had been at Forest Lodge from the beginning. He and Dad were the first to bring in a car to Middle, an old Model A, which they lugged in with a block and tackle.

> Ma said that Uncle Fred was "swept away" by Edith—Haas was her maiden name—and she was one of the teachers that boarded in Upton. There was an age difference between the two you wouldn't believe. Uncle Fred tried to be a kind of stand-in for my father, I guess. Kids never went to funerals in those days, so one day I had a father and the next thing I knew, I didn't.

Happy the Land (dedicated to Dinah) was published in 1946, and Louise took Rufus, who was about to turn ten, on her publicity tour in New York City. In preparation for the upcoming holiday season, Louise polled the family. Rufus wanted a watch and the board game Parcheesi, Dinah wanted a desk and a doll. The result of this simple exchange was Louise's last short story of 1946, "What Do You Want for Christmas?":

> It seemed to me that they [the children] had expressed in material terms the things that I and everybody all over the world, really, want. We all want a watch. We want time to call our souls our own, time to sit in peace and look at a tree blazing with autumn coloring—time to waste or spend wisely, as we see fit. We all want a game of Parchesi [sic]. We want a common ground on which to meet and make friends. We want to feel that we are part of the whole—a member of a close community of small interests or of the larger community of greater interests. We want to belong. We all

want a desk—some work to do that seems important to us—whether it may be coloring books with crayons, selling insurance, running a restaurant or putting words down on paper in the hope that someone may possibly enjoy reading them. And we all want a baby doll—the kind of quiet love that involves responsibility and care and the tremendous rewards which those things bring. We all want to be needed and loved.

So I couldn't think of anything I wanted for Christmas. No one could give me those things. The best part about them is that they are things anyone can have, quite independently of the whims and pocket-books of friends and family. And if we want them badly enough, we can have them. And if we'd concentrate on giving ourselves the things we really want for Christmas, it wouldn't surprise me a bit if everyone, everywhere, might finally wake up some December 25 and find that Christmas was exactly what it should be—the time of peace and good-will to all men.

That is undoubtedly what Louise wished for. Unfortunately, her reality was quite different.

On January 8 and 27, 1947, Jim Barnett legally filed two real estate attachments to Louise's property. Soon the *Rumford Falls Times* announced: "Author Louise Rich Is Served With Divorce Libel From Her Husband, James Barnett, Upton." Louise told reporters that Jim's grounds were "cruel and abusive treatment" and that he had attached her "property and bank account to recover alimony or a cash settlement of $50,000." Jim filed his petition at the March term of the Oxford County Superior Court, and it was set for trial at the June term.

Meanwhile, in April, Louise countered with attachments to Jim's property and filed her own divorce action, citing "non-support, gross and confirmed habits of intoxication, and cruel and abusive treatment." She asked that "a reasonable alimony" be paid by Barnett and that she "be allowed to resume the name Rich."

In the midst of these nasty divorce proceedings, Louise was confronted with yet another reminder of her renewed single-parent status when Rufus came down with a high temperature and severe stomach-ache. She described the incident in *Only Parent*: "I almost lost Rufus, when he was eleven, because of a lapse on my part. There is no one in the whole world to whom you can go for help, who will give his whole mind and heart to the problem, backed by an intimate knowledge of the mind and heart and body of the child. Only a parent has that, and there is no other parent."

They were in Bridgewater at the time. The family doctor agreed that it sounded like appendicitis, but the only surgeon Louise could find was one who "might" be back from a fishing trip when they got to the hospital. Once there, Louise was left with the sole decision regarding an anomaly in Rufus's blood-count test. After a short delay, she decided they should operate:

> . . . and a very good thing, too, as the appendix burst while they were taking it out and we had an awful time getting the kid back on his feet. The moral of this tale is this: Six years before, our local Maine doctor told me that Rufus had a funny type of blood, low on white corpuscles. What was normal in anybody else was a high white count for him. In short, he was an infector. I should have remembered and told the doctors, and saved the little time that might have made a lot of difference. If there had been two of us parents, one of us would probably have remembered. I might have myself, if I hadn't been so harassed with sole responsibility. Luckily, the consequences were not fatal, but if they had been, I would have been to blame.

She jumped from this right back into divorce litigation. Barnett's lawyer argued for more detailed libel "specifications." Lawyers for both parties reported to the newspapers that "the present libel [Louise's] is not in order for trial, service on the libelee not having been made on time, and thus both actions perhaps will be heard at the November term." The battle was stalled.

Rufus recovered enough to be at Forest Lodge for the summer, and a grateful Louise allowed him to start driving lessons with her on the Carry Road where he proceeded to run into a boulder—truly a metaphor for that tenuous, head-on time. In September, the children went to Bridgewater to live with their grandparents, and for them, this particular school year proved the beginning of more stability. Rufus says:

> Ma taught me to speak perfect English—no *ain'ts,* but I really did not learn to read until the fifth grade. When you go to a thousand different schools, it's hard to pick things up. When I went to Upton, I looked out the window. When I went to Andover, I looked out the window. Same with Rumford Point and Chesterville. Uncle

Fred taught me math, which I liked, and I also knew geography, but in Bridgewater, I studied every night with Miss Porteus and then I picked up reading.

This was Dinah's first year in school, a learning curve she remembers vividly:

I arrived only the night before school started and it seemed so different coming into the "real world." The little grades were on the first floor, so Rufus was upstairs. There seemed to be *so many* girls in the playground—here I'd thought I was just about the only girl in the world, you know! I was very conscious that they all had party dresses on and I was wearing a jumper with my hair in braids. I was so shy I'd go around the corner to meet Rufus. It was against the rules, of course, but Rufus told them, "She's my sister, and if she wants to come see me, she can." I could get along with adults, but I had no social skills whatever with kids. I remember the teacher read a story about an animal that died and I cried (all the Riches have a soft spot for animals). Well, the kids laughed at me and I was so hurt I ran out of the room. I thought it was all going to be awful, but the teachers were very smart; they solved my shyness by making me a recess monitor, and I eventually got used to things.

However, while the children were settling in, Louise was faced not only with her divorce case but also a "Bill of Complaint" and a "Petition for Removal [as executrix]" lodged by J.W. Brooks Ladd, contending that Louise had "secretly" tried to sell a portion of her Pine Point property without reporting to the court. She had not been able to pay her debts, and her creditors were becoming impatient.

By November 20, 1947, after nearly a year of legal haranguing and jockeying, Jim and Louise gave up any claim on each other's property and dropped requests for alimony payments. Louise was granted the right to resume the name Louise Dickinson Rich, and their divorce was finalized. Back with her children and parents in the family house in Bridgewater for Thanksgiving that year, one can only surmise that Louise must have offered up a silent prayer of gratitude for her freedom. But, depleted emotionally and financially, she also felt her options and horizons shrinking. She had been under siege for years, both from inside and outside herself, and as an indication of how bad things were, the well had run dry in her writing.

Transitions

Louise's personality held the contrasts of practicality and idealism in about even balance. She was hardheaded and softhearted, but as she kept busy fighting estate battles throughout the winter of 1947/48, there must have been times when she felt softheaded and hard-hearted! By April 1948, she still needed to raise about $4,000. Idealism reluctantly conceded to practicality, and Louise filed a petition with the court to sell Pine Point (for $10,000). Louise dearly loved Pine Point and could have owned the property outright had she sold off Forest Lodge. This move makes it clear where her allegiance and heart lay. The sale was allowed in June, and soon "Camp Rich" was no longer.

June 1948 was a month of loss and change not only for Louise but also for Alice.

Louise's and Alice's lives resembled a double-helix DNA: two independent strands intertwining. Though each had her own personality and inclinations, they seemed to serve as catalysts and change agents for one another throughout their lives. Louise paved the way socially at school for shy, precocious Alice. It was under Alice's instigation that Louise went to Maine, met Ralph, and settled down to write and raise a family—which provided the setting for Alice to meet her future husband, Travis. By 1948, Louise was shuffling back and forth to Maine, stalled emotionally and professionally. But Alice's life intervened again. According to Dinah, on the night of June 14, 1948, Alice's birthday, Travis came home from attending a sports banquet (he wrote articles for sports magazines). He paused at their bedroom doorway, started to speak, and then swayed a bit. Alice said her first thought was that he was drunk. But he lurched, fell to the floor with a massive heart attack, and died.

The consequence of this uncanny similarity in their circumstances was that Louise started to move away from her post–Ralph frantic self. Dinah explains: "Artists see life in a gentle way, and Ma wanted life to be lovely. But she kept finding life difficult. She had times of depression, but amazingly, she was never jaded. During this time she taught herself how to cane chairs and upholster furniture, tried to occupy her mind and do new and useful things."

And she returned fully to her work. Louise acknowledged writing's healing effect on her in the last chapter of *My Neck of the Woods*: "The writer … acts under a real compulsion which he cannot deny and remain whole." She began her first children's book: *Start of the Trail*. Rufus says the main characters—game warden Les Gordon and his son Bill, who has just received his Maine Guide's license—were patterned after Leon Wilson, the game warden, and Phil Learned, who had returned from the war and was guiding at Lakewood Camps, but they were really a "thinly veiled" overlay of the Rich family and its way of life. The target audience for *Start of the Trail* was "male juveniles," although Louise's particular audience was her twelve-year-old son. She wrote about a manhunt and natural disasters, but she also made a point of instilling a yearning for higher education in young Bill. She was speaking directly to Rufus on behalf of herself and Ralph at the end of the book:

> "Don't you see, Bill," Mom was going on, "that the reason you and I thought it was funny that time was that we had the background to interpret the [deer] tracks. Jeff didn't. Your father and I can interpret life into terms satisfactory to us, only because we do have education. It amounts to this; the more you bring to bear upon any situation or way of life, the more you get out of it."

On January 6, 1949, the family suffered another loss. James Dickinson, eighty-two, died of "heart failure/arteriosclerosis." Dinah and Rufus remember their grandfather as a quiet, stern presence. They were struck by his teetotaling, churchgoing life. Once Rufus put Dinah up to asking him if they could stay home from a church event. The approached their grandfather—little Dinah in front, Rufus towering close behind—and she pleaded their case. James lifted his walking stick, thumped it back down on the floor, and they knew it was a lost cause. Louise adored her father—respected him enormously—but she was denied any show of affection from him, and both she and Alice confided to Dinah that their parents did them a great disservice in this regard. Having never been hugged as a child, Louise carried this trait forward. Rufus has no recollection of his mother hugging him, and Dinah says she didn't know what to do when her grandmother (perhaps hoping to make amends in the next generation, or freed to show affection since it wasn't her own child?) hugged her. But James's death was deeply felt. He set a standard for integrity and intellectual diligence, and with his passing went the last adult male presence in the immediate household.

Start of the Trail was published shortly thereafter and proceeded to win the *New York Herald Tribune* Children's Festival Award. Despite the acclaim, Louise, in the summer of 1949, still had to sell off all the parcels of land adjacent to Pine Point to make the final payments to her creditors.

However, unencumbered with litigation, she was able to turn her attention to her next book, *My Neck of the Woods*, a series of character sketches, an expansion of the "who's who" of the area. She wrote that she was going to "forget about the scenery and the weather and tell about the people." And this she did with wit and wisdom. We read about guide John Lavorgna and his wife Mabel; Whit and Gertie Roberts (carpenter and cook); Alys and Larry (Parsons, of Lakewood Camps); Cliff Wiggin, "hermit" of Umbagog; game warden Leon Wilson; Elmer Rhodes, logging camp clerk; and scores of others. Rufus says, "You take one finger and put it on top of the other, that's how Ma was with these people." Gratitude was one of the best antidotes for fear and grief, and thinking/writing about her gifts of friendships was the perfect focus for Louise at that time:

> These are ordinary people, but it seems to me that they are nevertheless important. I do not say that here alone still exists the attitude that puts character above personality, principle above expediency, duty above pleasure, and independence above ease. I think it must be true of other places where people live as we do here, close to the soil and seasons, close to each other, if not geographically, certainly spiritually, far enough removed from the stress and speed of modern living so that we have time to form our own considered opinions and freedom to act in accordance with them. It may be that these qualities which I so admire and which were commonly possessed in the early days of this country's history survive here as an anachronism. It may be that they are no longer necessary in the world of to-day, where man's worst enemies are himself and his misuse of his own expanding knowledge. But it seems to me equally possible that these qualities may be the pinch of yeast in the bit of dough, with which, when the time is ripe, the whole mass will become leaven. When humanity gets tired enough of being hounded from pillar to post, when the powerful have sufficiently persecuted the weak and the envious weak have sufficiently obstructed the strong, perhaps our way of life will come to seem the true one, and people will awake in astonishment at having for so long neglected its simple wisdom.

Louise told Dinah she felt she was born in the wrong century, that she wished she could have been a pioneer. It is all a matter of perspective, because, for hundreds of thousands of readers, Louise was, in fact, a pioneer woman who embodied the very characteristics she espoused above. Fortunately, she was able to recognize her frontier.

By 1950, when *My Neck of the Woods* came out, Rufus was fourteen and Dinah, nine. Sally, twenty-five, was living in Maryland with a son, a daughter, and a husband studying to become a doctor. Terpe, who had been living with her sister Sadie in San Antonio, Texas, died that year. She had had paramours but never remarried. Louise, wintering in Bridgewater, bought the family a TV set, the newest rage (1.5 million people owned one; the next year, 15 million would). The assassination attempt on President Truman and Senator Joseph McCarthy's communist investigations were in the news. Benny Goodman's band was big, as was warzone nostalgia: Thor Heyerdahl sailed his raft *Kon Tiki* from Peru to Hawaii, James Michener's *Tales of the South Pacific* won the Pulitzer Prize, and Rodgers and Hammerstein staged the musical *South Pacific.* And in her writer's journal (a couple of dozen pages of quotes and literary commentary and ideas), Louise included the Nobel Prize in literature speech, entitled "I Decline to Accept the End of Man," that William Faulkner delivered in Stockholm on December 10. Louise penned, "Read the 4th of every month," above what clearly served as a source of inspiration. Some excerpts:

> I feel that this award was not made to me as a man, but to my work—to create out of the materials of the human spirit something which did not exist before.
>
> Our tragedy today is a general and universal physical fear so long sustained by now that we can even bear it. There are no longer problems of the spirit. There is only the question: When will I be blown up? Because of the young man or woman writing today has forgotten the problems of the human heart in conflict with itself which alone can make good writing because only that is worth writing about, worth the agony and the sweat.
>
> He must learn them again. He must teach himself that the basest of all things is to be afraid; and [then] forget it forever leaving no room in his workshop for anything but the old universal truths—love and honor and pity and pride and compassion and sacrifice. Until he does so, he labors under a curse. He writes not of love but of lust, of defeats in which nobody loses anything of value, of victories without hope and, worst of all, without pity or compassion. He writes not of the heart but of the glands.
>
> Until he relearns these things, he will write as though he stood and watched the end of man. I decline to accept the end of man. I believe that man will not only endure: he will prevail. He alone is immortal, not because he alone among creatures has an inex-

haustible voice but because he has a soul, a spirit capable of com-
passion and sacrifice and endurance. The poet's, the writer's duty
is to write about these things. The poet's voice need not merely be
the record of man, it can be one of the props, the pillars to help
him endure and prevail.

Also included in Louise's journal were a number of musings:

October 25, 1950—Doris, Alice, Jessie and I doing our shopping
and acting free and easy and at home all over town—A&P, 5&10,
etc.—like summer people. Regardless of the Natives. It is my attitude, I am afraid, to feel like a summer visitor in the world. Is this
reprehensible? Part of being a writer? What? Is this not the attitude that caused the downfall of Manley Halliday (protagonist of
Fitzgerald '20s) in Shulber's "The Disenchanted"?
        What the hell kind of person thinks like that? Right. Very few
ideas are abstract enough not to be qualified by the company
they keep.
        Outside looking in wistfully—Ralph & Harvard etc. I don't
believe there is anywhere a group quite like the Harvard–Boston
cabala.

And she described some "story themes and suggestions":

The First Snow—This is the story of someone who returns, tor-
tured and disillusioned, to the scene of a significant event in his
life during the first snow of the year and finds that all the geographical features have been wiped out. The point of the story is
that more than geographical implications have been erased. He
finds himself without any feeling toward a situation that had been
important to the point of obsession in his life.
        Story: A woman spent her life keeping things from happening
to a man, and in the doing got bigger. It doesn't matter what happens to a person, but only how he takes it.
        The Wholesome type: They hated her, but they missed her
when she was gone. (She was currying her dog, and sipping
bourbon, her long legs and spare shoulders denimed.)
        Rufus and the little people: Story about a mother and a
slightly lacking child, whose "deficiency" boiled down to simple
love, for everything that lived, the littler the better.

The Broken Leg: What did I learn? (1) Futility of combating the inevitable. (2) To be a clearing shop for other people's griefs. The pullman porter who carried my bags, and wouldn't take a tip, on account of he was sorry for me. What would it do to one to be crippled for life?? Phys. freedom hampers mental freedom. Phys. bondage frees the mind.

Mr. Leman's story of snow in October (12) when red leaves blew down on top of snow layer. Very odd and lovely effect.— The river was high, but not high enough to be silent.

[And she made a list of character names:] Serepta, Loma, Saretta, Velzora, Ismay, Basha, Winola, Ceylon, Saba, Letana, Lunetta, Minta, Hightower, Merle, Vernal, Pottle, Trimback. . . .

On May 31, 1950, Louise presented a final accounting of her work as executrix of Ralph's estate. She requested, and was granted, the appointment as trustee for the Rich Trust Fund (a fund set up by Ralph's father to pay for long-term care at a psychiatric hospital for Ralph's half-sister, Maud). By the 1950/51 school year in Bridgewater, the hemorrhage of funds had finally stopped. But life in civilization had its problems, and at the beginning of 1951, the entire family came down with the mumps. Louise, with her inimitable sense of self-directed humor, wrote a spoof of all the legalese she had finally shed. Her formal notification to all assembled read: "Sarah Louise Dickinson Bacon Rich Barnett Rich wishes to announce that she too has the mumps, as of Saturday the seventeenth of February, nineteen hundred and fifty one. Please omit flowers."

It was not long before Louise was at her typewriter working on *Trail to the North,* the sequel to *Start of the Trail.* Alice had also turned a corner and went to New York City to work as an editor for Franklin Watts and Sons publishers. As the summer of 1951 approached, Louise and the kids decided to rent a cottage on Cape Cod (Angelica Point, Mattapoisett), right at the water's edge, from Memorial Day to October. It was a real step away from the past. Alice came to visit (Rufus remembers examining tide pools with her), as did Louise's friend from Bridgewater, Alice Folsom. As Louise wrote, "To make things simple in my life, I seem to have collected a list of women friends a large percentage of whom are named Alice." During a great summer together, Dinah had a pet lobster, Rufus got to rush to the rescue next door as a junior volunteer fireman, they all made new friends, and Louise reconnected with a surprise neighbor— a fellow teacher from her first job in New Hampshire, and traveling companion to Europe: "To my great joy Bea turned up, this time as Dr. Kershaw, a pediatrician, married to a Dr. Gardner, a psychiatrist, and mother of two girls just about Dinah's age. What could be handier than having a good pediatrician and a good psychiatrist on tap? Now the kids could go right ahead and pick up viruses, and I could crack under the strain of adjusting to a new environment. Everything was taken care of; and possibly because that was the case, none of us developed anything at all untoward."

Dinah and Rufus left Angelica Point for school (in Bridgewater), and Louise spent all of September at the cottage finishing *Trail to the North*. As December approached, Dinah reminded her mother that Rufus had been in fifth grade, like she now was, and had been going on ten, like she now was, when he went to New York City. Louise acquiesced, and they trundled off to the Algonquin and took in the sights. Dinah was enthralled with the zoo in Central Park and named all the horses on the carousel. Ditto the Bronx Zoo. Between trips to the Empire State Building and FAO Schwarz for a "ray gun," Louise found time to touch base with Willis Wing. They discussed her next book, *Only Parent,* detailing some of her life as a single parent, more of an anomaly then than it is today. Louise was ahead of her time writing about, and being, a pioneering woman, as well as a female head of household.

Trail to the North was published in 1952, and Louise wrote *Only Parent* from March through December of that year. In the summer, they all returned to Forest Lodge with school friends in tow for Dinah (ten) and Rufus (fifteen), plus "Frank," Rufus's tutor. The following year, *Only Parent* came out. Not only does it allow us a glimpse into another era, it also provides insights into parenting that resonate today:

> Being a parent means being regarded, always at the moments when you are most painfully aware of your fallibility, as infallible; and at the times when you know with an absolute knowledge that you are right, as being a silly, old-fashioned type who has failed to keep abreast of modern thinking and up-to-date trends. For me at least it has meant living in places where you never intended to live, doing things you never planned to do, undergoing experiences you never had any wish to undergo, simply because your own wishes and plans and intentions no longer come first. Do you think that for one moment, had I been a free agent, I would ever have spent whole afternoons playing Pounce? Or belonged to the PTA? Or left the place I love and call home to spend winter after winter in a semisuburb? Ha! You can think again!
>
> But there is a special dispensation bestowed upon parents. On

the one hand they are given a terrible and frightening responsibility, so that they must at least attempt to be always wiser and calmer
and stronger than it is their true nature to be; and then, in recom-
pense, they are allowed to glimpse again the world of small things,
of wonder and delight. For a moment, on a clear and quiet evening, they may believe again in the spell of wishing on the first star,
hanging glimmering and far in an apple-green sky.

I hope that once in a while, because I have been privileged to
see what the human heart is like before it has grown its protective
casing, I shall be able to do unconsidered, generous, childlike
things. A child has nothing to give away except himself. As soon as
we begin to possess other things, we lock ourselves away; and yet,
in the end, our selves are the only things we have that are important and worth giving. That is what my children have taught me.

The Peninsula

For the previous eight years or so (aside from Mattapoisett), Louise and the children had been spending summers at Forest Lodge and winters in Bridgewater. In fact, the family was so focused on her hometown that Louise started writing her childhood memoir *Innocence under the Elms*. As the summer of 1953 approached, Louise was offered a house- and dog-sitting opportunity on Islesboro, Maine, for a Mrs. Luce, a fan of her books. "It was a monstrous place," says Rufus, who was in seventh heaven "fiddling with the dumbwaiter, learning how to run the pump, and making a trail with rock stairs to the beach."

They had visitors—David Sias for Rufus and Tina Venot, from Andover, as a sitter/companion for Dinah. Vaughn also arrived:

> You know, I only remember Louise being mad one time, and this was in Islesboro when Rufus was in high school, and at sixteen, now legally driving. He had a sweet tooth, and opened up a can of peaches and sweetened condensed milk that were sitting on the counter. I didn't like it, so he ate most of it. Louise came in and was cross at us because she'd had a special breakfast planned with it. Mostly, though, she was really easygoing and great about organizing stuff for us to do. She made arrangements for us to go clamming with the groundskeeper, and once we went to the Boston Maritime Museum. Louise never talked down to us kids, it was always on an adult level. To me she was something of a mysterious figure. When she was typing (which in the summer was in her bedroom), we had to be quiet in the house.

Their black-and-white collie, Caro, was with them and, as Rufus says, "He barked at the seals until he was totally hoarse. Ma also took care of Humphrey, Mrs. Luce's black Newfoundland, when she wasn't around. Humphrey had been the mascot for a submarine crew out of Rockport, but he had been left behind, and Mrs. Luce adopted him. She couldn't get him to do a thing. But as soon as she left, Ma would shout, 'Humphrey, you get your big, black ass down here!' and he was fine. I guess after living with a bunch of sailors that's the kind of talk he expected, and Ma was used to it after living around a bunch of lumbermen."

They all explored the area during Aunt Alice's annual summer visit, and she taught Rufus and Dinah how to make gravestone rubbings. Alice was now editing and writing scholastic books for Franklin Watt (including more than a half-dozen histories and biographies). She and her sister undoubtedly talked about Louise also writing something for Watts.

A very public indication of the inspirational and literary success of Louise's books, and of her popularity, came that fall, on the heels of *Only Parent*'s publication. She joined an illustrious roster of people broadcasting on Edward R. Murrow's *This I Believe*, a radio news program. Her segment pretty much sums up her life and her philosophy toward it:

I have met with poverty, flood, famine, hurricane, brutalizing labor and illness on extremely personal grounds. I have seen the sudden and tragic deaths of those nearest and dearest to me. I have had to shoulder responsibilities for which I was ill-prepared and the much more difficult burden of sudden, if brief, fame. I have been hard-pressed for money, as we say in Maine.

I'm not whining. I've had one swell life, with the joys far outweighing the sorrows. But still and all, there have been times when I was fair-to-middlin' desperate. There was the time [1937] when my husband and my year-old son and my mother-in-law and I had one meal a day. We ate baked potatoes and salt. It didn't do us adults any harm, and my neighbor, Alice Miller, provided me with six oranges and six quarts of milk a week—she kept two cows—for the baby.

Then there was the time in December when my husband . . . suddenly died. I don't know how I could have possibly survived that—because, you see, I loved him from the bottom of my heart— if it hadn't been for my other neighbor, Alys Parsons. She came and sat with me, not saying a word, just with infinite wisdom being *there*, all through the awful formalities of the coroner and the sheriff, who must investigate in Maine a case of sudden death.

There was a time after that when I owed a lot of money to a lot of people, I'm sorry to say. I went to the butcher and baker and candlestick maker and they all said, "Mrs. Rich, I'm sorry to hear about your trouble. Ralph was a good man. We'll miss him a lot. About the money—anytime at your convenience—and forget the interest.

So, I don't believe in myself any more; not in myself alone. I do believe in myself as a member of the human race. Nobody, not even Big Louise, can walk the trail alone. I know that now. I don't know about God. He's too big for me to understand. But I have seen His visage reflected in the faces of the people who have helped me through my hard times. I hope to live so that some day, someone will say, "Louise Rich? Oh sure, I know her. She isn't so bad. She's human." I believe in humanity.

These forthright words gave solace and inspiration to people during the holidays of 1953. In the winter and spring of 1954, Louise turned her attention to *Innocence under the Elms.* By the onset of summer, she completed her manuscript, but it looked as though the usually dependable concept of "family vacation" was about to be redefined. Louise, at fifty-one, suddenly felt everything was "disorganized, disturbed, and disturbing." Rufus informed his mother that he would be driving a tractor at a farm, and Dinah was not "enthusiastic about the exclusive society of bunnies, deer, and her mother" back at Forest Lodge. As she would later write in *The Peninsula,* Louise found herself

> . . . in that exhausted and depressed state that all writers know—a condition that lasts until you get another idea for a book and have it under way. As far as another book was concerned, my mind was a blank and I was convinced—as most writers are between books—that I had come to the end of the line and would never write another word. I was tired of writing anyhow. I was tired of myself and my life. I wished the West had not been opened up. I'd have been a big success as a pioneer woman, I was sure. I wished—I didn't know what. Oh, I was in a bad way, ripe for revolution. At that precise moment the letter came.

It was an invitation from Marjorie and Lisle Albright, a couple from Chicago who owned a log cabin on Maine's Gouldsboro Peninsula. On the strength of her previous books, they offered Louise the free use of their basic (no amenities) but beautifully situated cabin on Cranberry Point, Corea, for the summer. As soon as school was out, Louise took Dinah (twelve, "but I told everyone I was fourteen") and Caro up the coast and fell in love with the area.

> We must learn to distinguish between those things which are ornamental and the true necessities; and we must learn too the possibly more difficult lesson of letting go gracefully the superficial and of treasuring and nurturing the few basic realities which must be our support and comfort for as long as we walk about under the

light of heavens. Perhaps that is why, in that moment on the edge of the heath, something within me responded to the place. It was beautiful with the only kind of beauty that I was now beginning to recognize as authentic: the great, unadorned beauty and strength of the functional.

The country spoke to some inner need to know who I was and what I was worth. Here away from the pleasant, unintentional, fatal seductions and unplanned blackmail of friends and acquaintances, away from the facade I had built over the years to impress a world with the self I wished I were—a false front that I was obliged continually to reinforce—perhaps I could find my real self, whether it be good or bad.

During this pivotal summer, Louise wrote a new chapter in her own life. The peninsula made an indelible impression on her, and she brought to bear on the situation her usual curiosity, intelligence, and enthusiasm for her natural surroundings. She observed, and absorbed, and felt the exhilaration of a clean slate. Fate had brought Louise Dickinson Rich to the coastal equivalent of Middle Dam/Forest Lodge.

Back in Bridgewater, she decided her next book would be about the coast of Maine, and she began her research. That fall (1954) was Rufus's senior year in high school, and he was not interested. He still watched out for Dinah, though, and told her that if any of her teachers started to give her "the horrors," she should just tell them who her brother was, and "that should straighten things out...." In November, he signed up for weekends with the local National Guard.

Innocence under the Elms came out in the beginning of 1955, to much fanfare. Publication day, February 21, was declared "Louise Dickinson Rich Day" in Bridgewater, with all the festivities, speeches, and media coverage due a native daughter. Shortly thereafter Rufus's third-term report card came out poorly. Louise told him to "stick with it," but he countered that he wanted to enter the military. Louise's response apparently was, "I don't think you have enough guts to do it." That's all the encouragement he needed. In March, he left with David Sias, without a word, and enlisted in the army at Fort Benning, Massachusetts. Florence told her grandson that when Louise received the required letter home announcing this event, "It was a good thing your mother was standing by a chair at the time!"

Louise, back at Cranberry Point with Dinah in June 1955, kept busy researching and writing her next book, *The Coast of Maine,* an "informal history and practical guide." In it she tried to debunk the stereotype of the dour, stolid Mainer by quoting typical quips: "Only reason I found my way back into harbor was that I'd the foresight to stick my knife in the fog, on my way out, to mark the entrance." Also included were tales of some of the colony's colorful colonizers, such as William Vaughan and his "silly notion" (miraculously successful) to capture Louisbourg (Nova Scotia) from the French; "Willie Phipps, youngest of the twenty-six children of an impoverished gunsmith who became Sir William Phipps; Sir Ferdinando Gorges, who spent his life and fortune to prove that the coast of Maine was habitable, after it had been clearly demonstrated that it was not; Baron de St. Castin, who gave up vast estates in the Pyrenees to live among the Penobscot Indians; Captain Clough, who planned to rescue Marie Antoinette"; and many others. And she gave readers a literary walk up the coast, pointing out landmarks, historical tidbits, and things to do along the way. Besides being informative, and timelessly insightful, it remains eminently readable (Louise's trademark combination).

Engrossed as Louise was in those lives and locales, Middle Dam and the Rapid River were receding farther and farther in time and distance. A change in attitude had been coming on gradually, but her time at Cranberry Point proved to be the turning point at which she moved into her future. On October 27, 1955, Louise sold Forest Lodge. Fortunately it went to Catherine ("Katie" Jacobs) and her second husband Arthur Luce, so it would be in knowledgeable and loving hands. With the proceeds, and the sale of the Dean Street home, Louise bought a bigger house, at 74 Mount Prospect Street (in Bridgewater), for her mother and children. Her life had turned in a new direction: away from the vertical world of the forests to the horizontal world of the sea.

Within several months (1956), *The Coast of Maine* (Crowell Company) was out, her first book not published by Lippincott. That summer, Rufus was still in the army and Dinah stayed in Bridgewater, with her grandmother, to be near friends. But Louise needed to be back at Cranberry Point, where she spent the summer alone, starting a book about the area she had come to love and writing a poignant short story about letting go of her children (who were clearly on her mind) entitled "I Can't Find My Apron Strings." She also completed her first scholastic volume for Franklin Watts, *The First Book of New England*, published in 1957.

That same year, Dinah and her mother had a falling-out. Louise visited Hester, who says it was the only time she ever saw her friend cry: "She was deeply upset, drinking heavily at this point because of the stresses, and she just fell apart. I think she was also truly disappointed that neither of her children were going the traditional educational route."

Louise was a bit out of her element as far as her children were concerned. Rufus's slow rate of childhood development perplexed her; adolescent Dinah was more enamored of boys than books. Although she was determined not to impose strict controls on her children, she also carried on a family tradition that did not include hugging or overt affection. In addition, she was a working mother and needed time most days to attend to her job. Add to this the early loss of husband/father, the complications of remarriage and relocation. . . . The disarray is hardly surprising.

Hester's assessment:

> I have to say, my impression is that Dicky didn't always see her kids' lives from their point of view. It wasn't meanness, just the self-absorbed side of her. This was my impression of the whole family— her parents and sister, they were all self-absorbed. Not in a mean way, like I say, but simply intent about what they each were doing. Dicky didn't need people because she lived by her own abilities. On the other hand, she liked people enormously, was always interested in them, and could empathize with them. And this applied to her children as well. So, although she was practical, she also had this deep, highly tuned sensitivity (which may account for the binge drinking when she got unstrung).

During Louise's coming of age, the turbulent 1920s, the issues surrounding Prohibition provided the arena for making a statement (perhaps akin to the drug culture of the turbulent 1970s). Drinking was not simply a mark of "sophistication" but also an activist display of the power of the individual to buck the establishment, to create his/her own rules. In Louise's case, although her drinking was probably infrequent and surreptitious, her expulsion from college—for smoking, no less—was a blatant declaration of her own identity in the face of her nonsmoking, nondrinking parents. Years later, Louise was surrounded by hard-drinking lumbermen and married to a man who needed a weekly batch of fudge—"because otherwise," Ralph told Sally, "I'd be an alcoholic." Fortunately, drinking did not get in the way of Louise's writing, and Dinah says she would go for months without a drop. In the long term, Louise's parents could be proud of the integrity of her core values, as Louise could be of her own children's. But, as Dinah says, "She must have curled my grandparents' hair more than once!"

Hester adds:

> I think she questioned her worth as a parent and person at this point, you know. But then, she hadn't gone the traditional route herself, had she? Dicky was a truly good person, solid and sincere, but she made her own rules. That was one of her strengths, and it's what appealed to her about Ralph, too, I believe. He was apparently the same way. And her children were part of that gene pool. . . .

However, the predominant mother/daughter and mother/son interactions were positive and respectful. Dinah says that their house in Bridgewater was the local gathering place for kids:

> Ma was game for anything, and my friends really liked her. After my father died, she went to school to learn small-engine repair—she was really a ground-breaker. We had an old horsehair couch Ma learned how to upholster from taking a course. She made this beautiful piece of crewel embroidery and upholstered that couch and traded it for a sideboard with a marble top and dining room set with eight chairs that needed caning. Then she taught herself to cane those chairs by reading an article in *Woman's Day*. It seemed like we were either rolling or starving, but Ma subsidized us by being clever.

An additional sadness for Louise at that time was the loss of her collie Caro. As a child, Louise had never been allowed to have a dog because her father preferred cats, but Louise had been a dog owner for twenty-five years at that point. In her opinion, dogs were the bridge between beasts and people: "They are more than domesticated, because they have adopted/adapted to humans' ways and attitudes (they feel remorse, guilt, jealousy, and joy); they are 'civilized' . . . fringe citizens of man's world."

Louise said she was shocked that friends assumed she would not take on the "burden" of another dog when Caro died. In her writing, she paid tribute to all her dogs: Cookie, the Siberian husky who mothered the skunk Rollo and kept an eye on infant Rufus at Forest Lodge; Kyak, who sat by her side, consoling and attentive, the whole long, lonely night of Ralph's death; and Caro, who comforted her with faithful companionship when the children were gone and she was on her own. Caro also served as a role model:

He became arthritic and stiff. These limitations he accepted with sweetness and patience, never allowing them to rob him of his interest in the things that went on around him and never imposing his infirmities on the sympathy of others. More than anyone I have ever known, he grew old gracefully, with courage and dignity.

Remembering all my dogs, I knew I wasn't going to spend the rest of my life coming home to a silent and empty house, where no one was transported with joy at seeing me. It wasn't a question of burdening myself with another dog. It was a question of finding the right dog, one who had enough selfless patience and forbearance to burden himself with me.

Fortunately, Louise "fell afoul" of a five-week-old St. Bernard puppy. A week later, she and Hero were settled into a "gray-shingled shack ... the size of a kennel," a mile and a half from Cranberry Point at the head of Corea Harbor, for the summer of 1957. There she decided to teach herself the constellations while waiting for her puppy to do his midnight duties, and she explored off-road environs while taking him on his daily walks. Looking out onto an ever-changing rowan tree, Louise set up her typewriter and got to work.

Whatever it is that causes illumination, for Louise it seemed to be the physical act of putting one word beside another, of writing through the valley of shadows. She realized this intimately and poured herself into finishing her next book. Although *The Peninsula* did not receive the lucky (albeit deserved) media and print-run breaks of *We Took to the Woods*, many people consider it to be at least a coastal equivalent. (Not surprisingly, *We Took to the Woods* is the inland favorite, while most coastal dwellers insist *The Peninsula* is her best.) In *The Peninsula,* she describes an area in which, because of its relative inaccessibility, from both land and sea, time has slowed. The villagers are not backward, mind you, but simply living the lives, tempo, and values of an earlier era. Published by Lippincott in 1958, and dedicated to Lisle and Marjorie Albright (who introduced her to the area), *The Peninsula* received stellar reviews. Rachel Carson called it "a moving and beautiful book written with the insight and humility that her subject requires."

In the book, we read about the flora, fauna, geology, history, sights, and sounds of the area. We learn a host of Down East expressions, such as "By dear!" (translation: "By God!"); visit with neighbors and hear their stories; and enjoy gravestone epitaphs (her favorite— "The noblest work of God, an honest man"). We are taught how to gather and cook all sorts of fish; wild greens, such as goosegrass, dulse, and dock; and wild fruits/berries, such as sugar pears, highland cranberries, heath mulberries, and rowanberries. We attend a lobsterman's funeral and realize that villagers take time over death—people are not forgotten here. And they "endorse a philosophy that includes physical labor as inevitable and good rather than one which rejects it as being bad or degrading." Louise agreed. She felt: "The danger with the laborsaving device is that it too often produces idleness rather than leisure—and there is a big difference." We also find that village women are not "dependents or symbols of masculine success. They are vital and necessary for more than the raising of families and acting as housewives and hostesses." Louise said she "likes and respects these women. They're valuable, and they know it, and this knowledge colors their talk, thinking, and actions."

The Peninsula's conclusion came from the previous solitary summer Louise spent on Cranberry Point:

> Whatever I have been doing, there comes the time when I must return to the Point. As I pass through the village, single lights show golden in scattered windows, and then I leave them behind. Ahead lies the narrow track, pale and glimmering in the twilight, and the darkling empty shore, and the unlighted cabin.
>
> This is the saddest time of the day, the time when it would be possible to become unbearably lonely, not solely for oneself but for all mankind and indeed for the whole earth, spinning lost and alone into the coming darkness. The moor is dim and featureless, the sea is empty, and the surf breaks on the cold ledges with an endless, hopeless sobbing. For an instant it is possible to comprehend the meaning of panic—the unfounded terror that strikes those who wander abroad in primitive places.
>
> Then a rabbit flashes under the woodpile, and as I switch off the motor the sleepy chatter of the swallows under the eaves fills the silence. The dog trots to the cabin door, brushing a low bush in passing. Immediately it springs into trembling light as a hundred fireflies are disturbed, and glimmers like a Christmas tree. Somewhere inland a dog barks, the sound carrying easily in the still, clear air. Far away on the utmost horizon 'Titm'nan Light springs abruptly into being and shines bright and steady in the gloaming, and in the deep and limitless vault of the heavens the stars appear one by one.

And then I know that I am not alone, that none of us is alone, that the earth itself swings through space in brilliant company. The fireflies, the rabbit, the swallows in the eaves, the women in Peninsula kitchens and their men plodding up from tiny harbors, the solitary keepers of light on their sea-washed distant rock and I are all bound together as parts of a colossal plan, the success of which depends equally on the soundness of the greatest and smallest part.

Perhaps that is what I had come to the Peninsula to learn: that isolation is not estrangement from life, that across the void that separates man from man and from the wild things it is possible to flash a light, to transmit a voice, to send a glance or a thought; and that one cannot live in true community with others until he has learned to live with himself.

Reviewers, friends, and fans—even her detractors—agree that Louise Dickinson Rich could, if she chose, make even a phone book or tax code come alive. Clearly, with the Gouldsboro Peninsula as muse, Louise found inspiration for her words. It was the right venue at the right time for her talents, sensibilities, and inclinations. She was around her kind of people in her kind of place. There were drawbacks, of course. As she put it: "Nothing is free in this world." She mourned the characteristics that isolation creates in some: "Those girls—oh, so many of them!—not beautiful, but bright, lean, honed keen, so eager for life and all its wonders; and the women they become—dull, blunted, mean and spiteful, bent out of the marvelous mold for which they were intended." Louise had to learn to cope with pockets of insularity and provincialism in return for the nourishment of her soul. She obviously felt she was on the better end of the bargain.

Louise's children were going their own way, independent as always but still very much on her mind: "Lie down and roll over, she ordered her thoughts; but like disobedient dogs, they continued on their course." What to do, but write about young adults. Her third "juvenile" book featured a female protagonist. *Mindy* takes place in a "lobstering and fishing hamlet one reaches by crossing 'The Hayth' [in other words, a thinly disguised Corea]." Mindy takes the school bus inland along with her big brother, Freeman, who is attentive to his sister but otherwise spends much of his class time looking out the window (in other words, a thinly disguised Dinah and Rufus).

When the principal, in frustration, says, "Freeman, you don't even know the time of day," Freeman promptly answers, "Tide's just started on the ebb"—which, as Louise writes, "if the Principal had taken the time to check, would have been exactly right back at the harbor." In a meaningful family gesture of loving reconciliation, Louise dedicated the book to Dinah.

In 1959, Rufus, age twenty-two, out of the service and collecting unemployment, bought a motorcycle and headed cross-country; Dinah (seventeen) graduated from Bridgewater High School. During the summer, Dinah visited with her mother in Corea at the Crowley Island summer cottage of Grattan Condon (who did the pen-and-ink drawings for *The Peninsula*) and his wife, Hortense. Condon Rodgers, their granddaughter, and Louise were in residence there, looking after one another. Condon recalls being a bit awed by Dinah's worldliness and by Rufus's sheer size and energy as he roared into the backyard for a visit. As for Louise, she was "good company, a great storyteller—she talked as she wrote. She was medium height, solidly built, and pleasant looking, schoolmarmish, easy going and interested" in her (Condon) as a person when she wasn't writing; "unapproachable when working," or when she announced she was "having a bad day" (drinking). Condon's parents, Jackson and Floyd, and her brother Dwight, agree that Louise was "extremely bright, great at word games, up for anything, earthy, had opinions but wasn't a joiner of movements, and could talk on just about any subject. She wanted to be involved, and was accepted as part of the Corea scene. And she worked to get to know people before forming an opinion about them. Once you met her, you wouldn't forget her."

In the fall of 1959, Dinah went to Boston to attend business school. Rufus explored with his motorcycle and drove big machinery for the Massachusetts Park Service on Cape Cod. *Mindy,* published by Lippincott, came out, and Louise started writing more scholastic books for Franklin Watts.

The First Book of New World Explorers was published in 1960, and during the summer, although both Dinah and Rufus visited their mother in Corea, it was clear to Louise that her family had now dispersed. Once she was back in Bridgewater, rattling around the Mount Prospect Street house with her mother, Louise was faced with the age-old questions and re-evaluations that crop up when one's children go off on their own.

Let's review. Louise is now fifty-seven. She has lived for ten years full time, plus six years seasonally, at Forest Lodge. For the most recent ten years she has been in Bridgewater, spending the last six years seasonally on the Gouldsboro Peninsula. She has divorced twice, witnessed the death of her common-law husband, paid off his creditors, and raised and provided for their children. She has only one parent left, but fortunately her mother is relatively strong. And she has been working steadily as an author for twenty-six years, producing eleven books and more than thirty short stories. There are very few strings, and the world is before her.

At this point in her life, Louise decided she would make a few changes and do what was in her heart.

The Sands

Louise put her Mount Prospect Street home on the market and helped her mother look for another place to live. One of the many attributes Louise and Florence shared was flexibility. They moved around from place to place, were willing to tackle new things, and dodged the blows life dealt them. Life has a tendency to double back on itself, and those willing to ride the flow encode the form of that old toy, the "Slinky," dynamic and nearly unbreakable, within themselves. But a Slinky is not much to lean on. For that one needs the linear constancy of solid core values, and mother and daughter shared these as well. Florence was willing to strike off on her own, and she found a converted carriage house apartment at 27 Spring Hill Avenue—by a stroke of fate, the very same property that she and James had rented upon their arrival in Bridgewater more than half a century earlier.

As soon as the Mount Prospect Street house was sold (1961), Louise, given the chance to follow her inclinations, cleared out her things and moved back to the Gouldsboro Peninsula—as she put it, "for good"— with Hero. She rented a lovely 1790 Cape-style house called "The Sands" outside the village of Prospect Harbor, opposite a quiet beach with one neighbor and miles of heath behind her. She had pared down her belongings and divested herself of ownership responsibilities. Friends recall a tidy household with spotless hurricane lamps. Dinah says her mother used a few found treasures from the beach and heath for decoration. Louise was traveling light.

As for the variety of employment options open to her (including a well-deserved retirement), Louise sat right down, removed the dust cover from her typewriter, and started working up her next three books and a short story for *Outdoor Life* entitled "All This and Fishing, Too!" in which she extolled the virtues of Acadia National Park's Schoodic Point. Clearly, writing was her heart's desire. By 1962, Louise had produced two more "First" books for Watts—about Vikings and China clippers—and her naturalist book, *The Natural World of Louise Dickinson Rich*, was published by Dodd, Mead.

Written earlier in her little shack at Corea Harbor, where she was barely separated from the elements, *The Natural World* was something of an autobiography from the point of view of Louise's natural environments during different periods of her life. After an introduction that leaves the reader with a much-expanded understanding of the natural features of New England, the book is divided into three sections: The Plain (childhood in Massachusetts), The Highland (motherhood, Forest Lodge), and The Coast (middle age, the Gouldsboro Peninsula). Along the way, Louise shares some of what she learned about herself and the world by her wholehearted interaction with nature.

As a child, Louise learned to "identify a tree as far as I could see it, summer or winter," because of its climbability: "beeches were by far the best—they and apple trees." Early on, she knew the difference between five-fingered woodbine and three-fingered poison ivy (and "not to be seduced by the gorgeous fall coloring of the ivy into touching it with a ten-foot pole"). She'd been told that "the horsetail was the only plant left on earth whose form remained unchanged from prehistoric time, cobwebs on the grass no matter how cloudy a morning meant a clear warm day to come, and a mackerel sky foretold rain." She and Alice chose the wild things over "man and his works." And nature returned their attentions by teaching them many things: the ability to "recognize beauty in rather unlikely forms," the knowledge that "no matter what befell us, the earth would remain constant."

> We learned patience—you can't hasten the hatching of an oriole's egg, and acceptance—a familiar old tree felled by lightning cannot be restored to its former pride. We learned faith—that eggs would hatch, that new trees would grow up, that snows would melt. But the most important thing was something beyond learning. Perhaps we were born with it, or perhaps it simply grew from day to day on new discoveries and insights and in the end on memories. I only know that during my childhood, I fell in love with the world around me. For better or worse I was committed to the love affair, down to the present day.

The Highlands section relates the journey of finding one's own home: "The search for one's own place in the world—the actual, physical surroundings into which one fits—is as constant, universal, and real as the search for the right vocation, or for love."

She shrewdly noted that vocational and family guidance counselors, therapists and psychiatrists "all work on the premise that everything that ails you is within yourself; that if you have the right attitude toward your work and your family and your associates you will be, *ipso facto,* a useful, happy and complete person." However, some could simply be suffering from feeling physically displaced, "that the home for which each one of us hungers may well change for each of us as the years go by, to meet the changes within ourselves." Forest Lodge was the right place at the right time for Louise. It gave her a feeling of integrity and purpose knowing that everything she did was necessary, that very real challenges graced her with a very real sense of accomplishment, that the starkness of her life made her aware of true abundance. "As I look back," she mused, "it seems to me the time of my life when I was the richest. I was living just the way I wanted to live, with my own family whom I loved, close to a world with which I was almost obsessed. Nobody could possibly want more than that."

Whereas the first section deals mostly with plants, the second section is full of animal lore, such as this deer-hunting technique:

> Proceed fairly noisily through the woods, and then creep back along the trail you have come. The deer heard you the first time and stood still in a thicket to let you pass. But he can't let well enough alone. He has to find out all about you. So he steps out into the trail and stares after you; and there you have him, if you want him.

Louise wrote that living in the wilderness involves constantly protecting your own habitation from being overrun by animals (bats in the attic; rats, mice, squirrels in the pantry; mink, skunk, snakes in the footings; bear and deer in the garden). She wrote that what distinguished most of the people living in a backwoods environment—and she included herself—were those who would rather do daily battle with the wild animals than with urbanized humans—people "who did not fit well into the modern world of today."

As we know, circumstances showed her that she had come to a point where she needed people "to recharge and reflect the power and warmth that they give out."

> So, regretfully, I left the woods that had given me so much because of the one thing they could not give me. I miss them, still, at times, even now. One thing I know, one certainty cherish. They are still there, unchanged. The black tips of the spruces still stand motionless against an evening sky as they did when I was there to see, and the river roars with the same deep voice that filled the forest when I was there to hear. They are there. They will still be there if ever I need their strength and solace.

With the book's final section, The Coast, we have traveled geographically and autobiographically from a childhood home of discovery to an adult home of activity, reaching what Louise characterized as an older, cellular home of synthesis, the ocean:

> It is brought home to me that in the cosmic scheme I am of no more nor less importance and value than a blade of grass or a chirping cricket. Any impression that [the three] of us may make is at the most negligible and impermanent and, individually, of absolutely no consequence. This truth is everlasting, of course; but it's only in the presence of the sea that I am reminded of it and forced to acknowledge it. That is the reason, I suppose, that some people hate the sea.
>
> On the Point it is possible to think of yourself not as an individual, but as one manifestation of the living; and the evidence of the triumph of life—any type of life—over death and oblivion becomes a stirring and heartening and personal affair.
>
> As I write this, I am again in the shack on the Hill. It is early September and . . . I wonder again as I sit looking out the window at the rowan and the birds and the signs of coming rain, what art man that Thou art mindful of him? And suddenly I know at least part of the answer. Man who cannot swim as well as a fish, or fly as well as a bird, nor support himself on bare ledges as well as a lichen, is the observer, the recorder; because there is no one else—not the bird, not the rowan, not the lichen or the fish—who is capable of doing it. Perhaps all his other achievements are less than this, that he watches, and makes the record, and tries to find the meaning. He alone cares; and in that caring, perhaps, lies his weakness and his very great strength.

By early 1963, Rufus was staying with his mother at The Sands when not on the road driving his truck: "Ma probably wanted me to be more than a truck driver, but it was a great way for me to see the whole country. I took her for little rides once in a while." Louise said he became her eyes and ears for news of the area. They played cribbage and went out to dinner at friends' homes.

Louise had a variety of friends—some native to the area and some, like herself, "transplants." Author Sandy Phippen says she was one of a circle of strong, intellectual women in the area who had wide-ranging talents and views. Some in the group were heterosexual, some homosexual, some in the arts, some in business. She kept in touch with one friend, Hortense Condon from Atlanta, by mail. The extant letters—thanks to her granddaughter, Condon Rodgers—begin in 1963 and provide insight into neighborhood news and Louise's activities and thoughts for nearly a quarter of a century (through 1987). Here is an excerpt from the first note, which talks about the "village eccentric" we'll call Betty:

Dear Hortense:

I agree with you that the letter written from [Betty] seemed to have been written by a woman in unusually good control of her faculties. For the past three summers as I have walked for my mail, I've often exchanged the time of day with her, and had what *I* considered very bright and sometimes witty conversations. I have come to the conclusion that her chief trouble and tragedy is being set down in an environment far below her own level. They don't understand her, so she *must* be nuts. Or else I am nuts, too, so we understand each other. . . . This is all I know at the moment. Got to get to work anyhow.

Also in 1963, Lippincott reissued *We Took to the Woods* and *My Neck of the Woods* in one volume: *The Forest Years*. That *We Took ...* was still popular enough, after twenty years, to warrant a reprint, clearly puts it in the realm of being a "classic."

Rufus, during the holidays and between jobs, stayed with Louise, who was finishing her next book. She also wrote another "legacy" short story for her children called "A Good Bearin' Northern Spy," in which she admitted she had not yet written a will, and explained what she wanted to bequeath to Rufus (twenty-seven and single) and Dinah (twenty-one and married).

By the middle of February 1964, Louise wrote:

Dear Hortense:

The news of your impending move came as a surprise, although it shouldn't have. It is of course the sensible thing to do, but pulling up roots is bound to be hard. I was delighted to sell the Bridgewater house and move up here, and have never regretted it for one minute. But adjusting to the idea was a bit slow. Or maybe I'm reaching the age of inflexibility.

Now let's see what is new around here. Rufus has gone back to work, for one thing. I miss him—not only for all the work he did, but as company, too. He was here just long enough for me to get out of the habit of lugging in my own wood, etc., and of running around on a mess of paltry errands. Oh well, I'll get back into the old groove in time.

X is the same as always—at the moment dreading the return of the Ys. I said, "When do you expect them?" and she said, "It's only six months from to-day." Now I ask you. Isn't reaching six months into the future for trouble a bit exaggerated?

I guess this is all I know at the moment.

When the weather warmed, Florence arrived to spend some time with her daughter. She later told Dinah it was the best vacation she had ever had. The big event of 1964 was the publication of Louise's last adult-audience book, *State o'Maine*. Harper and Row had commissioned a handful of authors from across the country for their "Regions of America" series, and Louise was honored by being chosen to write the book about Maine. Similar in content and purpose to *The Coast of Maine*, this book expanded into the interior of the state. Hester (Hopkins) says that while Louise was researching the book, the two of them would take off on exploratory junkets around Maine. Louise also relied heavily on the reference staff of the Bangor Public Library.

In the book, she wrote that Maine's native and adopted sons and daughters were always inwardly "preoccupied and pre-empted by the tiny pinpoint on the face of the globe called Down East." Wherever they might be, "they try to live not in such a manner that they will eventually be welcomed into Paradise, but only so that someday they can go home to Maine." As for herself, she said that she had lived all her life in New England, and "travel outside the area has done nothing to convince me that I'd prefer living anywhere else." At The Sands, "the sea lies before me, and behind, beyond the lawn, the garden and apple orchard, rise the woods. I hope never to be obliged to go anywhere else." Not surprisingly, Louise started work on a book called *The House* and got as far as the following opening paragraph and outline:

It is very odd how much power a house has over the habits and conduct of its inhabitants. Silently, simply by being what it is, it dictates courses of procedure. Now that I have lived here at The Sands for a year, I suddenly look at myself and realize that I am not the same person at all that I was.

The House Outline:

Through woods—then out into the spaciousness of old Sands clearing with its brightness of sea and sky, its openness of beach and fields—then back into narrow passage of road with its walls of tough and twisted trees.

The house—easy enough to describe; but how to write a summer's day in an old orchard or an autumn night with the hunter's moon and surf on the beach?

Fire and moonlight meeting in middle of room—sunlight extinguishing fire temporarily.

Sea has crept into this house—shells and bailer, clam basket, buoys, floats, pebbles and rock doorstops.

Feeling of wildness engendered by sight of surf on outer reefs. Barrier reefs everywhere.

RFD—I love it. US Travel bureau urges entertain foreign visitors by (1) showing kitchen gadgets, (2) take to supermarket, or (3) drive-in hamburger stand.—We live here like foreigners to rest of US. We take our guests to see coons or watch the *Bluenose* [Ferry] come in.

GK Chesterton—"The telescope makes the world seem smaller; it's the microscope that makes it seem larger." The Sands=a microcosm of all country living.

Constant watchfulness of weather: everyone has barometer and weathervane. Weather news—poetry of broadcasts and weather talk. Examples: Hush before storm, hooter loud, can't hear in fair weather. Bell buoys loom up clearly on lovely weather-breeder. Cobwebs on grass.

The house induces one to take up the old skills: canning, pick "timber" oneself, bread making, house plants (Rockwell's words on calla, begonia). Gardening—old plants like lobelia. Old methods. Use of terms: "flax 'round" etc. Sewing. Also the old childhood amusements: blowing grass, frogs purses, blowing dandelion tops to get wish, counting daisy petals, skipping stones, leaf burning, ice cream making.

Legacies: white narcissus, purple lilacs (Miriam & Chen) [former owners of the Sands] and white from *long* ago, corset and birdcage in bathroom. Birthing and dying room.

Seasonal rites: Of spring—house cleaning, necessary here. Wash curtains. The spring urge to clean. Spring expansion—take stove down, open spare rooms, fling up windows, storm windows off, screens on, wash windows from smoke and sea spray. Furniture back in summer place. Rebirth—symbolic. Daily inspection of bulbs. Clean yard, spade under mulch (think of Aunt Dorcas, and outdoor women too). [The Sands is still called the "Aunt Dorcas House," after its original owner.] Birds arrive—plant seedlings. Lawn furniture out—painted. Plans for summer. Get a croquet set?

Of summer: Evening walk with dog on beach. One trip per summer—Andover–Campobello. Once around Cranberry Point (at least & Point Francis—seals). Hiding and hiking places. Walks to and from village. Once a week to Gossler's for pretty lettuce. Croquet. Zucchini. Guests. Eclipse.

Of fall: banking sills of house, storm windows, rockweed on garden (to be outdoors, lugging r-weed keeps one warm, winter confinement here all too soon). Cleaning gardens, digging and storing dahlias, re-setting spring bulbs. Lupin seeds in fields. Woodpiles, in and out. Stove set up. Hose away. Take up house plants. Close spare rooms.

Of winter: Fewer—chiefly struggle to keep warm and fed. Wood. Snow. Shopping to keep ahead in case of emergency. Eye on temp.—guard in advance against water freeze up. Longest season—"winter and the fourth of July." We work harder but have more time—it's nice. Drops frozen on apple tree twigs like pussy-willows of crystal, next time a moment later I look out they are gone. Wonderful beauty of blizzardy day. Night sky.

There were several pages of this book on country living (see Part II), but they were not expanded, so it seems likely that either the outline and sample chapters were not accepted or that Louise decided against the project. Whatever happened, *State o' Maine* thus marked the end of an era, and Louise turned her attention to writing juvenile scholastic books and a few more short stories. After a quarter of a century of steady, successful literary outpouring, Louise, at sixty-one, began to slow the pace just a little.

As did Florence. Although she was still in complete control of her faculties, Mrs. Dickinson was getting frail. Dinah had asked her to come live with her in Boston, and since Louise was too far from any hospital emergency room, Florence moved out of her apartment in 1965. She kept busy, knitting a lot and reading prodigiously. Dinah relates: "I used to go to the library each week and get her a load of books (she liked a variety of books, but mostly romance novels). But Grammy read so much, who could keep track of what she'd already finished? So we had this system—as she read a book, she'd circle page 100 in pencil. So [at the library] I would just turn to page 100 to figure out what I should bring home."

Louise, alone at The Sands with Hero and her two cats, Bargain and Bonus, was still churning out scholastic books for Watts. In 1966, *The First Book of the Fur Trade* was published, and she was in the midst of *The First Book of Lumbering*. Unfortunately, however, health problems were starting to crop up. Louise was diagnosed with breast cancer. Knowing that Dinah was already occupied with Florence and that Rufus was on the road, she valiantly, stubbornly decided not to "burden" them. With neighbor Marcia Spurling she set off for the hospital and removal of one of her breasts. Dinah only found out after the fact, because of her persistence in trying to find out where her mother was (which turned out to be at Marcia's). Louise, told she had a couple of years to live, refused chemotherapy. She told Dinah, "I figure I don't want to spend what time I have left vomiting."

As though this wasn't enough, Catherine Luce called Louise at the end of the summer to say she was planning to sell Forest Lodge. This must have been a difficult conversation, lingering emotionally well after the fact. Katie was essentially "family," part of the Rich heritage. Once she was gone from Forest Lodge, it would be the end of that era. Louise sadly determined that neither she nor her children would be able, as things currently stood, to buy and maintain the old homestead. Rufus says that he had told Catherine he wanted to buy Forest Lodge when she was ready to sell: "She spoke to Ma about it, but my mother said I wasn't in any position to buy it. Without talking to me." He adds wistfully, "So Katie sold it...."

In October 1966, Katie sold to Edgar A. French, whose son, Aldro, is the current owner and respectful caretaker. He has maintained nearly all of the interior of Forest Lodge as Louise and Katie left it, and hopes to entrust the place to some preservation-minded group or institution. Meanwhile, he hosts visitors from across the country and beyond, who walk down the Carry Road in hopes of seeing Forest Lodge. (Catherine Luce remained in her home at Rumford Corner, where she died in the mid-1980s.)

The cancer and the sale of Forest Lodge were a double blow for Louise, a stereo reminder that time was passing all too quickly. Nature, her family and friends, and the bottle—all provided solace for her.

They say that trouble comes in threes, and this unfortunately, proved true for Louise. In addition to her private sorrows, she became the brunt of very public ridicule—some gentle, some malicious—which everyone from the area who knew her remembers to this day. She was headed to have dinner with the Condon/Rodgers clan on Saturday, September 16, when she backed into a lobster boat outside the village store. The weekly *Ellsworth American* told the story:

We Vote for Mrs. Rich

Newspapermen, who by the nature of their jobs are privy to some of the least admirable human behaviors, are sometimes privileged to witness moments of personal grandeur as well. We tell this tale not to tattle on one of Maine's most popular authors, but rather to insure that one of her most splendid moments lives in history.

As we entered the Sheriff's Office recently, Louise Dickinson Rich of Prospect Harbor, who hasn't had a driver's license for thirty years, was about to enter the lockup after being booked for driving under the influence.

As the bars swung open to admit her, that grand lady turned toward Deputy Urquhart and graciously bending her head, asked with impeccable courtesy: "You will tell my dinner hosts that I am in jail?"

This is local legend—event as metaphor. Louise was viewed as something of a character, and her run-in with the law simply clinched it. Her detractors have called her blunt, opinionated, a part-time lush, too large in person and aloof in manner; someone who viewed both the natives and the well-heeled with disrespect. They have said she only showed working-class areas and people in her books, and in person shunned the prime social movers. Her admirers have described a capable, funny, intelligent individualist with sharp wit and silver pen; courteous, tolerant, but uninterested in social climbing. There is truth on both sides.

Typically, neither slander nor specter of death seemed to stop Louise from writing. She worked up "A Summer place," a short story published in *Woman's Day* that poignantly spoke to the evanescence and complementary contradictions of life (without divulging to her readers, naturally, why she had that on her mind). Also in 1967, her scholastic book, *The Kennebec River,* was published by Holt, Rinehart & Winston. Plus she started on her next juvenile book, *Star Island Boy,* which dealt with the topic of orphans-as-cash through the eyes of an eleven-year-old boy. (An island community off the coast of Maine supplemented its income by providing foster homes, with a resultant respect for one another growing out of this mutuality of need). Once again, Louise was writing topical books that provided food for thought, and fortunately she was starting to receive public recognition for her young-adult writing. *Mindy* was selected as runner-up for the Austrian State Prize for Children's and Juvenile Literature.

Meanwhile, at Dinah's, Florence was still holding forth. One day, Dinah returned home to find her ninety-one-year-old grandmother up on a stepladder taking curtains off the tall apartment windows: "I just stood there, motionless, afraid I'd make a noise that would cause her to turn around and fall. When she finally got down, I scolded, 'Grammy, why are you doing this?' And she looked at me, 'Dinah, anything I give up, I'll never do again.'" The following year (1968), Florence actually did fall and break her leg. Dinah provides the details: "She said she was 'fine,' and was otherwise, but of course she needed proper full-time care at a nursing home until it healed. Two weeks later, August 4, she had a stroke and was gone. So she basically died at home. She was cremated and her ashes were buried with those of my grandfather at Oak Grove Cemetery in Springfield, Massachusetts."

Louise and Rufus traveled down to be with Dinah and attend the funeral. Although not at all prone to morbidity, Louise must have been contemplating her own mortality. According to the medical establishment, her time was nearly up. She wrote "The Handing On of a Garden" for *Woman's Day*, offering an immortality-through-horticulture view from her backyard. *Star Island Boy* was published and gratifyingly won the Child Study Association of America's Children's Book of the Year award. By October, as she wrote Hortense, Rufus was in Florida and Dinah (unable to visit while taking care of her grandmother) had arrived.

In 1969, Louise wrote her next young-reader book, *Three of a Kind*, about an eleven-year-old orphan girl in a foster home in Maine who befriends an "emotionally disturbed" four-year-old boy. It came out in 1970, but the public appearance most on Louise's mind that year was the birth of her grandson, Matthew, Dinah's son. In September of 1970, Louise wrote Dinah about the doctor who had told her she had only a few years to live:

Well, Dr. Stadler finally died last Friday night after never having regained consciousness. We all feel terrible about this—he was only 36. No funeral and no flowers—the Stadlers evidently feel about these things the way we do.

We have no doctor at the moment except the new Navy man. Dr. Mace, who was going into partnership with Dr. Stadler, is in Vietnam, with three months to go in the service before they turn him loose. However, the hospital and Red Cross are trying to get him discharged on a hardship plea. We do need a doctor here, but no doubt Vietnam does, too. We shall see.

Dinah adds, "I liked to joke later with my mother—very dark humor—that, as it turned out, she outlived her doctor."

In August 1971, Alice, who was retiring from Franklin Watts, spent three weeks at The Sands—the last time the sisters were together in Maine. Louise was becoming increasingly arthritic, and Alice's eyesight was failing rapidly. One imagines, though, considering the Dickinson girls, that they managed to explore, discover, and discuss their corner of the world. Louise always said no one except Ralph could make her laugh like Alice. One hopes there was a lot of laughter during those long summer days.

Sally also arrived at The Sands in August, overlapping slightly with Alice. The visit brought back many memories for her: caring for Rufus while Louise worked at her typewriter, walking four miles for mail/supplies, polishing the big Pine Point tables with bacon-greased hands. She still recalls the Forest Lodge wall display of bottles but says she doesn't remember ever seeing drinking there (yes, at Pine Point and later). The only time she remembers Louise being "distraught" was when she (Sally) spent a night on the *Alligator* logging boat with the crew. "I credit Louise with much of my good sense. She never spanked, but this was our *most* serious conversation." She recalls fondly the day Ralph "really broke loose and had a good time. He was always working on something, no interest in playing with kids. But this one time, Pond in the River was frozen solid, the local loggers had the day off, and we all went skating. My father gave me a straight chair to hang onto. At some point, he sat down on it and I started pushing him around." Suddenly the chair hit something, Ralph flew off, and they both landed on the ice, laughing hysterically. Her enduring image has Louise and Ralph on two chairs positioned between the fireplace and the porch, in front of the windows at Forest Lodge. A table stands between them with a gleaming hurricane lamp and Rufus's crib is under the stairs. Sally's voice still conveys the sense of that contentment even now.

When Alice and Sally left, Louise started working on her next Watts book, *King Philip's War.* She was pleased to see both *The Peninsula* and *Only Parent* out in reprint editions from Chatham Press.

On October 14, she wrote Dinah: "Peaches [her dog] had her operation yesterday. I called up to inquire in the p.m. She was doing great. I remarked that she was a better woman than I and Dr. Toothacre agreed—maybe a little too readily. I get her Saturday. Bonus, who now rules the roost, is not going to be happy; but I miss the old fool. No one to walk the beach with."

In November, Louise wrote to Hortense: "Voted Tuesday—I *love* voting here! I feel like a character off an old Norman Rockwell *Sat. Eve. Post* cover. Lobstermen in boots and oilskins, old gaffers swapping lies around the wood stove, the local candidates tarted up in their High School graduation blue serge suits which they will eventually be buried in, all the women with hair set in ridged waves but still wearing their aprons—real old-time Americana."

She also began writing a book about aging. She figured it would "run to about twelve chapters, expanding from house to larger community, and from self to larger society," with the working title of *Tay's Book.* However, perhaps because of her failing eyesight, this book also remained unfinished (see Part II). Some fragments:

> The Beach—general aspect of the shore as a "shinbone coast" with the Sands as the exception, the only beach around. The beach connotes a worthless life—"on the beach." Our beach equals a breathing spell for people bred on the shinbone coast and raised on dried fish and stewed Jacob's cattle beans.
>
> Moonlit late autumn night—cold, dead still, but with the roar and rumble of sustained surf on outer shores, low and throbbing in motionless air, plus crash of breakers on own beach—spectral to see from upstairs in moonlight.
>
> Country Living: Use daylight and good weather to like advantages—"thought I'd take advantage of the day to wash" and "thought I'd take advantage of the lovely rainy day (or snowy) after long stretch of good weather to stay in and read, sew, or clean silver with a clear conscience."
>
> Words: Kerflummoxed, take a back seat to, lickety-larrup, flaxing 'round, slower than death's warping bar, spring out, down river (off island), shack it (not the same as shack up), feeling old-fashioned this morning, a month of Sundays, not fit for fencin' nor

firewood, after chores—as a time of day, also 'fore noon, and "e-ven-in" (three syllables).

So many things to see and hear and remember: dancing shadows from swinging lantern growing heavy when stilled, town lights reflected on low clouds in distance, pine cone rattling its way to earth, individual rain drops on roof quickening into roll of drums.

In 1972, Louise received her second Children's Book of the Year award from the Child Study Association, this time for *King Philip's War*. Three years after she was supposed to be dead, she was not only very much alive, but serving as a generous mentor to aspiring authors as well. Louise gave moral and professional support to her neighbor, Virginia Rich (yes, another Rich!) and probably a number of unrecorded literary hopefuls. In her July 1971 note to Peninsula regular Sandy Phippen, she offered advice applicable to any struggling writer:

I don't know what I can tell you. The one thing I had in mind without even reading the ms. was that the epistolary form just never is successful nowadays. But you have already been told that by someone really more qualified than I to judge. Actually, I'm a writer, not a critic; and therefore liable to grave error in that field.

There was one other thing. I gathered from your last letter that you were doing this partly at least for J's benefit. That is nice, but it is also dangerous. You are bound to have her in mind—and her reactions—with every sentence you write. This does not work. You'll have to try to put her out of your mind. You can write only to please yourself; that is the only way to please others in the end.

About agents, marketing, etc.—Help!! Agents are hard to get and getting harder all the time. Before one will consider you, you must have sold something. The only way to sell is to submit, submit, submit to magazines, and be prepared for rejection after rejection. Some make it, some don't. It's largely a matter of guts and persistence—and of course, ability, which maybe is last on the list. However—

Louise continued her usual routine, but in the autumn of 1973, she fell and ended up in the Ellsworth hospital. At that point, she was hundreds of miles from her recently divorced daughter, three-year-old grandson, and ailing sister. Rufus had been working on construction during the summers and a variety of other jobs otherwise, but at that point he was a motorcycle mechanic and organizer of the "JR racing team" for kids in Middleboro, Massachusetts, only a few towns away from Dinah. With some coaxing from the family, Louise made a practical, tactical decision. Time to be in an easier position to support one another and stop being so darned far-flung and independent. Time to circle the wagons.

Brockton

Louise left The Sands in 1973, after she got out of the hospital, and moved to 1070 Pleasant Street in Brockton, Massachusetts, with Dinah, who explains: "Ma said she was doing it to be with her grandson, but I know she had me in mind, too." Louise laid out the details in a letter to Hortense (Condon):

> Thank you, *thank you!* for your notes and the very appropriate card. (Didn't know they made cards for *every* occasion nowadays, except possibly an abortion, which will come soon, I'm sure.) I am at last moved in after two weeks with Dinah while the wall-to-wall was being put down. Dinah is not yet moved—her apt. is not finished—so I am alone with the dog. Since I was never in my whole life so exhausted, this is a welcome situation—peace and quiet—they are wonderful. This is an old one-family house made into two apartments. I am upstairs and simply *love* it! I'd forgotten after the old house at the Sands that in some places things really do work and heat is a matter of turning up the thermostat, not climbing into boots and sweater and lugging in wood.
>
> I have four rooms, but it seems larger as the ceilings are higher than at the Sands and the windows larger. They all look out into the tree-tops and so I do not feel in the least shut in and really don't miss the sea view. One thing I'm getting used to is keeping the door locked. First time in my life I've ever bothered, but the way things are. . . . Oh well. . . .
>
> The move was not difficult, really. Rufus has his own plane now and flew me down on a perfectly gorgeous day. [Louise, at seventy, apparently was still willing to try anything!] Believe it or not, we had a slight snow flurry here last night. I got out just in time.
>
> Last words from the Peninsula were that Bertha [Cameron] and Marcia [Spurling] seem to be in fine fettle. Mrs. W took her jewelry out of her safe before going home, left it in the house while she did some errands, and came back to find it gone. Value $25,000 and the insurance was not nearly enough. All of which goes to show that she could have spent the money to better ad-

vantage—or so I would think, but I am not a personal ornament addict. (As you and everyone else doubtless have observed.)

M. called me when I was in the Ellsworth hospital and it is my opinion that he is getting a little fed-up with his home situation. This is *only* opinion, so please keep it to yourself. *I* think he is ripe to fall into the hands of a young, healthy, silly woman who will be *fun*. I could easily be wrong.

My cat Bonus got left behind in the shuffle, but Rufus flew back and got him last Sunday. Dinah and Matthew are well. Dinah has given Matthew too much attention, which is perfectly natural under the circumstances. He has been all that she had. I hope to remedy this without antagonizing either one of them, but I am well aware of the perils of being an interfering relative, so will probably leave it to the nursery school to teach him the prime fact of life that he isn't the only pebble on the beach.

Several weeks later, Louise sent this holiday update:

Dear Hortense:

Dinah moved downstairs last Friday after the usual delays caused by workmen who don't show up when they said they would. She and Matthew and the dog and the cat spent one week with me during the moving orgy, and I am exhausted. But I really enjoyed it, too, since I knew it wasn't going to last forever. I'm too set in my ways to adjust to confusion at this late date. I still love living here and I'm still glad I made the break when I did.

Rufus, Dinah and I spent Thanksgiving together, since Mal took Matthew for the day. He will be home for Xmas, though. I'd hoped my sister would come, and she planned to until this damn fuel and energy thing. So many of her friends had a rough time travelling even this short distance at Thanksgiving that she decided Xmas would be even worse (and I guess it will). And she did not relish the idea of sitting around airports hours on end, or standing on buses or trains all the way from NYC to Boston. I think she was smart. I don't know what the fuel situation is with you [in Atlanta], but here in New England it's getting pretty serious. Or maybe it's only that people are becoming frightened. At any rate, there are no public displays of Xmas lights and very few private ones. It doesn't seem like old Xmas at all—which doesn't

hurt my feelings. I really *hate* Xmas, I always find it terribly depressing for some reason.

Bertha wrote me that there had been a lot of vandalism of
summer cottages in Corea, but she didn't specify whose. Do you
know anything about it? I'm sorry not to be able to pass on local
Gouldsboro gossip, except second-hand. Actually, I'm a bit
shocked at myself, I miss the place, people and goings on so little. Maybe I wasn't as involved emotionally as I thought I was. I
never was socially, of course, but I did think I'd miss the area
more.

This is about all, I guess. I do wish you and Mabel the happiest of Christmases and a nice New Year. I always feel foolish saying that, to tell you the truth. I know perfectly well that things
will go right along just as they have been going, for good or ill,
unchanged by the buying of a new calendar. But I wish you happiness anyhow!

By February 1974, the gas shortage was still a problem, but apparently
not to Louise:

I'm glad that I no longer drive and have to go through the hassle
of getting a pint of gas, not to mention paying for it! I've just
come back from doing the weekly shopping with Dinah and we
sat almost an hour in a line at a gas station. I don't know how
things are in Atlanta, but in New England the situation is impossible. We have the even-odd system, so if we didn't get gas to-day,
that was it until Tuesday, since no sales on Sunday.

Marcia and Bertha keep me fairly well informed about Peninsula doings, but I'm damned if I can at the moment think of anything startling to tell you. It all seems so long ago and far away,
although actually it isn't. The big house next door to me at the
Sands is for sale ($100,000 with a lot of land and the beach) and
there was a chance that it would go for a nursing home. But the
people decided not—too far from hospitals etc. Then there have
been the usual breakings and enterings, illegitimate babies, family quarrels, etc. Both Marcia and Bertha seem in fine fettle, I'm
happy to say. It's a good thing for everyone involved that I moved
away. Marcia—I'm sure this will delight you—and H. are becoming very buddy-buddy after years of loathing each other. She
chauffeurs him around in his car and he buys her dinners. Her

car is pretty old and decrepit and he has no driver's license, so it works out well all along. And Bertha—I think the two women at the Corea store are a big factor in making Bertha's life happy. When I think of her as she was a year or so ago, I marvel at the change and improvement.

I do not for a moment regret moving to Brockton. I honestly don't think I could have managed alone at the Sands another winter, and I didn't want to live anywhere else in the area. I'm terribly arthritic and no one yet has figured out why I run a temperature all the time. That I have learned to live with; I've got used to being exhausted all the time, which doesn't mean that I like it much. Here the necessary mechanics of keeping warm and clean and entertained are so much easier. No, I don't regret it at all.

Dinah is fine. I think she works too hard, but one thing I promised myself when I moved here was that I would not interfere or give advice unless asked. Matthew grows like a weed and talks incessantly. Unfortunately he expects a sensible answer— none of this "Hmm-hum, Umm-humm" business. I haven't seen Rufus for a while, but I talk with him often and he seems in good form.

I'm not sure whether or not I'll attempt Maine this year. Virginia Rich has offered me her apartment over the lower store, which would be convenient as I could walk to the PO and the little store. But Hester Rich Hopkins has offered me her house on Cape Cod while she and her husband are in Maine at So. Gouldsboro, so I don't know. Do you plan to go to Easterly [Crowley Island, Corea] this year?

I guess that's all—and not much, I must say.

Another letter from 1974 reports:

Easter next Sunday already! Rufus will be having dinner with Dinah and me and assorted friends, *not* including Matthew, who has been invited to Passover Feast at his grandmother's. He's certainly going to end up with a mixed bag of religious convictions—or lack of convictions—as the case may be.

I finally broke down and admitted to the Bangor Public Library, my super-source of literature, that I had moved to Massachusetts. I was afraid that they might have a rule against Out-of-

State clients, so I had been having my books sent to Prospect Hbr. and forwarded. Miriam [Colwell—postmistress, author, friend] was more than kind about this, but I figured enough was enough and there was no charity in working a willing horse to death, or something. I could have saved a lot of trouble—the BPL has no prejudice at all against us outlanders, and the books continue to flow. At the moment I am on *The Uneasy Chair,* the biography of Bernard DeVoto. I like it and think you would, too. It deals with an era we both remember, when we were young and starry-eyed and everyone was idealistic.

I haven't yet made plans for the summer. I did toy with the thought of accepting Virginia Rich's offer of her store apartment, but she is in the hospital undergoing heart surgery—which surprises as well as saddens me, as I thought she was the picture of health—and I don't want to bother her at this time.

As it turned out, Louise spent the summer of 1974 at the home of Hester and Tom Hopkins on Cape Cod. Rufus meanwhile headed back to Middle Dam with Jane Costa, a woman he met in Middleboro and had known for a couple of years. Jane had become friends with Louise and Dinah and wanted to go to the area in Maine made famous by *We Took to the Woods.* They wrote to Alys Parsons and got jobs at Lakewood Camps—Rufus as boat man and Jane as "back hall girl," a position Louise held briefly thirty years earlier. On September 6, their day off, they went into Rumford and got married, with a couple of friends standing up for them. Rufus relates: "I got married in my work clothes, and the next day we were back on the job." After Lakewood closed for the season, the newlyweds decided they wanted to stay in the area, so they bought a parcel of land along the access road to Lakewood's boat landing at South Arm and built a house. Rufus settled in to driving his own tractor-trailer or hauling for others. Jane went to work at the local store in Andover.

Louise, meantime, headed back to Brockton and by March of 1975 wrote Sandy Phippen: "Your proposed call [visit] won't be possible. What with Easter, my daughter's birthday, a house full of guests and—above all and always—the pressure of a looming deadline, I'm at my wit's end for time and energy."

She was finishing *Summer at High Kingdom,* her last juvenile fiction. Ever the rebel, ever tolerant of nonconformists, she hatched the idea of writing about members of a hippie community and their native neighbors coming to an understanding and appreciation of one another—a thoroughly appropriate swan song. She either decided or was advised to keep the setting in Maine. Between the time that her grandson started kindergarten and the family (Jane, Rufus, Dinah, and Matthew) gathered for Christmas 1975, Louise's final book was in print.

Matthew recounts:

Louise—I called her "Bana"—was a bit of a fireball. She taught me to ride a bike. She was very methodical. Her routine was in bed around nine and up early. We spent schoolnights together and we'd watch the weather report every night. I remember she had a cookie jar that was almost impossible to steal cookies from because it made noise.

Dinah laughs:

He seemed to get away with some things, though. I remember walking in to pick him up and there was Ma happily stretched out on her recliner all tied up with string! She said she knew I was about to show up and figured it would keep him occupied. Ma was a great sport. Even at this stage, I never saw her take a nap, never knew her to be sick in bed. You knew, whatever it was, you got up and got moving. She did her own cleaning (she actually was a good housekeeper, very orderly and knew where things were) and her own cooking—she was a very inventive cook, didn't do recipes. Her independence was very important and we helped each other out.

In January 1976, Louise wrote to Hortense that she was "trying to kid myself that I'm enjoying a new Siamese cat named Lenore, who stretches along the tops of doors and takes swipes at all who pass." She reported that Dinah had a new "beau—that word dates me but I hate boyfriend, especially for those over twenty-one." She concluded: "Now back to earning a living by writing (with taste and discretion, I hope) another juvenile about a teen-age girl becoming involved with an older lesbian. Times have changed. This is now considered an acceptable subject to present to the young."

Ultimately, however, the book was unpublished (no draft or outline remains). During this period, Louise had several books in the works that never came to fruition—either through her own volition or due to publisher/literary agent response—and that may have influenced her decision to call her career good. In what seems like a closing of the circle, Louise's last published short story had a connection to her friend Hester. "The Perfectly Proper Pig" was co-authored with Hester's husband, Tom. Printed in the November issue of *Yankee Magazine,* the subheading read: "In order to conduct an intelligent study of the effects of environment versus heredity you should look around for a worthy subject—a sort of guinea pig... or some kind of pig." The coauthorship seems appropriate not only because of Hester but also because Louise's first short story, "Why Guides Turn Gray," was also a collaboration—with Ralph. But that time, nearly forty years earlier, he had had sole billing, and no one had heard of Louise Dickinson Rich. This final literary collaboration was important on a personal level, because it gave Louise another opportunity to interact with Hester, and with Hester she would gain some perspective on herself and her life, and to gather the courage to face her infirmities.

Returning

Louise realized she missed the rigor of Maine and her independent lifestyle. What's more, she decided she was up to going back. So in 1977, at age seventy-four, she returned to Crowley Island (Corea) year-round, renting a little brown, one-floor bungalow facing the lobster pound. Hero had died by this time, so she took along Dreyfus, Dinah's big collie, for companionship. The following draft of an unpublished piece entitled, "I've Been Thinking about Death," provides a window into her life, and her state of mind, at that point:

> Last night I saw a discussion on public television about old age and the stereotyping of the elderly. The "experts"—both younger women (40 or so)—failed to take into account (because they couldn't know, not ever having been over 65) that age brings insight and tolerance. We really don't mind being considered slow, perhaps stupid, ineffectual, because we know better. Let the youngsters have their silly fun if they can't find anything better to worry about than us oldsters. Perhaps this is arrogance, but if so, make the most of it.
>
> Actually this youthful concern can be very harmful to us old dodies. [Many well-meaning sons and daughters] have made their mothers nearly helpless by over attention and solicitude. It's a very real danger that older people should be aware of, since you can't expect the blindered young to be. I was in real and present danger during the four years I was in Brockton. I was "Bana." I was old. I must be waited on, spared, etc. Muscles are kept in tone by exercise, and this includes mental and spiritual (spirit in the sense of fire, not in the religious sense) as well as physical muscles. You haven't the guts and stamina to rise to crises unless you have addressed your resources to minor emergencies (even such an emergency as making your own telephone calls) from day to day. You wear the coat that is given to you, adopt the image that is imposed on you. I was Bana, Dinah's old mother to her friends, ancient grandmother to Matt.
>
> I escaped by the skin of my teeth, thanks to Hester and Virginia [Rich] at precisely the right time, the time of Dinah's remarriage. I came to Maine, not really knowing if I'd survive the trip, found a house when there wasn't any, made the move that I dreaded phys-

- 143 -

ically (the actual move, that is) and returned not only to my own place, but to my own self, Louise. This is not something I've built up in my mind. This is very, very real.

I've been thinking about older people who retain their interest in life: Ma on her death bed being excited and thrilled by the proximity of a wounded thug, and his police guard, near her in the corridor of the hospital. . . .

Tantalizingly, the writing ended there—except for a few names she would probably use as further examples, followed by a final sentence: "Look on it as an experience."

This is quintessential "LDR" (as her family jokingly dubbed her during the FDR period)—informing others, sharing what it is like to live life on the edge of one's abilities. She is like the captain of a sinking ship, the astronaut crashing upward into the unknown, the journalist under fire—passing on essential information so that others can live or learn from their experience. Louise had the luxury for introspection and written communication, a silent conversation. But the compulsion is the same, the willingness to share publicly the gift of what one is seeing and feeling.

From this point, Louise's writing consisted of letters to friends and family, and notations to herself for future pieces. Like her much earlier diary, the letters shed light on her activities/thoughts, and she can speak for herself:

Sunday the 3 December [1977]
Dear Condon [Rodgers]

Your grandmother [Hortense] says that you would be willing to call my sister once in a while, and you don't know what a relief this would be to me. I feel very diffident about asking you to do this, as Alice is by no stretch of the imagination your responsibility, and it would come under the heading of plain good-heartedness and a generous spirit. The point is that Alice has lost the sight of one eye and has very little in the other, and we worry about her. She can't leave NYC at this stage of treatment (she hopes some sight can be saved), although later she will go to Dinah's. I guess what I'm asking you to do is keep a loose (very loose) check on her, since you live so near her, and let us know if she gets into real trouble. All of this sounds pretty alarmist and I imagine is unnecessary, but one never knows.

25 March [1978]
Dear Hortense:

Happy Easter! I've just celebrated the occasion by mopping my kitchen floor. The snow is shrinking, the yard is full of those damn starlings—driving my cat crazy—crocuses are in bloom in front of the Ellsworth City Hall, the roads are full of potholes and water, the remaining snow is filthy, in short, spring is upon us. Oh, and Bea Crowley has a new car, or at least new to her, another sign of spring.

There are two mobile homes in place at the Sands, which annoys me, and a small shack that looks like a privy, but is probably an office of some sort. Mr. Burrill evidently is ignoring public sentiment on the subject of his development.

I feel sorry for Jo, although I know she would not thank me for that, not being one who bids for sympathy. She seems at loose ends, and regrets having sold the house, but of course did what seemed best at the time. I hope she finds some solution to her problem. She will be here in May, and I am looking forward to seeing her and all of you at that time. It will be terrific.

Saturday, July 8 [1978]
Dear Hortense:

There! The Glorious Fourth is a thing of the past and we can relax for a minute. Rufus, Jane, Dinah, Ray and Matthew were here (R & J brought their camper as I don't have much room, as you know) and we had a very nice time indeed.

[After a lot of news of local people] I haven't seen any of them yet. I get more and more reclusive every year, which I know I should combat, but don't. [Followed by more news!]

Since I suddenly couldn't see much at all, I went to get new glasses. No luck. My old cataracts that I've had for fifteen years have taken a new lease on life and I'm supposed to be operated on at once. Since I can see well enough to function, after a fashion, I'm putting it off until after Labor Day. Frankly, I dread it, and have got to get used to the idea, which came as a shock. I guess I'm a coward. Guess, hell. I know I am.

Ruth Young is doing very well (*I* think) but she thinks otherwise. She can't spade up a full acre of potatoes, so feels she is failing. I just love Ruth. Marcia seems fine. She improves with age—or at least her attitude does. There are fewer tourists around than usual, it seems to me, but maybe that is because I live off the beaten path now.

I guess this is all. The radio keeps harping on how terribly hot and humid it is everywhere, but I have a sweater on and am none too warm. It's 59 here, 79 at Marcia's, and 89 in Ellsworth.

Sunday the 21 October [1978]
Dear Hortense:

I am typing with one eye and that one not very good, so you will have to bear with me. I'll do my poor best. Due to complications which were unforeseeable, Dr. Bromley could operate on one eye only at this time and I have to go back later—three months later at least—for the other. So here I am with a patch over my right eye, killing time. I'm not supposed to lift, bend, strain or do much of anything else, and it is frustrating and boring. Since I can take care of myself perfectly well, given enough time, I sent Jane home. [Jane came down from Andover for a couple of weeks to look after her mother-in-law.] She had plenty to do there getting ready for winter and all she could do here was put drops in my eye, which I can do myself. I may need her a lot more later and I don't want to wear out a good thing. Our relationship at the moment is fine and I'd like to keep it that way.

What is really disturbing me is my sister. She will be totally blind in a very short while—a matter of weeks. You can imagine how I feel about this so I won't dwell on that. At present she is still in the Eye and Ear Infirmary undergoing training for the blind so that they can function on their own. They like to start this while there is still some sight left. After that, I don't know what is going to happen. We'll have to take it one step at a time. Probably the best thing would be for Dinah to find an apartment near her, and Alice and I move into it together. But we'll see when the time comes.—Honestly, between my sister Alice, my friend Jo, and my dog Dreyfus, all in the past month, I'm beginning to feel a little paranoid:—afraid to answer the phone or read my mail lest I find out something else terrible has happened. Sorry to sound so full of gloom and next time I will do better. [Jane explains that Louise had gone out into the garden, a week or so before this letter, to find Dreyfus lying dead. "She was terribly upset; it was a real blow."]

Monday the 6 November [1978]
Dear Hortense:

Well, I hear on the radio that the *TIMES* [*New York Times*] is back on the stands to-day, so I assume that Condon has gone back to work. Things are very quiet around here [many people] have gone to West Medford Friday for the memorial service, so the neighborhood is practically in a coma. Bea is still staying here. She's taking Jo's death very hard—can't sleep, doesn't want to be alone, and looks terrible. I think Barbara [Crowley]—who is a very nice person—is worried about her. Evidently Bea is burdened by a feeling of guilt, although God knows she did all she could to get Jo to the hospital, but you know as well as I do that once Jo dug in her heels, there was no moving her. Actually I believe that Jo's life wouldn't have been very happy anyhow. She really did regret bitterly letting the old home go and things would have never been the same again with someone else in control. However, that is all conjecture and now we'll never know.

I hope this typing isn't too bad. I still have a patch over one eye. I'm coming along OK, but it takes time. Fortunately the weather is gorgeous so I can get out and walk some, which is a help. We need rain though, wells are going dry all over.

I am very much worried about my sister. Dinah wants her to come stay with her, and that's what she ought to do and wants to do, but her doctors say they don't want to interrupt treatment at this point. She is out of the Eye and Ear after a month, trying to manage alone, and I don't think succeeding very well.

There isn't anything I can do in my handicapped condition, and it's driving me crazy. I appreciate now what you felt when you were faced with the question of what to do about your sister. I can't even give Alice advice as I don't know what would be best for her. All this chatter about the blessings of a tranquil old age is a lot of nonsense. Problems increase as you grow older and you get less and less able to cope with them.

My cat is carrying on a war with Ruth Young's cat Baby. When Dreyfus was alive, he defended Audrey from Baby, chasing her up a tree at the slightest provocation. Now Audrey is on her own and I'm afraid, a coward at heart. I can't go out and throw stones at Baby or I'd find myself in a war with Ruth, which I definitely don't want. Problems, problems, problems.

Marcia is fine—calls me up several times a day to report on the activities of M's tenants at K's old house. They really do sound like a raffish crew, although I'm sure Marcia puts the worst possible interpretation on what they do. To-day she has them involved in drug smuggling and running a house of ill repute on the side. Their name is V. and they may well be perfectly responsible and hard-working people.

I guess this is all I know at the moment, which I'll be the first to admit isn't much.

Friday the 26 January [1979]
Dear Condon:

We're recovering from the latest storm (which I think you had, too) and you would not believe the surf I can see, over the roof of the Co-op, down on Cranberry Point. The Coast Guard report says, "seas from fifteen to twenty-three feet" and by God! I believe it.

And speaking of gorgeous, X is not his old beautiful self. The years (he must be crowding forty) and the various slammers have taken their toll. [He has the] well-known prison pallor and some prison mannerisms, like looking all around without turning his head, talking without moving his lips, and walking with a chain-gang shuffle. That sounds horrible and he's not horrible—just subdued on the surface, though I doubt if it goes very deep. There's still a spark in the eye. But then, I was always partial to X for some strange reason. Appeal to my baser nature no doubt.

As to Alice. Yes. One thing you could do, and I would be eternally grateful, is inquire about her food shopping. She tries to do it herself at some little neighborhood supermarket, but if it is cold, windy, stormy she can't go out. Wind bothers her eyes dreadfully and causes great pain. I get the feeling from talking with her that she is often without some basics that she needs and is getting by on maybe a can of soup. When she does shop she can't carry a hell of a lot. She hates to ask for help (so do I), but if you could offer to pick up a few items for her? I *know* this is a pain, so don't try to kid me. I loathe food shopping. But it would really be a kindness. Laying up treasures in Heaven or something.

Alice's landlady is going co-op. Alice has no intention of buying as she plans to move near Dinah as soon as her doctors say it is OK. (She has, by the way, *two* eye specialists, as her eyes present two different problems. Does that not strike you as being the last word in something-or-other?) Anyhow, Alice is afraid that the apt. will be sold out from under her before it is safe for her to go, so she keeps it looking like a slum so that any prospective buyer will take one look and say, "Forget it." So don't be appalled at anything you may find.

Monday the 5 February [1979]
Dear Condon:

Yesterday I talked with Alice and she said you had called her offering to shop for her and she refused. I asked her why, for God's sake, when it would be such a help, and she said because she just couldn't face you in her condition for fear of shocking you. She says she looks frightful and so does her apartment. She has lost weight (she was skin and bones already), one of her eyes is partially sewed shut and her hair is a mess as she can't see to comb it properly. I can see her point, and I suppose I ought to be glad she has enough spirit left to care. But I feel awful about asking you to do this only to be turned down, which I certainly didn't anticipate. I apologize and thank you from the bottom of my heart for trying. But I guess you can't help those who won't accept help. Anyhow, you have surely made points with me and with her (she seemed very touched that you offered) and with Heaven, for that matter. For what that's worth.

Did you know Jean Oser? (Made the movie *Lobstertown.*) Your parents and g'mother did, I know, so they may be interested to learn that last night he called up Joe Young from Saskatchewan (where he teaches) to say that he is going to re-marry. A Canadian girl (woman?) and he wants to marry in Corea in the spring. He wanted Joe to find out the law about marrying a Canadian in Maine. This will be a blow to Q who had plans of her own for him—and for any other pair of pants so misguided as to cross her path.

Friday the 23 Feb. [1979]
Dear Hortense:

Yes, I admit freely that I now owe you two letters, of which this is
#1. My problem is subject matter. There is very little going on
and practically nothing worth reporting. However—the weather
is always a good last resort. Lack of snow cover has allowed the
frost to penetrate and practically everyone has frozen water
pipes. I've escaped that fate so far. Two nights ago it suddenly
and mysteriously became warm (well, up to 40) and poured rain.
To-day is sunny, windy and not too cold. In fact, I was able to dry
my washing outdoors.

Alice arrived safely at Dinah's yesterday. I talked briefly with
both of them last night, and everyone seemed happy and relieved. Me, too. This is a load off my mind.

[No, I haven't read] *The Immigrants* because I had a fight
with Howard Fast some years ago and swore I'd never crack a
book of his. I know this is childish at this late date, but frankly, I
don't give a damn.

As you no doubt read in the Ellsworth paper one of the S
boys got murdered last week. This should have created a lot of
local excitement, but the timing was bad. It came during the
week of basketball tournaments and so caused hardly a ripple.
I'll be glad when the stupid things are over. That's all we can get
on radio or TV, and who cares? Well, lots of people, evidently,
but I'm not among them.

Wed. the 7 March [1979]
Dear Hortense:

Okay, here's the second of the two letters we agreed I owe you—
though I still don't have anything earth-shaking to report. At Town
Meeting the proposed new Town Office was turned down, which
is good for the tax payers.

My sister is installed with Dinah and by all accounts is happy
and comfortable. I don't think she realized how desperate her
straits were until the pressure was gone.

My friend Virginia Rich has had another heart attack, I'm very
sorry to say. She called me from Arizona the other day and didn't
sound too hot, although I could tell that she was trying hard for
the light touch.

My eyes are still driving me crazy, but I hope for better things after I get the other one done next month.

This is all—Happy Lent!

Saturday the 28 April [1979]
Dear Condon:

Daylight savings starts to-night, thank God. My damn cat goes by the sun, and I'm sick of being waked up at 4:15 a.m. and told to get up and on the ball with the can opener.

Not much news here, really. X has been out clipping the long grass in the cracks of the ledge by his garage. He's a terrible old woman—prissy, prissy, prissy. I don't think he and G. find life here quite the Pastoral Idyll they pictured.

Did you see X while you were here? Thank the Lord I have been delivered from the perils of homosexual love; so far, at least, and I figure I'm pretty safe at this late date. Heterosexual love has offered problems enough without fancy complications.

My sister is with Dinah and getting blinder and blinder. But she's learning Braille and taking a course at the Perkins Institute for the Blind, so hopes to get an apt. of her own in a couple of months. I'm going to have my other eye operated on next Friday, and after that hope to be better. I'm not too sanguine. I'm not sure whether I can take another long recovery period. It's one frustration after another, so that you end by being constantly irritated and therefore bitchy. Thank Heaven I live alone and can take out my spleen by kicking furniture rather than people.

Dwight just drove past with Stonewall [dog] regal beside him. I'll bet it's gorgeous over at Easterly II to-day. I can hear the sea pounding clear over here.

Sunday the 29 April [1979]
Dear Hortense:

. . . Rufus and Jane were here Easter. Jane arrives [back] Wednesday and I go into the hospital Thursday. I'm getting itchy—eager to have the whole thing over with. I really dread the long recovery period, but I've lived through it once and will probably survive again.

Wednesday the 18 July [1979]
Dear Hortense:

Dinah and Matt were here last week and I haven't gotten over it
yet, even though there were only two of them, they were no trouble at all, I was happy to see them, and Dinah did all the work—
what little there was. but to one who is used to being alone, just
having others around is tiring and confusing. Dinah reports that
Alice is doing very well. She hasn't found an apt. yet, as there are
a great many conditions to be met. It has to be on the ground
floor, near Dinah, small, etc. But Dinah is confident that if they
persist, the right one will eventually turn up. While Dinah was
gone, Alice did well on her own. Ray [Dinah's husband] was
home nights, of course, so she wasn't completely isolated.

Our recent soap opera is about the same except that G is
about to fight back a little. I had dinner with her over at Hester
Hopkins the other night and on the drive home she talked freely.
She has fallen in with some lesbians who rent a cottage over at
Birch Harbor and entertains them quite a lot and reported very
gleefully that this bugs Z—since she can see all this activity from
her Love Nest—and goes over to G's to tell her how much it
hurts. Tit for tat. I am happy to say that G keeps right on taking a
nice healthy bitchy pleasure in it. If things have not straightened
out by next summer, G is going to England with two of these
women. I hope she does.

The log cabin [Cranberry Point] is rented to a family from So.
Carolina, the head of which looks, and sounds, exactly like Billy
Carter before he was Reconstructed and stopped drinking and
lost weight.

Sunday the 12 Aug. [1979]
Dear Hortense:

I got my permanent glasses Friday and so far can see very little
improvement. My equilibrium is still off and I'm slightly nause-
ated all the time. However, the doctor said I'll have to allow
about two weeks for adjustment, so that's what I'm doing, having
very little choice in the matter.

The J [divorce/custody] mess is still simmering along its rather
sordid and stupid way. (*Why* do I dislike that young man so
much? He has never done a thing to me.)

. . . And I guess that's all, except that my sister is moving into her own apt. this week.

Sunday the 25 November [1979]
Dear Hortense:

Well, Thanksgiving and the deer hunting season are both over, so things can relax to their normal state of confusion.

I'm sure you must have known H, T's wife? Well, H died very suddenly on Thanksgiving eve. She was sitting in her living room, felt chilly, reached for a sweater, and toppled over. This was a great shock to everyone. T has been having an affair with J for the past two years, which made H's life miserable, and H's mother Mrs. D refused to go to her daughter's funeral as she never wanted to lay eyes on T's face again. You can imagine what grist for the gossip mill that was! She's gone now to live with her other daughter, which is probably just as well.

[Betty] continues to be not well at all and a real problem. She's abusive, which isn't like her at all. Most people now lock their doors when they see her coming, but this doesn't prevent her from using the telephone. She calls people up and gives them hell over things they never did. This is all sad, and someone ought to take steps, but who? ,

The weather here is very odd—really quite warm and a lot of fog. My forsythia is coming out, of all things. I can only assume that The Almighty is cognizant of the energy situation and taking steps.

Dénouement

By 1980, President Jimmy Carter was confronted with the Soviets invading Afghanistan and Iranians invading the U.S. embassy in Tehran. There were female heads of state in Iceland and India (which was also the seventh nation to put a satellite into orbit). John Lennon was shot, as was J.R. of the TV show *Dallas*. The U.S. population topped a quarter of a billion. Mount St. Helens erupted in the Northwest, and a killing heat wave hit the Southeast. Iran and Iraq went to war. Ronald Reagan became president and suspended aid to El Salvador. *Camelot*, on Broadway, and *Kramer vs. Kramer* at the movies, reflected family breakups and increased divorces. *Voyager I* reached Saturn and discovered six new moons. Microbes were being created synthetically.

Closer to home, Louise philosophically shared her latest news with Hortense:

June 18—Wed. [1980]

Did I tell you my landlord very apologetically told me that he is putting this house up for sale? I'm not especially disturbed. In the first place, at the rate real estate is moving here now, I've got plenty of time and will probably, in fact, be able to spend the rest of my Sunset Years right where I am, if I want to. In the second place, L. has been offered a job in California and gone out there to see about it. If he takes it, I can have his house, which he doesn't want to sell. It's a much better house than this one with a great view of the harbor. If he doesn't take it, I'm back to square one, but with plenty of time to worry about it.

Tuesday 5 August [1980]

The woman who now owns my old house at the Sands has had a well drilled in the front driveway. She is spending a lot of money on the place, which is a mistake, I think. I loved that house, but it was really gone beyond repair, even when I lived there.

L. is not back *yet* so I don't know when or where I am moving and at this point don't care much.

Virginia Rich just had her *fifth* heart-by-pass operation and reported doing OK. She wants to come here in Sept., but I doubt if she makes it. However, she's pretty rugged, so she may. X and Y almost visibly decline from day to day. It's really sad; feeble and can't remember a thing. (But which of us can?)

Saturday the 8 Nov. [1980]

Don't expect much from this note, as I haven't much to say; just thought I'd keep the lines of communication open.

Marcia reports that she has lost 45 pounds as a result of her brother's death; and in the telling of that, we (of course!) go back to The Passing of Saint George, told in every detail with embell-ishments that are blatantly Apocryphal. She forgets that I, too, knew George.

My friend Virginia Rich is on Cranberry Point [she built a house down the road from the Albrights' log cabin] and says she is recovering well from her heart surgery.

However, Louise's plans for staying in Corea soon fell through, and she moved into a house near Dinah (who was once again single):

I continue to love Mattapoisett, even though I get lamer and lamer. But I would have been just as lame in Corea, or more so, with no Dinah to do my errands for me. My poor blind sister, on the other hand, walks two miles a day with her white cane, more power to her. But I'd rather be in my shoes than hers, believe me.

Matthew remembers a "three- to four-room house across from Gib-bons Beach, near the town wharf, full of books and coastal things. It got blown away by a hurricane the year after she left it."

Saturday 17 January [1981]

. . . Thursday Matthew came over here on an errand and I asked him why he wasn't in school. He said they had the day off "be-cause it was King Luther's birthday." Wouldn't you think the teacher would have explained who Martin Luther King was and given a rendition of "We Shall Overcome"? They don't make teachers like they used to in my day. . . .

Last night we had eight more inches of snow and it's still coming down. It's very pretty since I don't have to go out in it or shovel it.

Enough of this hogwash. I love all of you!

Saturday the 25 April [1981]
[This note was written on Forest Lodge stationery.]

Just checking in to let you know that I am still alive and kicking, although with somewhat less vigor than of yore. Age taking its toll, I guess. At that, I've outdone the rest of the family. Dinah and Alice have both had the flu, Alice is having her teeth out next week, Jane had an automobile accident that put her in the hospital for a week, and Matt is still recovering from the excesses of a combined Easter and Passover, which fell on the same day this year and involved being whipped from Easter service at the Congregational Church in Mattapoisett to his grandmother Z's feast in Boston. He's nothing if not ecumenical—and probably confused.

Marcia informs me that H passed away last week at the age of ninety-odd—although I didn't think she was that old. Marcia's account would lead me to believe that she was drunk (Marcia, I mean) if I didn't know better. Either that or on dope. Which I also doubt, so will give you the story as truth until I find out differently.

It seems that H gave "Ann" and "Alan Adams" of Prospect Harbor, who worked for her and more or less looked after her, explicit instructions about what she wanted done after demise. She wanted absolutely no truck with undertakers, funerals, and all that nonsense, but simply to have her body carted to Auburn for cremation by the cheapest and most convenient method possible. And—Ann and Alan being very literal minded—that is just what H got. The Adams [sic] collected the body at the Nursing Home with their pick-up truck, wrapped it up in a blanket, stowed it in the back, and hi-ho for Auburn. Can you quite believe that? It seems to me that if Alan had been stopped by the police for any one of a number of reasons, he would have had quite a lot of explaining to do.

Tuesday, June 16 [1981]

Thank you so much for your birthday card. I can't tell you how wonderful it was to see your own handwriting after all this time! I deduce that your eyes are progressing well. Can you do any reading yet? To me, the ability to read again was the biggest reward of the operation. I am continually grateful. I swear I'll never, never again take sight for granted!

I had a chance to ride up to Corea the other day and turned it down. I found—rather to my surprise—that I had not the slightest desire to go there again. When I think of the place, what comes to mind is sunlight and long walks around the shore and the beauty of Cranberry Point and the Sands, and all of us whipping around like crazy. It has finally sunk in that there is as much (or more) fog as sunshine, I couldn't walk around the shore now if you paid me, Cranberry Point is built up with shacks and the boatyard, the Sands has changed, and my whipping around days are long gone. So at last I accept that one can't turn the clock back and if one tries to one is going to be very sadly disappointed. So Corea, R.I.P. You know, I think Josey left us at just the right time, for her. She was never happy with what was done to the old homestead and although she fought it bravely, she too had begun to discover physical limitations. Gee, I didn't mean to get into that morbid strain!

Dinah just came in moaning and groaning because tomorrow is the last day of school and she is not pleased at the prospect of three boys [she remarried and had two stepsons] under foot all summer. I did not sympathize, pointing out to her that it was the common lot of mothers and I, too, had been there; the chief difference being that while I only had two to cope with, one was a girl and the nuisance value of girls was about three times that of boys. She changed her tune with a paean of thanksgiving that she had no daughter to deal with. I didn't tell her that when she got to be my age, she'd thank God she had a daughter. I'll save that until later.

Friday the 18 Sept. [1981]

... I'm currently reading John Brook's *Showing Off in America* which I find highly entertaining. It's a sort of application of Veblen's theory of the leisure class to present day living. Unfortunately it tends to make one (this one, at least) a bit self-conscious, so that I hardly dare draw a deep breath for fear I'm exhibiting conspicuous consumption. . . . On the other hand, it points out a lot of things you can observe in others and feel superior about, which is always a comfort. If, that is, you are as mean-minded as I am.

I have a feeling that we are going to have an early fall and a long hard winter. So I am about to offer prayers of thanks that my landlord pays the oil bill and to go out and buy votive candles to burn in favor of his not raising the rent.

So toodle-oo!

Tuesday the 27 Oct. [1981]

By this time, you must be back from Corea. How was the trip? Did you have nice weather? What's the latest gossip? How did the Easterlies [cabins] survive the summer? . . . If I had any Peninsula news—which I haven't—I would spare you it, as you undoubtedly know much more at this point (In Time! GRRR—I hate that expression) than I do. Only one thing: Virginia Rich writes me that she receives visits frequently from Betty. What interested me was that—in spite of all she has heard about Betty's oddities (shall we say?)—Virginia finds her much more intelligent and entertaining than much of the rest of the local population. Since this corroborates my own long-held opinion, I was pleased to hear it.

Did you see Marcia? How does she look? She keeps telling me how thin she is, and how miserable, but I'd like a disinterested witness, as I can't judge how much of that is true and how much Marcia's well-developed flair for Tragic Drama.

Things here plod along routinely. Last week Dinah and Ray took a little vacation, so I went (with my cat) over to her house and rode herd on the boys. They were good as gold, but all that youth and activity exhausted me. The Young have never been my favorite people.

Harper and Row want me to revise *again* (I've already done it three times) *The Coast of Maine*. I said *no*. I'm too tired and besides, bored with the whole thing. However, they asked me to find someone else to do it, and Rufus' wife Jane said she would. (She is competent to do it, and willing.) So there that stands.

Went to the doctor for the first time in well over a year and wish I'd stayed home. He told me (a) that my blood pressure is dangerously high; (b) that the only thing that can be done about my rapidly advancing lameness is an operation on my hip (to which I responded with a resounding NO); and (c) that if I'd lose forty pounds I'd be a lot better off. I know he's right about that. What I resent is his cleverly shifting all the responsibility onto my shoulders—where, to be fair, I guess it belongs. Oh, well—

Tuesday the 9 Feb. [1982]

Thank you so much for the clipping about Emily Dickinson and for the snapshot. You've lost weight, haven't you, since the last time I saw you. Good—I guess. At least, "Lose weight" seems to be all doctors' theme song, including my own Dr. Howard, who assured me I'd feel *so much better* with less poundage. I'd like to know when this surge of well-being is supposed to begin. I've lost twenty-five pounds and feel not one whit better; worse, if anything. But I persevere, hoping to shed twenty more pounds and leap around like an athletic gazelle. Hah!

Marcia called the other night, and she was in fine fettle— more cheerful than I have ever known her to be. She has a new doctor (that old one was a public menace *I* thought) who has pre- scribed potassium for her, and she feels great. Didn't have a sin- gle catastrophe to report or a single character to destroy. This merits mention in the Guinesses [*sic*] Book.

Virginia Rich is still in Corea and loving it. Young Joey Young comes in every day and she loves him dearly.

Yes, I enjoy *Brideshead Revisited* very much, and you're right—it does follow the book very closely. I have Cable TV, which is loaded with worthwhile programs (as well as X-rated things which I find supremely boring. I really don't see how peo- ple can be shocked at them—they are so adolescent). I guess what I like most are the discussion programs, although Sunday I did watch Faulkner's *The Reivers* and simply loved it. But I'm a Faulkner fan from way back.

My family seems to be operating smoothly. Jane is visiting her mother in New Jersey, and I assume that Rufus is managing to feed himself. Dinah's shop [children's clothing on consignment] is doing very well indeed; Matt got a wonderful report card from his new private school; [his father] has remarried a widow with three kids; and Alice is absorbed in her music and talking [audio] books. She has adjusted so well to her blindness!

Now it's time for me to go prepare my feast of lettuce leaves, cottage cheese and diet pears, trying to make it look like a banquet on the plate. How I would *love* a banana split!

Saturday 8 May [1982]
Dear Hortense and family:

Right now, if I figure a-right, you must be almost in Corea. I don't know whether I envy you or not. At last Spring seems to have arrived here and Mattapoisett is simply foaming with spring flowers, blossoming shrubs and leafing trees. The harbor below my window is suddenly full of boats after an empty winter. I know all about the simple, cleancut lobsterboats—in fact, I have written my share of words in praise of them—but I must admit that some of these expensive pleasure boats are absolutely beautiful. If this be degeneracy, make the most of it! Marcia said the other day when she called me that Corea is still fairly bleak and cold, which accounts for my being perfectly satisfied with my present situation. These arthritic bones can use a bit of sunshine.

I have absolutely no news to pass on. In fact, by the time you get this, you will know a great deal more about goings-on in Corea than I do. I'm trusting you to pass on all the dirt.

Have you ever heard anything as silly as the Argentine–Great Britain business [disputing over the Falkland Islands]? Gilbert and Sullivan in full cry. It would be hilarious if it weren't so dangerous. Everybody involved should be sat down and given what my mother used to call "a good talking to." Though, as I remember it, from Alice's and my point of view, there was nothing *good* about them. Terrifying is more like it.

I have an ear infection so that my outer ear is three times its normal size and bright purple. I look exactly like an old beat-up prize-fighter with a cauliflower ear—a delectable sight in anyone's language.

Everyone else around here is about as usual which means that my sister can't see, Dinah is working toward getting into her last year's bathing suit (three pounds more to go, she estimates) and we'll happily farm Matthew out to anyone who'll take him. The pre-adolescent madness has him in its grip. I'm sure you remember putting up with those symptoms, most annoying of which (I guess) is the inability to remember anything for two seconds. And a Happy Mother's Day to you, Jack[son] and Hortense!

Sunday the 19 Sept. [1982]
Dearest Hortense

Since we talked Friday, I've thought of you a lot. I was distressed
that you seemed so sad and forlorn, somehow. I didn't understand exactly why you had been at High Ridge [nursing home]
for the past three weeks, but gathered that it had to do with a
health problem. If so, I certainly pray that whatever it was is now
under control. But I think the chief reason for your being at rather
low ebb is disappointment about not going to Corea with all the
family. Believe me, I understand how you feel. Left out and
alone, while everyone else is having fun. It's only natural. But
please try to remember that they all truly love you (They do, you
know!) and are acting out of real concern for your welfare. All of
us—and we are many—who love you want what is best for you;
and I honestly don't think that long trip and the isolation of The
Island are what is best. I'm sure they would worry whenever it
was necessary to leave you alone; and I'm equally sure you don't
want that. Growing old is not easy, I have found. I, too, have my
twinges of regret when Dinah and her family take off on an
expedition leaving me home alone. But I don't want to be a burden or a damper of spirits (who does?), so— For so many years,
you were the center and heart and guiding light of all your family. You gave so much of yourself. Alice and I were talking the
other day and both agreed that one of the hardest things about
being old is that one feels so useless, with nothing to offer. But I
guess nothing can be done about that except to try to learn to adjust and accept gracefully. Which—for me at least—is damned
difficult.

Hester Hopkins (friend of sixty years with a place in South
Gouldsboro) has just lost her husband of fifty years and has asked
me to visit her in S.G. I wish I could, but I simply can't. I would
only be a nuisance, I'm so lame and crippled. And I'm not sure I
want to, come right down to it. The Peninsula is not what it was.
It's seen its best days, and we were lucky enough to be there
when it was at its prime. For that we can be grateful.

I'm enclosing a review of Virginia Rich's book. (She will arrive in Corea Sept. 22 and stay at least until February.) I'm so
pleased for her that her book is doing well. After all, she's 65,
hampered by a very bum heart (five by-pass operations) and has

never written before, except [a magazine short story in 1945 and] a food column in a Chicago paper. She deserves a lot of credit.

Got to go and listen to David Brinkley now and see what he has to say about the simply appalling events in West Beirut [bombing of the U.S. Embassy]. All the news is so shocking now, it seems to me. I was really sad to hear of Grace Kelly's death, and so young. She was apparently a really lovely woman, in deed as well as looks.

Keep up a good heart and do know that I and all who know you, admire and love you!

October 31, 1982
Dear Sandy [Phippen]:

Thank you for sending me the copy of *The Police Know Everything* and for the flattering inscription, slightly inaccurate as it may be. It is my belief that nobody can help anybody to write. Either you've got it (in which case help is unnecessary), or you haven't (and there is no help). You've got it. I enjoyed the book thoroughly; felt right at home with the more or less zany characters, whose prototypes I know well.

Good luck to you in your future efforts, which I hope will be many.

Sat. the 6 Nov. [1982]
Dear Hortense:

The nicest thing just happened to me! I feel I must share it with you.

Right after reading Amy Clampitt's poem in the NYer [*New Yorker*], I wrote her a note and sent it to Corea—sort of like putting a note in a bottle and throwing it into the sea. It caught up with her somewhere in the mid-west, where she was travelling; and yesterday I received her answer. She said she'd been going to Corea since 1974 and was indebted to me for finding the place. Then—here comes the nice part—she asked if she could dedicate her next book of poems, which will include *What the Light Was Like,* to me. Can you imagine? I feel so flattered and honored; this on top of Virginia Rich dedicating her first book to me! I know I don't deserve this, but I like it anyhow.

Clampitt's first book of poems, *The King Fisher,* will be published by Knopf in January and she said she'd have one sent me, as several of them are about Corea. I'm looking forward to that, as I think her work is really outstanding. If Jack's [Jackson Rodgers—Hortenses' daughter, Floyd's wife, Condon's mother] library ever buys poetry, maybe she might keep this in mind. I know you'd like to see it.

The weather here has at last become seasonable—cold, windy, brilliant, after about six weeks of Indian summer. I really prefer this at this time of year, although it raises hell with the old arthritis. I can hardly get around, which affronts my pride. I never was the world's best housekeeper, and my "pad" (we must be with-it at all costs!) is a dusty shambles. A preview of things to come, like The Grave, no doubt.

Rufus fell down and broke two ribs. Matthew has poison ivy. Dinah is on a diet and slightly edgy. In short, everything around here is more or less normal.

Friday 31 Dec. [1982]

Ring out the Old, Ring in the New, and all that good stuff. It hasn't been a bad year for me personally; but for so many of my friends it has been; to say nothing of the state of the world in general. On the other hand, I really can see little hope for improvement in 1983. But let's not go into that—I shall celebrate the coming of the New Year by going to bed at 9:00 as usual.

I haven't much news from Corea. K just wrote that her mother-in-law fell down in her room the day before Christmas and broke her hip. (Let that be a lesson for you and me to be careful!) Marcia gets more and more cheerful every time I talk to her, which puzzles me some. Virginia Rich is still there and will be for an indefinite period. Her husband says that he prefers her to be there as she is much nearer a hospital and ambulance service than she would be on the ranch in Arizona. G. spent Xmas with L. and then took off for Cape Cod to see my old friend Hester Rich Hopkins, and then on to Connecticut to spend New Years with some lesbian friends.

It's still warm here, and I really don't like it, although I suppose this could be termed tempering the wind for the shorn lamb and its fuel bills.

Sunday, 13 Feb. [1983]

At long last it finally looks like a proper winter! We've had two serious snow storms in the past week; yesterday's netted us 23" on top of the 8" left from last week. I gather from the various news reports (which seem to be overly excited by a purely natural phenomenon like a blizzard) that you too got the storm, so I won't dwell on it further, except to say that to-day the sun is out and the glare is so terrific that I'm wearing sun glasses in the house and still am having more than normal trouble typing. So forgive errors.

Virginia Rich writes me that Sandy Phippen went to her house to tea last Sunday. She liked him and found him amusing. That must have been an interesting confrontation since both of them are (in my opinion) over-zealous self-promoters when it comes to their books. Having been brought up by the rule "Self praise goes but little ways" and taught from the cradle to keep a low profile, I find this slightly distasteful. However, I guess it's generally accepted as OK. In this particular case, I'd think probably Virginia had a slight edge, as she is older and Sandy is well-mannered. Virginia's husband has bought her a word processor "to make writing easier for her." I wasn't sure exactly what these things are, so asked my son-in-law Ray (who deals in them) to explain. His first reaction was, "My God, she'll have to sell a hell of a lot of books to pay for that!" Seems they sell for like $8,000 to $10,000. Virginia's husband is very much concerned about her health and really does want to do everything he can to please her.

You no doubt saw in the [*Ellsworth*] *American* about the drowning of A and T's son-in-law. I thought it was sad—only been married seven months. (The Albrights paid for the wedding to the tune of $6,000; most elaborate wedding in Corean history, I'm told, with the bride's train six yards long.) Anyhow, Ruth Young writes me that the young widow is carrying on like crazy (which seems normal to me), but my guess is, it won't be long before she's shacked up with someone else. Ruth incidentally writes very good letters, newsy and funny.

Marcia seems to be improving in health and spirits all the time. I'd almost say she's enjoying life. Too bad she didn't start sooner. Although, I guess her Calamity Jane role was her idea of fun, come to think of it.

Monday, April 11 [1983]

Dear Hortense

Well, I suppose by now the Rodgers are safely in China. That seems to be where everyone is going nowadays. I was trying to decide the other day where I would go if I had a choice, and the only thing I was sure of was that it would *not* be China or Japan. Spain, maybe? Or New Zealand? It's purely academic. I'm not going anywhere.

High Ridge sounds very nice indeed. I know it's not home, but at our age we've learned that the world is not run for our own personal benefit and to accept whatever comes our way. I imagine that you have your TV with you, and I hope it's as much company for you as mine is for me. The Public channels have so much good stuff on them now! I enjoy David Attenborough's environmental programs especially.

Virginia Rich is still in Corea finishing her third book, laid in Nantucket. The one laid in Corea comes out May 26. I've read the galley proofs and don't think she has caught the flavor of the place, though I didn't tell her that. Her characters are largely Paul Bunyan types, about whom I know little. One native is based on Forrest Young, with whom she was friendly. I must say that her Forrest and my Forrest are two different people.

My family is as usual. One of Dinah's stepsons has been accepted by Maine Maritime Academy and is happy about that. Matthew is entering his teens typically: suddenly fussy about his hair and clothes, and more or less a pain in the neck. I trust he'll grow out of that. Jane has been re-elected to her third term as selectman of Andover, Maine, so I guess she's doing a good job.

And this is all, except I love you!

Saturday the 30 July [1983]

Don't expect too much of this note. The heat and humidity have got me down and addled my brains—what there are of them. I really wish they wouldn't publicize all these new diseases all the time. Now they've almost convinced me that I have Alzheimer's disease: can't remember a thing from one minute to the next. Not that I have anything very important to remember, when you come right down to it.

I have been thinking a lot about you since our telephone

conversation, and I'm so sorry that you seem to be unhappy. It's very easy for me to say that happiness lies in the end within ourselves, and that we are in control of it. Very easy, but I'm not entirely sure that it's true, especially when we reach our age.

We are so at the mercy of our failing bodies and of other people. When we were young and full of energy, we could more or less direct our destinies: take a long brisk walk if we didn't like what was going on around us; cook up a great meal if we were bored; clean house if we were angry. Now we have to sit and take it—with a smile, if we can manage that. It's pretty frustrating. I guess what we're reduced to is developing the ability to take things in stride—difficult, because the older we get the tireder we get. Maybe that's a wise provision of Nature, to wear us down to the point where we no longer care what happens. I myself am getting to that point fast.

I didn't mean to get going like that. Just talking off the top of my head. Sorry.

I see in the *American* that Arline Shaw is selling her house at the Sands. Probably some developer will buy it and cut the 700 acres up into lots. There are some nice sites there, especially across the road from the house, by the beach. Too bad. It will ruin the area.

Ruth Young writes me that Shawn Benoit is the best and politest yard man she's ever had; she is not one to take much nonsense. She also said that Burnham's riding lawn mower rolled over on him, but luckily he wasn't badly hurt. Marcia seems in good shape. She's stopped driving her car but is keeping it for old times sake, and in memory of the sanctified George. I'd never dare say it to her, but the day she lost him was a turning point for the better in her life. After the initial shock, she became a free woman for the first time in her life.

Well, enough of this! I'm not even sure I'll mail this. It isn't much of a letter for one friend to send another. Love as always.

Thursday the 1 Sept. [1983]
Dear Jack[son]:

Thanks for returning the V. Rich book. I myself was not too impressed with it (and I'm a whodunit addict). But I think she deserves a lot of credit for starting a new career at the age of 70 and in poor health. It's not all that easy to break into print at any age.

I understand that your mother is back home. I do understand her wish to be there, but I also understand your pressures. I'd hoped she'd become oriented to High Ridge and settle content-edly to the life there. You'd all be a great deal happier. BUT—please don't tell her I said so. She'd with reason feel that I am being disloyal and be hurt, which is the last thing I want to have happen! But I also want you to know that I see your problem all too clearly and sympathize.

My life-long friend Hester Rich Hopkins of Truro, Mass., and So. Gouldsboro I never suspected of having a sadistic streak. But she writes me that J has a new car and a new lover. I don't give a damn what kind of car it is; but don't you agree that failing to name the new love shows a cruel streak? I'm dying of curiosity!

Matthew broke his collar bone last month and now has a terrible case of poison ivy. Rufus was in an accident and is in a hospital in Nashville, Tenn., with a crushed knee and will proba-bly be there for at least ten weeks. Aside from that, my family is just fine.

Love and all that.

Friday the 16 Sept. [1983]
Dear Hortense:

Your being back home makes me happy for you!

Last night Marcia called to tell me that Malvin Albright had passed away (aged 86) in Fort Lauderdale, where they had been spending the summer. (They spent winters in Corea. Connie and Malvin really did make an effort not to be in step with the Com-mon Herd!) God knows (I certainly don't) what will now become of Connie. I wouldn't be surprised if she married again at this late date (she must be crowding 70), probably some smart and per-sonable young fortune-hunter. (This is obviously my day for being charitable to my fellow woman.)

You probably remember how crushed G was when Y left her for K. Well, G now has a new lover, a Professor at the University of V, and has recovered bravely. The prof. spent the summer with her, and this new dame sounds much more suitable. G, for all her sexual preferences (or possibly because of them?) is one of the most able and intelligent women I have ever known, a really good person.

At long last the weather here is seasonable: cool and crisp and lovely after some horrible heat and humidity. My poor cat is infested with fleas in spite of my best efforts with sprays and collars. She's driving both herself and me crazy, scratching. Oh, for a nice killing frost!

I am waiting to learn the outcome of Rufus' operation. Did I tell you he was in an accident while driving a truck in Tennessee and has been in the Nashville hospital for three weeks with a crushed knee? They're going to try to put it together again. I'm concerned. Knees are tricky. He will be in the hospital for another month or so and then in a cast for five months. He seems to be taking the whole thing with much better grace than I would have anticipated. The State cops of Tenn. consider him a hero. He crashed himself rather than a solid line of passenger cars, which would have resulted in many deaths and more injuries. I'm proud of him, but I still wish it hadn't happened.

Aside from that, we all seem to be plugging along. Matthew is back in school and loving it. Dinah's stepson is at ME Maritime and loving it. (Whatever became of the old convention of hating school? In my day, if you admitted to liking it, you were considered an absolute drip.) My sister Alice seems fine. I get lamer by the minute. Dinah is well and has just had her hair cut because she thinks that long hair is unsuitable to those over forty, which she is.

And this is all.

Saturday the 22 Oct. [1983]
Dear Jack[son]:

I am very much distressed by your mother's condition; which means I am even more distressed about the situation it puts you in. She called me up a while ago and for the first time ever seemed to realize the stress she is putting on you. She also sounded sorry for herself, which is bad and I have never found to be typical of her. About now, I gather she will be going back to High Ridge—a very good thing for all of you. I found it hard to talk to her, as I wanted to give moral support, but didn't know what to say. What does one say? I think she called chiefly because she wanted sympathy from someone near enough her own age to understand. Believe me, I do! But I also understand that leaving one's husband's bed for whatever good reason isn't the friendliest thing in the world to do. In the early autumn of life it's cozy to have someone to cuddle with (if nothing else) on these cold nights. (I could pursue this subject further and in greater detail, but I guess I won't.) I'm not about to hurt my old friend your mother by drawing diagrams for her, but what I will do is write her in an attempt to cheer her up.

Rufus got back from Tennessee OK, but after two months in bed was very weak. Now, unfortunately he is back in the Rumford (Maine) hospital with several problems. But he's taking it pretty well, glad at least to be near friends and in Maine, his idea of Heaven. (Mine, too.)

Thursday the 1 December [1983]
Dear Hortense:

Rufus and Jane came down from Maine and I was very glad to see them so I could judge Rufus' condition for myself. He's in better shape than I had anticipated. He's at last—after three months—out of the cast and on crutches, and his morale seems good. He is confident that he will eventually be able to go back to truck driving. I doubt it very much, but perhaps I am underestimating his determination. I hope so.

We made a jolly pair. I have at last given in and got a walker. I hated to do it. It seems like a long step in the wrong direction. I guess my problem is mostly mental. I'll freely admit that physically it is a great help. I feel much more secure and have much less pain getting around. But it appears to me a stigma of age, which is no doubt foolish. Better [to] be an old lady in a walker than an old lady lying on the floor with a broken hip.

I saw in *Time* magazine last week that Ivan Albright had died in VT where they lived. He didn't outlast Malvin long, which really didn't surprise me. The two of them were very close indeed, even for twins. In fact, when Ivan married, Malvin went to bed with his face to the wall for two weeks—which seems a bit extreme. Old A finally forcibly hauled him out and onto his feet.

I did not get one of those cards from Virginia Rich promoting her books. I'll have to admit that the whole thing surprised and

rather shocked me. I don't know why it should, really. Just because I wouldn't dream of doing such a thing is no good reason
why she shouldn't. Everybody to her own style, after all. Only I
didn't think that was her style. She has always seemed to me
unassuming and low-key. But there is an awful lot about that
family that I don't understand at all. I certainly wouldn't ask her
any questions about her personal life. And she, in turn, never
asks me about mine. She just sent me a big box of citrus fruit
for Thanksgiving, which was nice of her and completely
unnecessary.

I suppose Jack and Floyd [Rodgers, Jackson's husband] were
at High Ridge with you for the holiday. That seems to me to be a
good arrangement for all concerned. I'm sure you must find—as I
do—that getting out and around and meeting a lot of people is
tiring and confusing. In fact, I'm bracing myself now to tell Dinah
that I can't make it to her house for Christmas—and that's only
two blocks away. I went T'giving and was completely exhausted
for two days. All that talking! Which may sound odd coming
from me!

Approaching Christmas [1983]
Dear Jack—

Shortly before Thanksgiving I talked with your mother, who was
at High Ridge. I was really surprised at her complete change in
attitude. She seemed to have become adjusted and satisfied with
the idea that she is to be there more or less permanently. She
sounded happier than I have heard her for some time, which
made me happy, too.

For one thing, I was bitching to her about being in a walker
now (which I am, but resenting the doddering category it puts me
into) and I remarked that I guessed I'd have to see about getting a
woman to come in once a week to vacuum, etc. She simply
amazed me by saying that having someone come in was very un-
satisfactory. Up to that point she had told me repeatedly how
well it worked out with her and you-all. So I guess it was just
wishful thinking on her part. Now she seems to be facing facts,
which is great. She was never going to be anywhere near contented until she looked the truth in the eye. I'm sure you know

everything I've told you, but it's always good to have outside confirmation, I think.

I'm catching up on Barbara Pym. She really is terrific in a
quiet way. Too bad she died. Or maybe I like her because she
writes about older people, and I can identify.

January 1, 1984
Dear Hortense—

This is my first letter since 1983, so Happy New Year! For me,
1983 was a so-so year, distinguished only by being the Year of
the Walker, adoption of which is my formal recognition of the
fact that I really am Old. I don't have any great expectations
for the New year; only hopes that I can continue to operate on
my own.

Christmas was snowy, bitterly cold and very windy here, so I
stayed home with my old cat. We both enjoyed our peace very
much. My sister Alice and I talked on the phone and agreed that
it was a great relief not to be involved in any Yuletide whoop-la.
Dinah brought both of us our dinners, which was very nice.

My old friend Hester Rich Hopkins is about to take off for
Florida for two months. Alice and I were discussing it, and she
said that Florida was the last place she'd want to go. I agreed and
said that if I had a choice, I'd go somewhere in the Southwest,
like Taos. She pointed out that that area is having absolutely brutal weather this year, as is almost everywhere else. So we came
to the conclusion that staying right where we are is our best bet.
Considering the fact that that's what we're obliged to do anyhow,
that's a very comforting decision to have made.

Love as always, and good cheer!

Sunday, July 22 [1984]
Dear Hortense:

By the time you get this, you will probably have read about the
Corea drug bust in the *Ellsworth American*. Here, however, is the
Bangor Daily News account. The coverage seems to be both good
and accurate, according to Marcia. Nobody knows (yet) who the
anonymous informer was, although I'm sure that will come out
sooner or later.

The local opinion is that of course Tish [Albright] is deeply involved (wishful thinking) which I think highly unlikely. In fact, ridiculous. But you know the native mind: always eager to think the worst of those From Away. This particular rumor is based on some pipe-dream that Tish has a boy-friend who is in some way connected with whatever real estate agent rented her cottage to the smugglers. All very vague and probably false. I'm not even sure Tish has a boy-friend at all, although she very well may have. Although she is into her sixties, the last time I saw her (four years ago) she looked thirty-five and getting younger by the minute. She is really remarkable.

Nothing else to add. The weather here is killing me—the heat I don't mind, but the humidity is brutal. If it's any comfort to you (it isn't to me), Corea is just as bad.

Sat. the 25 August [1984; written to Hortense]

It's been a rather miserable summer—first half damp, foggy and chilly; second half hell-hot and horribly humid. Excellent grass-growing conditions, so that Matthew has amassed a fortune from his list of mowing clients. (Usually by August lawns are drying up and need no mowing at all.) He has a bigger bank account than I have, and true to his Jewish-Scotch-Yankee genes, hangs on to his money, which is more than I can say for myself. (But I'll bet I have more fun spending than he will have saving.)

Next week he enters Bishop Stang, a parochial High School (with, like most parochial Highs, an excellent reputation). He certainly has an ecumenical record: Jewish name, Congregational religious training, and now a Catholic school. Makes one wonder what kind of hodgepodge his spiritual persona (if any) will eventually be.

I know absolutely nothing about anything. One of Marcia's cat's died, cause for full-dress mourning: "Now I'm all alone in the world except for Mindy" (the other cat). Virginia Rich is doing fine. Has completed another book. She really buzzes along, once she got going. She loves her new little retreat—calls it "The Dotage" although I'd say she's far from her dotage at the moment. J has aged and become waspish apparently, but H is flourishing. Dick Shaw has a bushel basket of zucchini by the road in front of his house with a sign "Help Yourself." This verifies my impression that if you plant zucchini you are asking for trouble. You have to decide whether to (1) eat them three times a day for three months (nauseating thought), (2) throw them away (unthinkable to the Yankee Thrift Ethic), or (3) give them away (impossible, because everyone else has too many). Better to forget the whole thing.

My friend Hester Rich Hopkins has about decided to sell her South Gouldsboro place. It's really a lovely house overlooking Frenchman's Bay and quite secluded. Some architect friend of the Viberts [potter friends of Louise and Hester] planned it. [She kept it.]

In closing I will say that I know we all have new zip code numbers, but I am refusing to acknowledge the fact. This thing has gone too far. One more step and we'll all have no names at all, just a string of digits, and I won't think of my friends and my- self that way.

Your little individual—

Sept. 22—first day of Fall [1984; written to Hortense]

Not that I have anything to say, but thought I'd check in with you before Winter sets in. Did you see in the August 6 New Yorker (which I've just gotten around to) the four poems about Maine by Amy Clampitt? The subject matter is familiar to both of us, but I find the language a bit too ornate for such simple things. How- ever, that is just one non-poetic woman's opinion. Her second book of poems comes out next month.

Marcia tells me that Tish has put up for sale the southwest part of Cranberry Point. Don't know the asking price. That would be the point of land across the cove from the cabin reaching over to Shark's Cove; a really lovely area, but I would think unsuitable for building. Much too exposed to storms.

Virginia Rich was interviewed by a Federal Agent about that drug bust next door to her. She wasn't able to tell him a thing, since she minds her own business.

Matthew absolutely loves his parochial High School. He's obliged to take a course called Religion and may yet end up a priest—if not a rabbi.

This is it.

Thursday the 8 Nov. [1984]
Dear Jack—

Thank you very much for the Clampitt piece. I don't know her, although we have had some correspondence; but she and my friend Virginia Rich have become friends, and Virginia likes her and her companion very much. They both come from Iowa, which is a bond. Not *everybody* comes from Iowa!

Your mother called me and sounded very contented, so for God's sake (as well as your own) get off this guilt trip! I know, I know, you can't help it, but— Your mother told me that even thinking about taking that long trip to Maine tired her out, and she didn't want to go anyhow. I gathered that her last hoorah to Corea was not 100% unalloyed joy. What she wants (and who doesn't) is to turn back the clock and have everything just as it was thirty or forty years ago, herself included. I think she felt last time that the place and her old friends of yesteryear didn't exist any more—and of course they don't, really. So—

[1985]
Dear Jack:

I'm glad your mother finally bowed to the inevitable and consented to High Ridge. I hope she is still there. However, she is about ten years older than I am, and in another decade quite likely I'll be as set in my ways (if I live that long which I sincerely hope I don't!). I hope you are keeping the old guilt under control, or should I give you another lecture?

No, I didn't get the bulk mailing [regarding Rich's book] from Virginia Rich's husband, but the personal letter he wrote me was terrific. He and Virginia have a relationship that I have never completely understood, but which has seemed to be satisfactory for both of them. He's certainly coming through this thing nobly. I think he's in Corea at the moment and plans to be there as long as necessary.

I was sorry to hear of J's seizure. I think you know (or you may not) that my sister is an epileptic. The secret of successful treatment (she says) is absolute faithfulness in taking the medication, which in her case is dilanthin (I think that's right). Do you think that J takes his pills regularly and on the split second? It's very important, Alice says. She has had the condition under control for sixty years except for a couple of instances when she got stuck without medicine. I hope they find the solution for J very soon.

Got a letter from Ruth Young practically accusing me of being the writer responsible for *Murder, She Wrote* on TV. Good God, I never even heard of it or watched it, let alone wrote it (worse luck). She based her claim on the fact that one episode was laid in Maine.

I sent to the Bangor Library for that Chute book "The Beans of Something Maine" two months ago, but have not yet got it. Too long a waiting list and God forbid, at this point, that I buy it. The review made it sound like the Maine I know from up Rangeley-way.

Back Home

By 1986, things were going downhill. Rufus and Jane were divorcing and Louise's health had deteriorated. Dinah explains: "I used to come home from work and rush over to check on Ma and on Aunt Alice, bring them each meals, do the grocery shopping and laundry. [It got to the point where Dinah convinced her mother that it would be easier for all concerned if she would move in with her.] Several times I'd wake up in the middle of the night, so worried that something terrible had happened that I'd drive over and just peer in the window to make sure everything was all right. It was a relief to have Ma with me."

(Later, in 1994, Alice would move in with Dinah as well. She'd had a couple of falls, one of which created small fractures in her back and necessitated recuperating in a nursing home for several months. She died of a heart attack on February 7, 1996. She was cremated, and Dinah scattered her ashes along the nearby shore, as she had requested.)

Louise, coping with a failing body at age eighty-three, was still able to inject humor, local Maine news (omitted here), and philosophical straight talk into her letters:

Thursday the 15 May [1986]
Dear Jack—

No, I do not feel better. In fact, I feel worse. Just out of the hospital for the umpteenth time: slight stroke, impairing speech temporarily, but that's OK now. To lose the Rich power of speech would be the final irony.

So—I thank you, *thank you* for the wonderful idea and invitation. Normally, there is nothing I would like better. But I guess my trips to Maine will have to be by memory from now on; and maybe, considering all the changes and loss of friends— that's the best way.

Saturday, March 28 [1987]
Dear Rodgers [Jackson, Floyd, Condon]

You are quite right. I have never seen the side of T that has been revealed to you (for your sins, I guess). But I can well imagine it. She has money and talent, which more or less add up to power, which (as we all know) corrupts. Or so they say. Her territory and mine have never impinged, let alone over-lapped, so she has no need to bulge her biceps at me. In fact, she has always been almost deferential to me, which used to make me nervous.

Marcia in her old age is really living it up. She bought a microwave oven and called me up to tell me what wonderful popcorn it made. Now she has bought a police scanner, so she can keep track of Crime in Hancock County. The only drawback is that the cops give no names but only locations in their calls. But she knows the area well enough to be able to guess fairly accurately who is being arrested for what. Can't you just see her with her bowl of popcorn listening to her scanner? It more than takes the place of the sainted George.

I trust you survived your Japanese guests. Was it an interesting experience?

My sister Alice is well, thank you, and I'm slowly getting no younger—but aren't we all?

Sept. 4 [1987]
Dear Jack—

I'm sorry and abashed at this long silence (throughout which you have been so faithful!) but I've had a perfectly hellish summer, in and out of the hospital at regular intervals with respiratory problems. I hope they are now past history!

Nope, I haven't heard "Boo" from *Down East* Magazine or any publisher's note about LDR. I trust my agent is aware, but who knows? So I'll welcome your photocopy.

Congratulations on graduation from walker! I'm utterly dependent on mine, but at least I'm not in a wheelchair or bedridden (yet, should I say, lest I be tempting Fate?).

Somehow I can't quite see Corea with an arty-crafty shop named Two Sisters. Too cute for words, and cuteness has no place in the Corea I knew. Virginia Rich's daughter, Susan, tells me that Amy Clampitt is now poet-in-residence at Amherst College.

And I guess this is all I know, except that Marcia has finally shed her mourning clothes for her old cat of sainted memory and got a new one.

Thus ends the collection of Rodgers family letters. From this point on, Louise continued to decline. While in the hospital during the summer, she quit smoking her Lucky Strikes cold turkey, and she was no longer drinking. Tests uncovered the fact that she had an enlarged heart, which was contributing to her respiratory problems. It was very difficult for her to get around because, in addition to her breathing difficulties, her arthritis was becoming more painful. Consequently, she was forced to sit most of the time. Dinah relates:

> Fortunately, she never lost her eyesight and could knit, watch TV, and, of course, read. She used to consult the *New York Times Book Review* and check off what she wanted me to get from that, in addition to her mysteries. She'd go through five books a week.
>
> Then Ma developed an abscess on her spine because she had to sit so much, and she went from her chair to a bed. It was tough because she was such an outdoors woman and now she couldn't get out. I bought a bird feeder, the kind you can attach to a window, so she could watch the birds. And the dog and cats loved her. In fact Trevor, my German shepherd slept with Ma in what used to be the den. I told her not to feed him sweets, but I could tell they had this thing going. One day I came in and found a treat on the floor and I asked her, "Ma, did you give Trevor a sweet?"
>
> "No, no."
>
> "Well, what is this here on the floor with teeth marks on it?"
>
> "OK, I gave it to him. But the damn dog wouldn't eat it, and I couldn't pick it up!"
>
> And she was always interested in Matthew.

Matthew picks up the narrative:

> I knew her as a large, white-haired woman with a sizzling intellect—eloquent. And she seemed very alive. She was independent, what you'd call a free spirit. I saw her all the time and we talked about baseball mostly (the Red Sox) and football (the Patriots). She didn't like basketball much. But we hoped the Red Sox would win the pennant, and they did, just around this time. *Star Island Boy* is my favorite [of Louise's books] because it was the first one I read, and then *Three of a Kind*. They were great. Louise had a sense of mission about her work, totally into her writing. She was a no-

nonsense person, but laid back, if you know what I mean. Fun to be with.

Dinah describes her mother's decline:

Her last years were very sad, painful. Even so, she was really easy to care for. I had home health aides come in from nine to three, and they all loved her. She never complained, which actually was a problem. One day we discovered this cyst on her spine. It was horrendous. Apparently, it had been getting worse and worse for two weeks and she hadn't said a thing. Stoic. Didn't want to be a bother. Earlier, while she was still in Corea, she told me she'd decided to donate her body to science. She was trying to be as little bother as possible and do something for mankind. I couldn't bear to think of her body held somewhere and then all chopped up and disposed of who knew when and where. Once I told her how I felt, I was able to talk her out of it. But this was typical—

Then I would say about a month before she died, she stopped knitting and read very little. She slept a lot and just didn't feel good. Our doctor told me Ma would either die from her enlarged heart or from her failing kidneys. "And just pray it isn't the kidneys, because that is a gruesome death." Finally, she was becoming dehydrated, and we couldn't get her out of bed. Our doctor said, "She needs to be in a nursing home." I didn't want this at all, but I couldn't get any more home help. I only needed someone on Saturdays while I was at the store—two more hours a week. So, I figured we'd go over, get things stabilized, and Ma could come right back. I went over every day right after work to comb her hair and talk—she was still sharp mentally, but once she went to the nursing home, she never got out of bed. She was gone within two weeks, so for all intents and purposes, she died at home. I couldn't understand why she went so quickly and I asked our doctor. Ma was wearing a patch to help with her heart and he said, "The day we brought your mother here, I took off the patch." "Why would you do that?" I asked. He just said quietly, "You think about it, Dinah." He didn't want her kidneys to take her. They were all so touched by Ma's courage.

That last day, I came into the room and she looked like she was dozing. I started to comb her hair as usual. She didn't move. And that's when I knew she was gone. But a couple of days before she

died, we had a talk; she knew it wouldn't be much longer and
seemed relieved. I don't want to go into our conversation in detail,
as it was between mother and daughter, except to say we were fortunate to have the time, and we were able to tell each other how
much we loved each other and how much we would miss each
other. Not everyone is lucky enough to have that, and I'll be forever grateful.

Sarah Louise Dickinson Rich died April 9, 1991. She was eighty-eight
years old. The *New York Times* ran her obituary. Her body was cremated.
And the ashes? The ashes traveled with Rufus past Bridgewater, Louise's
childhood hometown, went through New Hamphire, site of her first
marriage and teaching job, along the Maine coast, which she had loved
and written about, then veered northwest onto side roads through Rumford Point, along an even quieter stretch to the village of Andover, and
onto the fifteen-mile wilderness road to South Arm.

Eric Wight, the Lakewood Camps boatman, met Rufus at South Arm.
As they headed across Lower Richardson Lake, they passed nearly the
same view his mother described fifty years earlier: ". . . cris-crossed with
ridges, dotted with swamps and logans, and covered with dense forest.
The trees come down to the shore, the black growth of fir and pine and
spruce streaked with the lighter green of maple and birch. There is nothing at all on the hills but forest, and nobody lives there but deer and
bear and wildcat." Rufus walked up the lawn at Middle Dam and continued past Alys Parsons's cabin, past the Club Pool Trail and Black Valley,
up Birch Hill, along Pond in the River and what once was a logging-camp
wangan, around the corner and up a slight rise. Behind Forest Lodge,
the roar of the Rapid River called. Louise was home.

-- PART II --

Selected Writings

Fogbound (1922)

[Appearing in the Bridgewater Teachers' College *Normal Offering* along with her poems (see page 11), the following was probably Sarah Louise Dickinson's first published piece. It lends credence to her friend Hester's assertion that Louise could spin a good story—ghost or otherwise.

Strangely and prophetically enough, Louise's first published short story takes place in Maine. Although her flare for story-telling and setting gives a strong sense of place, there is no indication that Louise had ever visited Maine up to this point.]

The heavy, smothering fog hung in a dripping white curtain around our tiny cabin on the desolate, rocky Maine coast. It isolated us from the cherry everyday world. We could hear occasionally a dog barking, the sound being magnified by the mist, and always in our ears was the dull monotone of the heavy surf, creaming on the rocks.

It was my turn to row the two miles for milk, and I set out from the camp apprehensively. A dozen steps and I was cut off from all mankind by the motionless wall of fog. I entered the boat and shipped the oars with some hesitation. A heavy sea was running, and the harbor was blotted from view. But reluctance to face the derision of my friends urged me on. I had hardly rowed beyond the first line of breakers, when the shoreline completely disappeared. I was alone in a vast gray-white void upheld by the surging green-gray water, out of reach of time or event. Always in my ears were the voice of the surf and the thin plaintive cries of the gulls.

It seemed decades that I had rowed in that eternity of fog, and ages since I had heard a human voice, when suddenly the tone of the breakers changed, becoming deeper, heavier, ominous. At the same time the boat was caught in a black cross-current, flowing with the strength and speed of a mill race—the terrible irresistible undertow that had tossed so many lives away on Dead Man's Reef. None had ever yet escaped that remorseless, soulless monster!

Panic seized me, and I beat the ebony water furiously with my oars, which were as effectual as two straws. Then horrible, degrading terror came in a thin red mist, blotting out sanity. I do not know how long I cowered in the bottom of the boat, glassy-eyed, screaming, and biting my fingers and knuckles till my mouth was full of the bitter taste of blood and brine. It could not have been for long—Dead Man's Reef does not give its victims much time.

Then suddenly I heard the creak and rattle of oar and thole-pin, and dim through the pall I saw a large boat, driven toward me. What manner of men were these, to row against that relentless current?

Tall in the stern stood the leader, clad in mail and leather, a winged helmet on his head, and his long unkempt hair and beard streaming out behind him. On the thwarts sat fourteen men clothed as Leif Eriksson's crew was, when centuries ago, he had explored these waters. And as they swayed to the oars with mechanical precision, borne down the wind was the old, old, hail—faint, ghostly—"Skoal! Skoal!" Then the short hair on my neck stirred, and my blood froze in my veins, for *through* the boat and crew I saw the hungry black fangs of the reef.

I covered my face with bleeding hands, and waited for the end of the world. Aeons passed. With a sharp movement, I tore my hands away. My flesh crawled and my breath left my body. Far down through the planks I saw the cruel water, and beside me, gazing at me with flaming hollow sockets, was the tall Viking! I was in the spectral boat, rowed by the fourteen ghastly henchmen with "Skoal! Skoal!" on their bloodless lips. Behind, I saw my own dory, going to splinters on the black and jagged rocks, before fog shut us off again.

Back and forth, back and forth, back and forth swayed the unearthly oarsmen, hypnotizing me with smooth rhythm. And deep, deep into my eyes went that unblinking, blazing stare, till I felt my poor, imprisoned soul drawn out, and out—and out....

Then with the sudden effect of a bugle note, a strong east gale tore through the white, breaking it up, dispelling it. A crimson ray of sunlight fell on that unhallowed craft. Instantly I was struggling in the water, and the phantom ship, fleshless crew, and ghoulish chief were nowhere to be seen.

It was a long swim to shore, but I succeeded, helped by a strong incoming tide. That afternoon my milk can was picked up four miles away, battered flat; and pieces of my dory were found far out at sea. *They* had not escaped the Reef!

I have told this to many, many people, and most of them have laughed. But sometimes I have told it to men who are of the sea, and they have sat silent for a time. After a while they have told me strange tales from the ends of the earth—and all, all, I have believed.

Stories Written with Ralph Rich

[Although Ralph's name appears as the author of "Why Guides Turn Gray" and Louise's name is on "Wish You Were Here," their recounting of the production of these two stories was that both were a collaborative effort. There is the tone of Ralph's Harvard alumnae entries with Louise's additional infusion of strong observational detail and dialogue. "Why Guides Turn Gray," written first, appeared in *Outdoor Life;* "Wish You Were Here" was published in the *Saturday Evening Post.* A few paragraphs from each piece will give the general idea of topic and style.]

Why Guides Turn Gray (1937)

Hunters, fishermen, campers—call them what you will. To us natives of the North woods, they're all "sports." We could say, I suppose, "that fellow from Boston Bill is guiding." We'd rather say, "Bill's sport." It's shorter.

Because guiding is the major source of summer income up here, years of contact have finally taught us all there is to know on the subject of sports. We can classify them on sight. We accept their notions and humor their peculiarities. We know they want us to be quaint, so, as soon as the ice is out, we take out our old plaid shirts and moccasins, polish up our dialect, and recall our best tall stories. (The biggest liar, we have observed, is usually considered the best guide.) We try always to combine the best features of the packhorse, Fred Allen, and Job, rolled into one. Then we draw a long breath, and plunge into our May-to-November rush season. Probably the sports we have up here in Maine are typical of their class the world over. It's been our experience that all our troubles are caused by less than 20 percent of them. Take, for example, what we elegantly call "fish [hogs]." Probably they are nice to their mothers, love dogs and children, and only steal from blind beggars, but their one ambition in life is to catch all the fish in the state, and they have to prove their prowess by killing and bringing home every fish they catch. They are the lads who think a snapshot isn't the truth unless it makes them look like a Gloucester fisherman just home from the Grand Banks.

And these are the lads that complain the most that the fishing isn't what it used to be. Under our archaic game laws they have the right to the fish, but it is men like them who have ruined some of the finest lakes and streams in New England. They boast loudly of their catches, recounting faithfully each move of the twenty-minute battle, all unaware that down behind the cook shack Bill, the guide, is apologizing to Larry, another guide: "Say, I'm sorry about that sport of mine laying his fly down right over your sport's line. If I'd known, I'd have kept him over at the other side of the pool."

"That's all right, Bill," says Larry handsomely. "I saw he didn't know nothing when it took him half an hour to bring in that four-pound salmon. There ain't a fish in these here waters a man with the tackle he's got couldn't land in ten minutes. Just try to keep him away from me tomorrow. I'm guiding old Judge Martin, and you know how he'd act if anybody snagged his line."

I was working in my garden last spring when Will, a guide I know only casually, came along, and squatted down among the tomato plants. We exchanged amenities and chatted for an hour, during which I concealed my surprise at his unprecedented neighborliness. He's a man who drops in on a definite errand, never simply to pass the time of day. Finally he rose.

"Guess it's safe for me to go back to my sport now."

"Safe?" I said.

"Yes. He wasn't having no luck fishing legal, so he went ashore and dug him some worms. I told him these are fly-fishing waters, but he would-n't listen, so I left him be. If a warden showed up, I'd lose my guiding license for a year. So I came here. Guess he'll be sick of his worms by now."

The sport who insists on breaking the law can afford to pay the fine. His guide cannot afford to lose his license and means of livelihood for a year.

Wish You Were Here (1937)

[This piece was Louise's re-working of the "Why Guides Turn Gray" theme. Completed months ahead of the *Scribner's* writing contest, she sent it off to the *Saturday Evening Post*, where it has the distinction of being the first story published under Louise's name ("Louise D. Rich") in the national print media. What follows is an abridged version.]

As soon as the ice went out last spring, my husband sent to Augusta for his guide's license, and shed his old shirt which does him well enough in winter when only we natives are around, in favor of a grand plaid creation, carefully faded to a proper soft loveliness. Although normally the master of an extensive vocabulary and a purist in matters of pronunciation, he suddenly took to answering me in as few words as possible, and those of Grade-A Yankee.

No, I had no fears as to his sanity. I knew he was merely practicing for our silly season. The state requires that he be an expert woods and canoe man, camp cook and emergency doctor before issuing him a license to guide. But the summer people—"sports" we call them up here; they're like the "dudes" of the West—wouldn't hire Paul Bunyan himself on that alone. Be he ever so competent, if he fails to make the grade as "quite a character," the family bread will go unbuttered and the cakebox echo hollowly. My husband could do his work as well, if not better, in a pair of mail-order overalls. He would be fully entertaining, and considerably easier to understand, if he spoke the excellent brand of the king's English that cost his father, himself, and the school authorities money, tears and nervous energy respectively. But he wouldn't be picturesque, and the customers would feel cheated. Actually we differ very little from the average man and woman the country over. We are as good, and no better. Some of us say too little, some talk too much. We are intelligent and stupid in about the same proportions as you will find elsewhere. But the "furriners" want us to be picturesque, and although we may not be able to define the law of supply and demand, we can certainly make it put up its little paws and beg. We know what is expected of Maine guides, and do we dish it out!

First, a man must look as though he wrested his livelihood from Nature, decidedly against the lady's will. If he bears visible scars, so much the better. They're always good for a yarn. Pete fell off a stepladder a few years ago while—whisper it!—helping his mother clean house, and gave himself an awful gash over the eye. But, as he tells the story, it isn't a patch to what he did to the bobcat. Lenny lost three fingers in a mowing machine, and I'm afraid he's going to get in trouble about it too. He's told three versions of the affair already, involving respectively a beaver set, a defective shell in his gun, and a blizzard at thirty below. Sooner or later he's bound to lose track; he'd do better to think up a humdinger and stick to it. My own better three fifths, I unblushingly admit, is not above laying on the local color a bit thick at times. Last month, in lifting a kettle of raspberry jam off the stove for me, he spilled some of the juice on his pants. Later, as he was embarking on a three-day canoe trip with some New Yorkers, he suddenly remembered it.

"I ought to change my pants," he explained. "But I'm late. I'll tell 'em it's bear's blood. They'll be tickled simple." He did, and they were.

First Monday in March (1938)

[This is the short story that won one hundred dollars in the 1937 *Scribner's* magazine contest and launched Louise's career as a working writer. Her connection with literary agent Willis Wing followed from this piece. This and the previous two stories were all written at Forest Lodge during a period of great personal privation, and their financial success was instrumental in allowing Louise and Ralph to continue their wilderness lifestyle.

The venue for "First Monday" is most likely an Upton town meeting, though "somewhat elaborated," as friend and neighbor Alys Parsons would say.

What follows is a slightly condensed version.]

Town Meetin' day in New England is a gala occasion, combining all the better features of Old Home Day, a session of the Lower House, a barbeque, and an encounter between the Hatfields and the McCoys. This year's proceeding offers a very fair sample of what takes place on the first Monday in March, from Long Island Sound to the Canadian border.

Everyone in the township who was able to stand on his feet was present in the big, bare, wind-beleaguered town hall half an hour before the meeting began. The village idiot, a man of forty-one, stood at the door, a broad smile on his vacant moonface. He had constituted himself the welcoming committee, and he pumped the hand of each newcomer. The village drunkard sat on the step, singing softly to himself, already well on the road to what looked like a big day. The noise within the hall was deafening. School had been dismissed for the day, and the children, giddy with freedom, ran and shrieked about the room. Around the red-hot stove, the women had congregated in triple phalanx, and were making the most of this unequaled annual opportunity to exchange gossip, recipes, and symptoms. About the speaker's table stood the white-collar class—white collar in name only as, like the rest of us, they wore sheepskins, flannel shirts and corduroys—the minister, the hotel proprietor, the schoolteacher, and the storekeeper-postmaster. In the middle of the floor, a group of respectable farmers exchanged views on politics, prices, and crops, while over in one corner a dozen lumberjacks in colored plaid jackets and high boots had their heads together, alternating rapt attention to the mumbled repetition of the latest smutty story with uproarious appreciation. The game warden, trim in his blue uniform, stood near the door, exchanging amiable back-chat with our leading poacher. The fact that the one had been instrumental in having the other incarcerated the preceding fall seemed no hindrance to social amenity. The town's oldest citizen, in whom we all take a personal pride, was holding court down one side of the room. He had failed considerably was the general verdict. Last year, on his eighty-seventh birthday, he had leaped into the air and clicked his heels three times. If he could manage twice this year, it would be a wonder.

At nine o'clock the meeting was called to order, and a hush fell over the room. The men tiptoed to seats near the speaker's table, and the children were sent outside to play. The women about the stove continued their parley, but in subdued tones.

"I nominate Jake Chadwick for moderator," came from the front row. This is routine procedure. Jake, the storekeeper-postman, is our perennial moderator. But this year he dealt precedent a blow.

"Nope, I can't do it," he said, turning a perspiring face from the stove which he was stoking. "I'd like to, but y'all know my woman's mother's sick, and she's got to stay with her, so there ain't no one to tend the store. I got to be back and forth twixt here and there all day. Ye'll have to git someone else."

"But gosh, Jake, there ain't anyone else knows this parliamentary procedure!"

"Wal," conceded Jake, "I'll be in an' out. If ye git stuck, I'll try to help out."

A flurry of nominations, all declined with panicky haste, succeeded this announcement. Finally the hotel proprietor allowed himself to be persuaded, for as he observed, "If someone don't, we'll never git started." He added as he climbed onto the platform, "I don't know how this is goin' ter go, but I guess we'll weasel through some way."

Once again the cloak of comparative formality was donned, and the town officers were elected with suitable decorum. It is largely a matter of re-electing the present incumbents, as the most suitable candidate for each office has been determined long since, and only death can dislodge one. In that event the office in question is apt to be subject to some few rough years, until its fore-ordained occupant is found, when it again becomes stabilized. It is true that the three selectmen, having the most to do, are most liable to censure, but we have a pretty system to take care of that. To fill the three positions, we have four likely men. Each year the one in great-est disfavor is deposed and the spare elected to his place. By the following March, his crime has been eclipsed by time and the black deeds of one of the trio in office. So he ascends again to power and the doghouse has a new tenant for twelve months. It works out very well.

Article 10 of the warrant was the big bone of contention at this year's meeting. We always manage to have one issue over which men fight, bleed, and die, figuratively speaking. Once it was whether interest should be charged on overdue taxes. Once it was whether the constable should receive a salary of three dollars a year, or should, instead, be furnished with a star at the town's expense, rather than buy his own. And once, oh lovely year of which fables still are told, it was whether or not the renting of a bull by the town for the convenience of its cattle-owning citizens would be advisable. This year the Article read: "To see what sum of money the town will grant and raise to purchase or repair snow-removal equip-ment." Snow is our one sure crop, and "breakin' out the roads" costs us annually more than educating our young.

"Mr. Moderator."

"Mr. Hart."

"I been runnin' that danged plow for seven years, ever since we bought her, an' she was secondhand then, an' I'm here to say she won't go through another winter. She's all tied together with haywire, an' every time I take her out, somethin' else falls off her."

"I don't see's Bill's got no kick comin'," announced a truculent voice from the rear. "He gits paid by the hour, whether he's plowin' or sittin' tin-kerin'. 'Twas in the agreement that he keeps her in good shape, an' if he ain't done it, why it ain't no skin off our noses."

"God A'mighty, man, they's limits to what a feller can do with a bunch of junk. If you, or any of the rest of the shif'less Gorham tribe can do bet-ter, yer—"

"Shif'less, are we?" roared the Gorham. "Why you— you—" Words failed him. "I won't take that kind er talk from any squirt that lets his wife buy store bread 'stead er bakin' her own. Shif'less! What about that—"

"Address the chair! Address the chair! shrieked the moderator. "You fellers is way out of order!"

"We need a new snow plow," shouted Bill Hart at the top of his lungs.

"We don't neither! We can send that one back to the factory an' have 'em undo the damage Bill done."

"I ain't done no damage. I—" There's no telling what might have taken place, had not a din of such volume as to drown the voices of the two broken out beneath the window. Those nearest stampeded for the door.

"Hey Bill," reported a tall lanky farmer, "yer heifer's out here, stuck in a drift, bellerin' her fool head off, an' doin' her durnedest to break her leg."

"Now how in tarnation'd she git out?" and the harrassed Mr. Hart vanished. He was gone for several minutes, during which a stream of mingled profanity and bovine protest penetrated the double windows, augmented by a chorus which seemed to indicate that the juvenile population had turned to help, as one man. To continue the meeting was impossible, until he returned, his temper somewhat cooled.

"Now 'bout that plow. Honest, folks, why don't we buy a new one? Fixin' this one up is jest pourin' good, hard cash down a rathole."

"Couldn't we appropriate some money an' leave it up to the selectmen what ter do?" suggested a mild-mannered little farmer.

"NO!" from one of the town fathers. "That's what was done fifteen years ago when we put in the cement bridge. I was selectmen then too, and some there be who still ain't satisfied. So it's up to you folks. Tell us what to do, an' we'll do it."

"Wal then," stated Bill Hart, before the opposition had a chance to advance further, "I move we appropriate the thousand dollars an' buy a new plow." His motion was seconded by his wife's sister's husband's brother, with a promptitude which suggested prearrangement, and the vote was called for by one of the Hart uncles-by-marriage.

A buzz arose as the votes were written on slips of paper brought from home (no sense in wasting the taxpayers' money on printed ballots), and a straggling procession started for the ballot box, an ex-canned-beef crate, over which the moderator and clerk stood guard to insure an honest vote. The town idiot voted with the rest, and as soon as his back was turned, the clerk fished his ballot out and pocketed it, a flagrantly illegal procedure condoned tacitly by all present on the grounds that there "warn't no need ter hurt his feelin's." It was a close matter, but the new plow won.

A nondescript man who had been figuring feverishly on an old envelope rose to his feet. "Mr. Moderator, we hadn't ought to do this. It'll raise taxes 'most sixty percent. I got the figures right here."

Consternation reigned. Touch a Yankee's pocketbook and you touch the very core of his being. All over the hall voices were raised in recrimination of the entire sly Hart outfit. The moderator pounded the table until his gavel broke, and then cut loose with a stentorian bellow. "There's no use losin' our tempers now," he said, demonstrating the why and where-fore of this title. "It's too late to change our minds."

"Why is it, if we want to?" demanded a lawless spirit.

"Wal, I don't rightly know, but it seems as if I heard somewhere it's agin' parliamentary law."

"Where's Jake at? Git Jake!"

Jake had gone across to his store, but answered the call of duty on the hotfoot.

"I don't rec'lect anything 'bout that in the rules," he said when the problem had been put to him, "but I don't see why we can't fix it up. How many want to back-water?" The walls bulged. "Wal, then, if someone'll put it in the form of a motion, jest so's it'll be legal...."

The matter was put through with almost indecent haste, the clerk's notes on the previous appropriation destroyed, and the sum of two hun-dred dollars voted to repair the old plow, an amount much smaller than would have normally been named, since a resentful citizenry felt the need of retaliating for almost having one slipped over on them. Let Bill sweat, come next February, to get his plow over Mill Hill.

The women had withdrawn some time before, and now one spoke from the door.

"Les, if you've come to a good stoppin' place, dinner's on the table." No other motion to adjourn was needed.

Trestle tables in the basement were loaded with more food than I would have believed available in the state—ham and chicken, salad and hot rolls, pies cut in quarters, layer cakes laced with jam and topped with yellow whipped cream, and urns of strong, clear, steaming coffee, all do-nated by the women of the town. As soon as the sharp edges of appetite had been dulled, the talk broke out.

"...ain't layin' so good. I guess I'll have ter hire me a dozen or so Rhode Island Reds to git me through spring."

"...that's what I'd er done if the Soopreme Court had uphelt pertato control. Seems like the Gov'nment can't keep their noses outer nothin' nowadays."

A woman's shrill voice soared in a sudden hush. "Extravagant! My land, you ought to take one look in her swill bucket!"

And a man's nasal Yankee twang sawed the air. "... Don't blame them none. When them crazy Democrats comes 'round, shovin' money at us, y' can't expect us ter put our hands behind our backs, can yer?"

The afternoon session proved rather an anticlimax to the fireworks of the morning. Routine matters were quickly disposed of, although the final Article, "To see what sum of money the town will grant and raise for support of the poor," occasioned a little discussion probably unique in this day. The customary amount is five hundred dollars, which is never wholly expended, so that now the Poor Account shows an accumulated balance of almost eight hundred dollars. It was suggested that this year no money be set apart, necessary funds to be drawn from this balance.

"Wal, I dunno," said one of the selectmen. "Course, we never do use it all, but yer never can tell. 'Twon't do no hurt to have a backlog. We could, mebbe, cut it down ter four hundred this year."

This compromise was effected, and the meeting was adjourned. Farmers went back to the stables to hitch up, or dig out the Model T's, while women bundled up the children and hustled down into the kitchen to reclaim pie plates and cake tins. Word was passed around that Bill Hart and Sy Gorham were having it out down behind the cemetery, and the sporting element departed in all haste in that direction. Town Meeting, another town meeting not in the tradition of our historians, was over for another year.

Don't Worry (1938)

[Originally titled "Husband on Ice," this was the first short story Louise wrote for her agent, Willis Wing, to submit to *Woman's Home Companion* (a magazine no longer in publication). "Don't Worry" proved very popular and gave Louise a huge boost in name recognition, as it was reprinted both in the U.K. and Sweden.]

Caroline York moved briskly about a well-defined triangle—its points marked by the glowing range, the supper table with a kerosene lamp shining goldenly on the red-and-white checked cloth and the blue plates, and the sink with the two pails of spring water on the drainboard—as she gave her husband a spirited résumé of the day's news. She had been alone, except for year-old Joey and the dog, since Jed's early morning departure to tend his trap line. The three-room cabin which the Yorks called home was set down in the middle of two hundred square miles of frozen timberland through which rivers and lakes served as the only highways and the only semblance of civilization therein was a handful of lumber camps; but these facts did not mean that she had none to relate. Jed, changing his gum boots and sodden wool socks in the shabby comfortable rocker beside the stove, gave her his grave half-amused attention.

"Well, in the first place, some man called up about ten minutes ago and wanted to talk to you, so you'd better call him right back. His name's Stuart and he's over at the Number Ten lumber camp at the head of the lake. Now let's see what else I've heard today." She emptied a jar of piccalilli into a glass dish and set it on the table. "Dan Corbett, the clerk up at Number Ten that I told you about, you remember? He's the one had such a bad cold last week. Well, he must be younger than I thought. I thought he was about sixty-five judging from his voice, but that must have been that cold of his. Anyhow, his wife just had twins yesterday, so he had to go out this morning and they don't know when he will be back. He'll probably get drunk to celebrate, so—"

"Now Caro," interposed Jed mildly, "you've got no business saying a thing like that about a man you never laid eyes on. He—"

She peered into the oven and shifted a pan of biscuits from the bottom to the top shelf where they could brown evenly. "Oh, I didn't make that up. I heard the clerk at the Moose Mountain camp talking to the cook at Black Cat about it. They're so sure of it that they've sent out for a new clerk to take his place till he comes back, Smarty. Then I heard the dam keeper talking, but I had to hang up before I found out whether they were going to change the water, because Joey started crying and I was afraid they'd hear him."

"That's too bad," Jed sympathized, a twinkle in his eye. "I'd hate to think there was somethin' going on my wife was missing, after the comp'ny was kind enough to hitch us up on their private woods line."

Jed hauled his lean length out of the chair with a groan and went to the telephone. He depressed the hood with his left hand and turned the crank vigorously, one long and one short.

"If he wants to give us the whole shebang, Caro, what'll I tell—oh, hello. Mr. Stuart there?... This is Jed York, Mr. Stuart. Did you want... Why yes, I got an old jalopy that we use to go back and forth over the carry road in summer.... Sure she's runnin'." He was silent a long moment, listening. "Why, sure, I'll be glad to do what I can. Where was they last seen? . . . What time was that? ... Two o'clock! They shoulda been in to your camp three hours ago.... No, 'tain't no use sendin' men out on foot this time of day.... Sure, I'll start soon's I get my supper under my belt.... O.K., I'll keep in touch with you as much as I can, but there's a lot of lake to cover and some of it's a long way from a phone.... Sure." He hung up.

"Jed, what—?"

"Look Hon, get supper on the table quick, will you? I'll talk while I eat." He sat down and helped himself hastily from the steaming platter she set before him. " And find me some dry mittens. Thanks. Well, it seems that new clerk they're getting in to take Corbett's place decided to drive his car into camp over the ice. He left the main camp down to the foot of the lake 'bout two o'clock and they ain't seen him since. There was another feller with him, a scaler, but neither of them's ever been up in this country before. They tried to tell them down at the foot how to come, but you know how the lake is, so full of coves and inlets and arms that they could get lost twenty times over. What Stuart's afraid of is that the ice has reefed, or they struck a spring hole and went in. Anyhow he and his whole crew's been out in the cuttings all day, and he just got in and heard about it. There ain't no use sending men out on foot to hunt in the dark and horses wouldn't be much better. So he thought, seeing's I had the only car round here, I might be able to at least get track of them—piece of that pie, Hon—though if they've gone through the ice, we won't see hide nor hair of them till the spring break-up."

Caroline paused abruptly on her way to the sink. "But Jed! What's to prevent your getting drowned? That ice is treacherous. You've told me a dozen times how the current from the river shifts and scours it out. Jed, I don't want you to go."

"Now, now, Hon. I ain't going to take any chances. You know I got to go. Even if their car has gone through, they maybe jumped clear and are out there holding on, waiting for help. Or like as not they just got lost and are pulled up in a cove, settin' till they get found. Any case, I got to go, if only to show Mr. Stuart I appreciate his getting this phone put in for us."

"Oh, I suppose so. But Jed, you be careful now. If you get drowned, I—I—"

"You'll be right put out 'bout it, won't you, and I won't blame you a mite. Cheer up," he added as she essayed a feeble smile. "You can't get rid of me that easy." He rose and patted her shoulder. "Look, while I get into my boots again, find a piece of rope and chuck it in the back of the car, will you? And you might dig up that pint your brother gave us. It may come in handy."

• • •

Caroline was up back in the lean-to that served as garage, stowing the rope in the back of the car, when Jed joined her.

"Looks like it might blow up a gale," he said. "Don't you stand round here in that thin sweater, Hon; you'll catch your never-get-over." He kissed her briefly.

"Jed, you will be careful?"

"Sure I will. Now don't you worry. I'll be back 'fore you know I'm gone, and you might have a pot of coffee ready. She's going to be a mite breezy out on the ice." He turned her about and spanked her smartly. "Scat now."

She returned reluctantly to the kitchen, a forlorn place now in spite of the rosy stove and the contented gurgling of Joey, happy in his pen. Just as she started to pick him up the telephone rang shrilly, two long and three short—her own number.

"Hello." She was surprised to find that her voice shook. She must be getting the jitters. Jed was all right. He hadn't even left the yard yet.

"Mrs. York? This is Stuart. Jed gone?"

"He's just starting the car."

"Good. Look, Mrs. York. Get this. Tell him for the love of Mike not to cross the channel. They've opened up the gates of the dam above and there's an awful lot of water going through. Got it? Tell him to keep to the east shore."

Caroline dropped the receiver and let it swing as she raced to the door. As she flung it open she heard the gears mesh and the motor rise in a crescendo above the sound of the rising gale.

"Jed!" she screamed and started running up the trail through the grove to the road. "Jed." The lights of the car swung in a swift arc, gilding the tree trunks briefly and steadying as the car swung into the road. "Jed! Wait!"

The gears meshed again and the lights moved on. Then Jed was gone, leaving her stumbling after him in the sudden dark. She came to a halt and stood a moment looking after him. The wind moaned in the tops of the trees and she felt a cold prickling on her bare arms. It was beginning to snow, she realized. She turned and went back to the cabin. The receiver still hung at the end of the cord. She picked it up.

"Hello? Hello? Mr. Stuart? He went before I could stop him. What shall I do?"

The voice that came back was comforting. "There, Mrs. York, don't worry. I'll get word to him down the line somewhere. He's bound to stop in at some of the camps along the lake and I'll leave word at them all. Don't worry." He hung up.

. . .

"Don't worry," Caroline snorted, snatching Joey up with a violence that drew an outraged howl from him. "There, there, Lamb. Mama didn't mean you. See the nice teddy bear." He stretched out his fat little arms, quickly appeased, and she hugged him close for an instant. "Don't you ever grow up into the kind of man that tells women not to worry."

The telephone rang two long and she set him back on the floor, put her hand hard over the mouthpiece and pressed the receiver to her ear. Mr. Stuart's voice came clearly over the wire. "—started a few minutes ago and he'll prob'ly go straight to your camp. Tell him to keep to the east shore. They're running a lot of water and—" Caroline hung up silently. Mr. Stuart was as good as his word.

The next hour went fairly rapidly. There was the baby to put to bed, the supper to clear away and the dishes to wash. For the first ten minutes the telephone kept up a constant jangle as Mr. Stuart called the camps strung along the lake's thirty serpentine miles of shoreline and left word for Jed. Caroline checked the calls against a mental list. Two rings—that was Black Cat, just below; three long—that was Moose Mountain, high on a slope halfway down the lake; two long and two short was Number Eight in the pocket ten miles away as the crow flies; and one long was the main camp at the foot of the lake. The phone fell into silence.

The last dish polished and put away, Caroline determinedly picked up a half-made sock. There was no use getting into a state, she told herself, knitting and purling doggedly. The lamp whispered softly to itself; from the stove came the muted roar of the fire; the dog under the table stirred in his sleep and whined. But the room seemed empty and deathly still without Jed's deep slow voice and Joey's cheerful chirping.

Suddenly, shattering the quiet with the violence of an explosion, the bell jangled—two long. That was the first camp Jed would come to. Caroline was on the line seconds before the legitimate recipient of the call.

"Black Cat Camp," she heard.

"That you, Olsen?" It was Mr. Stuart's voice. "Say, did you get that message to York?"

"Why, we ain't seen him, Mr. Stuart. We been watching but either he got by before you called or else he was so far out we couldn't see his lights. It's snowing some and blowing to beat the band, so they's quite a smother out front. Anythin' we can do?" asked Olsen.

"No, except get off the line so's I can use it. Or wait. You got horses there. Find someone can stick on one and send him over to the Big Island

Camp. They ain't got a phone in and they might know something, though it's doubtful, they being off the main track. Call me when you find out."

"O.K. But it's over a mile—"

"Oh, hang up. Stop talking and hang up!" Caroline cried silently over the wire. She replaced her own receiver and stood shivering, pressing her forehead to the cool mouthpiece. The next call was to the Moose Mountain Camp.

"No," said Moody, the clerk there, "we couldn't reach him. We see his lights a piece out, but there wa'n't no way of stopping him. Way he was heading, seems like he was digging right for the foot of the lake where them fellers was seen last. He was all right when we see him, way this side of the channel. Whyn't you call the main camp at the foot— His advice was cut short by the click of the boss' receiver.

The one long ring of the main camp rang out next. Caroline's knees were trembling when the clerk fifteen miles away spoke across the intervening reaches of black ice and wind-racked forest.

"Look, Eddy," Mr. Stuart was not quite so calm and confident as he had been. "That feller I sent out to find them two men—has he come in your place yet?"

"No, he ain't. We see his light, though, 'bout a mile up the lake, near that bunch of little islands. He kept stoppin' and startin' and stoppin' and startin' till we figured he was in trouble, so I sent a couple men out to help him and tell him 'bout the channel.... Wait. They just come in. Want I should put them on?"

"Put them on," ordered Mr. Stuart and Caroline's heart echoed, "Oh, put them on!"

There was a moment's pause and then a rough voice spoke.

"Boss? We couldn't catch that guy. We got almost up to him and then he went off lickety larrup. He couldn't see us, 'count of the snow blowing, and we yelled our blooming lungs out, but he couldn't hear. She ain't making much snow, but it's blowing and drifting and the wind's terrible."

"What in tunket was he doing?"

"Well, Jerry Fayette was with me—he's part Indian—and he doped it out. He musta been looking for the tracks them fellers left this afternoon. That's why he was stoppin' and startin'. They was all blowed over most places but we found them in the lee of some of them islands , and this guy was follerin' them right along. Trouble is, they's no telling which way they went after they got out on the main lake, and there ain't going to be no tracks out there. Why the Sam Hill them two fellers wanted to take a car on a lake they never see before—"

Mr. Stuart hung up and after a moment Caroline followed suit. She stared at the telephone.

"You devil," she thought. "You took him away from me. I'd like to tear you out by the roots and burn you."

The next moment, as the little cabin shuddered under the impact of a tremendous blast, her blood ran cold. It was so frail, so slender a thing, that lone strand of wire strung through the woods from tree to tree, sagging over gullies, spanning ice-locked brooks, swinging from camp to warm bright camp in the bitter windy dark. It was her only possible link with Jed and it was so vulnerable. A shattered treetop crashing across it, too heavy a load of frozen sleet upon it and—she quivered and came to the realization that she had been staring at the silent black mouthpiece for minutes.

The telephone shrilled a long and a short—a call for Mr. Stuart at Number Ten. Her hands fumbled at the receiver.

It was Olsen at Black Cat. "—that I sent over to the island on the horse just got back and they got one of them lost men over there."

"Which one? How'd he get there? Where's the other one?" Mr. Stuart's voice was sharp.

"It's the scaler, Abbott. They don't know where the clerk is. Seems just 'fore our man got there this York come driving up in front, ablowing his horn, and hollering. Course they didn't have no inklin' over there what was going on, so they all piled out to see. York had this scaler dumped in on the seat 'side of him, his clothes all froze. Nigh dead, he was."

"Where'd he find him?"

"Dunno. Somewhere's out on the ice. He was unconscious. They got him wrapped up in blankets, pumping liquor into him. Our feller stuck round a while and then he see there was no use waiting, so he come on back."

"Where's York?"

"He'd gone 'fore our feller got there. Seems he never even got out of the car; just handed Abbott over and put out of there. Said somethin 'bout getting another one, and high-tailed."

"They give him my message 'bout the channel?"

"Jeepers, no. They didn't know nothin' 'bout anything'. Might's well be in Siam as out on that there Big Island. Comp'ny ought to run a line out there and put in a phone and things like this wouldn't—"

"Send that man back and tell him to stay there till there's some news and then hotfoot it back." Mr. Stuart hung up.

. . .

Caroline pressed her knuckles to her mouth and bit them—hard. The pain steadied her.

"I won't be a silly fool," she said aloud. "He brought one in; he can bring the other. What I need is something to occupy my mind."

She glanced around the room. Everything was neat and shining, everything except the shabby cushions in Jed's old rocker.

"I'll cover those cushions," she told herself and added firmly, "there ought to be just about time enough before he gets back."

The phone rang again as she was cutting the bright calico on the kitchen table. She leaned a moment against the wall before she took the receiver down.

"Moose Mountain?" It was Mr. Stuart. "Say, Moody, there's the devil to pay. That feller York I sent out to find them two men brought one into Big Island 'bout an hour ago and now he's lost. You're pretty high up there and get a good view of the lake. You ain't seen his lights, have you?"

"Yeah, we did, boss. I was just going to call you. Half, three quarters of an hour ago, feller come busting in here from the bunkhouse and said they was a car skitterin' round out there, heading straight for the channel. Sure 'nough, they was. We couldn't see very good 'count of the snow blowing and while we was looking and speculating, the lights went out. 'There he goes,' says I to Bill Page. 'That's the end of that joker.' Bill's a betting man, as I s'pose you know, boss, and a blamed unlucky one too. He says to me, 'Two to one he ain't in the lake at all but just back of one of them islands.' Well—"

"Why didn't you do something, 'stead of standing round laying bets? I'll have your hide for this!" The receiver crashed down.

For a merciful moment Caroline's mind refused to act. She saw the line of snow creeping higher on the window pane and the gaily patterned bits of cloth lying in the pool of lamplight.

Then the full force of Moody's words struck her. It had happened, the thing she had known would happen. The current, lashing back and forth under the ice, wearing it, rotting it, turning eight inches of solid blue crystal to a thin treacherous shell, had reached out and taken Jed. Her head felt funny, she heard noises. It was a moment before she focused on the sound of the bell ringing one long and a short. When she took up the receiver Mr. Stuart was answering.

And then a deep slow familiar voice came over the wire. Jed! It was Jed's voice!

"Hello, Mr. Stuart. Moody says you hung up without hearing his story. He's a mite put out."

"You tell that long-winded old fool—say, who's this talking, anyhow?"

"Jed York, last I heard. Well, I got your men for you. One's over on the island and the other's here. So I'll be heading for home 'fore my wife commences worrying."

"Hey, wait. Where'd you find them?"

"Seems their car went through the ice, right out on that sunken reef. One of them got caught in the car—it didn't more'n three quarters sink and you can get it out with a team, come daylight—and the other made it to solid ice and started for help. He musta wandered round for hours. When I found him he was down on the ice, half-froze and more'n half covered with snow. Lucky I see him. Took him for a log, first, till my headlights caught him just right."

"I'll say it was lucky. Where'd you find the other one?"

"This first one come to enough while I was getting him in the car to tell me where to go. Soon's I got rid of him—took him to Big Island, that being nearest—I went back. He'd got out of the car and was setting on top. He'da fallen off and drowned, sure, shape he was in, if I hadn't showed up when I did. He's a kind of frail feller. I brought him in here and that's that. So I guess I'll be getting home, 'fore my wife—"

"How'd you get him off?"

"Oh, I brought a short ladder 'long with me, just in case. Handiest thing in the world, on ice. And now I gotta start—"

Mr. Stuart laughed. "For home 'fore your wife starts worrying. She won't worry. She strikes me she has her head screwed on right."

Jed's voice came back strong and full of pride in her. "You're telling me? She ain't one of these fool panicky females."

"Oh, Jed," she thought, "if you only knew! But you never will."

Mr. Stuart went on. "Well, you had me worried. I don't mind saying I sweat some when I couldn't get hold of you to tell you they raised the water."

"Oh, that. Say, after you've lived round here long's I have, you don't take no chances. First thing I did was go up past your camp and look at the river. I see she was way up and acted according. Now I gotta—"

"O.K., Jed. Thanks a lot. Good-by."

Caroline hung up too, weak with relief. She hurried to the stove. The fire was almost out. She put some bark and kindling into the fire box and opened the drafts. Jed would be cold when he came in. She'd make that coffee and perhaps some sandwiches wouldn't go badly. And those cush-ion covers—she'd try to get those done.

The telephone rang, her number. That would be Jed.

"Hello, Hon. I'm leaving Moose Mountain now. It will be an hour maybe 'fore I get home."

She forced herself to speak as matter-of-factly as he did.

"All right. How'd you come out?"

"Pretty good. I found them and brought them in. And Caro, it's drifting some, so don't worry if I'm a mite late."

Men, thought Caroline. Them and their "don't worry's."

Then, "Of course not. You know I never worry," she said indignantly.

Stories for
Women's Magazines

[By 1940, Louise was under contract with Willis Wing to produce one short story a month in return for a monthly check. Although she wrote a variety of pieces, the ones that made print were period pieces along the lines of "Written in the Stars," which appeared in *Farm Journal*. She called them her "Madonna Stories"—tales of idealized, suffering, or upright women.

Although her women's-magazine stories tend to feature the prescribed self-effacing, girl-meets-boy females, Louise's twist on the generally prescribed format portrays capable women, often outsiders, who prevail because of the inherent goodness of their characters. Her abilities with plot, characterization, and dialogue hold up under the constraints of the magazine world's boiler-plated expectations of her day.]

Written in
the Stars (1942)

Janet, Professor Stevens' younger daughter, lay flat on her sister's bed, her chin on her crossed forearms, watching Clarissa dress. Clarissa was the pretty one. "Which would make me the homely one, regardless," reflected Janet without rancor. She raised her head, turtle fashion, and peered over Clarissa's shoulder into the dressing table mirror. "And, as it happens, a very fair appraisal," she decided, seeing her round, freckled face and straight, sandy hair alongside her sister's honey-colored loveliness. If she were thinner, now—

"It's no good, though," she sighed. She lay still a moment, listening to an ancient car cough and rattle past the house.

Funny, she thought, how those sounds could still, after more than two years, make her heart turn over. She knew that it wasn't Larry Grigg's old rattle-trap, even though it did sound like it. But it was a lesson her heart could never seem to learn. It had been too thoroughly schooled in adoration for Larry, through the years the Griggs and Stevens children had been growing up together. Well, it'll just have to change, she told herself impatiently. Larry had graduated and gone half way across the country to work, and it was evident from his sketchy letters that she was just what she had always been to him—the sexless, pug-nosed brat next door.

The garden gate creaked and banged, and footsteps sounded on the flagged walk.

"That my date?" exclaimed Clarissa in alarm.

Janet craned her neck and gazed down through the autumnal red-and-gold glory of the maple outside the window. "Just Dad," she informed Clarissa. "I never saw you in such a stew, Cas. Who's this man you're expecting?"

"Tom Hunt. He's wonderful. He really is, Jan. He's the instructor in the new aviation class, and if you want to know, he's My Fate. If I can get him," she added. She emerged from the closet, pulling a blue linen dress over her head. "Look, Jan. Let me wear that new apricot sweater of yours, will you? And you can take my black for the Get-acquainted Party Friday."

"Sure. Take it. But I'm not going to the party. This year I'm giving up all that sort of blather."

Clarissa was aghast. "Giving up parties? But what's the point of living in a college town if all you do is study?"

Janet rolled over onto her back. "Last year I went to every party there was. Ten million of them. And I had ten million rotten evenings. You don't know," she said suddenly vehement, "what it's like to be homely and self-conscious at a party. It's hell," she defined simply.

"Oh, Jan you—"

"Nobody'll take me," she swept on, "except the ones who are flunk-ing Dad's courses and want to make 'character' with him. Anyway, I get stiff and tongue-tied, and can't dance, and can't talk. Until I find a fool-proof system, I'm all washed up with social life."

Clarissa eyed her closely. "There's something about this whole thing that eludes me," she stated. "When we were kids you used to be all im-patience and scorn toward the social act, and you had a whale of a time, too. I used to envy you. Why do you want to change? You were doing all right the way you were. Why, you and Larry Griggs—my gosh!" She stopped abruptly. "Have I been dumber than usual, or what? I don't want to pry into your private life, Jan, but was it Larry's going away that knocked the bottom out of things?"

Janet nodded mutely, her eyes suddenly filling.

"Why you poor kid!" Clarissa thought a moment. "But look, dummy. He'll be back."

"Oh Cas, that's just it." It was a relief to talk about it. "He's been gone two years. He's traveled and met people. He's grown. When he went, I thought it was my chance to change, too. I had an idea that I'd turn into a raving beauty, and just knock him off his feet when he got back, the way girls in stories always do. But here I am, the same homely, awkward mutt I always was."

"But why? I mean, he always liked you the way you are, so—"

"Oh, he liked me all right," admitted Janet bitterly. "He liked me when we were in rompers because I didn't squeal at tomato worms, and he likes me in just the same way—and no doubt for the same reason—to this very day. That's not the kind of girl he's going to marry though."

Clarissa applied lipstick thoughtfully. "I see your point," she conceded. "Well, if that's the way things are, something will have to be done." She thought a moment. "Anyhow, don't worry. Before we're through, old men shall tell you their sacred memories, and the young shall pour their dreams into your ears." She paused admiringly. "Isn't that a swell line? It's the effect of that course in Irish poetry I've been taking."

The gate creaked and banged again, and Clarissa jumped. "Oh! This time it must be Tom."

"Aunt Gert's downstairs," Janet reminded her. "She'll entertain him."

Clarissa groaned. "Aunt Gert! And I'm trying to impress him with the culture and intelligence of my background. Please, Jan, go down and head her off. She'll get started on all that astrology stuff of hers. Go down and talk to him about the economic situation. He'll eat that up."

Janet stood up and straightened her skirt. "All right. I'll give him the lowdown on inflation. That ought to hold him till you're ready."

Janet found, however, when she reached the long, sunny, book-lined living room, that her Aunt Gertrude was before her, looking distinguished and aristocratic in lavender lawn, her silvery head cast into effective relief against a huge bowl of bronze and rose dahlias. That was the insidious thing about Aunt Gert, she thought. She looked so much like Queen Mary that you never guessed what you were letting yourself in for when you answered her well-bred questions about your birthday.

Things had progressed beyond the initial, fact-establishing stage. Aunt Gert was well under way. "You should go far," she was assuring the young man in the maroon chair. "You must, however, guard against a tendency all very intelligent people have, and particularly those born under the sign of Virgo, to be so critical and discriminating that you hesitate and delay until action is impossible."

Great governor's catfish, thought Janet. He'll think he's in a crystal-gazing parlor. "Good afternoon," she said aloud. "I'm Cas's sister, Janet."

The young man sprang to his feet, and she decided at once that she liked him. He looked humorous and kind. She sat down and prepared to discuss world events. But he had turned back to Aunt Gert.

"It's odd, your remarking on that," he said. "Only yesterday I found myself in that very predicament. There's a chap I know, who—" and he talked on, explaining, enlarging, and Aunt Gert listened and nodded from time to time. Both had apparently forgotten Janet.

I'll give him credit, she thought. He certainly gives the impression of being genuinely interested. Cas will kill me. She didn't see, however, how she could very well launch her bolt about the national debt smack into Mr. Hunt's story about his failure, when he was ten, to buy his mother a Christmas present.

"She was sweet about it," he concluded, "but she was hurt, I know."

Aunt Gert smiled. "And you couldn't tell her how sorry you were, and how you wanted the very best for her, and couldn't decide which was best."

Mr. Hunt looked startled. "How did you know that?"

"That's typical. You find it hard to give expression to your feelings, and you acquire an undeserved reputation for coldness and lack of sympathy. Really you feel more deeply than most people."

Janet snorted softly. Aunt Gert had over-reached herself there. This young man of Cas's certainly knew that his conduct had been nothing out of the ordinary. But to her amazement, he was leaning forward eagerly.

"That's remarkable," he was saying excitedly. "I remember dozens of instances of that very thing. There was the time our puppy got run over and—"

Janet suddenly sat up. Good grief, he wasn't putting on a polite act. He was having the time of his life telling Aunt Gert all about his boyhood. She looked at her aunt, charming, gracious, and, so they all thought, a little balmy. She and Cas habitually referred with pity to the other victims their aunt roped in to listen to her screwball ideas, but perhaps it wasn't like that at all. Perhaps people liked to talk to Aunt Gert! If that was so—

Cas came sweeping into the room, lovely in the apricot sweater, and Janet was not surprised to see the look of adoration on Tom Hunt's keen, dark face. But, she noticed, he turned back to finish his sentence, and to say to Aunt Gert, with every appearance of sincerity, "I don't know when I've enjoyed talking so much. I hope I'll see you again."

"Just like that," murmured Janet. "At sixty odd, she can snaffle Cas's best beau."

Janet was in bed when Clarissa returned, and she hastily thrust a small paper-covered volume under the pillow when she heard her sister's step. "Have a nice time?" she inquired.

"I would call it a successful outing," said Clarissa judicially. She smiled secretly. "Definitely successful." She flung herself across Janet's feet, stretching luxuriously, and then sat up. "Look, Jan. About Friday. If you'll go, I'll organize my friends and—"

"That's sweet of you," Janet acknowledged, "but never mind. I've already decided to go and take one last crack at the thing. I think," she added, "that maybe I've got a system."

The Get-acquainted Party was always held in the gymnasium on the first Friday of the fall term. It was distinguished by its informality, and by the fact that everybody went.

Janet drew a deep breath as she stood near the head of the long line of girls at one side of the gymnasium, and looked down the long line of men opposite. In a moment the orchestra would start the Virginia Reel, the traditional inauguration of the first dance of the year. She knew the routine by heart. Somewhere in the course of the dance, the music would be cut short, and there she would be, holding hands with Heaven knew whom, irrevocably committed to him for the ensuing waltz. She lifted her chin resolutely.

The violins struck up, and she found herself moving forward, curtsying, smiling, moving back, Cas's cherished "black" flowing in soft ruffled folds about her. So it went for a moment, then in the middle of a bar the music was pinched off, leaving the dancers suspended, the pattern shattered. An arm went around Janet's waist, and she found herself staring straight ahead at a neat black tie. The music softly launched into a swing version of the Blue Danube, and not until then did she lift her eyes to the face above the tie.

She didn't know what she had been hoping for, except that it be someone easy—a homesick freshman, perhaps, or one of the shy studious unknowns. But she had drawn bitter old Professor Granby, whose corroding tongue and intolerance for what he termed "fuzzy thinking" struck terror to the hearts of the political science students. It was enough, she reflected, to make a woman spend every one of the thousands of evenings remaining of her three-score years and ten at home with a good improving book.

"If I pass him up," she thought desperately, "I'm sunk. He's my guinea pig, for better or for worse."

She wet her lips and plunged. "When were you born?" There, it was out.

Professor Granby faltered in the sprightly hopping exercise that he fondly considered to be the waltz, and regarded her with cold amazement. "February second, 1872, if I have not been misinformed."

Janet had learned her lesson well. "You're an Aquarian," she informed him, and added glibly, "You're quick, active, far-seeing, and intuitive." That wasn't very skillful, she knew, but there was something about Professor Granby's gimlet gaze that discouraged any more personal questions for the moment.

"My dear Janet," he said with elaborate patience, "what is all this claptrap?"

Wow! She'd have to shift her ground and shift it fast, if she wanted to retain an iota of his respect for her intelligence.

"You know my Aunt Gertrude, of course," she stated. "Well, I'm trying to wean from her that so-called science of hers. You know—astrology. I'm trying to collect enough case histories that definitely contradict her data to prove to her that there's really nothing in it." There, that had a nice, sound, scholarly ring. He nodded agreeably.

"That seems to me a worthy project. It's too bad that such a fine and charming lady as Miss Stevens should be so misguided." Something in his tone made her glance at his face. Why the old boy was soft about Aunt Gert!

"I want to be perfectly fair, of course," she continued, "because that will make my case all the stronger. Tell me, would you consider yourself oversensitive?"

There was a moment's silence, and Janet's heart sank. She had had experience with that silence before. It was the sign that Professor Granby was marshaling his forces for a swift and complete annihilation. She looked up again. His face was thoughtful.

"Why do you suppose, my dear young lady, that I've spent thirty-five years building myself a reputation for being the crustiest, most unfeeling old devil that ever marked E on an examination paper? My parents were poor. We lived on the wrong side of the tracks. It was torture to me to go to school, because the rest of them laughed at my clothes. Why, I remember one time—it was bitterly cold—I had to wear my sister's sweater, a pink sweater, mind you, with some sort of ribbon doodad at the waist. I can see that sweater yet, and the sight of the pink makes me sick to this day. There was a boy named Harold Fay in the class, and—"

Why the poor old darling, thought Janet, as he rambled on. The sweet old thing. And to think that she had been afraid of him. She wanted to pat his head and tell him that she understood perfectly.

The music stopped, and he blinked uncertainly.

"Now how in the world did I get started on that?" he asked. Then he smiled. "Anyway, you're a very sympathetic listener," he said, and led her toward a place in the huge double circle that was being formed in the middle of the floor.

"Why, it worked!" Janet told herself incredulously as she marched clockwise in time to the music. Scientifically, astrology might be questionable, but it certainly had its points socially.

She watched the faces of the men who formed the outer circle moving counter-clockwise. The music stopped on a high note, unexpectedly, and Janet clutched at the black sleeve nearest her, then almost dropped it in dismay. That campus dud, that snake-in-the-grass, that smart-alecky, too-handsome, too-rich, too-everything Jack Shrewsbury, her pet detestation. And here she was obliged to probe his innermost soul, in whose secrets she hadn't the slightest interest. Besides he was a smooth article, who wouldn't be deluded by her astrological chit-chat.

However, what he thought didn't matter. She was out to make a conversational success of herself, by her chosen method, come what might. "When's your birthday?" she asked, too much irked to employ finesse.

Jack Shrewsbury executed a talented variation of rumba, which Janet had no difficulty in following.

"April eighteenth, he replied. "Why?"

"That makes you an Arian," she told him.

"Well, I've been called a lot of things, but that's a new one. What does it get me?" he inquired good-naturedly, smiling over her shoulder.

"It means you were born under the sign of Aries, and your ruling planet is Mars. You're very magnetic and witty and a good conversationalist." That ought to get him, she thought. She looked up at him. His expression was bland and satisfied and it did something to her. "You're also conceited, intolerant, and headstrong," she added viciously, overcome with rage, "and spoiled." It didn't say that in the book, but it was true.

"Here, here!" He was suddenly looking down as if he had discovered a hedgehog in his arms. "What *is* all this? What did I ever do to you?"

"Don't misunderstand me. There isn't anything personal in this at all. I'm just telling you what's written in the stars." That was a line right out of Aunt Gertrude's book.

"Well, the stars are screwy, then," announced Jack flatly. "There isn't a more tolerant fellow in college than me. Why when I was at school—" Janet preserved her air of detached and polite disbelief throughout the recital that followed. He was still trying to convince her when the dance ended.

Why, this is fun, she thought. It's like a game.

Across the floor she caught Clarissa's eye, and the slight imperative lift of her chin.

"Excuse me, please," she begged Jack. "I think my sister wants to speak to me."

She found Cas in the cloakroom.

"First," Cas began without preamble, "did I or did I not hear old Granite-face Granby telling you he is at heart a big softy, or words to that effect?"

Janet smiled. "Well, more or less."

Clarissa whistled in admiration. "And you were howling about your lack of social technique. Baby, you're good! But what I really dragged you in here for—" she searched her sister's face—"I thought you ought to have some warning. Larry Griggs came in the door two minutes ago."

Janet sat down abruptly. "Larry— Why he isn't coming home until—"

Cas explained swiftly. "The Griggs family itself didn't know until today. His brother Bill just told me."

Janet stood up quickly. Her knees were shaking. "Cas, I've got to get out of here. I can't meet him here of all places, where I'm at my very worst. I— What'll I do, Cas?" she asked miserably.

"What'll you do, you prize idiot? Why stick to your system, whatever it is. Don't give up a line when it's working."

"But you don't understand, Cas. This won't go over with Larry. He'll—"

"Any line that'll work with Professor Granby will leave Larry Griggs on the ropes. After all, he's just the red-headed boy next door, no matter where he's been for the past two years," said Cas briskly. "Now look. The next number is Ladies' Choice, so just go right up and grab him. He'll be up with the Faculty, saying howdy, and the presence of so much authority will keep the little gals from out of town at bay for a few minutes."

Well, why not, thought Janet. What had she to lose? Only, she reflected, I wish I'd had a chance to try out my system a little more thoroughly before I had to put it to the big test.

She followed Clarissa out into the gymnasium, and there he was, talking to his mother. He really and truly was there, just as tall and broad, just as red-headed, just as unutterably dear, as he had always been. With a quick intake of breath, she started across the floor toward him.

"Janet!" He flung an arm around her. "Where've you been? I've been looking for you." The same old greeting, she thought, looking up into his eyes. "You haven't changed at all," he said. "Remember the time we dug up the Ivy Day ivy and planted poison ivy instead? To celebrate my return let's—"

Her heart sank. He was starting in right where they left off. She was still his good, obedient, little man Friday, unromantic as his shadow. But at least she wouldn't give up without a struggle.

"It's the old Geminian strain still showing, isn't it, Larry?" she said as they moved away to the music. "Your birthday's in June isn't it? You're dual in character and mentality. You've always been that way—serious and sensitive about some things, and a complete clown in your off moments." She looked up at him, meltingly.

He held her at arm's length, studying her face gravely. Then he gave a great shout of laughter, gathering her close, and galloped her at double time down the floor. "Wonderful, Jan! That's a swell new line! Why didn't we think of that before, with Aunt Gertrude right under our noses?" He chuckled, then sobered. "You had me worried for a moment," he confided. "I thought you'd changed—gone smoothie or something. Don't ever change, ever, Jan. I like you just as you are."

"I won't change," she said soberly. "I guess I'll always be the same, freckles and all."

"That's the girl." They danced silently for a moment, then Larry said the thing she had been afraid of. "The only trouble is that it's too late now for that swell approach to do me any good. You see, I've found out in the last few months that there is only one girl in the world that I really want to sell myself to, and I don't think she'd fall for astrology."

She'd always known it would be this way, Janet thought drearily. Larry used to tell her everything, and it was, she supposed, really a compliment that he should tell her first about the girl he had finally fallen in love with. In a minute, when she could get rid of the lump in her throat, she'd say something comradely and understanding. She swallowed hard.

"I could try it on her, though," said Larry thoughtfully. "In fact, I guess I will."

He grasped her by the elbows and looked deep, deep into her eyes. "Your birthday is in March, isn't it, Miss Stevens?"

Wartime Columns from
Woman's Home Companion

[Following on the heels of her wildly successful *We Took to the Woods*, Louise wrote a monthly column in *Woman's Home Companion*. It was here, rather than in the longer and earlier love-story format, that she was able to convey her lifelong themes of tolerance, the power of good humor, fortitude under duress, and personal responsibility—universal themes that provided solace and strength to a wartime readership. The following six pieces are all from her monthly column.]

Grandma and the Seagull (1943)

My grandmother had an enemy named Mrs. Wilcox. Grandma and Mrs. Wilcox moved, as brides, into next-door houses on the sleepy elm-roofed Main Street of the tiny town in which they were to live out their lives. I don't know what started the war—that was long before my day—and I don't think that by the time I came along, over thirty years later, they remembered themselves what started it. But it was still being bitterly waged.

Make no mistake. This was no polite sparring match. This was War Between Ladies, which is total war. Nothing in town escaped repercussion. The three-hundred-year-old church, which had lived through the Revolution, the Civil War, and the Spanish War, almost went down when Grandma and Mrs. Wilcox fought the Battle of the Ladies' Aid. Grandma won that engagement but it was a hollow victory. Mrs. Wilcox, since she couldn't be president, resigned from the Aid in a huff, and what's the fun of running a thing if you can't force your mortal enemy to eat crow? Mrs. Wilcox won the Battle of the Public Library, getting her niece Gertrude appointed librarian instead of my Aunt Phyllis. The day Gertrude took over was the day Grandma stopped reading library books—"filthy germ things" they'd become overnight—and started buying her own. The Battle of the High School was a draw. The principal got a better job and left before Mrs. Wilcox succeeded in having him ousted or Grandma in having him given life tenure of office.

In addition to these major engagements there was constant sallying and sniping back of the main line of fire. When as children we visited my grandmother, part of the fun was making faces at Mrs. Wilcox's impossible grandchildren—nearly as impossible as we were, I now see—and stealing grapes off the Wilcox side of the fence between the gardens. We chased the Wilcox hens too and put percussion caps, saved from July 4, on the rails of the trolley line right in front of the Wilcox house, in the pleasant hope that when the trolley went by the explosion—actually a negligible affair—would scare Mrs. Wilcox into fits. One banner day we put a snake into the Wilcox rain barrel. My grandmother made token protests but we sensed tacit sympathy, so different from what lay back of my mother's no's, and went merrily on with our career of brattishness. If any child of mine—but that's another story.

Don't think for a minute that this was a one-sided campaign. Mrs. Wilcox had grandchildren too, remember; more and tougher and smarter grandchildren than my grandmother had. Grandma didn't get off scot free. She had skunks introduced into her cellar. On Halloween all loose forgotten objects, such as garden furniture, miraculously flew to the ridgepole of the barn, whence they had to be lowered by strong men hired at exorbitant day rates. Never a windy washday went by but what the clothesline mysteriously broke, so that the sheets wollopsed around in the dirt and had to be done over. Some of these occurrences may have been acts of God but the Wilcox grandchildren always got the credit. I don't know how Grandma could have borne her troubles if it hadn't been for the household page of her daily Boston newspaper.

This household page was a wonderful institution. Besides the usual cooking hints and cleaning advice it had a department composed of letters from readers to each other. The idea was that if you had a problem—or even only some steam to blow off—you wrote a letter to the paper, signing some fancy name like Arbutus. That was Grandma's pen name. Then some of the other ladies who had had the same problem wrote back and told you what they had done about it, signing themselves One Who Knows or Xanthippe or whatever. Very often, the problem disposed of, you kept on for years writing to each other through the column of the paper, telling each other about your children and your canning and your new dining-room suite. That's what happened to Grandma. She and a woman called Sea Gull corresponded for a quarter of a century and Grandma told Sea Gull things that she never breathed to another soul—things like the time she hoped that she was going to have another baby but didn't, and the time my Uncle Steve got you-know-what in his hair in school and how humiliated she was, although she got rid of them before anyone in town guessed. Sea Gull was Grandma's true bosom friend.

When I was about sixteen Mrs. Wilcox died. In a small town, no matter how much you have hated your next-door neighbor, it is only common decency to run over and see what practical service you can do the bereaved. Grandma, neat in a percale apron to show that she meant what she said about being put to work, crossed the two lawns to the Wilcox house, where the Wilcox daughters set her to cleaning the already immaculate front parlor for the funeral. And there on the parlor table in the place of honor was a huge scrapbook; and in the scrapbook, pasted neatly in parallel columns, were her letters to Sea Gull over the years and Sea Gull's letters to her. Grandma's worst enemy had been her best friend.

That was the only time I remember seeing my grandmother cry. I didn't know then exactly what she was crying about but I do now. She was crying for all the wasted years which could never be salvaged. Then I was impressed only by the tears and they made me remember that day. Now I know that something happened that day worthier of remembrance than a woman's tears. That was the day when I first began to suspect what I now believe with all my heart; and if ever I have to stop believing it, I want to stop living. It is this:

People may seem to be perfectly impossible. They may seem to be mean and small and sly. But if you will take ten paces to the left and look again with the light falling at a different angle, very likely you will see that they are generous and warm and kind. It all depends. It all depends on the point from which you're seeing them.

The Red Slipper (1943)

When my Cousin Eben was ten he decided to marry a girl who wore red slippers. My grandfather took the whole bunch of us to a little circus that was touring rural New England, and that's where Eben got the idea.

We were all impressed with the circus and most of all with The World Famous Equestrienne. To our unworldly eyes everything about her was wonderful—her orange hair, her spangled tights, and especially her high-heeled red shoes. Nobody wore colored shoes in those days. So we were entertained to the point of hysteria when Eben, the baby of the lot, announced his presumptuous marital intentions.

Eben learned then and there that a member of a large and lively family does well to cultivate a close mouth. No one ever lets you forget an unguarded remark. We were still rubbing it in five years later when Eben was in high school. "You're wasting your time, Eb," we'd say if he was caught carrying a girl's books. "Her best shoes are black."

Red slippers became a family byword. If we said a girl was the red-slipper type it meant she was gay and glamorous and fascinating, even if she'd never had such a thing on her foot. We abandoned the fact for the symbol—all except Eben. He was pretty literal. When he said red slippers he meant red slippers and not just an attitude.

Eben was also both proud and sensitive, for all he looked like an amiable prize fighter, so instead of eventually laughing it off he just got rock stubborn. He even made himself some rules. For example it wasn't fair to suggest to a girl he liked that she'd look cute in red slippers. No, she had to really wear them and they had to be her own idea. It would have been funny if it hadn't been rather tragic.

What made it tragic was Nan Haskins. From romper days she'd thought that Eben made the world and set it going. He liked her too to play tennis with and take fishing. She was a swell girl, generous and gentle and humorous; but she definitely wasn't the red-slipper type. I guess that's why Eben never thought to ask her for a real date. She'd have died of joy if he'd even taken her to the movies. It was too bad.

After Eben went to college, things looked up a little for him. Colored shoes became stylish and he had quite a field to pick from. He got around, but none of his affairs seemed serious. We asked him about that one Christmas vacation.

"Don't worry," he said. "I'm still interested in what a girl has on her feet. But now I'm also fussy about what she has in her head and in her heart." Pretty fancy talk for our baby, we thought. Baby was growing up and getting sense.

Eben was twenty-seven when Pearl Harbor was attacked and he joined the navy the next day. A year later he came home on what was called recuperation leave. Somewhere he'd met up with a piece of shrapnel. But instead of recuperating, he came down with pneumonia.

The little town had no hospital so my Aunt Serena took care of Eben daytimes and the district nurse stayed at the house nights, sleeping on a cot outside Eben's door. The district nurse was Nan Haskins and she was a good one—calm and strong and competent. She and Aunt Serena between them put Eben on the road to recovery.

· · ·

I went to see him as soon as he was out of danger. He was in bed, very thin and white, but looking rather pleased with himself I thought. "My Lord, Eben," I said with a cousinly candor designed to cover my real concern, "you look smug. I'd almost think you'd found the girl in the red slippers."

He smiled obliquely. "Yeah? Well, Smarty, it so happens that I have. We're getting married week after next."

Then he stopped being flippant. "I've been in some spots in the last year, but the toughest spot was right here in my own bed. I guess I was off my nut; but honest, I could actually see death laughing in a corner waiting to get me. I was scared. Then Nan would come in in that old bathrobe she wears, with her hair on end and no lipstick on, and she'd hold my hand and talk to me and then I wouldn't be scared any more. But I'm dumb. I didn't catch on until one night I noticed her feet. You know what she had on?"

He reached under his pillow and drew something out, cradling it tenderly in his big hands. It was probably the most disreputable sloppy old knit slipper in the world—comfortable and warm and all that but about as glamorous as a saucepan. It was scuffed and faded and looked as if a puppy had cut his teeth on it. But it was unquestionably red.

"There are red slippers," Eben said softly, "*and* red slippers."

The Gift (1944)

[Written at the height of Louise's popularity and financial stability, "The Gift" covers the autobiographical topics of the different faces of poverty and the down side of being on the receiving end of fame and fortune.]

Nobody in our home town would have said that Miss Letty Lord and Serepta Fenwick had anything in common. They were both poor, it is true, but poverty served to emphasize the difference between them. Miss Letty Lord was fastidiously and proudly poor, the way old maids of a certain age and excellent family can sometimes manage to be. Miss Letty Lord allowed herself to be beholden to no one. That was her only luxury.

The Fenwicks weren't like that at all. They were shiftless and lazy. If Serepta Fenwick was any different from the rest of the family, certainly nobody ever suspected it. She was in my class in high school but I never really knew her until Miss Letty Lord broke her ankle. Then the members of the Browning Society to which Miss Letty Lord belonged decided that the invalid ought to have someone stay in the house with her. Somehow they got hold of Serepta Fenwick.

Before she had been at Miss Lord's a week I heard my mother and the other members of the Browning Society laughing a little about how much like Miss Lord Serepta was growing to be. "Ladylike" was the word they used, and in those days that was praise. Certainly Serepta gained poise and a quiet assurance as well as manners and an appreciation of neatness and cleanliness. And then the ankle mended and Serepta went back home.

The Browning Society should have known that Miss Lord would never let a kindness like that go unrepaid, and sure enough at Christmas time she gave a tea. All the members were invited and Miss Lord had Serepta in to help her with the refreshments. I hate to think of the penny-pinching that went into that tea. The food was marvellous, and at what sacrifice will never be known, Miss Lord had managed a Christmas present for everybody there. My mother's was an exquisite hand-embroidered hand-kerchief, and my Aunt Agnes received a pair of beautiful knit gloves. But when they got home they were much too indignant over Miss Lord's treat-ment of Serepta Fenwick to be truly appreciate of their own gifts.

Miss Lord had not given Serepta any Christmas present, although Serepta had been the only one who had brought a present for Miss Lord.

"You would have thought," my mother said, "that when she opened that box and saw that beautiful silk nightgown—it must have cost that poor child every cent she'd earned there—you would have thought that she could have scurried around and found something to give her!" The whole affair caused a lot of talk for all of a week.

It wasn't until about a year ago that I gave the matter another thought. I heard a woman at a table next to mine in a city restaurant say, "Look, that's Serepta Fenwick; you know, Aunt Serepta on the radio." I looked too, although that stunning creature couldn't possibly be my Serepta Fenwick. But it was. I don't know how we came to speak of Miss Letty Lord's recent death, but when we did I was surprised to hear the genuine regret in Serepta's voice.

"She was a wonderful woman," she said. "She did more for me than anyone else has ever done."

"What are you talking about?" I asked. "The only thing I remember about her and you is how mad the Browning Society was when she didn't give you a present."

"That's just it," said Serepta. "You know how my family was—take, take, take, take all the time. Miss Letty Lord was the first person who ever allowed me to know what it felt like to be the giver. The Browning Society didn't know it, but she gave me the thing I needed most in the world, my self-respect. Right then I decided to stop being one of the other-side-of-the-tracks Fenwicks."

I said, "It's wonderful it worked out that way, Serepta, but she certainly didn't plan—"

"Oh, but she did!" Serepta contradicted. "That's what makes it so wonderful. She had a present all ready for me, a simply lovely old garnet necklace. You knew Miss Letty Lord. You know what it must have cost her pride, just to say, 'Thank you,' to me and put herself into debt to one of the awful Fenwicks. But she did it, and I never knew, until she died and left me the necklace done up in faded Christmas wrappers, the way she'd kept it all that long time. She knew, you see," said Serepta Fenwick, "that sometimes it is more blessed to receive than to give."

Our Growing Backyard (1944)

[In the following story Louise's themes of tolerance and open-mindedness during wartime hostilities are expressed in her inimitable way by showing the universal through the down-home. I have abridged this story somewhat.]

Something is happening to the village near which we live. It's a little place, really not much more than a crossroads. The hills crowd in on it from all sides, and the lives of the people who live there have always been as closely circumscribed by their own immediate interests as their farms are bound by the dark mountains. The village has not changed much, I imagine, in the last century, nor have the people; yet something is happening to change them now.

People are talking. That's nothing in a little village. People always talk about the weather and crops, about the oldest Johnson girl and her shameful carryings-on, about the minister's wife and her inappropriate hat. That's the sort of talk that has gone around our village ever since it was founded a hundred years ago.

I was out in the village last week. I haven't been there for a long, long time. People were talking, of course, but the talk was new and strange. In the bleak and frozen backwoods of New England's autumn, people were discussing monsoons and temples.

And they're talking about the people of Sydney, Australia. Five years ago nobody in the village cared about Sydney, if indeed they even knew where it was. They care now about the people of Sydney, Australia. They say they are nice people, just like the folks at home. The people in the village are talking about the English. It seems they're not the cold and haughty race the village had always supposed. They've been very nice to Nellie, who's been in England with the Wacs.

"The hot springs of Iceland aren't what they're cracked up to be," the people of the village say, "and Chinese children are cute. They got a scheme for keeping water cool in Morocco. It's a sort of earthen jar, porous-like, and you hang it up and the water gets cool–something about evaporation. Ned's going to bring one home, if he can. 'Twould be an awful handy rig to have when you're haying on a hot day in June." That's the sort of talk that's going around our village now.

I suppose I shouldn't have been so surprised because what it amounts to is this: People in small towns everywhere talk mostly about the things which touch them closely. When the boys were putting up the winter's wood, what happened in the woodlot was important. The boys are doing another chore now, a long, long way away; but our village doesn't recognize time and space anymore. We've simply taken the whole world over as an annex to the woodlots and back pasture.

Our village isn't a special case. What's happening here is happening in thousands and thousands of little places from coast to coast. Every time the mail comes in, there's handfuls of letters from all over the face of the earth. I think it's wonderful that each letter has written in the upper right-hand corner of the envelope the word "Free."

We have talked of ourselves as a free people, but we haven't been free. We've been free of political oppression, but not of the oppression of provincialism. We've been free of physical bondage, but not of the bonds of ignorance and prejudice. With every "Free" letter that drops into an RFD box, those bonds loosen a little. Every time a boy writes home, "You know, the people here aren't so dumb after you get the hang of them," the world comes nearer to the size of a man's own backyard and the barriers of race and religion and language and custom shrink nearer to the height of a plain stone wall across which you can smile at your neighbor or shake his hand.

The Martyr Wife (1945)

My Aunt Agnes, to hear her tell it, was a martyr. She didn't really complain—martyrs don't—but you couldn't be with her for ten minutes without realizing that she was a sadly overburdened woman.

You'd say innocently, "Have you read Such and Such, Aunt Agnes?" and she'd say, "When do I have time to read, with a husband and four great boys to do for? Not but what I'm glad—" Or she'd ask, "What's your mother doing today, dear?" and if you told her, "She and Aunt Susie have taken a day off and gone to Boston," she'd say, "Some people are lucky. I don't know when I've been to Boston. Just once I'd like a day to myself. Well, I mustn't complain—" That sort of thing, you know.

None of us paid any attention. Her remarks went in one ear and out the other. We knew it was just habit and she'd gladly give any one of us the shirt off her back; and if afterward she might mention being chilly— that was just her way. Being a martyr was her idea of fun, so we cheerfully let her be one.

But I suppose it was different with strangers who weren't used to her, and especially with the four strangers who came to be her daughters-in-law. I can see how her attitude could get under their skin and I suppose that's why, one Fourth of July, they all four ganged up on her. Anyhow, I came through the kitchen door just in time to hear Brad's wife say to Aunt Agnes, "—and sit on the porch where it's cool and read a nice book. You've been wanting to read—"

"How can I read a book?" Aunt Agnes wanted to know. "With so much to be done—"

"And four grown women to do it," Mart's wife finished for her. "This is your chance to have a whole day to yourself. Now take off that apron—"

"But the Fourth without any ice cream—"

"We'll make the ice cream," Phil's wife said.

She didn't want to give in, but they made her and I went out onto the porch with her. It seemed odd to see her sitting in the shade of the trumpet vine with a book in her hands. She didn't turn a page all the while I was there. Her eyes were on the book, but her ears were cocked on the laughing and the bustle inside the house. Finally she got up. "I think I'll just go—"

"You better not, Aunt Agnes," I said. "This is your day of rest." So she sat down and I went home.

When I went back in the afternoon, Aunt Agnes was lying in a hammock between two trees and I remembered that one of her favorite remarks was that she wished she could lie in a hammock and do nothing for once, like some people. As soon as she saw me she said, "Louise, go in and see what they're doing. They won't let me in the door and I don't know what's going on—"

Just then Brad came out with a glass of lemonade on a tray. "Service, ma'am," he said and I remembered Aunt Agnes' oft-repeated wish that just once someone would wait on her. "Want a pillow or a magazine or a sandwich or something? No? Well, I got to get back. Why don't you take a nap, Mother?"

"Nap!" said Aunt Agnes bitterly to our retreating backs.

They were having a high old time in the house. Two of the boys were finishing up the dishes and Uncles Leslie and Ben were waxing the dining-room floor. The four daughters-in-law were putting up a huge picnic lunch. "We're going to take supper up to the ball field," one of them explained, "and then we'll be there ready for the fireworks. Will two dozen deviled eggs be enough, do you think? If you want to do something, Louise, you can hull those strawberries."

So I sat down and started hulling strawberries and laughing and singing and joking with the others, and we forgot all about Aunt Agnes until the screen door slammed and there she was. She didn't say a word— just put on an apron and took the strawberries away from me and began hulling them herself.

Well, of course everyone started objecting and talking about her day of rest. Finally she put her hands on her hips and faced them. "Now that's enough," she said. "I don't want to hear the word rest again. I appreciate your thoughtfulness, but I'll finish my resting after I'm dead, thank you. Maybe I won't feel so out of it and grave as I did lolling in that damned hammock while everyone else was pitching in together."

And that was that, except that I think about Aunt Agnes sometimes when I hear people fussing about the demands made on their time and money and strength and sympathy in these days of stress. I wonder if they'd like it any better than she did, to be left out of it, lolling in a damned hammock while everyone else is pitching in together.

My Wills (c.1945)

When I was about ten years old I wrote my first will. My great-aunt, a woman to whom none of us gave a thought and about whom none of us cared a hoot, had died and left a sizeable estate. This she disbursed by means of a will, the terms of which, for several months, I heard mentioned more or less acrimoniously whenever two or more of the relatives got together. It occurred to me sometime during that period that if this aunt, to whom no one paid any attention in life, could set the family by its ears simply by writing a will, I, to whom no one paid any attention to either, might do worse than to emulate her. Posthumous attention left something to be desired of course, but it was better than none. The fact that I didn't have any money and little else to bequeath was the least of my worries.

I still have that will, thanks to my father, who for inscrutable reason of his own saved it and sent it to me recently. It is couched tersely, in pencil on blue-lined yellow paper, and it reads:

"My sister Alice can have my tree I planted if she won't let anyone cut it down. My father can have my bantam hen because he will take good care of her. My mother can finish the quilt I am making. My best friend Ruth [Hunt] can have the secret [place] I found that is good to hide in. It is on top of a rock with moss on [it] beyond Brown's strawberry bed, but she mustn't tell anybody about it. My second-best friend Bernice can be Ruth's best friend. Signed, Sarah Louise Dickinson."

My father let me keep this document in his safe deposit box, as befits its importance.

The following quarter century my fortunes have fluctuated considerably and I have kept on writing wills. This is not a symptom of morbidity. I simply like to write wills. It's an interesting literary exercise and the best way I know of taking inventory of oneself and all one's blessings.

There were times when I literally didn't have more than the clothes on my back with which to bless myself, but I wrote wills all the same. When things were at a particularly low ebb I would write a will leaving my view of a brilliant sun-drenched autumn day to all lovers everywhere. Then I'd leave the reading of a book I particularly loved to lonely people or people in distress. It's amazing the things you can think up to give away, if you put your mind on it, when you haven't a penny to your name. It's amazing and very heartening.

Then there have been times when I have had enough of this world's possessions so that I've had to pay a lawyer good money to help me with my will. I tell him what I want to give to whom and he translates it into terms of the first and second aforesaid party, interlarding the whole thing so generously with whereases that I have to pay him more money to explain to me what it means. Then we round up some witnesses and everyone signs, and we put it into my lawyer's safe until I get mad at someone, or acquire something new, when we drag it out and go through the whole business again.

It was after the latest of these sessions, when my poor lawyer was at some pains to make me see why, under the existing statutes, I couldn't forbid anyone, ever, to cut some standing timber that we had bought solely to prevent its being cut, that I came home and found in the mail my first will.

Maybe it was only because I was tired and exasperated, but when I read it, it struck me that it was the best will I ever wrote. None of the things that I'd been fussing about all day compared in value to the things listed in that first will. Perhaps the quilt I was making wasn't much of a quilt, but it was my work, and where would I be, how could I live, without some work that I liked to do? What would I amount to without some responsibility, even if then it was only the responsibility for a little bantam hen?

You can't will friendship, I know now, or the spiritual and mental independence that makes sitting alone on a rock and thinking an exciting thing to do, or real love of the earth, so fundamental that planting and caring for a tree brings a sense of fulfillment; but oh, how I wish you could! Those are the things that have made my life worth living; those are the things that I want my children to have.

And those are the things they are going to have, God willing. Since marks on a piece of paper are powerless to confer them, I've stopped writing wills. If I start living my will now, with all my heart and soul, perhaps I can yet provide my children each with his rightful heritage—a tree, a hen, an unfinished quilt, a friend and a secret place on a rock, to comfort and sustain him as long as he lives.

Other
Wartime Stories
═══════════════════════════

[Both published in 1943, "That Little Bit Extra" (*Good Housekeeping*) and "Road Commissioner's Report" (*Country Gentleman*) are in the same genre as the *Woman's Home Companion* columns.]

That Little Bit Extra (1943)

When we lost our old cat—Thomas Bailey Aldrich—I set out to acquire a new one. As all cat owners know, when you have a cat, friends and strangers approach you daily, saying: "Know anyone who would like a nice kitten? We've got a new litter." And when you have no cat and are looking for one, everyone says: "Oh, I wish you'd asked last week! We had ten then, but they've all been given away."

So it was when we lost T. B. Aldrich. I asked the game warden, the fire warden, and the dam keeper. Over our battery-operated woods line, I called up Joe at the Brown Farm, and he sent scouts all through Magalloway Plantation (Maine) and Wentworth Location (New Hampshire); but nobody knew of a kitten. Finally Larry Parsons, who runs the boat, spoke to Freeman, who carries the mail, and Freeman spoke to his mother. The next day along with the mail came six ounces of tiger kitten tied up in a tomato-juice crate.

We named him Carter Glass, partly because we admire the Senator and partly because Freeman's mother made such a point of the fact that this was no ordinary, riffraff, native kitten. The kitten's father was "summer folks" from Boston. We felt that he rated a distinguished name, and he has not disgraced it. Before long he was a handsome, swaggering cat, with a delicate, arrogant air. He sat in the best chairs and refused to eat his cereal in the morning unless it was hot and well laced with sugar and undiluted canned milk.

And then we acquired Pinky. The stove in the living room was red hot that night; but it was thirty below outside. The wind shrieked over the roof, and the boards of the house snapped and split with cold. It was a terrible, desperate night—an iron hand of a night, which would squeeze warmth and life from any creature who was abroad. Unbelievably, we heard a wailing thread of sound at the door, and when we opened it, a black shadow flashed in on the icy draft and was lost in the deeper shadows of the corner of the room. It couldn't be a cat, but it was a cat—if you can call huge eyes blazing out of a fleshless rack of bones by any name. He was so thin that picking him up was like picking up an empty twist of fur. We could see that if he stayed with us, if after the cold was gone he didn't go back to the wild state to which he was born—for he could have been only a woods kitten, born of an abandoned lumber-camp cat, knowing nothing but hunger and terror and cold all his days—he would never, never be much of a cat. Malnutrition had warped his bones, and countless fights—not for fun or for love, but for life—had left him scarred and battered. He expected little of life, and of man he expected nothing. Only the last bitter extremity of suffering and desperation could have driven him to our door. If he had had it in him to hope, all he could have hoped for was an end.

We called him Pinky because he wasn't pink and was hardly worth the trouble of thinking up a better name.

I don't like cats. They are selfish, self-seeking creatures with no love in them except for the comfort that their cleverness teaches them to exact from man. A little purring, a little stropping against human legs, a little show of spurious affection—and there they are, full as ticks and lapped in comfort and admiration.

That cold December night, however, Pinky wasn't a cat. He was Need, and he had turned to us out of all the world. We fed him and kept him warm, and after a while, he stopped being afraid of us and sat in our laps. He had lovely manners and never took things for granted. He never sat in the best chairs or complained about the food, and when we went into a room, he always got up and waited until we were seated, to be sure he wasn't in the way. He was the only considerate cat I've ever met, and I should have been pleased, but I wasn't. It isn't natural for a cat to act that way, and until he could act as a cat should act, we had somehow failed in the responsibility that had been laid at our door—that of giving Pinky what he had never known, faith in the goodness of mankind.

Well, today I went into the living room, and Pinky was asleep in the best chair. He opened one eye and looked at me and closed it again. I said: "Come on. Get up. I want to sit there." He pretended he didn't hear me. When I picked him up and dumped him on the floor, he gave me what can be described only as a dirty look and went off the way Carter does when he feels I have been uppity with him, walking stiff-legged and muttering curses to himself. So I thought: "There. I don't have to bother about him any more, thank goodness."

But I find that I still bother about Pinky. Where I feed Carter as a matter of routine, I feed Pinky with concern. When Carter stays out all night, I think only that he'll show up when he gets around to it; but if Pinky is missing, I wonder if he's all right. I owe Carter a living because I brought him here, deliberately taking over the liability of his well-being. I don't owe Pinky anything. I never asked for him or wanted him, and he's no duty of mine. What I give Carter is according to the terms of tacit bargain I entered into the day I sent out word that I was looking for a kitten. What I give Pinky I give freely. That's why I give Pinky just a little more than I give Carter—the same food, but seasoned with good will; the same shelter, but doubly thatched with hospitality.

Oh, well, that's nothing new. Other folks' dishes are always more fun to wash than your own; and loads of people who wouldn't lift a hand for pay work themselves to the bone as volunteers to a cause. And that, if we want to go further, is why democracy is such a good and successful form of government—good for its members and successful in its enterprises. People always give that little bit extra that makes the difference when the giving is their own choice. They always hold back that last crumb in the bottom of the bag when someone has demanded it of them. It's much better to give everything. It accomplishes more and it leaves you with a fine, careless, invincible feeling.

Road Commissioner's Report (1943)

Miss Minta Trimback, her delicate, middle-aged features severe with concentration, moved the ruler with which she was keeping her place on the road commissioner's report down a line and frowned over his difficult penmanship. Might as well try to read hen tracks, she thought impatiently, but let her make one error in transcribing his notes into the copy for the town report, and the whole town would be on her neck. She rose and put another stick into the kitchen range, drew herself a glass of water and drank it slowly, and came back to the scrubbed pine table where what she called My Books were spread out. Sometimes if you sneaked up on them when they weren't lookin'... Sure enough, viewed afresh and caught off guard, the pencil scratchings on the yellow paper resolved themselves into sense.

She picked up her pen, dipped it in the ink, and started copying in her own beautiful and precise hand: "Jan. 1. To W. Treadwell, for breaking out the Abbott Notch Road—

...

The storm started along toward noon. Shortly before two o'clock the teacher let the school out. The snow was piling up in the schoolyard at an alarming rate, and some of the pupils had miles to go before the early dark. Along toward milking time the wind came up, piling the drifts between houses and barns so that the men came in with the pails of warm milk, snow plastered to the hips.

"Desperate out," they said all over the countryside, pulling off gum boots and shaking out sleet-encrusted Mackinaws. "Good night to be under cover."

Their wives hurried the steaming platters of supper to the tables. "It's down to zero on the back porch, and dropping all the time," they said. "Pull down that curtain before you sit. The cold comes in around the sash."

By seven o'clock the whole valley was dark, all light sealed in with all heat behind drawn shades, and the snow blew unhindered across the roads about Hilton, and packed, under the wind, solid and trackless from wall to wall.

Inside the General Store, Post Office and Telephone Exchange, old Silas Pease, the storekeeper, turned a page of the mail-order catalog and said over his glasses to Jim and Frank Evans, sitting beside the red-hot, pot-bellied stove, "She's a terror this time. Jake Haswell's going to have a day for himself tomorrow with the old tractor and plow. Lucky if he gets the village plowed out, let alone the roads in."

Frank Evans hitched closer to the stove. "Heck, Jake went down country this morning. He won't get back now."

His brother Jim chuckled. "Kind of puts it on Bill Treadwell, don't it? He run the plow last winter, time Jake had sciatica. Do Bill good. If I ever see a young feller too big for his britches—"

Silas Pease said mildly, "Well, now, Bill ain't so bad. Bill's had a lot to contend with, what with his pa stealing that money and running off when Bill wasn't out of short pants. He's been supporting his ma ever since he was fifteen, and doing a man's work's bound to make a kid cocky. Then he's got the notion folks expect him to turn out like his pa, and that's made him sort of tough and hard to get along with. But let him get married—I hear he's courting Anne Ring—and he'll settle down.

"Anne Ring," said Jim Evans. "Now there's a nice girl. Quiet, pretty, well brought up. But Bill ain't going to marry her or nobody else. What his pa done to his ma soured Bill on marriage."

"It ain't that." Frank Evans recrossed his legs, preparatory for a long discussion. "Thing is, Bill figures he's got to amount to something, to make up for what his pa done. And he figures the feller travels fastest that travels alone. Now his ma's dead, he ain't planning to have no wife hanging onto his coattails."

Jim Evans snorted. "I'll give the devil his due. Bill's honest and hard working. But he's too damn brash. Why—"

The door opened abruptly, and brief and icy eddies circled the pool of warmth and quiet that was the store. The day-old newspapers on the counter lifted and hung poised for a second, and then sank slowly back to rest as old Doctor Phipps fought the wind to close the door behind him. He leaned against it for a moment, his breath short, his eyes red and wind-inflamed. Frozen snow dragged at the hem of his long buffalo-fur coat, and his mittens, when he pulled them off, kept the shape of his hands, icy woolen molds.

Doc was an old man, Silas Pease thought, and he should be warm at home on a night like this. But try to tell him that. "Where you been at, Doc?" he said instead. "I been trying to get you for the past hour. Jessie Bartlett, up in the Notch, phoned. Her youngest's down with pneumonia."

Doc dropped his mittens on the candy counter. "I been over at Hog-back." He turned the hand crank of the wall phone briskly. "Had a hell of a time getting back.... Hello, Jess. What seems to be the difficulty? . . . Yeah... Yeah... Well, you do just like you did last year for Jeannie, keep pumping the liquids into her, and I'll start up soon's I can lay hands on Jake Haswell to plow out ahead—"

"Jake's out of town," Frank Evans said tersely. "You'll have to roust out Bill Treadwell."

Doc nodded, and his tone never wavered from its sure note. "Have Ewen start down to meet us. . . . Oh, he ain't there? Working in the woods? Well, it may take us longer but we'll get there—"

The door opened again, and again the newspapers stood up in their places, and sank. Silas said, "Evenin', Bill." And Frank Evans exclaimed, "Speak of angels!" Jim Evans said nothing. He had no truck with Bill Tread-well.

Doc looked over his shoulder and resumed his shouting into the mouthpiece. "Feller drives the plow just come in, so we'll start up right away. Should be there long before daylight. Now don't you fret, Jessie—"

Bill Treadwell looked from face to face, his mouth sullen, his young eyes hard and unhappy. "Hey, what is this?" His tone, rough and defensive, spoke louder than he knew of his conviction that every man's hand was against him. "I ain't going no place tonight."

"Not to Anne Ring's?" Jim Evans asked slyly.

"No."

"She turn you down?"

Bill swung like a baited bear, powerful and hurt and confused. "I never asked her. I got troubles enough—"

"Cut it out boys," Silas said, and he meant it. "The thing is, Bill, Bartlett's little girl is down with pneumonia, and Jessie's up there alone with the kids. Jake's out of town, so it looks like it's up to you to take out the plow and open up the road for Doc—"

"Listen. I ain't going up into no Abbott's Notch on a night like this. We'd never make it. That's the last road Jake plows out, she's such a heller."

Doc Phipps was shouting. "Tell her I'm on my way. That'll put the heart into her. And don't—" He broke off to crank furiously, listened, and hung up with a bang. "Line's out. Damn the thing. I got no idea how long I been talking to myself. Well, get your shawl and bonnet back on, Bill. We got a trip ahead of us."

"You crazy, Doc? You got any idea what it's like out?"

The old doctor looked at him from under shaggy white brows. "I'd ought to have. I just walked in two miles from the crossroads. Left my car in a drift out there. I'll ride the tractor with you that far and pick her up."

Bill shook his head. "Unh-unh. Not me. Just because I drove the tractor three-four weeks last winter, I ain't required—"

"Well, I am." The lined old face flushed and the faded old eyes turned suddenly icy blue. "But I can't make you go. However . . ." His blue-veined old hands trembled as he tied his muffler over his ears and under his chin. "However, I guess the town will trust me with the plow."

"Use sense, Doc," Bill urged. "You'll never get through. Nobody'd blame you for not trying."

"Nobody but me." It was hard for Doc to close the door behind him against the storm.

"Why, the old—" Bill said into the silence that followed Doc's departure. "I never thought he'd try it alone. Well, he won't get far. Not tonight."

"Maybe not." Silas Pease turned a page of the mail-order catalog. "But he won't come back neither."

"What does that mean?" Bill wanted to make something of it.

"Doc's going on seventy."

"More fool him, then."

The words rang and rang in the still room. Nobody answered. The wood shifted in the stove and the snow beat on the window, and in a brief hush, while the wind gathered itself for another attack, came a clattering from up the street.

"Doc's on his way," Frank Evans said. "He was tough—"

His brother answered roughly. "He might get through. They made men when they made Doc."

"Better men than they do now." Three pairs of eyes measured Bill and discarded him. "It ain't going to be no picnic, sitting out in the open saddle of that tractor and taking it. Not for no old man without a bite in his belly and a day's work behind him." The clatter of the tractor grew louder, and Silas raised his voice. "It ain't as if he was young—"

"Aw, shut up." Bill reached for his mittens. "I'll go, damn it." They weren't going to have a chance to spread it around that Bill Treadwell was a coward like his father. To hell with them.

Doc was making rough weather of it, he saw, as the tractor drew abreast of the store. He clung to the control levers desperately, his slight frame racked in the single seat. If the level of Main Street did this to him, the Notch would tear him to pieces. Bill stepped into the headlights and held up his hand.

Grapevine for OPA (1945)

[Between 1938 and 1945 Louise wrote dozens of stories for the major magazines of her day. Toward the end of this period, most of her pieces were autobiographical, such as this account of the difficulties the Rich household experienced juggling wartime rationing with the exigencies of living in the backwoods.]

If I should ride up to you in a hack—or to a fisherman's wife in some little coastal village, or to the man who brings our mail in here to the remote backwoods twice a week—and ask, "How many points is a pound of butter worth now?" you'd be able to tell me without even stopping to think.

But if I should ask, "How'd you find that out?" I doubt very much if you'd be able to tell me exactly. You'd probably say, "Oh, I read it in the paper, I guess. Or maybe it was on the radio. Or—oh, I don't remember. What does it matter anyhow, as long as I know?"

It doesn't really matter, of course, just as long as you do know. But the fact that you do know is about the best tribute that can be paid to those friends and neighbors of yours who are serving on that part of OPA War Price and Rationing Board called the Community Service Panel. Recognition of their efficiency is all the pay they will get, too.

In the early days of rationing and price control, the information service was very badly handled. That isn't a statement that I made up myself. It is generally admitted by administrators of the OPA to be true. The result was that none of us knew quite what was expected of us, or—even more important—why it was expected.

This was a situation that had to be remedied before the rationing system could possibly operate with anywhere near the degree of success that was vitally necessary. So, about a year later, the Community Service Panels were organized.

I myself am not particularly enthralled by anything that goes around calling itself a bunch of letters, like CSP. There is a certain inhuman, dry-as-dust quality there that leaves me unmoved. It wasn't until recently, when Catherine Jacobs, who keeps house for me, announced with every appearance of authority that the blue tokens were no longer to be used that my natural curiosity began to percolate.

How in thunder, I wondered, did she know that? Neither of us had been Outside—that is, across the two lakes and five miles of tote road that separate us from the dead end of the road that leads fourteen difficult miles to the fringes of civilization. No one had been In—In is the deep woods where we live—to tell her. The radio had been busted for three weeks, and we take no paper. I could see why she, as housekeeper, might make more of an effort to keep abreast of rationing affairs than I. But the most passionate interest and the best will in the world couldn't, I was sure, enable her to go into a trance and pick a thing like that out of the air. So I undertook to investigate.

Maine is a very good state in which to carry on an investigation of this sort. We have cities and farms and forests, and islands out at sea. Any information system that will work in Maine will work anywhere, I verily believe. You can't use the same methods everywhere, of course. But Americans from way back are old hands at cutting the coat to fit the cloth, and that, after all, is the working principle of the CSP. If you've got a local radio station, use it, is the idea. But if you haven't—well, there are other ways of getting word around.

Bangor, for example, has everything, including a Community Service Panel right out of the book. Radio is represented by Mr. Edward Guernsey, the manager of WLBZ, the station to which everyone in Maine who has a radio listens. The press is represented by Mr. Palmer and Mr. Morgrage from the two Bangor dailies. Through the superintendent of schools, Roland Carpenter, and the Rev. John Feaster, the facilities of the schools and churches are made available. And Mrs. John Quinn, the only woman on the Bangor CSP, represents the Catholic women's groups of Bangor. There isn't anyone who can't be reached, the Bangor chairman, Mr. Mc-Manus, assures me, and I believe him.

The papers give free space for the spreading of information. If pork is point-free this week, you read about it there. If you happen to miss it in the paper, you hear about it during the fifteen minutes of free radio time given the panel by WLBZ on Friday nights. If you miss it there, having gone to the movies instead, your child will come home from school with a little mimeographed note for your attention.

The Community Service members will catch up with you somewhere along the line, and don't think that they won't. And, mind you, these people aren't professional advertisers. They're just people, serving free. They all have other jobs to hold down—except maybe Mrs. Quinn. She says all she does is keep house. But she has five children, including a pair of twins, so I think she doesn't sit about the house with folded hands when she isn't distributing posters to stores or preparing the five-minute information period which most women's clubs now use on their programs in the Bangor district.

A far cry from Bangor is the little fishing village of Stonington in Hancock County. I wish I could make you see Stonington. It's on the farthest-east end of Deer Isle, out in Penobscot Bay. The main street runs along the waterfront. There are wharves and the ocean on one side, and great ledges rise up on the other. The houses cling to the ledges precariously, and where it is too steep for a road, narrow footpaths over the wind-scoured stone wind from house to house. The sea lies all around, shimmering and restless, dotted with a score of islands.

The Stonington Community Service Panel isn't at all like the Bangor panel. There aren't any representatives of press or radio, because there isn't any daily press and there isn't any radio. There's Mrs. Laura Morris and Mrs. Mary Gray and Miss Ava Rich, working under the chairman of the local rationing board, Mr. James Stinson. They don't have very much to do with, and they have a lot of territory to cover. All those islands aren't just scenic effects to them. They're parts of their district, peopled with folks who have to be kept informed when it's time to apply again for boat gas, and there are more than five hundred boats registered—trawlers and seiners and lobstermen.

The CSP of Stonington meets in a little room about twenty feet long and ten feet wide, with a window looking out over the bay. On the table when I was there was a vase of fall flowers—nasturtiums and dahlias and feverfew. But the thing I liked best—next to the members of the board—was an unframed quotation tacked on the door:

> If I tried to read, much less answer, all the criticism made of me and all the attacks leveled against me, this office would have to be closed for all other business. I do the very best I know how, the very best I can. I mean to keep on doing this down to the very end.
>
> *Signed,* A. Lincoln.

Mrs. Morris comes from Minturn, on Swans Island. To get to board meetings she rides over on the mail boat one day and back the next, spending twenty-four hours away from her home. She finds out what is going to happen next, and when she gets home she tells the folks about it. Some she calls up on the telephone; or she gives a bunch of the newest ceiling prices to her husband, who sells fish, and he distributes them when he goes to work. She mails out quite a lot of information to the 450 people on Swans Island, but everyone there knows she's the one to ask, if they have any questions, so she spends quite a good deal of her time answering her telephone and doorbell. She spends a lot more time helping people who are handy with bait and marine engines and lobster pots—but not quite such good hands with application blanks and pens—to make out their forms for new boats, or oil, or gasoline. She's a comfortable, pleasant woman, but you can't make anything very dramatic out of her. She doesn't feel dramatic. She's just a woman who was asked to do a job and is doing it the best she knows how.

Mrs. Gray lives in Stonington, and she has four children, including a son in the navy. "He was just bound to go, for all he was only seventeen. He went down and enlisted, unbeknownst to us. Well, we thought if he had his heart set on it, there was no sense in our refusing to sign his papers. He was under age, you see. So we let him go. And then when they asked me about serving on this board—well, I thought it was the least I could do."

And that wasn't any speech Mrs. Gray had memorized from a book. She meant it from the heart. So did Mr. Stinson mean it when he told me in his slow, low voice, "I'm too old for the service. I'm too old for the shipyards. A man has to do something at a time like this. A man can give his time anyhow. That's what time is for."

The best method of spreading news in Stonington is by word of mouth. "Everybody goes to the store and sits around and talks. Or we call folks up. Word gets round."

But on Isle au Haut, where Miss Rich lives, there isn't any telephone service for the ninety-seven people. "Ava's sister is postmistress, though," Mr. Stinson said, and that didn't need any footnote. Everyone calls for mail, sooner or later, everywhere. "And they're all like one family out there, anyhow. What one knows, they all know, come nightfall."

It's the same on Eagle Island, where there are a light and fifteen people, and on Sheep Island, which is only ten acres large. Where the mail launch doesn't go, the fishing boats do. And if all comes to all, as we say up this way, there's always a dory available and someone who can swing a pair of oars.

The Rumford Board, which is my own board, although it's forty miles from where I live, and which in the final analysis was responsible for Catherine's knowing about the blue tokens, has a combination of Bangor's and Stonington's problems. There are good-sized towns in the district, and tiny hamlets, all surrounded by what is called unorganized territory—that is, simply wild land under no form of local government and inhabited thinly by trappers, woodsmen, and fire or game wardens. In most places there are no roads and no regular mail service, and when there is a telephone, it's only the lumber company's private woods line.

The chairman of the Rumford Community Service Panel is Douglas Fosdick, who owns the *Rumford Falls Times* and who is, incidentally, the president of the Maine Press Association. He uses his paper to keep the public informed of the latest rationing developments.

Mrs. Sarah McCaffrey is a valuable member of his panel, because, as he says, "She knows who'll do things. If you want someone to explain to the women over at Labrador Pond, for example, about applying for canning sugar, she knows who over there isn't afraid to stand up in meeting and talk."

Mrs. McCaffrey is the president of the State Federation of Women's Business and Professional Clubs, which probably has something to do with her specialized knowledge.

It is one of the principles of the CSP to have different racial or religious groups represented, and this district has a large French population. So Father Boivin, the head of the French parish, sits on the panel; and the schools contribute Lawrence Peakes, their superintendent.

Mr. Peakes commented on a fact which I, from my old schoolteaching days, know to be true: The little grammar-school kids are suckers for taking things home from school and faithfully delivering them, but the highschoolers are more blasé. They throw things away, or lose them, unless you

sell them on the importance of delivery. So when there is rationing information to be given out through the schools, Mr. Peakes has his teachers explain and emphasize its importance. Once, to see how fast the school children could cover the town in case of emergency, Mr. Peakes set out to
place a poster in every single one of five thousand homes scattered over
an area of twenty square miles. It took exactly one hour and three minutes.

That reminded me to ask Mr. Fosdick what he'd do if some crisis made
it imperative to reach everyone in his far-flung districts within twenty-four
hours. "Could you do it? There's a lot of territory back yonder, after all."

"Sure we could do it," he said. "Remember that little boy that was lost
last summer? We had two hundred people out looking for him in less
than an hour. The school children would cover the towns and villages.
Then the *Times* has a local correspondent at every crossroads. I'd call
them, or, if necessary, send men or women in cars out to them. From then
on it would be up to the local folks who know the country. They'd put it
on the grapevine."

When he said that, I was right back on familiar ground. I know all
about the grapevine, and I could just see it going into action. Jenny Judkins, the *Times* reporter in our almost invisible little village of Upton,
would get hold of Jim Barnett, who drives the stage, and Jim would stop at
every house on his route with the news. Then she'd give the general-alarm
ring on all the party lines which center in her husband's store, and when
successive clicks meant that all the receivers were down, she'd make her
announcement. Then she'd call up Joe Mooney at the Brown Farm, and
he'd send out the message along the woods lines which loop from tree to
tree through the wilderness to every lumber camp and warden's post between here and the Canadian border—including the Riches.

Within fifteen minutes kicker boats would be starting up rivers and
across lakes to remote camps, and bearded gum-booted woodsmen would
be setting out over narrow trails to isolated cabins. In the meantime Jenny
would have corralled all the boys in Upton who owned bicycles and
started them out to the farms which are not on the mail route or have no
phones. It could be done all right. It has been done before now.

And, by the way, that's where Catherine found out about the blue
tokens—off the grapevine. It seems a local guide stopped by to see if we
could let him have a sheer pin for his outboard. Up the lakes, he'd run
across the game warden, who had just been to the Dam to collect his mail.
The damkeeper's mother-in-law had come in from outside the day before
and brought with her the latest on the blue-token situation.

So—it's simple when you have it explained, you see. Only we never could have got it off the grapevine if the CSP hadn't put it on in the first place. That's what I mean by their cutting their coat to fit the cloth.

Backstairs (1946)

[A classic Louise Dickinson Rich version of "what I did on my summer vacation," her story "Backstairs" was at least partially written in 1945, the first summer after Ralph's death.]

The trouble with life is that it isn't long enough. You can't possibly learn even a little about all of its phases that touch you, let alone the many that never will. That's why I'm so glad I became involved for ten weeks last spring in the hotel business. I'm going to be a lot nicer hotel guest from now on.

This is the way it happened. I had left my home in a hurry, with the doors unlocked, the windows unshuttered, and valuable tools and equipment strewn all over the place under the snow. It was all right then. My only neighbors are so honest they hurt. But as soon as spring came I knew the place would be teeming with strangers, so it behooved me to go home and stand guard over my property before the ice went out.

So one cold March day Catherine, my housekeeper, and I took the long road trip up to the lakes to tough out the break-up and get the house into living order before the children came home from school. It was after we'd been there two weeks that Al Parsons and I started talking about the opening of a hotel at Middle Dam, which she and Larry own and which is two miles above us on the Carry Road.

She said, "The ice is going out early this year, and I'm going to have my hands full cleaning cabins and getting the place into running order. We can't get any help in now, with the ice so soft."

"Look," I said. "How about me and Katie coming up for a week or so? We haven't anything else to do now."

"Do you really mean it?" she asked. And I did. I thought it would be fun, and it was. The next day Catherine and I waded through the snow up the Carry, with our clothes on our backs.

I don't imagine anyone who hasn't been through the mill knows what it means to get a hotel into running order, especially a hotel which depends on boats for its transportation, fishing for its popularity, wood stoves for its heat and cooking, and luck and a long-handled spoon for almost everything else. You have to get the guests' rooms ready. You have to get the dining room set up. Hotel dining rooms always seemed to me to be places of permanence. I'd never seen one undressed, and it's something to see.

The tables were all bare and piled up on one side of the room, because that spring they painted the dining room floor. The tables go in rows down the length of the hall. That sounds simple enough, but it wasn't so simple when we came to do it. In the first place, they differ in size. Some are six-seaters and some are four-seaters. You can't just chuck them in anywhere, because at Middle Dam the dining room has supporting posts down the center and the tables have to fit in around them. Well, that could be done, with a little figuring, except that the floor of the building heaves with the frost and never was very level to start with. So some tables have two short legs, and some have one, and some have all alike. If you can get them into the right places, turned the right way, they'll set evenly and not wobble when anyone leans an elbow on them. Al, who has a truly remarkable memory for detail, could remember where they went. But during the course of a cold winter some of the bumps in the floor had heaved higher and some of the valleys had sunk lower. So we had to put cardboard props under a few legs, and in really serious cases perform delicate operations with a saw. We finally got them in place.

I'd never in my life been in a hotel kitchen until that spring, and I found it a fascinating place. There is a range for the chef and a stove for the pastry cook and a charcoal burner to heat the steam table. There's a gas plate for waffles and griddle cakes and a gas urn for coffee, both fuelled, in this remote section, by portable cylinders of gas. There are four sinks— the pastry cook's, the chef's helper's, the white dish (dining room dishes) washer's, and the back-hall girl's. There's a big refrigerator that belongs to the chef and a little refrigerator that belongs to several other people, and heaven help you if you stick your nose into either one of them. Heaven double-help you if you put a dish back into the wrong dish closet, or take hot water out of the wrong faucet, or use a wrong dish towel, or throw the pigs' garbage into the refuse pail or the refuse into the pigs' garbage pail. Or wash with water the pastry cook's bread pans. Or drink a glass of milk out of the wrong can. Or leave the steam table lid open. Heaven help you, period, I found out later; but that wasn't until quite a lot of water had gone through the sluices.

That wasn't, for example, until after I'd spent two days being plumber's helper. The plumbers came in from Rumford, as planned, to repair and connect the network of pipes that lead to the cabins, each of which has its own bathroom. I started out to do no more than point to the taps that leaked, and the taps that wouldn't work at all, and any other feature of the plumbing that seemed out of kilter. I ended by crawling under cabins with a hazel-eyed plumber named Gordon—I never did find out his last name—and holding matches, wrenches, pipe solder or anything else his errant fancy dictated. I learned a lot about elbow joints and shut-offs, but I gave up on the day that he herded me into a bathroom, asked me to hold up the end of a bathtub while he tightened the connection, and then left me standing there lifting while he got out the makings, rolled and lighted a cigarette, and went out to find the proper wrench. I'm good-natured, but enough was enough; and holding up the end of a bathtub for fifteen minutes, more or less, was more than enough. I resigned my commission as plumber's mate.

We opened on time, in spite of hell and high water and the fact that one of the waitresses who had been engaged couldn't come for a week because she was having an impacted wisdom tooth treated. Catherine took off her cabin-girl slacks, put on a green uniform and apron, and went into the dining room. I did a quick shift from the scrub woman to chambermaid, and Larry and Al doubled in brass and practically everything else. We got by.

I liked cabin work. I really did. I was a good cabin girl, if I do say so as shouldn't, leaving my cabins neat and clean and getting through my work by noon. That last item is important. No guest liked a chambermaid barging about his cabin while he is trying to take a nap or promote a game of poker or relax with a good book.

During my free afternoons I thought I might as well be useful to Al in the laundry. She hadn't been able to find a laundress, so she was doing it herself on a sort of catch-as-catch-can basis. In other words, she'd run through a washerful of clothes in odd ten minutes between answering the telephone, making out the menus, answering questions, hunting up spare blankets for the man who was cold last night, and finding a box of paprika for the chef.

I liked the laundry work. There was a certain amount of social life connected with the job. Anytime anyone of the other help had nothing better to do, they'd drop in for a minute to exchange the time of day, sitting on the table by the mangle and swinging their legs. Catherine and Rose Howe—another waitress—would tell us that Mr. Smith was a funny eater who didn't want anything for lunch except crackers and milk; and I'd volunteer that I should think he would be, judging the amount and variety of pills he had standing on his bathroom shelf. Or they'd say Mr. Jones was fresh, and Dr. Abbott was simply swell, and we'd all tear them to pieces. Believe me, next time I go to a resort to stay, I'm going to be careful. I never realized before how much the back hall knows about the front hall, nor how accurate their diagnoses can be. Then Al would say to me that another basket of clothes was ready to hang out, and I'd grab it and run into the clothes yard, with a parting plea not to say anything important or interesting while I was gone.

Ah, happy days as chambermaid and laundress. Too soon were they over. I wandered into the back hall one afternoon to find the chef's helper obviously coming down with something. She was miserable, and looked it, but she was trying to keep on the job. She was a nice woman and I liked her, and we couldn't wash because it was raining, so I told her to go to bed and I'd do her work. This wasn't pure generosity. I wanted to see how the kitchen functioned, and the best way to find out was to work there myself. A writer never knows when miscellaneous information will come in handy.

The title, chef's helper, is extremely misleading. It sounds very grand and important. Actually it means that you peel vegetables, wash pots and pans, and scrub floors. You're the kitchen scullion, in short. At Middle Dam, you also make the salads, and that's all I did like about the job, except that it was An Experience. I was a simply terrible chef's helper, as anyone who was working in the kitchen will gladly testify. I ended by working there for a month, during which time everyone was nice and patient with my shortcomings but I was very definitely considered the not-quite-bright sister of the family.

It was the vegetables that got me down. Did you ever sit in front of a bushel of potatoes? Just as you get into the swing of things, the chef starts hollering about where are those three large kettles? He needs them right away. You fish them out of the sink and scour them down. By that time the chef wants to know whether those potatoes are for lunch today or next Sunday's dinner, and don't forget to scrape the ten bunches of carrots. And the salads. This noon we'll have green pepper and beet, so how about cutting them into fancy shapes. In vain do you plead for something easy like sliced tomato. We had that the day before yesterday and he has a reputation to think of even if you haven't. So you shove your sleeves a notch higher, push back your hair, and redouble your efforts. I hated those darn vegetables, and those persons whom I discovered not to eat potatoes won my personal popularity contest hands down.

I did learn some things from the chef, though. I learned that if you haven't any parsley, you can chop celery tops fine and get by with it. I learned that to slice an end of ham thin without cutting yourself, you put it face down on a board at the very edge of the table, place another board on top of it under pressure, and work with your knife between them. I learned that any knife less than razor-edged is an insult to a chef and that anyone who abuses the chef's knives, cutting with them on a metal surface or chucking them into the dishpan with the other cutlery, might just as well leave the country at once, if she values her life.

There's a lot to serving a meal in a hotel kitchen. Up until about eleven o'clock, everything is very easy and comfortable. The waitresses are buzzing around in their old clothes, which they've changed into from uniform right after breakfast, polishing glasses and cleaning silver, and asking each other highly technical questions like, "Are you going to change your table-cloths this morning?" The two dishwashers are discussing their operations and returning dishes that somehow have wandered into each other's sinks. The chef is drinking another cup of coffee before emptying the urn and trying to sing harmonizing bass to his helper's erratic version of "Bell Bottom Trousers." (I was the helper and I can't keep a tune.) The pastry cook and one of the guides are fighting good-humoredly about the fate of the two chocolate doughnuts left over from breakfast. Al comes in to take the chef's list of things he wants from the store room and stays to eat a warm cookie. Swene, who has been icing up the big refrigerator, drops a splinter of ice down my neck, laughs at my yowl, and tells me that's for putting a coffee can in the pig's pail yesterday. It's fun.

But along around eleven o'clock the tension begins. The chef starts watching the clock and his braised beef. The waitresses say, "Now that's my tray and I don't want it touched. I just scoured it"; take a last look at their tables, and run along to change their clothes. I think, "Heavens above, I forgot to wash the coffee urn," and ask the pastry chef how many there are in the front hall, because I want to know how many salads to make. She doesn't answer me, because she's worrying about the meringue on her pudding and anyhow, she's mad at me for not returning a spatula I borrowed from her. The tension increases. I'm never going to get the salads out on time, and who hid the mayonnaise jar? I left it right here and nobody had any business moving it. The waitresses come back, all crisp and clean, with new faces on and their aprons tied back-side-to to save them from spotting. they start cutting their butter and getting their ice-water ready, and asking each other with restrained curtesy to please not use the center tray stand, because that's the one that goes with the six-seater, and you can't serve that big table from the end stands. The pastry chef announces under her breath that they'll just have to eat that pudding or go without; it's probably as good as they get at home, at that. The clock moves around to twelve. It's time to ring the gong, so I say, "All right to ring, Pat?" The chef scowls at me. "Oh, hold your horses. The guests aren't going anywhere," and tastes his cream soup. Then he gives me a nod, and I go out and beat on the gong. The waitresses run for the dining room—they're supposed to be standing there when the guests enter—but one of them comes back and asks frantically, "Has anyone got a safety pin? My slip strap just broke."

The chef takes his place behind the steam table, the pastry cook starts laying out individual servings of the pudding and cutting the pie, I count my salads and find I'm two short—someone stole a couple while my back was turned—and the dishwasher announces that she hopes the girls will bring their dishes out promptly, because she has to wash her floor after lunch. I groan loudly. If she washes her section of floor, I'll have to wash mine. The chef gives me a dirty look and says, "Quiet! The guests are coming in now!" I'm quiet, properly rebuked.

Then the waitresses start coming out, and you'd never know them. They're full of business. Even their voices, which were normal and warm that morning, have changed. They're sharp and crisp and inhuman. "Four cream, two tomato soup. Five braised beef coming up." They take the appropriate dishes out of the steam table and line them up on the shelf in front of the chef. All normal conversation stops. The chef may say, "You didn't put your dishes up, miss," or "Whose order of turnip is that? Take it out of here."; or one of the girls may say to another, "Hey, that's my ham!" But that's all. The entire attention of everyone in the kitchen is on getting food onto the front-hall tables, hot and with quiet expedition. It's nerve-wracking.

Then the peak is passed. I'm coming out even on salads after all. The pastry cook looks into the pigs' pail, sees no pudding, and remarks, "Well, I guess we got away with that." She grins at me. "You didn't have any lunch. Want a piece of apple pie?" The chef says, "Heck. Make yourself a hot beef sandwich, first." Catherine comes in and says, "Whew! Everybody's out. Hey, did you see me almost dump soup down Mr. Tarbell's neck? Look, what do you do about serving your corner tables? I can't get in behind mine. Chef, four people commented on how good the beef was. Anybody care if I have a cup of coffee, and could I snag one of those hermits? They look swell." The meal is over. We're all friends again.

But I'm glad I don't work in a hotel kitchen for keeps. I couldn't stand three nervous breakdowns a day, day in and day out. Whenever I eat in public now, no matter how quiet and efficient the service or how good the meal, I picture to myself the silent inferno out back. I don't know whether this clairvoyance spices or ruins the meal. But I do know this: it would do a lot for general good will all around if life were long enough and we all had opportunity to do for a little while the other fellows' jobs. I'm a good hotel guest now. If only I knew more about what lies behind the things and people that irritate me, for whom I have little tolerance and no patience, I'll bet I'd be nicer about them, too.

Molly Ockett (1946)

["Molly Ockett" is a contemplative piece written in the spring of 1946. Louise had recently married Jim Barnett and was living in Rumford Point. Katie had left and Louise had creditors howling at the door. This short story reflects Louise's personal search for meaning, for a role model, at a time when her reality consisted of absent loved ones, poverty, and an unhappy marriage.]

The first time I ever heard the name of Molly Ockett was upon a day when my husband Ralph and a man who sometimes works for us were discussing the building of a small water-powered sawmill. I wasn't paying much heed to the conversation, but since I have a very lively curiosity about the people who live around me—even if I never see half of them—that new name brought my wandering attention back, as the presence of a covey of quail arrests a questing bird dog.

"Molly Ockett," I said. "I don't believe I know her, do I? Where does she hang out?"

Whit laughed. "Well, for the last hundred and twenty-five years or more, she's been hanging out in the Andover cemetery, so I don't believe, either, that you know her." And he and Ralph went off to look at the site of the proposed mill.

But the seed had been sown. I went about my business wondering why in the world a woman dead over a century and a quarter should be mentioned in connection with water power, of all things. Who was she anyhow? What had she done that the syllables of her name should roll casually off the tongue of an old countryman? I was consumed with a fever to find out about this Molly Ockett; and I did, but it took some doing. There is no record of her life, so I had to depend on word-of-mouth accounts, handed down from generation to generation. In the end I decided that Molly Ockett was a woman after my own heart.

Did you ever try to determine the character of an individual from the reports and opinions of a variety of persons, from the known facts about him and the conjectures concerning him? It's a fascinating occupation, a sort of psychological hare-and-hounds. This fact is at wide variance with that; this opinion contradicts utterly the other. Somewhere through the maze of fact and personal bias and legend and distortion flees the hare, the true identity of the individual; but where? Every man has as many personalities as he has acquaintances. Which is the real one? Who and what was Molly Ockett, whose very bones were now dust, with whom I now could never talk, forming my own opinion from a flash of expression, an inflection of voice?

She was, so they told me, a St. Francis Indian, and her name was really Mollockett. She was, they said, a very pretty genteel squaw—this came from the granddaughter of a woman who had known her—with a nice way about her. A pretty genteel St. Francis? But the St. Francis were those limbs of Satan who burned and ravaged and plundered the colonies of New England with such fiendish ferocity that a punitive expedition finally had to be organized under Major Rogers to wipe out their village. Who ever heard of a genteel St. Francis Indian? She'd been baptized into Christianity under the name of Mary Agatha and she was very pious, she frequently registered complaints with the local distiller that his rum would be all right if it didn't have quite so much brook in it, and she lived with the Indian Sabattis and bore him three children, but she finally left him because he drank too much. Now where in that collection of contradictions lay Molly Ockett?

The living in sin, I decided, we could discount. Things were a bit less formal in this country a hundred and fifty years ago, and she was no doubt following the practical custom of the time. Sabattis came back from his trip to Quebec with Arnold, more or less of a celebrity. Molly wasn't the first—nor the last—woman to be impressed by a hero returned from the wars, and Sabattis was a very handsome Indian, they say. So when he suggested that they set up housekeeping, and there was no minister handy, she decided, no doubt, that if she held out for book and bell some other pretty genteel and more co-operative St. Francis would toll him away from her. There was no telling when the circuit rider would be along again, if ever. She'd better grasp opportunity while it was offered.

I don't think she left Sabattis because of his liking for the bottle. After all, as far as I can find out, he was almost never at home. He was off with Arnold, or guiding posses in pursuit of raiding parties such as the Indian Tom Hegan's. In all the reading I have done about the history of this country, I have come across the name of Sabattis often and often—but never in connection with Molly Ockett, except parenthetically. A woman of spirit can't take that sort of treatment. Here he was off covering himself with glory, having a whale of a time, and never giving her a thought. What's more, she had to support the family. In Molly's time that meant tramping through the woods in search of game. At this she became so proficient that to this day she is remembered as a tracker of uncanny skill and a dead shot. She was a competent little piece, and I like competency.

Finally the day came when she was fed to the teeth. What was the point of all this hanging about for that no-good handsome hulk of a Sabattis to get around to coming home? Next time he showed his face.... The upshot of it was that the next time he showed his face she pronounced the Indian equivalent of "You go your way and I'll go mine." From what I later found out about Molly, I gathered that she was not a woman for half measures. When she was through, she was through, and we can forget about Sabattis. Nobody remembers having heard of his being seen around these parts again. He apparently appreciated, if no one else did, that under the pretty gentility beat the heart of a true St. Francis.

By this time the country around here had become settled to some extent. There was a fair sized colony at Bethel and a few families at Andover, with two or three farms dotted along the Androscoggin and Ellis Rivers in between. Molly, solely responsible now for the children, appeared at Bethel one day and put in a claim for a free grant of land due her as one of the original proprietors. This she succeeded in getting, and she established her home there. Possibly headquarters would be a better term than home. She left the children, who were now old enough and, being Indians, self-reliant enough to take care of themselves, in residence there, and she devoted her days to tramping over the countryside.

She had no practical purpose in doing this. She simply loved the woods and hills and lakes of this country. She loved to travel about in them, observing the flight of a bird, the fall of a leaf, the rise of a cloud over a mountain. This country is lovely today, even after having been partially logged off and settled slimly along lake shore and wood road. What it must have been then, when the first growth pine—the pumpkin pine—towered a hundred and fifty feet into the heavens and over-shadowed cathedral aisles, when game was plentiful on the slopes overlooking wide lonely reaches of lake, is something to stir the heart to imagine. What sights she must have seen! There is nothing prettier in the world than the leap of a deer, white flag flying, over a fallen tree, or the romping of a litter of fox cubs, coats red, small pointed faces bright with fox laughter, around their complacent mother. How many times she must have stopped and stood and stared, even as I do today, still and enchanted. I envy her and I wish I could have been with her then.

Molly used to climb Whitecap, a mountain near here with a crown of bare white ledge, to pick blueberries. I've been up there myself, on the same errand. It's a stiff climb, but it's worth it. The whole world lies spread out before you, when you reach the top, like a map. Below are the lakes, running like inquisitive fingers into the folds of the hills, and to the west the White Mountains climb higher and higher to the flawless sky. It's gorgeous.

Molly went up there one Sunday and spent the day, coming down to Andover early the next morning with her bucket full of berries. She stopped at the house of the minister and gave his wife the fruit. She had, as a result of her travels, a wide and good acquaintance among the settlers of the district, and she often stopped in at their homes to pass the time of day. On this occasion, however, a little difficulty arose. When the minister's wife emptied the berries into a dish, she found them remarkably fresh. "Why, Molly," she exclaimed reproachfully, "you picked these on Sunday!" Molly admitted without apology that such was indeed the case. I suppose her private comment was her version of "So what?" The minister's wife was horrified. "But Molly! You did wrong! That was a sin!"

Molly drew herself together, got to her feet, and put on her jacket, and although the minister's wife had set a place for her at the table, she refused to stay and eat. "It would choke me," she said. "I was right in picking berries on Sunday. It was so nice up there on the mountain; I was so happy and all the while I felt so thankful to the Great Spirit for providing them for me. I know it was not wrong." And that seems to me as truly religious an attitude as I have ever heard expressed, and as free from hypocrisy.

As more settlers drifted into the territory, Molly's acquaintance naturally expanded, and she found herself called upon very often when she happened into a cabin in a remote district to render medical assistance of one sort or another. She was a very successful midwife, for example, and helped into this world the first baby born in Andover. The descendants of this child cherish to this day the distinction of having sprung from one of Moll Ockett's cases. She was very skillful with herbs and home remedies, too, and without doubt saved a great many lives. She wouldn't take any pay for this service, beyond one penny, which she put into a bag about her neck. Her attitude was that if a friend couldn't help out a friend in a pinch it was just too bad. The pennies she never spent, and I have no idea what became of them. I think she collected them simply as souvenirs of interesting occasions. What did she want of money? She was happy as she was. Food and clothing were provided her by the wilderness she loved. She lived the kind of life she wanted to live, and she had a lot of friends who were always glad to see her coming.

Molly must have had many adventures of which she never told, and she must have had many more that have been forgotten. She spent one day, though, the story of which everyone around here knows and tells upon occasion. It's this day, incidentally, that was responsible for her name being mentioned in connection with water power. She was in Andover and she decided to go to Paris Hill for unstated reasons of her own. It wasn't a very good day for traveling, as it was cold and raw, with a snowstorm brewing in the east. But weather was little or nothing in Molly's life—she'd seen a lot of it on its own grounds and none of it had ever got the better of her— so she set out anyhow.

The snowstorm turned out to be worse than it had any right to be, and Molly began to tire. It's hard work breaking trail through ten inches of snow. She had not the foolish and stubborn pride that insisted on finishing a stint laid out for herself by herself when it became apparent that the end wasn't worth the grief involved, so she started looking for a place to spend the night. She could, of course, have laid out, as we say—that is, made a fire and slept by it—but the road she was traveling had some dwellings along it, and she saw no point in being wet and cold and uncomfortable if she could find shelter. In this frame of mind she arrived at Snow Falls.

I know Snow Falls as it is today. It's right beside the Bethel-Rumford Road, a boiling drop of water between two ledges into a pool below. There's nothing else there now; but at the time Molly stopped, there was a mill which used the falls for power, and the residence of the miller and his family. Molly stopped and asked for shelter, and was for some unknown reason—because she was usually made more than welcome anywhere— refused admittance. Possibly the miller was new to the country and didn't know her and her reputation, so the sight of an unknown and rather bedraggled squaw on his doorstep frightened him. Whatever the cause, he turned her away.

Well, naturally, she was furious. She stood right there in the road and pronounced a curse on the place forever. Nobody, ever, should be able to live there and prosper. Then she spat, turned her back, and tramped off down the road, in no very amiable humor.

At the next place she approached, the family was in trouble. The baby was deathly ill and not expected to live the night out. However, in spite of her worry and distress and preoccupation with her child, the housewife asked Molly in and provided her with dry clothes and food. As soon as she had eaten, Molly took over the nursing, and before morning had the child out of danger. She left then, after thanking her hosts and assuring them that the baby would not only recover completely but would grow up to be a great and distinguished man. Her blessing was on it.

And that's all there is to that, except that to this day, in spite of the fact that Snow Falls looks like an ideal site for any power project, no one has ever encountered anything but grief and failure there. Even in modern times, with modern financing and modern methods and equipment, the old curse still holds. Something always happens—something outlandish and unforeseen—to ruin anyone with the temerity to try to establish a business there. Finally the place has been abandoned. No one ever thinks of using it any more. When Moll Ockett cursed, she cursed for keeps.

And when she blessed, she blessed for keeps, too. The baby did get well, and when he grew up he became Vice-President of the United States of America under Abraham Lincoln. His name was Hannibal Hamlin.

I like the story of her later life and death, too. Even when she was quite an old lady, she still liked to travel about the wilderness, looking it over and checking up on it. One day when she was over in the White Mountains, she ran into an Indian acquaintance of hers. He was a little drunk and he confided in her the intention of his boss, Tom Hegan, to ambush and kill a certain Captain Clark from Boston who was at the moment fur trading in the vicinity. This Captain Clark had, through many years of fair dealing with the Indians in the matter of furs, established himself firmly in their good graces—except obviously in Tom Hegan's, and he didn't like anybody. Molly at once determined to warn the Captain of the plot and save his life if it were at all possible. This project involved a long night trip over very rough and difficult country, further made dangerous by the presence of the raiding party, which, although it hadn't anything special against Molly, still wouldn't hesitate to kill her if she seemed to be a menace to the plan. She made camp successfully, and just in the nick of time. Two men whom Clark had stationed as outposts had already been killed and scalped, and Tom Hegan was closing in on the rest. But thanks to Molly's warning, they escaped.

The Captain was overcome with gratitude for what he called in the lofty language of the day "the noble act performed by this courageous and faithful squaw," and he insisted on rewarding her suitably. His idea of a suitable reward was to take her to Boston and set her up in comfort for the rest of her days. She fought the plan for a long time. In the first place, she didn't consider what she had done anything so remarkable. Traversing the woods at night was child's play for her, so why make a song and dance of it? In the second place, I'm sure she resented the patronizing flavor of those words "noble" and "faithful." Noble and faithful nothing. She was just being a pal. In the third place, she didn't want to go to Boston. She wanted to stay where she was. She couldn't see—nor can I—why people insist on rewarding you according to their own ideas instead of in the light of what you'd really like. However, Captain Clark finally wore her down, and she said she'd go. She went and lived there in the city for a year, and it nearly killed her. She just couldn't stand the restrictions of civilization, and she at last announced that she was going home where she belonged. Once back on her old stamping ground, she felt, she'd at least die happy.

But she didn't die at once. She lived to be over a hundred years old. In the end, when it was obvious that her days were numbered, some people named Bragg took her in and cared for her. The house still stands, overlooking Andover Common. At the last moment, however, she couldn't stand to die under a roof. She begged that she be taken outdoors to breathe her last breath. Can't you imagine the consternation of the Braggs? What would the neighbors say when it was discovered that they'd turned that poor old woman out to die on the ground like a dog? But old as she was, Molly still could impose authority if necessary. So they carried her out into the Common in a blanket, and there she died. More power to her memory.

So that's Mollockett, commonly called Molly Ockett, a woman of ability, sense, and simplicity, a woman who knew what she wanted and got it through her own efforts, a woman I should like to have known.

Can't Find My Apron Strings (1957)

[For the past eleven years Louise had been concentrating on writing books—six to be exact. This was her first published short story since that time. Rufus was in the army, Dinah was with Florence in Bridgewater. Louise was all alone at Cranberry Point, in Corea. In this piece she writes about the bittersweet ache of letting go one's children, of coming to the realization that one's offspring are essentially adults and on their own, leaving you on your own.]

There was a time when I would have said with all confidence that the life of my only son Rufus was an open book to me. I was acquainted with everyone with whom he was acquainted; I recognized his limitations and abilities; at any hour I could tell approximately where he was and what he was doing; and I knew that were anything troubling him, I would sense it. At least, that was my smug assumption.

Then one blizzardy Saturday afternoon he asked me as a favor to drive him around his paper route. I'd never had a paper route myself, but naturally I knew all there was to know about the business. You left the paper, collected the week's tariff, and that was that. If it had been any more complicated, my son couldn't have held the job for the past two years. He was, after all, only a child.

I not only agreed to furnish transportation, but, in my innocence, I offered to help him in the delivery. "All right," he said, "you take the left-hand side of the street and I'll take the right. That's 14 *Enterprise*s for you, six *Globe*s and two *Record*s. The first three houses are all *Enterprise*s. Stick the papers inside the storm doors, and the money will be on the porch rails. The fifth house, you have to ring the bell or she'll holler. The seventh and ninth houses are *Globe*s, and the eighth you have to deliver at the back door. She owes for two weeks, and make her give it to you. Seventy cents, and don't let her talk you out of it."

I was lost. "Wait. The first three houses the papers go in the storm doors. Then the next you ring the bell ... "

"No, no," he said indulgently. "Wouldn't it be simpler if I did them all and you kept the route book?" Keeping the route book consisted of checking off payments. I guessed I could do that.

For about three streets everyone paid on schedule. At the end of the fourth street, pencil poised, I asked, "Check them all?"

"Yup, all except number 39. I collect there on Mondays instead of Saturdays."

I asked why.

"Oh, he's always drunk on Saturdays. Half the time he doesn't understand what I want and the other half he tries to give me all his money." My face must have reflected my horror. "Don't start worrying about it," my sheltered little lamb begged me. "Him and me understand each other all right. Now," he changed the subject with finality, "want to count out eleven *Enterprise*s for me?"

It took me two streets to recover. Then I came to a name about ten weeks in arrears. When Rufus came plowing back through the drifting snow, I said, "How long are you supposed to let them go without paying? This one here . . . "

"Yeah, I know. We're supposed to drop them after a month, but the boss says to use our own judgment." What judgment of dead beats can you have at twelve? I wondered. "This fellow's been having a hard time. He's been out of work for a long while, and now his wife's in the hospital. But he's just got a job, and he says he'll pay me when he gets caught up with himself."

"But what if he doesn't?"

"It comes out of my hide. But don't worry. He'll pay."

I kept my mouth shut, since this was my son's affair and he had to learn the ways of the world sometime, probably the hard way. For weeks I studied his face every collection day, trying to read in it any signs of disillusionment. At last I couldn't stand it any longer, so I asked.

"Who?" Rufus looked blank. "Oh, him. Oh sure, he paid me up a month ago and gave me an extra buck for carrying him so long."

I never did find out much about Rufus' job at the garage. In theory, he washed cars and pumped gas. However, I came out of the chair store one day to find my son in deep consultation with a well-dressed stranger. Rufus was shaking his head and looking judicious. "She shouldn't do that," he said. "Let me take a look." The man climbed into a brand-new Lincoln parked at the curb, released the hood, and Rufus plunged elbow-deep into the innards of the motor. I prevented myself with difficulty from screaming, "Don't touch! Those things run into money!" I was in no financial position to replace Lincolns ruined by my son's feckless attention.

"Now try her," Rufus instructed with the confident aplomb of a high-priced specialist. The owner stepped on the starter, the motor purred into life, and Rufus announced, "She's okay now."

When the stranger had driven away, I told him, "You mustn't fool around with other people's cars. Who was that, anyhow? What were you doing under his hood? You might have busted something, and . . . "

"Gee whiz, Ma," he expostulated, "you'd think I was born yesterday! There wasn't nothing much the matter with that Lincoln. You ought to have seen the job we had last week. Oh boy, timing off, feed line plugged, wiring shorted . . . "

Last winter Rufus told me that he was going to spend his Christmas vacation working at a turkey-processing plant two towns away where they killed turkeys and prepared them for market. He'd arranged for transportation: he'd meet Norm at Charlie's Diner at six in the morning. All I had to worry about was putting up a lunch and seeing the alarm clock was set for five-thirty. This seemed within my limited capabilities. But one night I forgot to set the alarm. Rufus wasn't at Charlie's the next morning, Norm went off without him and it was up to me to see that he got to work, since I was the one who had failed with the alarm clock.

Shivering and hungry in the pitch black of winter predawn, I drove him by obscure back roads to a long tumbledown shed in a field. Dim lights burned within, illuminating vaguely some sinister figures bundled against the cold wearing rubber aprons. An ugly black mongrel came tearing out, slavering and snarling savagely. Good Lord, I thought, what a horrible setup! I can't leave my child here with this bunch of thugs. That dog is only waiting to rip his throat out. I'm going to take Rufus straight home.

But before I could open my chattering teeth to say so, he'd jumped out of the car. "Hello, Bandit!" he greeted the dog affectionately, and the great beast swooned with silly joy. The men in the shed crowded to the door, laughing. "Sure as heck thought you weren't going to make it this morning, boy!" they shouted, and all the unshaven, villainous faces were transfigured with good humor and friendliness.

"Okay, okay," said one who seemed to be in charge. "We haven't got all day. Shake the lead out of your pants, Rufus, and get an apron on. I want you to shackle today."

That's when I gave up. I didn't know what shackling was, and I didn't try to find out. Driving back home alone in the red sunrise, I faced the fact that my child had a life of his own that he was perfectly competent to handle. He'd been doing it for years, during which most of my fussing and worrying had been so much wasted energy. From now on, I resolved, I was going to bear in mind the truth that the young are much more resourceful, adaptable and capable than their poor mothers, who foster a delusion of indispensability, are willing to accept.

It'll be very good for both of us, if I can do it.

All This, and Fishing, Too! (1961)

[After 1945 Louise concentrated almost exclusively on writing books, but she sent the following piece (which I've condensed) off to *Outdoor Life*. The story was written at The Sands after

Louise had sold her Bridgewater house and moved back to the Gouldsboro Peninsula. It is a celebration of getting back to Maine "for good."]

DEDICATED TO THE MEMORY OF JOHN GODFREY MOORE 1848–1899

A Maine man who loved his native state, wherein he spent,
with his family, some of the happiest days of his life.
He owned Schoodic Peninsula, built the first road upon it,
and opened it to the public in the year 1897.

That's how the simple bronze marker on the ledges overlooking the North Atlantic reads. That's how it happens that this rugged and beautiful tongue of land across Frenchman's Bay from Mt. Desert Island, washed on the east by Prospect Harbor and facing south to Spain over 2,000 miles of empty sea, extends its wordless welcome to all people.

Schoodic is a fairly common place name on this part of the Maine coast. The word is Indian, meaning a burned-over area. So wherever there was a long-ago fire, today there's a Schoodic. [Schoodic Peninsula] is perhaps the loveliest place I've ever been or am likely to be.

Though [a] glacier created Schoodic's beauty, the [Acadia national Park] administration should receive credit for preserving it. Other beautiful places have been changed out of all recognition and ruined by man's improvements. On Schoodic, the narrow roads, surfaced with native pink granite, follow the natural coastline. The necessary bridges are abutted with boulders and look almost like the careless work of storm tides. There are no precise plantings on Schoodic. Even the large terraced parking area at the outmost tip is more like a part of the gigantic ledges stepping down to the sea than a feat of engineering.

There are as many reasons why people go to Schoodic as there are kinds of people. Two hundred sailors go because they work there at the Navy's Radio-Direction Finder Station, located in the middle of the peninsula behind a dense growth of fir and spruce. Through some quirk of the sound waves, this particular spot has better reception from Europe than any other point on the Atlantic coast.

Thousands on vacation go to Schoodic in summer, simply to soak in the beauty, to carry away mental pictures against the winter's routine. They take home real pictures, too, since many artists and photographers frequent Schoodic. The photographs and paintings show spruce-crowed islands on a diamond-bright sea, little lobster boats sturdily going about their business against a backdrop of all infinity, an ocean lively with leaping fountains of spray as far as the eye can reach, the sun sinking in purple and gold behind the great loom of Cadillac Mountain across the bay.

Serious naturalists go to study plant and animal life. Like all national parks, Schoodic is a wildlife refuge. It lies in the middle of one of the three great migratory lanes of North America, and also in the band where northern and temperate forms of vegetation meet and overlap. Consequently there's a great variety of animal, plant, and bird life to observe, some of it rare and all of it interesting.

There are those who drive out to the tip of Schoodic at dusk to see the *Bluenose* go by, slatting up over the eastern horizon like a great ball of fire on her way from Nova Scotia.

Finally, there are people who go to Schoodic to fish. Purists who consider dry-fly fishing the only proper angling would shudder at the sort of thing that goes on at Schoodic. Once they've overcome their first shock, however, a surprising number of them join the crew on the rocks. To their own amazement, they thoroughly enjoy themselves. From start to finish, fishing at Schoodic is fishing at its simplest. To begin with, no long trek to a secluded stream is involved. You drive to the end of Schoodic Point, park your car in the parking area, and there you are, 50 feet or so from where the ledges drop straight into the bold water. *Bold* is the word used locally to indicate water that comes straight in from the open sea to the foot of steep rocks, with no flats or beaches intervening. That's the water at Schoodic.

You don't have to scheme, either, to acquire one of the "good" places. They're equally good from one end of the ledges to the other, a distance great enough to accommodate scores of fishermen. You don't need boots or waders. You don't need skill or experience. You don't even need a fishing license, since this is ocean fishing.

All that is necessary to know in order to fish successfully at Schoodic is to fish on an incoming tide and fish on the bottom. When the tide goes out, so do the fish. If you think you have something on your line, you're probably right. Because of the conformation of the rocks, this is an unusually clean coastal stretch, with very little debris or rockweed to fool you. Some kinds of fish grab hold firmly and some sneak up on the bait. So it's better to reel in each time you feel a nudge. If you don't have a reel, just yank or haul in hand-over-hand. It works as well, if less stylishly.

One thing about fishing off Schoodic ledges, nobody cares about your technique. I've fished in places where I knew I was being judged not on my ability to catch fish, but on my tackle and casting style. There's none of that nonsense at Schoodic. Nor any nonsense about correct tackle. Whatever works is correct. The same applies to bait. Dry flies won't work, that's for sure. And I don't think wet flies would, either. Worms are good, and so are clams. If you're too busy or lazy to dig them, you can always buy canned clams at the chain store. Or you can use any scraps from your lunch that won't disintegrate too rapidly in water—ham, sliced chicken, Spam, anything of that sort. I once caught a cunner—a solid, deep-bodied fish something like a cod—on a sliver of dill pickle, but I think it must have made a mistake. It never worked again. Usually I bait with small herring.

Nobody bothers to dress for this fishing. To one who lived long in a country where it was *de rigeur* to dress formally and properly for fishing (waders, plaid shirt, and hat-band stuck full of flies), the outfits worn on Schoodic are downright fascinating. Dungarees are very common, as are shorts and swimming trunks. Once in a while you'll see a man in a business suit, a salesman snatching time between calls to relax his nerves. Once I saw a woman in a beautifully tailored silk suit, veiled hat, and stocking feet hauling in a flounder of considerable size.

But the group I've liked best so far was a family come to Schoodic on a picnic. There were the mother and father and seven children aged from about fifteen down to the baby, and an older woman who must have been the grandmother. She was my pet. She was wearing the type of housedress called a Mother Hubbard, sensible shoes, and a clean, starched apron. I decided she was going to be the one who laid out the lunch and minded the baby. But oh, my, no! The others amused themselves in various ways, but grandma sallied down to the water's edge and started fishing. She looked perfectly ridiculous, as though she should be leaning over a big wood range in a comfortable country kitchen instead of perched on a jagged rock at the edge of a wide and restless ocean; but if she realized it, it didn't trouble her a bit. She was catching fish and having a wonderful time.

In October last year I went to Schoodic to get my quota of scrod for the season. Scrod is, correctly, the fillet of small cod, not over two pounds at the most. Properly broiled (lightly, with butter) and served with lemon juice, it's the best-eating fish there is. Bitter experience has taught me that even the good restaurants sometimes cheat when it comes to scrod. They serve you cut-up fillets of large cod, or of some other fish altogether. So now I have control of the situation.

I had the ledges to myself (the park was technically closed), except for one man fishing on the nearest ledge. He wore the turned-down hip boots, oil-skin frock, and billed cap of a lobsterman. We both said, "Howdy," although we were strangers. I added, "Nice over here this time of year." It was, too. The thin October sun was warm on the pink rocks. Dark blue swells rolled in slowly and gently. Patches of late-autumn color stained the flanks of Cadillac Mountain, seen clear but far across the bay. Over and around us the gulls inscribed their intricate geometry against the sky.

He gazed around him. "Guess 'tis, at that. I ain't had time to notice. My wife's folks showed up unexpected from Illinois and she promised them chowder for supper. A treat, them being from inland. So I come over here. We live outside Bar Harbor."

I was amazed. Bar Harbor, although within sight across Frenchmans Bay, is 50 miles away by road. "Can't you catch fish nearer home?"

"Mebbe. Mebbe not. This bein' what you might call an emergency, figured I'd best not take any chances. Always sure of somthin' over here, the tide bein' right."

He'd about summed it up. Whether you're fishing for fun, for food, or to meet an emergency, you're almost sure to catch something at Schoodic. Even if you don't, it will be a day to remember. Walking in peace and beauty is never a waste of time.

A Good Bearin'
Northern Spy (1963)

[This is a legacy short story for Rufus and Dinah. Rufus, 27, when not driving trucks, was staying at The Sands with Louise. Dinah, 21, was married. During this time Louise was also doing the research for her last adult book, *State o'Maine*, and welcoming her mother to Maine for Florence's last visit. Clearly, Louise had her children and the passage of years in mind.]

The other day I met a lawyer friend of mine. During the course of our conversation, it was brought to light that I had not made a will. She was disturbed. "You really ought to attend to that," she said. "If you only knew the trouble we lawyers see resulting from people's dying intestate, estates tied up, family quarrels, you wouldn't put it off another day."

I laughed and told her that my estate, so called, wouldn't be worth tying up, and that my heirs, my two children, loved each other enough, I was sure, not to fight over anything I might leave behind on my departure to another plane. She shook her head. "That's what everybody thinks," she warned. "You may be right as far as Dinah and Rufus are concerned them-selves, but whoever they may marry may not feel the same. Husbands and wives can exert a lot of influence. You'd better see about making a will."

I promised her that I'd think about it, and that's just what I've been doing. In fact, that's the sum total of what I've done so far. Oh, I'll get around to writing a will; the trouble is I keep getting sidetracked. I consider my material possessions, the ramshackle old house, the scarred pieces of furniture, the dog-eared books, and am forced to the conclusion that al-most nobody would take the lot as a gift. I'm accustomed to my things, and we get along fine together; but they're a far cry from what I'd like to hand on to my son and daughter. I'd like to bequeath them—what? Suddenly I am reminded of Gerrish and the apple tree.

Gerrish worked for my husband and me for years when we were liv-ing in the Maine woods, and he was much more a member of the family than an employee. We were very fond of him, and he was fond of us, and especially of the children. The day before he left to go "outside" he spent planting some little apple trees. This was his own idea. "I'd like there to be something for the kids to remember me by when I'm dead," he explained. "I ain't got much to leave, but I don't know of nothin' they'll take more comfort from than a good bearin' Northern Spy." We never saw him alive again; but every spring when the grown trees frothed in bloom and every fall when they bore fruit, they renewed the testament of a fine man.

That's the sort of estate I'd like to leave my children, something lasting from which they'll take comfort all the days of their lives. Houses burn, fur-niture falls to pieces, and books are borrowed and never returned. Money in itself is nothing. Again I am sidetracked by a memory.

Once when he was small, Rufus lost his entire week's allowance, the princely sum of a quarter. When I sternly took him to task for carelessness, he looked at me in honest amazement. "What the heck, Ma," he said, "it's only money." At the time I felt obliged to lecture him on the value of money; but now I'm not so sure. There are things of much more value that I'd like to will him and his sister, were it in my power.

I'd like to will them what all parents wish for their children, success and happiness. But success and happiness are almost impossible to define, meaning as they do such entirely different things to different people. No parent, however well meaning, can bestow them full fledged upon his child. The best he can do is to provide the materials from which each may build his own happiness and success. I'd like to leave my children the means of doing this.

I'd like them to have minds of their own, so that they do not fall easily into popular patterns and attitudes that are too often superficial and sometimes actually injurious. I'd like them to have the courage to think and act for themselves, even if such thought and action cuts them off from the herd and isolates them at the other end of the pasture. Maybe they'll be lonely there; but the lot of mankind is a great and irremediable loneliness.

I'd like them to have eyes and ears that not only look at and listen to the natural world around them, but that really see and hear it as well. Governments may fall, fortunes may be lost or friends prove false; but still the Big Dipper wheels around the Pole Star, anemones toss in the warm spring wind, birds sing, tides crash on far-flung beaches, and ants go about their involved daily business. These things are permanent and predictable. To one who is truly aware of them, they can be a constant source of wonder and delight, a comfort in adversity, a bulwark against despair, a last security.

I'd like each of my children to find some kind of work that he wants to do above all else. It doesn't make any difference whether it's important in the worldly sense, so long as it is important to him. My daughter's name will never be spoken in the same breath with that of Mme. Curie, I feel very sure; but she might become the best possible wife and mother. Nobody who is anybody will have heard of her, and that couldn't matter less. What will matter is that she'll be filling her own shoes more than adequately.

I'd like to add a short codicil to this mythical will I'm thinking about. I'd like to leave each of my heirs a small fund of discontent. Not that vague discontent with life in general that has no focus and only succeeds in making the victim miserable, but the kind of discontent that recognizes the imperfections and inadequacies and inspires the bearer to set about remedying them. Complete satisfaction with one's life can lead only to smugness and self-satisfaction, a deadly combination that kills growth of mind and spirit. A constructive dissatisfaction is a very healthy condition.

One of these days I'll write the kind of will my lawyer friend was talking about. There's not much I can do now about the bequests in the will I'd really like to write. In the past twenty years of bringing up my children, I've already either succeeded or failed in giving them the things I want them to have. Like Gerrish, I've been planting a few little apple shoots for them. If the saplings grow well in the soil of their minds and hearts, in time they'll have an orchard of good bearin' trees in which to take comfort. They'll probably never be rich or famous; but they'll be busy, useful, interested citizens. That's really about all the success and happiness anybody could wish them.

A Summer Place (1967)

[This one was written during the time after Louise had been diagnosed with cancer and only given a couple of years to live; when she, binge drinking, was prevented from driving a car again; and when Katie sold off Forest Lodge.]

Whenever I hear the words "summer place," a feeling of felicity flows over me. I can't say that I think of certain things because what happens can hardly be called thought. It's more a matter of the senses and the emotions than of the mind. It's rather as though we're riffling the pages of a catalog of pleasure and catching quick glimpses of a hundred delightful items. All mixed up together are long sea beaches, white under a flawless sky, and dark, mirror-still mountain lakes, and surf crashing on pink granite ledges. There's the scent of bayberry and sweet fern, and the taste of wild straw-berries, and the softness of a dusty country road under bare feet. There's the drumming of rain on a cabin roof, and northern lights in a midnight sky, and the breathless hush of high tide at noon in a tiny down east har-bor. Then there are all the summer faces, brown and merry and friendly; and above all else, a sense of tremendous well being. In fact, my immedi-ate, unconsidered definition of "summer place" would be "a sunny, lovely, outdoor place where it rains only at night, where there are no responsibil-ities and where people are always happy."

I don't need to be told how ridiculous a definition that is. I have spent summers in a variety of places, none of which was in actuality the attained Utopia, the Ultima Thule. Experience as well as common sense informs me that while the north woods are beautiful in June, they are also infested with black flies and mosquitoes. I know perfectly well that the sun-drenched days on Cape Cod about equally balance days when a mean, raw wind drives the cold rain in around window frames; and that the coast of Maine, which can produce weather of a blue-and-diamond-dust perfection un-matched anywhere, can also produce clammy fog so thick that you can't see your hand before your face. I have learned that the roofs of summer shacks, which reverberate so soothingly to the drumbeat of the rain, fre-quently leak; that the brown vacation faces are as capable of anger, sulkiness, and sorrow as they are of joy and laughter; and that no normal adult, no matter where he may be, is ever without responsibility.

Nevertheless, my impression of a summer place as an eternally happy, sunlit place persists. So unshaken is it by evidence to the contrary that I am forced to conclude that there must be a truth of some sort underlying it.

It isn't, certainly, that summer people spend all their time playing. A great many—artists, scholars, writers, for example—bring their jobs with them and work as long and hard as they would at home. Many more—all housewives and all parents on family vacations—work even longer and harder. I'm both, so I know. It's not easy to keep a family adequately fed and reasonably clean with only an old oil stove and a pump in the kitchen sink to work with; and it takes quite a bit of agility, both mental and physical, to size up the strange new surroundings and lay down the new ground rules before some child, through inexperience or vacation-time madness, gets hurt, lost, stung by wasps, or drowned. It may be more fun to pick two quarts of blueberries than it is to go to the chain store and buy them, or to dig two pecks of clams than to ask the fishman to deliver them; but it's also a lot more work and takes a lot more time. Long days of careless play and lazy leisure are definitely not the program in the kind of summer place to which I am accustomed.

Nor is it true that being only a temporary resident in a community absolves one from community responsibility. It's easy and probably valid to argue, "I spent all last fall on the Visiting Nurse Association fund drive and half killed myself on the Red Cross blood bank this spring, so I deserve a vacation from public-spiritedness this summer." But somehow you still find yourself involved in a two-day auction up on US 1, a good tourist trap, to raise money to equip a playground for the local school; or an all-day fair with bingo . . . ; or a baked-bean supper to reroof the poor little village church. Before you can say "civic duty" you are, in spite of your resolutions, driving around the countryside prying auctionable articles from their lawful owners, or trying to keep up with the demand for hot dogs at the refreshment booth of the fair without making too many mistakes in the mustard-and/or-relish category, or shredding tubfuls of cabbage for coleslaw because those in charge don't dare trust you, an outlander, to bake beans acceptable by their standards. The cares of the world press just as heavily on your shoulders in a summer place as they did at home, and you're just as concerned about reaching the thousand-dollar goal for the playground as you were about the hundred-pint goal for the blood bank.

All this being true, there remains only one explanation for the golden glow that surrounds the words "summer place." It must come from the

people of the summer, although that seems absurd. They are the same people with whom you have associated all winter, or people exactly like them.
They have the same vanities and virtues, the same abilities and weak-
nesses, the same differing tastes and opinions. People, unlike some of the
lower forms of life, don't change with a change of season and background.
That's ridiculous to suppose.

But do you know, that's exactly what I do suppose, and I'll tell you why
I think it may be true. In the first place, each of us, whether he recognizes
it or not, suffers a deep nostalgia, a sickness to return home. This home for
which we long never actually existed for any of us. It's a racial memory of
the uncomplicated lives of our ancestors. We can't go home, but for a
while in summer we can harbor the illusion that we have gone. The very
discomforts we suffer from wind and weather and inconvenient shelters
and unsophisticated food meet an inner need; and so especially does near-
ness to the soil—to the grasses and trees, the tides and the rocks, the running water and the quiet stars. The Greek myth of Antaeus, who when he
was thrown to earth rose with redoubled vigor, is not without meaning.
We are minor Antaeuses, and in the summer places, where we have our
feet literally on the ground, we are stronger, more composed, and better
people.

More than that, we entertain an easy-going bird-of-passage attitude.
"The whole thing's not worth fighting with her about," we think, "because
after this summer I'll never see her again." Or, "I can afford to be agree-
able about having all the dirty work shoved off on me because where there
is no future to worry about I'm not establishing a dangerous precedent."
It's only a summer place and you're not going to be there forever so there's
no object in battling tooth and nail to place yourself high in the pecking
order. What's the sense in making yourself disagreeable in a competition
for something that you're going to have to abandon soon anyhow? No
sense at all, so let's go swimming instead.

That's a fine little theory, I think to explain the magic of summer
places, but it occurs to me that possibly I'm being much too profound and
elaborate about the whole thing. You don't suppose, do you, that it really
all boils down to my own improved summer approach to life and people?
Could it be that the world seems sunny and pleasant because I'm prepared
to find it so, that the merriment I see on summer faces is reflected from my
own to a degree, and that I find people more friendly and easy to get along
with because I myself am easier to get along with?

It's a very sobering thought. If it's true, then there's no good reason why
I can't be a summer person all year round. Nobody prevents me from liv-

ing as simple a life as I choose wherever I may be, or from seeking strength
and healing from the natural world in winter as well as in summer. As for
being a bird-of-passage, what could be more temporary than any individual's stay on earth?

There's really no good reason, except my own disposition, why I
shouldn't find the whole world forever a happy summer place.

The Handing On
of a Garden (1968)

[This story, featured in *Woman's Day* magazine, takes us into the
backyard of The Sands and beyond to talk of immortality.

Originally titled (by Louise) "The Lovesome Thing," and actually started in 1964, this is a piece about Louise's move back
to the Gouldsboro Peninsula. It is her last published short story
(other than a 1976 piece she coauthored with Thomas Hopkins,
Hester's husband).

The Miriam and Chen mentioned are Miriam Colwell, author
and postmistress, and Chenoweth Hall, sculptress—neighbors
and former residents at The Sands, who were part of her larger
circle of friends. By the time this story was published Louise's
mother had recently died—and her doctor had erroneously pre-
dicted that Louise herself had little time left.]

When I moved into this house three years ago, it had been unoccu-
pied for a long time. It is an old, old house, with all the inevitable signs of
age about it; but in addition to these—the uneven floors, the sagging
doors, the windows that must be propped open with sticks—it had about
it a sad air of neglect. This was particularly evident in the yard. The lawn
was full of arnica, the ancient lilacs sprawled across the stone steps, and
weeds and grass grew tall and rank along the foundations. It was high time,
obviously, that someone employed a firm hand around here.

I like to work outdoors, although I wouldn't go so far as to call myself
a gardener. I don't know much about mulches, suitable varieties for shady
spots, or what to do about thrips—whatever that may be. I simply like to
dig in the dirt. I like to lop off a branch here and there, restoring symme-

try to an untidy shrub; to edge a walk with seashells; to plant bulbs and seedlings that will, I hope, reward me in time with a riot of bloom.

Sometimes they do and sometimes they don't. In either event, I've had the pleasure of dreaming the dream, beholding the vision, and striving to bring then to actuality. This must be a reward in itself, or else I wouldn't keep on trying to make gardens in places I know I'm going to occupy only temporarily.

It has sometimes seemed to me in the past that the minute the perennial border on which I have spent a lot of time and some money begins really to show signs of amounting to something is bound to be the minute I'm obliged to pull up stakes and move elsewhere. On these occasions I tell myself that the whole routine is nonsense and that I'm not going to all that bother again. It's a waste of time and effort.

Nevertheless, even before I had my furniture fully settled in this house, I got out my meager collection of garden tools and started hacking at wild raspberry canes, yanking up twitch grass, pruning the lilacs and spading a strip against the south wall of the house. This was in May, which in Maine is early spring, too early to plant but not too early to prepare the ground, especially ground that has never been cultivated before. If I wanted any kind of a garden at all, it behooved me to get started in good season.

Almost at once I discovered that I had made a miscalculation. Appearance to the contrary, someone had had a garden here before. The line that I had established mentally as the limit of my border was already marked off by partly decomposed bricks sunk in the earth, and every tangle of sod that I shook out yielded handfuls of narcissus and daffodil bulbs. Smothered in the matted grass were struggling little columbine and delphinium plants, and others that I did not recognize. Someone had labored here before me, and labored with love.

Who this someone was I did not and do not know—not her name nor her age nor her circumstances. I do not know whether she was beautiful or plain, happy or sorrowful. Only this I know from that first day: once upon a time another woman who liked to dig in the dirt lived here. It took me quite a long while to clean up that south bed and restore it to its original order, but it didn't seem very long. I truly felt that I was not working alone, that I was doing this as much for someone else as for myself.

Since then I have grown closer to her. There is at the back of the lawn a huge and lovely old tree stump, exactly the right background for clumps of phlox and daisies. When I started to put this idea into effect, I found that she had been there before me. Her brick retainer was crumbling and her plants almost strangled by weeds—but they were there. When I decided that the ledge by the fence would make a wonderful rock garden, if it were cleaned up, I found sedum and hens-and-chickens bravely fighting for existence under the debris.

But she and I were not the only ones who, grubby and contented and full of plans, had worked in the soil of this small holding. Once, walking after a rain through the tall wet grass beyond the chopping block, I smelled something marvelously fresh and aromatic—mint, catnip, marjoram and tarragon, the survivors of an old herb garden. When I mentioned this to a neighbor she said, "Oh yes! Miriam and Chen planted that when they lived in your house—it must be twenty years ago now." Before Miriam and Chen, I learned, Bess Ray put in the little old-fashioned roses by the kitchen door; and after them came Arline Shaw with monkshood and globe flowers. Only this spring I decided that the lilacs were getting completely out of hand and that I would cut down the strangling old bushes and give the strong young ones a chance. As soon as the earth beneath was exposed to sunlight and fresh air, it blossomed forth with lilies-of-the-valley, sweet rocket and veronica, the descendants of old Aunt Dorcas Allen's long-forgotten flower bed. She lived here almost a century ago.

Over a century ago a poet wrote, "A Garden is a lovesome thing, God wot!" I like that word lovesome. It does not necessarily mean breathtakingly beautiful or rare and exotic—terms that certainly don't apply to my modest plots. It means—or so it seems to me—fashioned with love, expressing love, handed on with love. That's what my little garden is—a legacy of love from all my predecessors.

Of all the gardens that I have slaved over and perforce abandoned with regret and a feeling of wasted endeavour, I hope that at least one has found somebody to love it and care for it and pass it along down the years. Then after I am gone and forgotten I will have what all the known and nameless women who helped make my garden have—a small but lovely form of immortality.

Examples of
Louise Dickinson Rich's
Unpublished Writings

Excerpts from
LDR's Steno Book (1942–1945)

[A simple stenographer's book was lodged among a pile of papers and magazines Aldro French and I uncovered in the attic of Forest Lodge. I found someone who could decipher old stenoscript (thank you, Eleanor Trask!) and, when translated, the following draft of a chapter from *Happy the Land* emerged.

This, and the other entries, were penned between 1942 and 1945, and show Louise's work before it got to the editing, revision, publication stages. (Incidentally, the steno book contains very few self-corrections and edits—her writing just flows, clean copy.) Try comparing chapter four in *Happy the Land*—"The Whirl Around the Lakes"—with the following whirl.]

As in any other way of earning a living, there are things to be said both for and against writing. The most obvious thing to be said for it is, of course, that you can do your work anywhere you please. You aren't chained down to a desk in the city. You can even live as we do, so far back in the woods that when you mention your place of residence nobody ever heard of it.

I will admit there is one disadvantage to being off in the sticks where your neighbors make their living by straight-forward methods such as guiding, trapping, or lumbering. They're all convinced there's something faintly disreputable and probably more than a little dishonest about anybody who actually gets money for sitting on their tails all day long putting words down on paper. But, if you don't mind the slight aura of suspicion that's around to creep into all your relationships. . . .

And the best thing I will say about writing for a living is that there's always a chance one fine day you may wake up and find yourself in the money, ankle deep at least. You may sell a story to the movies or a book may become a best seller. Of course, these things mostly wouldn't happen to you yourself that happened to Margaret Mitchell, for example. Mostly, you go along the even tenor of your stay one short jump ahead of the sheriff. But, in the back of your mind, you can always hope, even when with the front of your mind you are debating whether to try to shove the wolf, [starvation] hind and forequarters, back onto the porch with the broom, or lure him into the kitchen and butcher him for supper.

Where we live, in the back woods of Maine, not being in the money is fortunately comparatively easy to take. There is absolutely nothing to spend on, for the nearest movie, beer parlor, or beauty shop is 40 miles away on the Outside, and there's no easy way to get there through dense forest and over long stretches of lake. In order to buy an ice cream sundae, we would have to walk from where we live on the Rapid River, (which connects two of the Rangeley Lakes), two miles to Middle Dam. At Middle Dam there's a dam, a fishing camp, and nine people. No ice cream. So then we would have to take a boat five miles to South Arm. But that's only the beginning because at South Arm there's nothing but garbage pickup bins, boat houses, a falling-to-pieces dock, and the end of a road. By taking this road for twelve miles we would arrive in Andover, which is important, because that's where our mail comes. But you still can't buy an ice cream sundae there. So we would have to go 30 more miles to Rumford. Rumford, in addition to being our nearest rail head and our shopping center, does have drug stores where they serve fancy ice cream. But you can see it would be hardly worth the bother of going down there on any such picayune errand as that. In summer, the whole trip from our house to Rumford takes from 2½ to 3 hours.

The winter is another story. Then you must snowshoe from our house to Middle Dam and sometimes from Middle Dam to South Arm, depending on the condition of the ice and whether or not it's safe to put a team onto it. When you get to South Arm, you frequently discover that the road in from Andover has not yet been plowed out. So you go into a shack, build a fire, and wait for the snowplow. Sometimes you wait an hour, sometimes you wait all night. Supposing the road is plowed out. You might then sometimes discover that a car which has been sitting for a week in temperatures of 30 below won't start as easy as you might think. Sometimes you spend the whole morning getting it going. So frequently, you might say, all is not smooth sailing. Although technically plowed, the road in no time is drifted so badly in exposed spots that you spend more time shoveling snow than riding. Sometimes it is so badly rutted up by heavy pulp trucks that it's impossible to keep your car on the road. And once you have fallen off, you have a choice of two courses. You can either walk back home. Or you can walk out to Andover, depending on which is nearest to the scene of the incident. It is not unheard of to have all the men of Middle Dam go out for a day of shopping and disappear into the blue for days. These are a few of the reasons why, by and large, we so seldom go Out but prefer to amuse ourselves at home.

So during the first six years of my married life we two, Ralph and I, and our little boy Rufus and Ralph's daughter, Sally, and our hired man, Gerrish, just stayed at home in our little woods-and-water-bound clearing and entertained ourselves in our own tried and true and inexpensive ways. We fished and hunted and picked berries and worked and read and tied flies and painted boats and patched our clothes and told each other what we were going to do when our ship came in. This ship coming in business is the index by which I know that, while we often didn't know where our next pair of shoes were coming from, we were never actually poverty-stricken. As long as you can say, and believe, that your ship is coming in, you are only poor. It is no disgrace. It's when you lose faith. After that, you cross the line into poverty. The lack of money starts to grind you down, wear away first your sense of humor, then your imagination, and last of all, your self-respect. Then, though you may still be up and walking around, you are as good as dead.

We never got to that stage, and we certainly never plan to. Nothing was ever too slight an occasion to set us off inventorying the cargo of our ship. Not even so everyday an affair as going out onto the porch, looking up the river, and seeing fishermen on the dam. Our house is situated on a knoll, just at a bend of the Rapid River which goes roaring and curdling white down over the rocks beneath the door. From the porch we can look up across the rapids between the thickly-wooded banks and have a perfectly lovely view of everything that goes on at Rapid River Dam. If someone happens to be fishing off one of the piers, we rush into the house and grab the field glasses off the bent deer foot driven into a wall stud by the door and rush out again adjusting them feverishly. If the light is right, we can then identify not only the fisherman, but the fish he is netting as well. "Trout," we say to each other. "About three pounds." Or, "Salmon. Nothing to write home about." If it is something really impressive, like a five-pound, square-tailed Gerrish always said wistfully, "Gee. I wish I knew what fly he was using." And we would shake our heads sadly because we knew that's one question no fly fisherman would ever dream of asking another fly fisherman. Should we so far forget ourselves to ask, a lie would be the only proper answer. "Oh well," he would say, "just wait 'til our ship comes in. We'll buy a pair of 30X glasses. Then we can count the stripes of body tinsel."

Or supposing we are having some freight land in Rumford from what is locally called simply "the Mail-Order." Freight in Rumford is a far, far cry from freight on the premises and requires some negotiation. First, it must be arranged with Larry Parsons, who runs the fishing camp at Middle Dam, to have his driver pick up the shipment and truck it to South Arm. Then it has to be arranged to have it brought up from South Arm to Middle Dam on Larry's boat. It always develops that the same day our freight comes in, Larry has some freight of his own and there isn't room for both. Tomorrow seven guests are coming by train and, with them and their luggage, there will be no room either. The next day is always Sunday, when the boat isn't running. Monday is grocery day, when the truck will again be full. But maybe Tuesday... So far, so good. But on Tuesday it seems the cows are coming in for the summer and Larry won't have time or room for anything else. After he brings the cows in he might have to go back to the Arm for some people who maybe are driving in and, if he does, perhaps he'll bring in the freight...

Beyond that point hours ago, everything went to Hell in a hack. At noon the wind started blowing blue blazes out of the northwest, boiling the water down four miles of open lake. Meanwhile, the cows had been delivered to the Arm. Larry knew he would never make it, so he herded the cows aboard the boat and sat down to wait until sunset when the wind would probably calm down. Even tied up in partial shelter the boat pitched and rocked and water foamed over the bow. The cows staggered around for a while and then gave into the inevitable and, when a cow is seasick, it's seasick! What I mean is, it wasn't a pleasant afternoon for either the cows or Larry. Finally, the wind went down a little and Larry set out. The health of his passengers had improved somewhat and he comforted himself in the fond belief that in half an hour he would be in Middle Dam and rid of them. In half an hour he was in Middle Dam, alright, but his wife, Alys, met him with the information that just after he left, the guests who were driving in had arrived at the Arm. So he would have to go right back there soon as he had unloaded the cows, who by this time were completely recovered. In fact, so completely recovered were they that they decided that they simply loved boat riding. Get off? Not on your life! Not while they had legs to kick and horns to hook with and voices left for protesting. If the boat was going back again, they were going back with it. And they did. You can't keep paying guests standing around cold and hungry in the dark of the US of A while you play games with cows. Our freight? Oh naturally there wasn't room for that. It stayed down at the Arm for days and it was then, too, that Ralph issued the ultimatum: "When our ship comes in, we're going to have a boat of our own, by God!"

Or Gerrish and I, according to our custom, would decide to go fishing at the head of the pond after supper. Pond-in-the-river is a widening in the Rapid River just a little way above our house, Forest Lodge. We kept a rowboat and canoe at the foot of the pond for getting to the head of the pond where the best fishing is. This involved about a mile of rowing. As we shoved the boat off the skid, I would repeat my usual formula: "We'll each row one way. Would you rather row up or back?"

Gerrish took off his sweater, "If we're gonna have any time to fish before dark, I'd better row up. Won't make no difference what time we get home, or how much floundering around we do, so you can row back."

Technically speaking, I was Gerrish's boss, but actually I usually came pretty close to doing what he said. So I would climb into the stern seat with the rods and net and he would shove us off shore adding, "It would be nice to have a kicker with about $3\frac{1}{2}$ horsepower to get us up there in no time."

"When our ship comes in," I would promise him as he laid the rods down very carefully because mine only cost $3 nine years before and his was a haywire rig he'd improvised from various discarded rods he'd found around the country. "We'll have new rods," I'd tell him. "And reels." The click on mine is almost worn out.

"I'd like to try one of the synthetic gut leaders. They'd ought to be good for dry flies." That needed no comment from me. Of course we'd have boxes and boxes of leaders.

Or take Forest Lodge, where we live. I better say right now that I love living here because before I get halfway through telling about all the things that are wrong with the place, it's going to sound as if I were serving time instead of living a life. The reasons I love living here are manifold. I like to be isolated, with no one to bother about except my own household. I like to feel that on every side forests and lakes and mountains stretch for mile after mile with no one in the whole territory except the Parsons and Millers at Middle Dam and old Cliff Wiggin (Wallis) and Ben Bennett down at the other end of the railroad at Umbagog. I like never to have to dress up and be polite to strangers. I like to live in a house the rooms of which are full of the sound of rushing water which, to me, is one of the two loveliest sounds on earth. Whenever I go anywhere else away from the sound of the river, the air seems flat and dead and life tastes strangely empty.

But I don't like it so much when the water itself actually rushes into the rooms as it did years ago the first night my new baby, Dinah, spent under the parental roof. I put her to bed in her crib and, babies being what they are, I put a rubber sheet under her. I was awakened in the middle of the night by her crying and stepped out of bed, in the middle of the dark, into a puddle of water. It took me a minute to realize that in addition to the roar of the river, there was a roar on the roof. It was raining as it had never rained before, or since, and my poor infant child's crib was directly under the worst of the many leaks in the roof. There she lay, in a rubber sheet full of rain water, and it's a wonder she didn't drown. It sounds easy to say that we moved the crib, but it was a little more complicated than it sounds. In order to get the crib to a place where it wasn't under a leak, we had to move everything else in the room. And no matter how we arranged things, something was bound to get wet. Definitely a new roof was one of the things the house needed.

Most of the other things the house needed aren't brought home to me quite as forcibly as that. Most of the time I can ignore the lack of a real honest-to-God bathroom of earlier times. Most of the time it doesn't bother me that our furniture looks as though it had been through a hurricane. We haven't any rugs on the floor because what rug could stand having snow and mud tracked on it twelve months of the year? The fact that we have to carry water into the house in pails rather than have it run in pipes doesn't bother me most of the time. It's only when some sport—that's what we call people from the city who come up to the fishing camp for their vacation— some sport drops in and looks at me with such a mixture of horror and pity that I begin to feel definitely feeble-minded to put up with this way of living and that I begin to wish a few things were different. She will say—it's usually a she because men are either less observing or more polite than women—"But you stay in this house all winter?"

I patiently explain to her that no, we live in the big house by the river only in the summer. In the winter, we move to a little cabin by the road because that is properly insulated and we can keep warm there. Then she says, "Do you have a kitchen up there, too?" Then I explain to her that no, we don't have a kitchen up there. I have to do my cooking in the kitchen of the bigger house. She either says, "Oh" or "Isn't that really inconvenient?" In either case, she makes me realize that it is real inconvenient, although I have just been happily through a winter and not minded the inconvenience at all. And I make a mental note that one of the first things we will do when our ship comes in is somehow or other get complete, all-year living quarters under one roof.

I don't mean that the lack of material things was constantly on my mind. I have heard it said that money may not bring happiness, but if you have it you can at least be unhappy in comfort. This seems to me not only a too sophisticated point of view, but actually a false one. The truth about being poor, I conclude from my own experience, is that you have no time to be unhappy. Particularly if you live as we live, with no necessity for comparing our standard of living with that of anyone else. Ideally, I suppose it should be possible to achieve a detachment of mind even in the midst of a group whereby possessions, or lack of material things, would not matter. Actually, it's probably very difficult not to care if you are wearing the shabbiest thing even though you are convinced that your own mental and spiritual life is a good deal more richer and satisfying than the housewife with the prettiest new mink. So, I'm not trying to say that when I had one pair of ski pants and the seat of that was patched, I developed a philosophy that lifted me above such worldly considerations. What I'm trying to say is that no philosophy was necessary because there was no world to consider.

In the summer, while all the whole tribe of us is riding up the lake through the narrows, we start playing a game of ours. It's a simple game that causes us to forget that the reason why we were going up the lake to the low, windy, burned-over point, called Prospect, is to pick the enormous blueberries that grow with such crazy prodigality out of the thin, fire-scorched soil. We pretend that this is virgin country and that we are the first white men ever to set eyes upon it. You would be surprised what a freshness this gives to cool little coves and wild, half-moons of beach. We nearly manage to feel that around the next point we'll come upon something wonderful and rich and new. Although we know perfectly well that all we'll see is the west landing of the upper dam carry. But if only instead of going straight ahead to Prospect we were going across the Carry, then we really would see something new. At least to Gerrish and me. Neither of us had ever been above Upper Dam, and the names of the lakes stringing along to the north fascinated us. We'd say them over to each other just because we like the sound of them: Mooselukmeguntic, Cupsuptic, Aziscoos. How beautiful and wild lakes must be with names like these. Some day, we'd see them. Some day, when our ship came in, we'd take a canoe trip all around the Rangeleys. We'd go clear to the end and then cross on the long Carry from the mouth of the Kennebago River to the headwaters of the lower Maggaloway and follow that stream down to the Androscoggin, paddle over into Umbagog, then turn north again from

Umbagog to Sunday Cove to the end of the Carry, and so home. One year we were playing this game and Gerrish snapped, "Look, Louise, let's take that boat ride around the lakes. If your book takes aholt—"

For by now the ship had a different form: that of a book I had written which pretty soon now would be published. I think I happened to write a book also because I was about to have another baby. And let me tell you, if you're planning to write a book at all, while you wait to have a baby is a good time to do it. The months stretched out before me, long and dull and boring. Sitting and brooding over your condition is no good. And you can't knit baby garments all the time. Had I been home, I would have managed to have kept busy. But Ralph, having acted as midwife at the birth of Rufus five years before, was definitely not sticking his neck out again. He insisted that I go to my mother's in Massachusetts where a hospital would take over in his stead. At my mother's there was nothing for me to do, used as I was toiling with wood stoves, kerosene lamps and buckets of spring water. Housework in a modern house was child's play for the two of us. The friends with whom I had grown up were all married and moved away or working away from home. So my social life was almost non-existent. There was naturally nothing else for me to do but write a book. And that's what I did. This book, which I called *We Took to the Woods,* was written under the spell of acute homesickness.

I would sit at the typewriter and look out the window at the street and the shops and the people and think of home. Of the long, lonely reaches of the lakes stretched out to the Canadian border. Of the wild, black mountains that hold the lakes in the hollows there as gently as cupped hands. Of the bodies of water moving from level to level southwest to the Androscoggin which turns again east to the sea. Of the large silence and completeness of forest and swamp that surrounds us here at home. Of the snow lying league after league unmarred except by the delicate imprint left by the feet of fox and mink and partridge and deer.

I would look out the window at the hard surface of the street that goes by my father's house and think of the Carry Road that passes Forest Lodge. It is presumptuous to even call it a road. It's really just two rough ruts winding through the woods with tall grass and wild strawberries growing between them and trees crowding in at the sides. If one car meets another on it, someone often has to back up ¼ of a mile before he can find a reasonably clear space and so get out of the way. But since the road only goes 5½ miles from one lake at lower Richardson to Umbagog, and since there are only three cars on the road—the Parsons, Millers and ours—that's no great inconvenience. Even if we all have the animated heaps of junk that we call cars out at once, the traffic problems never become acute. It's impossible for foreign upstart cars from the Outside to get on to our Carry Road, sealed off as it is at both ends by miles of open water.

Sitting in the silence of my father's house, I would think of my own home where the rooms are always filled, summer and winter alike, with the sound of water rushing over stone. I do think of the Rapid River boiling green and white past our door, no less quick and beautiful because I was not there to see it than when it seemed I couldn't stand it any longer. I would write about that—for lost country and the life we lived there. It seemed at the time that I was wasting the winter—because any time I spend on the Outside is wasted time to me. But at last, in the spring, I had a book and a baby to show for it. So as soon as the ice was out I could come back home and everything would be just as it had been before.

But you can't go back it seems. The characters may seem to be the same, but the subtle erosion time makes flowing imperceptibly from day to day sums up the damage. The new life may be better, or it may be worse, but certainly it will be different. The first effect of this came on the day I got home with the matter of Rufus' attire. He announced while he was dressing that morning that he wasn't going to wear the overalls I had bought him any more. Daddy and Gerrish wore blue denim pants with belts, and that's what he was going to wear from now on. I said that as soon as he had worn out the overalls, he could have pants and let it go at that. That was only a symptom. He went outdoors to help Gerrish make the rounds of the rat traps that were set out in the garden. Rats had been brought into a nearby lumber camp in bales of hay during the winter and the minute we had the corn planted, they came running miles to dig it up and eat it. So Gerrish and Rufus ran a trap line. The next thing I knew, Rufus strode into the kitchen, threw a humble dead rat down on the table and told me to cook it for lunch. Naturally, I screeched the house down, ordering him to "take that thing out of here," and bellowing that if he ever brought another one in I'd pound the living daylights out of him. He went, alright, but when I looked out of the window to see what he was going to do with the corpse, I saw him and his father and Gerrish standing in a tight little knot behind the woodshed slapping each other's backs and laughing their fool heads off. I had lost my baby. He was a man now and equal with his father and Gerrish. In a stupid game they played called "getting Louise started raving." Even the catch word, when our ship comes in, had changed to "if the book goes good." And this rather bothered me because, while I think I'm not superstitious, I have firm convictions against counting chickens before they are hatched.

And then one morning, Joe Mooney called me up from the Brown Farm. Joe Mooney and I were great buddies, although I have never laid eyes on the man. He tends the switchboard and takes care of things generally at the Brown Farm (which actually isn't a farm but a headquarters for the Brown Company lumber operation through this entire district). There's a storehouse there and a bunk house for lumberjacks arriving or leaving the woods, stables for the horses used on the operation, and a switchboard from which single strands of telephone wire ran out for miles all over the country. These telephone lines are private, owned by the company, and used chiefly by the various lumber camps. But the few people who do live in the country are allowed to hook on which is a great convenience. Joe said, "I got a telegram for you, Louise." He cleared his throat and then he cleared it again. Nobody ever gets telegrams in this country because nobody knows how to go about sending them. It's a very complicated procedure and by the time the average uninformed person has doped it out it would have been simpler, less expensive, and a lot quicker to have written a letter.

"It's from the people who are publishing your book," he said. "It says 'We Took to the Woods chosen by the Book of the Month Club, putting you in upper income bracket.' Jesus! I wish someone would send me a telegram like that!"

It took me a minute to dope out that the last was Joe's footnote and not a message from J.B. Lippincott, Company. He added, "Congratulations" and I don't know to this day whether they were his or Lippincott's.

I said, hotly, "That's not funny, Joe." And he said, "Honest, Louise. I wouldn't make up a thing like that if I could." I said, "Are you kidding?" and he said he wasn't. And he really wasn't!

I sat down and looked at the stove. It needed polishing, for crying out loud. And what was going on. . . ? Because, you see, although I had written the book, I hadn't known anything about writing the book. Its stories were my life. A book, I knew, demanded a different and special technique. I didn't know anything about that technique and I wouldn't know where to find out about it. So, I had just plunged ahead and written it the best I could and hoped rather desperately that honesty and accurate reporting of our odd way of life would cover for a complete lack of story line and literary style. Apparently, it had.

I got my feet under me and went and hammered on the old three-foot saw that we had salvaged from the ruins of a fallen-down saw mill and were using both as a dinner gong and an emergency warning system. Since it was already half past nine in the morning, I felt sure that Ralph and

Gerrish would clearly interpret the racket as announcing a crisis and not a meal.

"Listen," I said in a voice that sounded a little queer even to me, "Joe just called up. The Book of the Month Club has chosen our book"— because you see, it was their book just as much as it was mine. I may have done the actual writing, but if we hadn't all done the living of it, there would have been no book. "Listen—our ship has come in!"

They stood and looked at me. Then Ralph said, "By God. Now we'll have a new roof on the woodshed." Gerrish said, "Gee. We can take a trip around the lakes." And I said, "Yeah, and at last I can see Joe Mooney."

In spite of the fact that Gerrish and I had talked so blithely about taking a jaunt around the lakes, when the time came to do it, obstacles began to pile themselves in the way. In the first place, you don't take a four months old baby on a forty mile canoe trip. Or at least I don't. You don't leave her home to shift for herself either. I thought some of simply parking her with the neighbors. But in the summer the neighbors homes are just as full up with sports as mine is. It began to look as though we would have to postpone the trip until Dinah was old enough to paddle a canoe by herself.

And then, one evening when Gerrish and I were fishing at the head of the pond he said, "Got a letter from Catherine today." Catherine is Gerrish's oldest daughter. I had met her and her uncle Edward and their little boy, Vaughn, the year before when they had come up here to spend the fourth of July with Gerrish. Since that time Gerrish had always kept me posted on the doings of the Jacobs family.

"What's she up to?" I asked.

Gerrish cast his line out and started reeling it in slowly. "Well, she doesn't know." It seems her husband, Jake, was going to be drafted. So he decided he might as well join the marines and be in the branch of the service he wanted to be in. "Catherine's got to get a job," Gerrish continued, "but there's the kid to think of, too."

I dropped my rod and looked at him. "My God," I said, "You don't suppose she would want to come and work for me?"

Gerrish was never one to stick his neck out. He cast again before he answered. "Twant hurt to ask," he said with native caution. So I did ask. And she said yes, she would like to come and work for me. And that's how we came by Catherine.

Much as I hate to admit it, sometimes I think she is a better woman than I am. For example, I can drive a car and she can't. On the other hand, she can wheel a wheelbarrow and I, for some unknown reason, always dump the load out in the first six feet. She can make pies that turn out well every time and, while mine are sometimes wonderful, they are equally often completely inedible. But, I can write a short story and she can't. For the rest, we can swim and handle a boat and do two weeks wash or start a fire in a balky stove with about equal facility. So, I guess it's about a standoff.

The arrival of Catherine solved the problem of what to do about Dinah while we went on this trip around the lakes. So I wrote to our friends, the Wings, and asked them if they would like to go, too. I had discussed the possibility with Barbara Wing the year before as something that maybe, sometime, might take place. And I thought, rightly, as it developed that they would like to go with us on the trip.

The idea was that since there were to be five of us, Ralph and I, Willis and Barbara Wing, and Gerrish, it would be best to have another guide and take three canoes. Lots of people do take trips around these lakes with three or even four people in a canoe, but it's a very bad practice. An overloaded canoe is not only heavy and hard to handle, but it's also dangerous. These lakes are subject to sudden squalls when, from a dead calm, six-foot waves suddenly spring up. They are nothing to fool with in an overloaded canoe or boat. All of the disasters that have occurred around here, with one or two exceptions, have been completely unnecessary because they are always the result of overloading. The only other guide that we would consider taking with us, if we could get him, was John Lavorgna. He was the guide with whom my sister and I were traveling the very first time I was ever in this country. That was the time when I first saw Ralph. John was shepherding us along the Carry Road where we wouldn't have been at all if he hadn't insisted. And when we went past Forest Lodge, Ralph was splitting wood in the yard. We stopped to pass the time of day. One thing lead to another with the result that I have now been married to the man for 10 years. I have always felt that John was more than half responsible for this and so have entertained a particularly friendly feeling toward him. He is one-half Yankee, one-quarter Indian, and one-quarter Italian. He is a mixture of bloods which results in the best G.D. guide in the state of Maine. He looked like an Indian, worked like a horse, tells a story like an experienced after-dinner speaker, and has a disposition that is proof against anything.

So the next time I saw John, I asked him if he would take us on this trip and he was very much pleased at the prospect. I think he gets a little tired of showing sports around the woods. He knew that with us, at least, he wouldn't have to think up innumerable answers to a lot of foolish questions. So we set the date and everything seemed to be fixed.

The first thing that happened was two days before the proposed take off when Willis Wing sent me a wire that all his children had whooping cough and probably he was going to have it, too. He did. So we postponed the trip for two weeks to give him time to recover.

Before that Happy Day arrived, Ralph came down with something which is always referred to in the family as "Ralph's mysterious Oriental disease." The only symptom was a temperature of 104 degrees which held with no variation whatever. He insisted that he felt alright, although I thought it unlikely he wouldn't want anything to eat. We put up with it for two days and then called the doctor who, after a complete examination, agreed that there was nothing whatsoever the matter with Ralph except that he had a temperature of 104 degrees. I like my doctor. He could have given me some name for it which would have meant nothing to me. But he admitted, quite freely, that he didn't know what the matter with him was. You can have confidence in a doctor that will be as honest as that. He said it might just as well be a mysterious disease as anything else. He left some medicines and told us to keep Ralph in bed.

I began counting the days to the canoe trip. If Ralph wasn't any better the day after tomorrow, I decided, I would wire the Wings and put the trip off another week. But before the day after tomorrow arrived, Catherine and I decided that we were getting nowhere fast. The place for Ralph was in a hospital. Whether due to fever or starvation, he had got to the point of where you couldn't keep him in bed. The minute we turned our backs on him, he would get up and wander around at great danger to himself and anyone else that he might fall downstairs on top of. We decided that he should be in the hospital. So at five o'clock one morning we went to Middle Dam and called up the doctor and told him to send an ambulance in to the Arm. Then we went home and told Ralph he was going to the hospital.

I'll never forget that ride. It was raining, in the first place, and in the second place, Rufus had also come down sick. So we decided that if we were going to the hospital anyway we might as well take him, too. The ambulance was also used occasionally for the hearse so the sides were all clear glass so that the floral tributes to the deceased could be viewed by the bystanders. The driver had a stretcher between the two windows on which Ralph could lie and look out at the passing scenery if he chose. Rufus sat in front with me and the driver. We had barely left the Arm when a fox jumped across the road and the driver leaned on the siren just to make him run. Rufus had never heard a siren before and the sound fascinated him, of course, necessitating that the driver do it again. So we went the entire 15 miles from the Arm to Andover, on a completely deserted road, through thick wet woods, with that darned thing making like a banshee. There was nobody to hear but I imagine the entire population of game in Oxford County is running yet.

In the middle of the racket, the driver glanced into the rear view mirror and said, "Jesus, lady! He hadn't ought to do that, he's got a fever. He'll get pneumonia."

I turned around to see that Ralph had taken off not only his bathrobe but his pajamas as well. There he lay, as naked as a jaybird between those two windows, like a turkey in a showcase. It was alright on the lake roads, but as the driver cried out, "My God, lady. We're going to hit Andover in a minute and you know those old dames out there."

So I climbed over back and made Ralph put his clothes on again. It was sort of a hopeless job. As fast as I'd put them on, he'd take them off. The result was that we sailed through Andover, with the siren wailing, at about 70 miles an hour so that all the citizens would see was a blur. It was a very harrowing experience but apparently it had some theraputic value because when we arrived at the hospital in Rumford shortly afterwards Ralph's temperature was normal, and it never went up again. Apparently all he needed was a ride in an ambulance.

I didn't wire the Wings. But I think they were a little surprised when they got off the train at the station, the same day that Ralph got out of the hospital, to have him meet them on the platform dressed in a bathrobe, slippers and pajamas. He said he wasn't sure whether he would be strong enough to go on the canoe trip or not, but by that time I had decided I was going on the canoe trip if I had to go alone. And the result was that we got out from South Arm on the day appointed.

It was a perfectly lovely day when we arrived at the Arm. We were a little bit early and had to wait for John. We spent the time lying on the float in the sun and I planted a tree two inches tall in a knot hole in the corner of the float. The last time I was down there, after three years, I was very happy to see that it was still growing, although Larry Parsons, who owns the float, was much less pleased about it than I was because it had reached a size to spring the planks. I think he only waited until my back was turned before ripping it up.

While we were waiting there the glassy calm was disturbed by a faint breeze out of the northwest and we, dopes that we were, thought how nice that it wasn't going to be hot paddling up the lake. Little did we know. No sooner had John arrived and we distributed our duffles and provisions among the three canoes, than the white caps were rolling into the Arm. We set out bravely into the teeth of the gale thinking then what a lovely and exhilarating jaunt this was. If you have never paddled a heavy canoe into the wind, you have no idea how tiresome it can get. It isn't that it's such terribly hard work, but you can never stop the working. The minute you relax, you go backward twice as fast as you were going forward. You can't stop to look at the scenery. All you can do is dip the paddle and push, and dip again and push until you think your arms are going to drop off.

We had decided to have lunch at Pine Island, which is up at the further end of the narrows between the two Richardson lakes. That's about ten miles from South Arm. On Pine Island there's a state camp site with fireplaces, a very nice sandy beach and a fire warden. It seems terribly organized to have official camp sites in the middle of the deep woods, but it is absolutely necessary. If people go camping about any old place summer or winter, a forest fire ensues. And forest fires in this country are no joke.

Also on Pine Island is a two-quart bottle of gin buried under a birch tree that the fire warden before this one left. When he went to go out in the fall he had to leave over the ice. But he had too much to carry. So he buried the gin against his return. Unfortunately for him, he couldn't remember which birch tree he buried it under. And, while I'm sure there isn't a birch tree on the island that hasn't been investigated—I did a little investigating myself when I was there—so far the gin has not been found. I think either he forgot what kind of a tree it was, or else the tree blew down. Anyway, it's interesting to have some form of treasure to look for when the fire warden's life gets too monotonous.

At the time we were at Pine Island, Ansky Hines was the fire warden, Ansky Hines is not only a very nice man, but he's a terribly good fire warden. What's more, the story of his marriage is one of those things that you read about in books. One time when he was in Andover, he met a young Englishman. And this young Englishman showed Ansky a picture of his sister. Ansky was very impressed with the girl and corresponded with her for a couple of years. Finally, he invited her to come over. And, to show his honorable intentions, he invited her father to come with her.

Ordinarily you know how this would have turned out. They would have taken one look at each other, screamed, and started running in the opposite directions. But it didn't work out that way. Each one turned out to be just as nice as the other had supposed. And so they were married and their married life is a companionably happy one. I met Mrs. Hines for the first time on that canoe trip. She's sweet. She still talks with an English accent and everybody round about here calls her "the Duchess." Because obviously anybody with such an English accent as that must be at least a duchess.

We were a little disappointed that the Hineses were expecting us because we had planned to surprise them. But it seems that while we were paddling up from South Arm, Ansky had been down to Middle Dam and had seen us going up the lake. We hadn't seen him, but it's amazing in this country what you can't do without everybody knowing all about it. We had a very good lunch that noon which consisted of bacon, scrambled eggs and canned peaches. Maybe this doesn't sound like much. But after you've paddled ten miles into a headwind, I can recommend it.

I was also very pleased to teach John, who was a very good woods cook, how to make scrambled eggs. I myself learned out of a book: "How to Cook a Wolf" by M.F.K. Fisher. Mrs. Fisher says that she makes the best scrambled eggs in the world and that she has tried to teach a great many people to make them as well, but that while many of her pupils were professional cooks, and all of them were willing, nobody has yet ever managed to make them as good as hers. Never having tasted her scrambled eggs, I couldn't say that mine are as good as hers. But at least they are much better than the ones I used to make, and are probably the best ones I have ever tasted myself. This is how you do it. Take eight good fresh eggs. If you can afford it, take half a pint of rich cream. I've never been able to afford that, so I take a can of condensed milk and a can of water. Add a touch of salt and a little pepper. If you want to, you can also add grated cheese, herbs, or whatever. Break the eggs into a cold, iron spider (skillet to you), pour the cream in, and stir it quickly with a fork until it is all blended, and not (!) frothy and whipped up together. Put the spider where the flame is warm not hot. Every now and then take a spoon and scrape the eggs off the bottom of the pan in large curls, as seldom as possible. Don't break these curls up. Never, never allow any part of the mixture to bubble. Just keep scraping gently off the bottom every few minutes. This takes at least half an hour. It cannot and must not be hurried. This seems like a lot of work for a few scrambled eggs, but believe me, it's worth it. If you're going to add any cheese, or chicken livers, or anything of that sort, do it when the eggs are done.

I didn't feel offended at Mrs. Fisher, nor do I think she is showing objectionable complacency when she brags about her scrambled eggs. In my opinion, if you know how to do something very well you should certainly be allowed to say so. Most people will admit their shortcomings, so why

shouldn't they be allowed to admit their strong points? Mrs. Fisher's attitude about her scrambled eggs has given me courage to take an attitude
about my own chocolate fudge. I say, without exaggeration, I think I can
make the best chocolate fudge in the world. Like Mrs. Fisher, I have tried
to teach others to make it, but nobody yet has been able to. If you're not
interested in chocolate fudge, skip the next paragraph.

You take two cups of sugar, three squares of cooking chocolate
(unsweetened) or three and a half tablespoons of cocoa, as generous a
piece of butter as conscience will let you, and three-quarters of a cup of
canned milk with three tablespoons of water added. This you stir up. You
put it on the back of the stove, where it will not boil, until all the sugar is
melted. To determine if there are any grains of sugar left, use the unscien-
tific and sloppy procedure of putting your thumb and forefinger into the
brew and rubbing them together. If you feel grains, it isn't melted. Then
you move it further over into more heat and allow it to boil gently. The less
you have to stir, the better. But you do have to stir once in a while or it will
catch on the bottom. When you think it's done, that's when it boils rather
thickly, drop a spoonful in a pan of cold water. If it forms a firm ball it's
done. If the water around the ball is chocolaty, even if the ball is firm, it's
not done. If you have any doubts, cook it a little more. Then you take it off
the stove and beat the living daylights out of it. I'm not sure if this is the
secret of good creamy fudge, but I think perhaps it is. I don't mean stir it,
I mean beat like the devil—fast and hard. When the mixture begins to
grow less shiny-looking on top, and the spoon makes a kind of sucking
noise when you beat, it's time to pour it into the pan (which you will have
greased thickly with butter before you even started this operation or else
you're going to find when you get ready to pour that you have forgotten to
butter the pan). I'm sorry I can't be any more definite about the length of
time to beat, or the temperature on a candy thermometer, or exact time to
boil. These are things you have to learn by instinct. If you do just what I
said, you ought to have good fudge. But unfortunately, experience has
taught me that very likely you won't have.

Now, as to our canoe trip: the very idea of our taking it was unusual.
In the first place, in this country canoes are not used very much by us natives. They are strictly a sport's boat. The boat most used is what is called
a "Rangeley boat," a type invented, I think, by a man named Jim Bernier.
This is a rather heavily constructed wooden boat, high at both ends, very
easy to maneuver and very difficult to sink or swamp. Everybody who
knows his way around owns a Rangeley boat. Flat bottom boats are held
in very low repute. The general opinion is that anybody who amounts to

anything, or who knows enough to come in out of the rain, wouldn't be caught dead in a flat bottom boat. We sometimes refer scornfully to "flat-bottomed Frenchmen from Berlin." This term is not intended to be any slight upon their nationality or the place of residence, but only upon their insistence on using flat bottomed boats.

We had intended to continue after lunch to Upper Dam, cross over the Carry to Mooselukmeguntic, and spend the night at a campground at Schaefer's Island. But instead of going down, the wind increased in fury, and it seemed much more sensible to stay where we were for the rest of the day. Then followed one of the most unearthly afternoons I ever spent. Nothing happened except that the wind blew and blew and blew. It should have been a great afternoon, but it wasn't. In spite of the wind a dense haze, almost like a smoke, lay over everything. You couldn't see the opposite shore of the lake. Out of an impenetrable curtain which extended, as far as we could tell, to eternity, the wind blew and the waves came rolling in. The nearer ones were clear and green with falling white tops. Fifty feet offshore the waves began to diminish in outline. Ten feet beyond that we could see only gleaming white crests apparently materializing out of nothing. It was weird. But weirder even than the appearance of the water was the appearance of the land.

Connecting Pine Island with the mainland on the East was a narrow spit of white sands which continues north as a wide white beach. We wandered over there to go swimming. The beach disappeared ahead of us into the haze. All along it, looking like the skeleton of big historic monsters, were great bleached pieces of dri-ki. Dri-ki, in case you don't know, is long-dead wood, not logs, but whole tree tops or entire root systems, or great branches. The bark has long-since fallen away from the wood, is bleached by the sun, and scarred by wind and sand out of any semblance of the original tree. Some of the pieces along that beach stood higher than our heads. The whole scene, discovered as it was in the haze, was something out of time and space. It looked exactly like an impossibly improbable landscape conceived by Salvadore Dali. You had the oddest feeling that you were dead, surrounded in a world between worlds where nothing you did or said could be held against you because neither the place not the time nor yourself existed.

I can't remember what any of us said or did except that Ralph and Willis and Barbara and I swam. I can remember that it was with almost a feeling of being rescued, from what unnameable peril I cannot say, to hear John shout from over on the Island that supper was ready and to get back to such familiar things as the smell of coffee, the hiss of steak frying in a pan, and the sight of the two guides moving about the fire as domestic as any housewife in her kitchen.

We thought the wind would go down at sunset. But it didn't. It blew all night long. We slept on the ground and felt it rush over us. A little after midnight, a sudden sharp shower came up. But it passed over quickly. Willis was thrilled because never in his life had he slept outdoors. And he felt that it was more or less a gift from the gods that he should be given a sample of everything, even rain. I myself like to lie under a tarpaulin and listen to the rain patter on it and feel it wet on my face. If I can be sure that it's not going to amount to more than a shower, but of course, the trouble is that you never can be.

In the morning, the wind hardened again. Darn it all. All it had done was change its direction slightly so that we would again be heading straight into it. However, we decided that we were supposed to be on a canoe trip, and no more fooling around on islands. We loaded everything aboard and set out north toward the Upper Dam Carry. It was early, about half past seven, and we thought how surprised Mrs. Grant at Upper Dam would be to see us at the door of the hotel, cheerfully announcing good morning. "We were rather looking for you last night," she greeted us. So there went that surprise. I haven't found out yet how she knew we were coming. She gave the vague impression of having picked it out of the air. And maybe she did. She showed us all over the place and we bought some postcards, among them a picture of Fly Rod ["Fly Rod Crosby," a famous female angler of the Rangeley area].

Above Upper Dam, Mosselukmicuntic starts. Mooseluk is purely a sportsman's lake. It is referred to hereabouts as the "big lake." It is a big lake, too. About ( ) miles long and ( ) miles in width. They say that the big lake is lovely, and I suspect that it is. But the mysterious, smoky haze of the day before continued. All the day the wind blew. The wind should have displaced the fog, but it didn't. There is something wrong about a high wind and a thick fog. Something against nature. The sun moved over our heads and shone with bright, diffused light all about us. It was hot enough to burn the fog off, but it didn't. This whole unnatural combination gave the day the same weird dream-like quality of the day before.

We were following the left hand shore and that we could see dimly. To the right, as far as we could tell, there was nothing from us to eternity. We met the big, white boat that carries the mail from Oquossic to Upper Dam. It was impossible to see the outline of it. As it passed us, it was a flash of blending light, the sound of a motor, and voices calling back and forth. Now and then we saw other small boats. They appeared suddenly out of nothing, black, distant outlines on the edge of a void. Once we saw, silhouetted darkly against the shining curtain of the fog, a small boat in which two men stood struggling fiercely while a third sat quietly in the stern and watched them. What were they fighting about? We didn't know. Why was the third man so unconcerned? They disappeared as quickly as they had come, without a sound.

I said to Gerrish once, "When we get around this next corner, the wind ought to be behind us."

He answered me kindly, with the gentle, patronizing manner of one speaking to a not-quite-bright child, "You mean, when we round the point into the lea, she'll be astern."

That was what I meant, all right, but it never worked out that way. Every time we changed course the wind changed, too. This doesn't seem possible, but fortunately I have five witnesses that it's absolutely true. Never once that whole trip did we have anything but a full headwind. At first we thought nothing of it, and then it became irritating. But finally we passed the point of irritation and grew rather proud of a wind that could be so consistent.

I would never again be able to find the place where we had lunch. I don't know how John found it then. At noon he pointed out into the fog and said, "Over there is where we'll stop to eat." We obediently headed over there and in a minute saw the white glimmer of a grove of birches through the fog. Out of nothing, a little island resolved. The beach was clean and stony and a path led through the tall grass and raspberry bushes and a clearing under the birches. It was a lovely spot, all the lovelier because it seemed to have been plucked out of nothing.

We ate corn chowder and chocolate cake and were just about to re-embark when Ralph discovered that the tall growth of raspberry cane and little spruces hid the remains of what at one time must have been a very elaborate camp. Gerrish and I looked at each other and groaned. Gerrish set down the pack sack that he had started to take to the canoe, lay down under a tree, and tipped his hat over his face. I got a cup and started picking raspberries. We both knew from long experience that we'd be there an hour, easy.

Long years of living in the woods, where the general rule is fix up what you've got instead of getting a new one, has developed in Ralph what amounts to a mania for junk. I think he sees every new bit of territory which he covers, not in the light of scenic or geographic interest, but in the light of future possibility for salvage. He will say when rigging up a motor, for example, "What I need is about a three-foot piece of one-inch angle iron." Then he'll squat on his heels and stare into space with the same fixed stare as you sometimes observe on a cat. At the end of a minute, he'll announce, "And I know where there's one." It may be six miles away at Sunday Pond. It may be at South Arm. It may be over at Black Cove, where a sawmill burned down fifteen years ago.

I never used to understand how he could be so sure. But I'm getting to be the same way myself. Once you get the junkman eye, the mental cataloging of junk becomes purely subconscious. I remember Ralph saying to me once, "I wish I had a piece of strap iron." I had my own answer, "I know where there's one six-feet long with holes for bolts at one-foot intervals." It wasn't until I said it that I realized that it was true. I did know where there was one. It was in the yard of the Thurston's #3 camp, long since deserted and fallen down, lying about ten feet from a spring on a rock with a split in the middle. I honestly don't remember ever truly noticing that piece of iron. And yet, when we walked the mile and a quarter over B Ridge to look, sure enough, there it was exactly as I thought. I almost credited myself with second sight.

Once you get the junk-picking-up habit, it persists wherever you are. Ralph found a brand new spark plug on the sidewalk of Canal Street in New York City. And once I found, and picked up (because you must never let an opportunity pass) a pretty good lock washer by the intersection of Fifth Avenue and 28th Street. The cop on the corner gave me a hard look, but I put it in my pocket just the same. As it turned out, this new junk mania wasn't a very profitable one. Most of the metal—and there was quite a lot of it—was galvanized and, it seems, is inferior. I found a good piece of iron rod, just the wrong length to be conveyed comfortably in a canoe. It didn't quite lay flat on the bottom, so that every time you got in or out of the canoe, or tried to lift something else in or out of it, the darn thing tripped you. In addition to that, it periodically stabbed me, sitting in the bow seat, just above the kidneys. But we took it on the whole rest of the trip around to all the lakes and back safely home.

That afternoon we spent looking for dead men. John planted this delightful thought in our minds just after we had left the lunch grounds and headed again into the teeth of the wind. We now had to cross the widest part of the lake and would be out of sight of land in the haze for about an hour or two. John said cheerfully, "They say she's rolling up now. Those Frenchmen ought to be coming to the top." About a month before, two men had been drowned in this stretch of the lake under rather mysterious circumstances. Their bodies had never been recovered. This in itself was rather a peculiar circumstance, for while people drown in this country, they're frequently not recovered until spring. In this country, people drowned in the spring almost always rise to the surface within a few days and are found. These Frenchmen had never come up and never been found, and they haven't yet been found to this day. I don't know whether John thought we might be bored with nothing to look at except the fog and the waves rolling around us, or whether he really thought we could find the bodies (not that we wanted to, heaven forbid), but he got us into the state of mind where every time you saw a floating branch we were sure the dead men were coming aboard. It lent a certain spice to the canoeing, but I'm glad we didn't find them.

One of the most delightful things about that afternoon's paddling in the windy, sun-shot fog was the social aspect of it. It had some of the features of a big reception where you mill about with a cocktail glass in your hand, talking first to one person about the international situation then another time to a matron from Long Island about the breeding of guinea hens, and finally to a gentleman from Illinois about the trials of strip mining. We didn't have any cocktails in our hands, we had only paddles. We weren't milling aimlessly about in our best clothes, we were working like hell against a headwind in denims and checked shirts.

But Gerrish and I would be carrying on a conversation something like this, Gerrish: "Why don't you take that wool jacket off?" Me: "With the wind blowing like this, wild horses couldn't get this jacket off me." Gerrish: "Whenever I hear anybody say that I just wonder how a wild horse would go about getting that jacket off you. It wouldn't make sense."

This struck me funny, and from then on we were analyzing other meaningless catch phrases when John and Barbara Wing drifted within hearing. They were talking about the best way to conquer mosquitoes. So we joined the conversation. The upshot of that was that we all agreed in order to slap many you should first wet your hands. No matter how quick and careful you are, mosquitoes somehow fly out between dry hands and fly happily away. If your hands are wet you can almost always get them. My theory was that the wings stick to the water. But John was of the opinion that the water on the hands cushions the air so that since there is no draft to blow them out from between your hands, then...They drifted out of hearing. Then Gerrish and I overtook Willis and Ralph. They were talking about the proper way to build a rotary saw. Gerrish and I added our two cents worth to that before we were blown beyond earshot. I think that due to the fluid nature of the group, we covered more topics and conversations, in the three days of the canoe trip than I have in any given three years before or since.

Finally we saw, through the mist, something shining large and white and distant in the diffused sunlight. It was there for a moment and then it was gone. John said it was the Mountain View House and we were about to enter the narrows between Mooseluc and Cupsuptic where our course turned at abrupt right angles and we, again foolishly, anticipated a wind that would be at least deferential. Experience should have taught us better. We rounded Blueberry Island and the wind shifted immediately into the north and again we plowed right into it. We followed the shore very closely here and I wish it hadn't been so hazy because Cupsuptic must be a beautiful lake. The Rangeleys down our way have black growth [spruce forests] to the water's edge with an occasional sandy beach. Cupsuptic is all ledges. And if there's anything I love it's ridges of rock that thrust out from the woods and then drop off into the deep water. Along the top grow tall trees and the gullies are usually filled with whinnigan. A whinnigan is an impassable tangle of black spruce growth, of blow downs, or the like. And I have never heard the term used unless prefaced by "God-awful." If it isn't God-awful, I guess it isn't a whinnigan.

We were going to spend the night on a little island just north of the Pleasant Island camps and it was when we got to Pleasant Island that I witnessed an astounding gastronomic feat on the part of Barbara Wing. First she bought an ice cream cone and ate that. Then she bought four chocolate bars, the kind filled with marshmallows and nuts and other goo, and ate them. Then she asked John what we were going to have for supper, and how soon. What's more, when we had supper three-quarters of an hour later, she ate steak and onions, french fried potatoes, two pieces of cake, and two dishes of pears. And she only weighs about 120 pounds! There must be something in the theory that many thin people who eat a lot put such a burden on their systems that the work of digestion keeps them worn down.

The next morning we hired a truck to take us over to the headwaters of the Magalloway. The Magalloway is never referred to in our family as anything but the "noble Magalloway." This is because we once read a book called "Grant Henley or, The Trapper of Umbagog." The book was written probably about 1880 and is a melodrama of very low style with stilted language and stilted sentiments. In it, the characters are always going on trips up the "noble Megalloway." We didn't think the Magalloway was so very noble. It's a somewhat wide stream meandering down a valley.

The wind had at last stopped blowing—when we could have done with a little—and the sun shown through the still-existent haze 'til we felt as if we were confined in a warm oven. The water was low so the banks of the river were muddy and altogether uninspiring. The only thing I remember about the Magalloway, besides being too hot, was that I lost one of my shoes overboard and never found it again. Gerrish picked me a bunch of white water lilies which were perfectly beautiful, and at last, after ten years of conversations with him, I met Joe Mooney.

We had to go by the Brown Farm anyway, so we thought we'd stop in and see him. Joe Mooney is almost blind. He can, I think, distinguish figures, but that is about all. He depends entirely upon his sense of hearing. I walked into the office and said, "Hello, Joe." He turned around and said, "Well hello, Louise." I said, "Oh, you knew we were coming?" He said, "No, but I recognized your voice. What in hell are you doing over here?"

Ralph explained we were on a canoe trip. "Jesus Christ," said Joe. "What in hell are you doing on a canoe trip? You gone crazy?" Ralph said, "No. We got some people from New York staying with us." "Oh," said Joe with sympathy and understanding. No native would ever go on a canoe trip just for the fun of it. The idea of pushing canoes around and walking long distances through bad going mile after mile, simply because of liking to do it for pleasure, doesn't enter the mind of the natives. Their idea of pleasure is to sit. We wouldn't have to explain this to Joe. But people from New York, they would do anything.

We finally got down to Umbagog just before sunset and we saw, across the lake on Pine Point, a flag flying. This meant that Mr. Lehman, an acquaintance of ours, was in residence at his camp. Since he is almost never up on the lake, we immediately decided to go over and call on him. We would surprise him. But the moment we pulled up at his dock his man, Wilbur, met us. "Hullo," he said, with no show of surprise at all. "We heard you were up on the Magalloway." I asked him who told him and he just shrugged. "Oh, the grapevine," he said.

The woods grapevine is a strange and wonderful thing, the workings of which I do not yet fully understand—and I expect never will. Simple examples can be doped out. For example, early in the spring, when we are cut off completely from the Outside, someone will say to us, "They have started the Cambridge drive, and Mike Murphy is bossing it." Nobody has come in and told us that and the telephone is down. This isn't, however, an example of telepathy. For days, at intervals of perhaps an hour, we have been hearing the dull boom of distant dynamiting from over south, where the Cambridge is. Dynamite in that direction, at this time of year, can only mean one thing—that the drive has started and the logs are jamming. But that being a year of plenty of snow and heavy spring rains, there certainly should have been enough water in the Cambridge to get the drive down with very little dynamite. Some bosses wouldn't have used any, but Mike Murphy is a man of very short patience. His answer to every problem is, "Put a stick of dynamite under it." Therefore, conditions being what they were, nobody else but Mike Murphy could be bossing the Cambridge drive. It's very simple, you see, when you understand it.

This same Mike Murphy, it is reported, once took his passion for dynamite too far. An inexperienced "bull cook"—a bull cook is a general handyman around a lumber camp who keeps the fires going, gets water, and does whatever odd jobs there may be—was told by Mike Murphy that it was time to clean out the latrine. This looked like quite a job to the bull cook because a camp of 150 men required a fairly large and elaborate latrine. So he asked Mike, in all innocence, "Just how would I be going about that?"

"I'd stick five or six sticks of dynamite under the seat," Mike told him. Whether this was from absent-mindedness, habit, or just general impatience with stupidity no one will ever know. The bull cook took him seriously. And after the resulting blast, not only had the latrine completely vanished, but it was necessary to abandon the camp and build another a half mile away.

If you are standing on a mountain in this country and you see a man rowing a boat across the lake a thousand feet below and two miles away you can, if you are a native, say with complete confidence, "There goes old Hank Bemis. He's rowing over after his milk," because you know that every day at 4 o'clock Hank Bemis does row over after his milk. By and large, the working of the grapevine depends, I think, on complete familiarity with the country. If you know everybody and their habits, then you can interpret whatever a man does or doesn't do correctly. It gets to be second nature. You don't have to figure out a line of reasoning. A man shows up in his best plaid shirt, for instance, and you are instantly sure that he has heard that his son is coming home on leave. He's going down to Lewiston to get him. One thing is going to lead to another so that he will land in jail. Then his wife will go down day after tomorrow and bail him out. So you can count as a fact that Lettie is going to Lewiston and you will be absolutely right.

That's the way the grapevine works. I suppose that's the way it worked on our canoe trip, although I have never been able to uncover all the details. No one along the way, except Joe Mooney, was surprised to see us.

Ansky Hines at Pleasant Island and Mrs. Grant at Upper Dam and a guide named Archie Bennett at Pleasant Point all had been expecting us hours before we showed up. They didn't get the news over the telephone because, if they had, it would have come through the Brown Farm where all the telephones center, and Joe would have been expecting us. Nobody saw us because the haze was too thick. There is some explanation, of course, but I'm damned if I know what it is.

Notes for a Christmas Story, from LDR's Steno Notebook

[Here is a wonderful example of Louise's gift at brainstorming and creating a story line. I assume this is something she sent either to Willis, her agent, or to *Women's Home Companion* in connection with her monthly column. An accompanying letter indicated that this was worked up in October, getting ready for the holiday edition.]

This will be a story about Christmas based on Dean's making all those wreaths and decorating the Parson's barn. There might be enough parallel, not too close, between this story and the story of the birth of Jesus because Jesus was born in a barn. Maybe some guy lives up in the woods and he works all fall making wreaths and garlands out of evergreens which he plans to take out, as he usually does, to sell in the town just before C.

We'll say he's a hermit and a little queer. He'll have some special reason why he needs the money this particular year. He loads all the stuff onto a sled with a couple of horses, and starts down out of the mountains. But before he gets anywhere near civilization, he is overtaken by a terrible snowstorm and is snowed in. The place he is snowed in is a sort of squatter's camp where some people live that have practically nothing but a mess of kids and some livestock like a couple of mangy cows, a donkey and some old broken-down horses which they keep out back in a shanty.

There is something wrong with these people. I think they're in trouble or else they're doing something illegal. We'll say that the husband is a sort of overbearing brute who has a wife who is a very nice woman—intimidated. The wife is all the time trying to do something for the kids to give them a little pleasure in life. But she has pretty tough going because the husband is against "spoiling the brats."

The guy comes down with his load of wreaths and they won't let him in the house. So he asks to go out and stay in the barn. Instead of having the husband a brutish man, maybe we'll just have him a discouraged man. Life is very much against him, he thinks. He really wanted to do things for his wife and the kids, but he just can't. He hasn't any money and everything he has ever done has failed. And he might be going out and homesteading on this place. He might get ahead some, but that was a failure too. And now it's C. and he can't even give the kids any presents and it looks like the end to him.

Or maybe we'll say that there wasn't any husband. There was just this woman with a couple of kids. And she is trying to make a life for the kids. And she is discouraged. And the reason the hermit had to have a lot of money this year was that he was sick of living alone and he was, I think, going to write a matrimonial agency and get a wife. Or else, he had already written a matrimonial agency and was on his way down to sell his wreaths and get this wife who was a perfectly impossible woman.

We can show how impossible she was by having the hermit show her letters and picture to the woman when he gets snowed in there. She can tell that the woman is nothing but a gold digger…just from reading the letters and from the look of her. Naturally, the hermit thinks she's wonderful.

Maybe it would be good to have had the woman, with a great deal of work and deprivation, manage to scrape up a present apiece for her kids. But, unfortunately, on C. eve, the house burns down and everything in it but the people barely manage to escape. And they have to go live in the barn.

Instead of having the hermit going to be married, we'll have him sour and discouraged, too. But, against his nature really, he has found himself in the two or three days he has had to stay there, getting sorry for the woman and the kids. Although he has always believed that when you started getting sorry for people, then you let yourself open to getting hurt, this is based on some old experience of his—probably with a girl years before that led to his becoming a hermit. But on C. eve, when the house burns up, they all have to go up and stay in the barn where he has been sleeping.

Anyway, because the woman is a nice woman and hasn't felt that it is proper for him to sleep in the house and he sees how terrible she feels because now she hasn't anything for her poor kids, he can't help himself and he really does get awfully sorry for her.

The kids go to sleep in some hay in the mangers and the man and the woman sit around a fire he has built in an oil drum, and talk all night. During this conversation somehow will have to be brought out some of the basic principles of Christianity. Without stating it in so many words, it must be indicated that Christianity is especially for the weary and over-burdened and that it is based largely on an unselfish love for humanity (read in the Bible for specific definition).

The woman, exhausted, goes to sleep, and the hermit finds that he wants to do something. So he takes all his whole lot of C. wreaths and dec-

NOTES FOR A CHRISTMAS STORY   291

orates the barn, both inside and out, so that it looks perfectly wonderful and not like a barn at all. The kids, when they wake, are nearly overcome. And they ask the hermit [if] the reason he trimmed the barn like that is because Jesus was born in a barn. And he says, yes, it was. And he also tells them what they don't understand, and that the mother does—that Christ was reborn in that barn that very night. She understands that he means that that night the principles of Christ were reborn in him and that he has begun to live again like a human being. And she feels that the same thing applies to her because she has had hope reborn in her.

Maybe we can imply a little love is to come a little later. Or maybe it would be better to have the experience an isolated one and have them never see each other again, but to be two quite different people for having spent a night in a barn together. In the latter case, it would be necessary to outline quite clearly the problems with which each was confronted before the night in the barn. They had each reached a crisis in their affairs where they could take an easier wrong road, or a very different right road, and because they had both lost hope or belief in decency they were both about to do the wrong thing. It must be made clear that not only in their particular characters is Christmas a purely personal and wonderful thing, but it should be in all cases.

Notes for
Other Stories and a Book,
from LDR's Journal

The Country

[Written probably in the mid-1960s, when Louise moved to The Sands, in Gouldsboro.]

I have never lived in a city, but this is the first time I have ever lived in what I understand to be meant by the words "the country." Neither the Maine woods, my home for many years, nor the several New England villages I have inhabited for longer or shorter periods, seem to me to have been really the country. In the woods there was no discipline whatsoever. The forest stretched for miles on every side, unaltered by the hand of man; and what I did with myself and my time was dictated only by necessity and my own good sense, or lack of it. Look and listen as hard as I might, never could I see a light in a neighbor's window or smoke from his chimney, nor hear his dog barking or the sound of his ax. It wasn't the country; it was the wilderness.

Everything in the villages spoke of discipline: the neatly painted houses, the close-clipped lawns, the trim flowerbeds, and ornamental shrubs, and sidewalks under well-tended trees. Neighbors were everywhere, their voices calling back and forth in the daytime and their lights glowing soft behind drawn shades in the evening. Their rights and their feelings must be respected, and so a discipline of conduct was imposed.

Allowing the dog to run loose and tip over garbage pails was creating a nuisance, laughing loud and long late on a summer night when all the windows were open was inconsiderate. And hanging out a tremendous washing to dry on Sunday morning was a true offense to many churchgoers. These restrictions were legitimate and I have no quarrel with them. But they were things of the town, not the county.

To me, the country is a place between the wilderness and the town. Both the land and the people are under moderate discipline, other than that which everyone everywhere must impose on himself. The chaos of the virgin forest has been replaced by the order of meadow, field, and orchard, but a certain tolerance prevails. Weeds that would be stamped out like vipers in a town grace the roadsides and flourish along the fences—daisies and joepye-weed, buttercups, and steeplebush, meadow rue and touch-me-not....

Blizzard

[Louise started this piece while living in Corea, on Crowley's Island, probably in the late 1970s.]

Our sense of isolation increased. Now we really are on our own. The causeway is blocked by an ice cake jam which plows can't move. No vehicle can get on or off.

Nobody seemed much disturbed by being isolated. I knew I wasn't. Our routine was very little disrupted. Everyone had plenty to eat—you learn in the deep country and along untenanted coasts to stock up ahead for emergencies—and all the houses were warm. No mail of course; but the general attitude was, so what? If it's good news, it will keep and if it's bad, we don't want to hear about it. There was a little more calling back and forth between dooryards than usual, ("She's a corker, ain't she?" and "Blowin' hard enough for ya?") and a little more gathering in kitchens to discuss the situation; but we're always pretty neighborly over here on the island, even in the busiest peak of the balmy tourist season. Manny Young asked me if he could leave his truck in my yard for the duration. I have no car, and my driveway was swept clean to the frozen gravel by the wind; while his, several hundred feet long, was waist deep in snow which terminated in a twenty-foot drift against his garage. That was about the only visible departure from the normal.

We take things like blizzards less hard here in the country. We are better prepared for them: better clothes, better equipment, more experience with them. Most important, we are better prepared emotionally. We don't let them fret us, we don't have to go-go-go in the face of the impossible. I saw the TV news pictures of conditions in Massachusetts and Rhode Island, and I talked to Dinah in Massachusetts, and I was appalled. Roads closed all over Massachusetts. Hundreds of cars abandoned on highways. All of this was completely unnecessary. People were warned well ahead in no uncertain terms. They simply wouldn't believe, wouldn't heed the warning. And they won't next time, either.

[Additional notes and lines of text relating to "Blizzard" come from an earlier period at The Sands]:

Wonderful feeling of blizzardy day—can't go out so can relax and catch up on chores. Plenty of food, fires blazing, warm snug and safe. Outside wind terrible and snow thick and streaming downwind; can't see sea or Shaw's and cars infrequent and dim and slow. Don't feel confined–confinement is not space anyhow, but time, commitments and deadlines.

Fringe of icicles all slanting seaward on shed eaves.

Wind swooping from north across Point through orchard and lawn where in summer...etc. Now white and sculptured waste.

Mixture of blowing snow and spray in winter's crystal light.

Re-learning about not trying to go anywhere, lesson learned in woods. Just hole in and enjoy it. Arvid and plow finally–next day or two; Navy goes past, but almost no one else.

The great golden glitter of southerly sun on snow and sea, trees dark cut-outs against crumpled gilt paper. Shining path moves from east to west as day moves on.

Contraction of life in cold—back entry, summer and winter.

Night sky—new moon and 1 big star through bare lilac tree.

Winter scene in late afternoon up-road: black, white and pale gold with gold reflection on ice in brook.

Old Age/Desolation/
Women Alone

[Written in the late 1970s when Louise had returned to Crowley's Island for her last hurrah at living independently in Maine. This, and the preceding pieces on country living and the blizzard and isolation, are part of a book that, unfortunately, never materialized.]

I remember the houses to which, as a child, I was taken to call by my grandmother and mother and aunts [at] the old houses of their spinster or widowed friends. I remember the geraniums, the ferns and Christmas cactuses, the sleek, spoiled cats sleeping curled in cushioned rocking chairs, the seashells as doorstops and striped lucky stones serving as paper weights, the Boston *Transcript* or *Christian Science Monitor* folded on the table with the reading glasses beside it and the wildflower and bird guides stacked neatly, shed wing feathers or blades of ribbon grass used to mark pages. I remember those houses and those women in their starched cotton dresses or afternoon voiles, pouring tea and passing sponge cake, talking of gardening and bird-walks and last Sunday's sermon at the Congregational church, smiling their bitter-sweet smiles. They were the ones who had come to terms with loneliness and the passage of the years, learned to accept with wry humor the solitary lives that were the price of independence.

I remember those women well because now I am of your company. Oh, Miss Sykes, Miss Lewis, Aunt Julia Dickinson, and Miss Hermann, Mrs. Martin, and Mrs. Swift, I remember you all and I know you far better now than I did or could when I was eight or ten. Never mind that I wear mail-order jeans and sweatshirts instead of dresses and read *Time* instead of the *Monitor* and haven't been to church in a month of Sundays. I have the cat and the houseplants and the reading glass and beach-stone paperweight.

I live alone from choice, as you did and I, as you were, am well along in years. I know things about you now that I had no way of knowing, could not imagine, as a child. That as soon as the "company" had left, waved and smiled down the path, you thought, or even said aloud to the cat—"There! Now I can get back to my letter-writing." I know about the warm comfort of that cat on a bitter winter night, snuggled on the bed in the small of the back or the crook of the knees. I know about fighting the temptation to just slap together a sandwich and brew a cup of tea to eat, standing up in the kitchen, instead of getting out a placemat and the silver and china, preparing a decent meal and perhaps reading while eating it, to give a semblance of civilized company. I know about playing solitaire and scrambling the cards together to stuff into a drawer when someone knocks at the door, lest whoever it is decides I'm in my dotage or very hard-up for an occupation. I know about watching for the mail, but not running right out to the mailbox, for fear someone might observe and think that's all I had to live for. People like us can't abide even a whiff of pity, in ourselves or others.

I know about deciding at nine in the evening to clean the woodshed. When you're elderly and living alone, no one says, "This is no time of day to do that. Wait until tomorrow and I'll help you." Or "Don't do that now. You'll tire yourself out." So what? Who cares? I feel like doing it now, and if I haven't any more sense than to over-do, that's my business.

Laboratory animals, although well-fed and housed, and in good health, become snappy and then vicious when forced to live under even moderately crowded conditions. They have room enough to move about comfortably and easily, but they cannot get away entirely from others of their kind. The same, I think, is true of people. Being herded together brings out the worst in them. They stream past you on the street, jostle you in stores, fidget in lines at bus stops. Their faces are tense, irritable, intense, even scowling, and more often than not unhappy. Very seldom do you see a sunny, open, contented countenance. Those who show happy faces are at once suspected of being drunk, doped, or feeble minded—a very sad commentary. Oh, sure, you see groups of young people gathered on corners and hear their laughter; but it is terrible laughter, harsh and derisive, cruel, more the yelping of a pack than the expression of shared gaiety and joy. In Brockton, although I lived alone theoretically, I was constantly exposed to people, in stores, on the street, in my own home, even just looking out the window and seeing them walk past the house. They really bothered me; all those people scurrying around. What earthly good were they? They wore on my nerves so much that one day when I was sitting in the sun on the lawn and a group of young men and women passed on the sidewalk, I felt such hatred for them that had I been possessed of the power, I would have killed them. There was no excuse for me. They were minding their own business, talking and laughing quietly among themselves, their conduct in no way whatsoever objectionable. I understood then why the placid laboratory rabbit, without provocation, tries to murder his cage mates. Their mere presence is provocation enough. These people all need to learn about being alone. It would do them a world of good. And I'm not talking about the kind of being alone accomplished by going into one's own room and closing the door or by taking a solitary walk of ten blocks. That's an artificial situation, as easily terminated as created.

I seem to be hearing an awful lot about the horrors of loneliness nowadays, mostly from people concerned with the problems of old age, which they are trying diligently, and with the best will in the world, to solve. These are always younger people with active social lives and an admirable desire to serve humanity; but what do they know about it? Age has its problems all right. There's arthritis, failing sight and hearing, the diminishing buying power of the fixed income, and hardening of the arteries for starters on a long list on which loneliness does not necessarily place high, if at all. What these earnest young people don't know, and won't know for a few decades, is that loneliness isn't all that much of a problem to the elderly. The picture of the poor old lady sitting alone with only her cat for company is pretty pathetic until you are that old lady sitting alone with her cat. Then it's not pathetic at all, but thoroughly enjoyable. Through a wise dispensation of Providence, the years have slowed the old lady down considerably, so that there's so much now to occupy the time and mind.

All this and much more I know about old women living alone. Some people can live alone, and some can't. We're talking about able-bodied people now. Some people have to have the company of others, if not constantly at least most of the time, in order to function properly and for the good of their mental and emotional health. About the others, the ones who move in with children or relatives, who enter Homes for the Aged, who hire a companion or invite a friend to live with them—anything, anything at all rather than live alone—I don't know. And, if I am lucky and retain some semblance of what are known as "my faculties"—meaning eye-sight, hearing, use of my limbs, and enough sense to come in out of the rain—I never will.

Once I rode a bus through east-central Maine in the early dusk of midwinter. I was taking the all-night trip to Boston. Travelling through a long stretch of sparsely settled country, I saw, stark on a ridge, silhouetted against the apricot afterglow, a solitary farmhouse. One light showed in the window of the kitchen ell; and immediately I was out of the over-heated, crowded bus with the long journey ahead of me, transported to that kitchen. No one else was there: no man in rough boots and barn-reeking mackinaw; no children, red-faced and chap-handed from the cold; no other woman, aproned and sweatered against the icy drafts that creep around the ill-fitting doors and windows of old weather-worn country dwellings. I was alone, looking out the small window at the snow-covered fields slowly drowning in darkness; alone with no long journey confronting me, only a short twilight and the oblivion of sleep. And I liked it. I wished that it were true and that I were not going to Boston, not obliged to deal with people, to smile and ask or answer questions. I liked it up there on that bleak ridge.

When I arrived at the Sands, I often stood at the sea-facing windows on blustery winter days and scanned the ledges a mile or so off-shore through field glasses. The thermometer often stood at ten above zero, though the sun was shining brightly, and gale-force winds were blowing. With the naked eye, I could see only the sun-shot towers of spray rising thirty, thirty-five, forty feet above the ledges, shining angels standing in unearthly beauty on the desert of the sea. But when I put the glasses to my eyes, ah then, then I could see the gray-green waters gather themselves together in gigantic combers and march magestically down the screaming wind to shatter themselves upon the stubborn granite. The explosion would have been ear-punishing, if there had been an ear out there to hear.

Spray leaped high and streamed down-wind in tattered banners, the wave surged on, and the ledges reappeared, shedding water from their kelp-clothed backs like shaggy, drenched dogs. I always longed to be out there in the middle of that desolate turmoil. I wanted to feel the gale, taste the sea, to be surrounded by the mindless power and inhuman purity of the off-shore ledges at half-tide.

One summer night a friend and I stood in a salt-water pasture and looked up at the sky. Those who live in cities can have no conception of what the night sky is on a cloudless, moonless night, viewed from an almost uninhabited stretch of coastline. The sky is everything. The land is only a low, dark shadow and the sea a dim, sensed presence; but the sky is a vast canopy pricked with a million stars. There are no ground lights to confuse, no city glow on the horizon, no smog to blur the brilliance of the smallest asteroid. The stars are imperturbable in the limitless vault, sublimely unaware and uncaring in their awful splendor.

Earlier that day the first man had been put into orbit, and as we stood there in the rough grass beside the whispering sea, we knew that he was up there somewhere among the Heavenly bodies. Of course we couldn't see Sputnik, but we were aware of it making its soundless way through space above us. "It must be lonely for him up there," my friend said; and I said, "Yes." But I thought how marvelous it must be to wheel through all that glory alone, to experience the ultimate isolation this side of the grave; and I envied that Russian from the bottom of my heart.

This craving for isolation—for desolation, if you will—has nothing to do with the intellect. My intelligence, such as it is, tells me that actually I wouldn't like any of the situations I have mentioned. I know farm kitchens and they are more often than not cluttered, cheerless places, lighted by one drop bulb in the middle of the ceiling, either too hot or too cold, sometimes not particularly clean, and seldom really comfortable. The water pipes freeze in the winter, and in the summer flies from the barn have to be battled constantly. I don't really want to be planted in one of them, any more than I want to be transported in the middle of the winter to the off-shore ledges. I wouldn't survive there for two seconds; nobody could; even the gulls are blown and frozen out of the sky. It would be hellish out there. As for being launched into Outer Space—hah! In the extremely unlikely event that the opportunity should arise, I would run and hide under the bed rather than grasp it. Being slightly claustrophobic, I wouldn't like being sealed in a small capsule at all; and having had some unhappy encounters with mechanisms that malfunctioned, I'd be too worried about splashdown to savor my situation. My better judgement tells me to forget the isolated farmhouse, the distant ledges, the solo orbit and all the other symbols of loneliness that sometimes move me unexpectedly and deeply.

The quick flood of emotion, as I have said, has nothing to do with reason or mind. Its source lies hidden deep below the intellect. It is a gut reaction that feels like nostalgia, that overpowering sickness to go home. There is the same hollowness, the constriction of the throat, the dry-eyed inner weeping, the wave of utter despair. Perhaps it is nostalgia, an inborn longing for a world where it was not only possible but common for a person to be alone for long periods of time. I cannot believe that I am different from others. I believe that in everyone lies this atavistic craving for loneliness. Some recognize it and some do not. Those that do are the ones who take off for the bush of Alaska or the Outback of Australia or become sheep herders or lighthouse keepers. Those who recognize it vaguely become irritable and speak crossly of needing a little time to themselves to plan their new wardrobes or make out their shopping lists. Those who don't recognize it at all are headed for trouble.

[And finally, here is an unpublished, undated poem. It is doubly poignant in that it was composed sometime during the dark days after Ralph's death.]

A Prayer of Thanksgiving

For all the good things of the earth,
For friends and laughter and companionship
For bright fires roaring up the chimney on a winter's night
For bread upon the table and warm clothes against the cold
For long summer hours of leisure and days spent in the sun
For books to read and sunsets to admire, I give thanks.
But these are not the things for which my greatest thanks are due.
More than for my friends, I give thanks for my enemies.
They are the ones who stand guard over my character
To preserve the wandering of my feet and the flagging of my spirit.
They are your shepherds over me, Oh Lord.
More than for leisure, I give thanks for hard work that must be done.
For only through hours of toil and days that end with weariness
Is it possible to know accomplishment, contentment, and restful sleep.
More than for warmth, I give thanks for the sharp edge of cold,
The biting of the wind that I may feel.
I give thanks for all the times that I have been hungry.
For greater than the close companionship of those who feast together
Is the deep and unforgettable brotherhood of all those who cry for bread.
I give thanks for the privilege of membership in that brotherhood.
I give thanks for the tears I have shed.
For more than laughter, they remain the symbol of humanity.
For all the things I couldn't have, I give thanks.
For more than things is an appreciation of the glorious benefits,
given equally to all:
the earth beneath, the heavens above,
the wonders of thy changing seasons,
bright air and swiftly running water—
all the myriad wonders of thy world.

Conclusion

What makes certain books classics and carries their authors forward in time? Probably insight into the universal through the particular—keen observation and an engaging depiction of a time and place, and insights into the human condition—words for growing the soul. We are seduced not only by information and images but also, ultimately, by insight. We are drawn inexorably to it. Insight is not linear. It doubles back on itself, restated in illimitable nuances. It is like sitting across the table from a compassionate friend, crusty as an old shoe but as supple and sure; or walking with a wise one who points out landmarks and offers sage perceptions that speak directly, you feel, and appropriately, to you. We are drawn to the storyteller and her stories. Louise not only had a way with words, she had a way with life. You relate to her and see more of yourself through her.

People who know of Louise Dickinson Rich often seem to feel a real connection to her and her writings. Their faces light up when they tell which book(s) they've read. During my short stays at both Forest Lodge and on the Gouldsboro Peninsula, I met individuals who had traveled hundreds (sometimes thousands) of miles on what basically was a pilgrimage. A couple from the Midwest had come to Maine with the sole purpose of visiting Louise Dickinson Rich sites. (Aldro French reports that there is a steady stream of admirers walking the two-mile stretch of Carry Road to get a glimpse of Forest Lodge.) She has something of a cult following. It goes beyond mere enjoyment; there is a real yearning to connect with, to be somehow a part of, her and her world. Just as Bridgewater was the microcosm of Town Life, the Peninsula was Country Life, and Forest Lodge was The Wilderness, so Louise—capabilities, contradictions, clay feet and all, by her own admission—was and is a microcosm of ourselves.

Louise spoke—in a manner simple, funny, and wise—about a time and place and things we wish to remember, even if somewhat idealized, because the story and the personality of the storyteller still hold out the hope of possibilities. And when a favorite or formative author dies, you wonder at what was left unsaid, what in their lives can still inform.

Thus, a biography. Louise's life and work provide clues of how one person confronts the human characteristics up for review within all people in every generation. A life laid out before us, in retrospect, is, if truly told, full of contradictions. It is ambiguous territory. Louise was shy, and protected her sensitivity by staying apart, by performing in high-school drama, by brashness, by internalizing her emotions. She was also capable and self-confident, covering this with self-effacement and humor, or celebrating with unedited bravado. She had an enormous interest in human nature and people, but she disliked crowds, specific individuals, social conventions, fads, and causes. She wrote in a seemingly straightforward manner of a seemingly simple life. The reality was much more complex and demanding—requiring skill, dogged determination, and creative intelligence. Her wholesome accounts of a wholesome life were true and not true. They talked of virtues and underplayed the drinking and dark times. They espoused ideal love and omitted failed marriages. They professed an "aw-shucks" stumbling into the world of letters that belied her diligence and dedication to writing. Her actual practice of motherhood often fell short of her written portrayal. On the other hand, she often minimized or trivialized her own role in caring deeply and providing for her family. Louise showed great courage in adapting and learning, in surrendering to the unknown. She showed vulnerability, creativity, anger, humor, fear, and diligence in coping with the losses of loved ones, fame and fortune, dreams and hopes.

The stories and impressions of Louise are also contradictory. She said what was on her mind. Some have been offended; others have seen this as an asset. She was "lithe and dressed well," had "little interest in fashion." She snubbed and "was patient" with sycophants. She "put on airs" and was "down to earth." Sometimes the speaker knew her well; sometimes he or she was reacting to a snapshot impression. And sometimes the impression reflected the speaker's preconceptions of womanhood: soft-spoken, house-and convention-bound, slender, intellectually and physically inferior—pick one, or a combination—any of which Louise was not. The general consensus, though, is that Louise loved nature; was adventurous; had bouts of drinking; had a soft spot for animals; was her own person; was bright, tolerant, and blunt; and had a way with the written word. She definitely was not invisible or dull.

We can thank Louise Dickinson Rich for her insight into the ambiguities within herself and others, and for her considerable skill in creating a sense of time and place. And we can thank her for her generosity: Writing is a public, personal, and permanent act of sharing with others. We are the lucky recipients of her gifts. As the ages pass, rather than the ruler, it is the artist/scholar who speaks to us, who carries forth humanity: emperor, caliph, queen, and priest exist in time because of the scribe, the writer of lives. In *This I Believe,* her 1953 radio essay, Louise said, "I believe in humanity." This is true; we can feel it. And it is truest because it was a conviction that came hard fought, had been tested many times. In this same piece, Louise wrote that she hoped to live so that someone, someday would say the following. So here it is, on behalf of all of us who see something of ourselves in her, or who hope to see something of her within ourselves: "Louise Rich? Oh sure, I know her. She isn't so bad. She's human."

LDR's Published Works

Here is a list of louise's published books and stories that I compiled based on my perusal of dozens of old magazines; scrutiny of Louise's journal, five-year diary, and scrapbook; and interviews with classmates, family, and friends. There may be a couple of short stories missing—Louise was a prolific writer—but I am confident that this is the most complete list anywhere. —A.A.

BOOKS

We Took to the Woods (1942)

Happy the Land (1946)

Start of the Trail (1949)

My Neck of the Woods (1950)

Trail to the North (1952)

Only Parent (1953)

Innocence Under the Elms (1955)

The Coast of Maine (1956; revised 1962)

First Book of New England (1957)

The Peninsula (1958)

Mindy (1959)

First Book of Early Settlers (1959)

First Book of New World Explorers (1960)

The Natural World of Louise Dickinson Rich (1962)

First Book of Vikings (1962)

First Book of China Clippers (1962)

The Forest Years (1963)

State o' Maine (1964)

First Book of the Fur Trade (1965)

The Kennebec River (1967)

Star Island Boy (1968)

Three of a Kind (1970)

King Philip's War (1972)

Summer at High Kingdom (1975)

POETRY

(ALL PUBLISHED IN THE 1922 *NORMAL OFFERING*,
BRIDGEWATER STATE TEACHERS COLLEGE YEARBOOK.)

The Lure of the South Seas

Appreciation

Swamp Maple

SHORT STORIES AND ARTICLES

Fogbound (*Normal Offering*, 1922)

Why Guides Turn Gray (cowritten with Ralph Rich and
    published under his name, *Outdoor Life*, 1937)

Wish You Were Here (*Saturday Evening Post*, 1937)

First Monday in March (*Scribner's*, 1938)

Skunk in the Home (*New York Herald Tribune*, 1938)

Don't Worry (*Woman's Home Companion*, 1939)

Party for Phyllis (*The American Magazine*, 1939)

Little Matter of Politics (*Woman's Home Companion*, 1939)

Another Breed of Cats (*Liberty*, 1939)

Until Isobelle Came (*Good Housekeeping*, 1941)

Rainbow Chase (*Woman's Home Companion*, 1942)

No Story (*Family Circle*, 1942)

Written in the Stars (*Farm Journal*, 1942)

Road Commissioner's Report (*Country Gentleman*, 1943)

The Ship (*Liberty*, 1943)

The Wonderful Mrs. Rogers (*Family Circle*, 1943)

Ten Paces to the Left (*Woman's Home Companion*, 1943)

Pinky and Carter Glass (*Good Housekeeping*, 1943)

Grandma and the Seagull (*Woman's Home Companion*,
    Reader's Digest, 1943)

That Little Bit Extra (*Good Housekeeping*, 1943)

The Talisman (*Country Gentleman*, 1943)

Supposing Something Happens (*Glamour*, 1943)

Drama in Everyday Life (*Reader's Digest*, 1943)

What to Do When They Write (*Saturday Review
    of Literature*, 1944)

Luck for the Bride (*Woman's Home Companion,* 1944)

Althea (*Woman's Home Companion,* 1944)

Miss Pollard (*Woman's Home Companion,* 1944)

Tolerance (*Woman's Home Companion,* 1944)

The Red Slipper (*Woman's Home Companion,* 1944)

Paid Notice (*Woman's Home Companion,* 1944)

Share My Secret (*Woman's Home Companion,* 1944)

The Gift (*Woman's Home Companion,* 1944)

Our Growing Backyard (*Woman's Home Companion,* 1944)

Secret of the Island (*Woman's Home Companion,* 1945)

Grapevine for OPA (*Liberty,* 1945)

The Most Unforgettable Character I've Ever Met: Gerrish
     (*Reader's Digest,* 1945)

My Wills (c. 1945)

The Martyr Wife (*Woman's Home Companion,* 1945)

Molly Ockett (*Woman's Day,* 1946)

Backstairs (*Woman's Home Companion,* 1946)

What Do You Want for Christmas? (1946)

Leon and the Squarehead (From *My Neck of the Woods;*
     Reader's Digest, 1951)

This I Believe (*New York Herald Tribune,* 1953)

I Can't Find My Apron Strings (*Woman's Day,* 1957)

Friend in Need (*Reader's Digest,* 1960)

All This and Fishing, Too! (*Outdoor Life,* 1961)

A Good Bearin' Northern Spy (*Woman's Day,* 1963)

A Summer Place (*Woman's Day,* 1967)

The Handing On of a Garden (*Woman's Day,* 1968)

The Perfectly Proper Pig (cowritten with Thomas Hopkins,
     Yankee, 1976)

Index
